D1254240

The
Environmentalists

The
Environmentalists

*A Biographical Dictionary
from the 17th Century to the Present*

**Alan Axelrod
and
Charles Phillips**

Facts On File

WILLIAM WOODS UNIVERSITY LIBRARY

The Environmentalists: A biographical dictionary from the 17th century to the present

Copyright © 1993 Zenda, Inc.

All rights reserved. No part of this book may be reproduced or utilized in any form or by any means, electronic or mechanical, including photocopying, recording, or by any information storage or retrieval systems, without permission in writing from the publisher. For information contact:

Facts on File, Inc.
460 Park Avenue South
New York NY 10016
USA

Facts On File Limited
℅ Roundhouse Publishing Ltd.
P.O. Box 140
Oxford OX2 7SF
United Kingdom

Library of Congress Cataloging-in-Publication Data
Axelrod, Alan, 1952–
    The environmentalists : a biographical dictionary from the 17th
century to the present / Alan Axelrod and Charles Phillips.
        p.   cm.
    Includes bibliographical references and index.
    ISBN 0-8160-2715-3 (alk. paper)
    1. Conservationists—Biography—Dictionaries.
2. Environmentalists—Biography—Dictionaries.   3. Naturalists—
Biography—Dictionaries.   4. Conservation of natural resources—
Societies, etc.—Dictionaries.   5. Environmental protection—-
Societies, etc.—Dictionaries.   I. Phillips, Charles, 1948–
II. Title.
S926.A2A94   1993
363.7′0092′2—dc20
[B]   92-38773

A British CIP catalogue record for this book is available from the British
Library.

Facts On File books are available at special discounts when purchased in
bulk quantities for businesses, associations, institutions or sales
promotions. Please call our Special Sales Department in New York at
212/683-2244 (dial 800/322-8755 except in NY, AK or HI) or in Oxford at
865/728399.

Composition and manufacturing by the Maple-Vail Book Manufacturing Group
Printed in the United States of America

10 9 8 7 6 5 4 3 2 1

This book is printed on acid-free paper.

Ref.
S
926
A2
A94
1993

Contents

WILLIAM WOODS UNIVERSITY LIBRARY

Acknowledgments

The environment is a vast, complex and ever-evolving field with a long history that is often as controversial as its present state. We have done our best to make this book a comprehensive and objective resource that includes the most recent and accurate information available. In this task, we have had a great deal of help.

First on the list of those we wish to thank are the individuals and organizations included here who have responded quickly and generously to our questions and requests for information. Those organizations that supplied visual material are credited in the captions that accompany the illustrations.

We were assisted in research and writing by a most able team that includes Candace Floyd, Alison Mitchell, Curtis Utz, Philip Reynolds, Amy Handy and Nanette Maxim.

Our publisher, Facts On File, Inc., and especially project editor Kathy Ishizuka have been understanding, helpful, and generous to the point of out-and-out indulgence. We are very grateful to Gloria McDarrah, who handled a formidable copyediting job with great intelligence, vigilance and not a little fortitude.

A Note on "Further Reading"

A great many of the subjects profiled in this book are authors in addition to being activists, administrators, scientists and so on. In the case of such persons, we have listed their most representative publications within the running text of the biographies. For many individuals or organizations about whom useful and informative books have been written, we have also appended to the entry proper brief suggestions for "Further Reading."

Introduction

This book is a guide to individuals and organizations, present and past, who influence or have influenced the environmental movement in the United States and the world.

A book on the environment? Soon after we undertook this project, it became apparent that we might as well be writing a biographical and institutional guide to the universe, since *universe* is perhaps the only concept that encompasses more than *environment*. Environment is that which envelops us: the elements of nature and of nature modified by human action. A list of these physical elements would be as arbitrary as it is endless, and yet it would be incomplete. For the subject of the environment entails more than its physical constituents. Our environment is the product of nature and humankind, which means that it is the product of industrial activity, government activity, politics, culture, religion, greed, wisdom, stupidity, ambition, dreams, faith, hope, charity, et cetera and et al. Nor does reaching back toward the origins of the scientific study of the environment help us much to narrow our subject. The term *ecology* was coined in 1866 by Ernst Haeckel (whom the reader will meet in these pages), the leading German disciple of Charles Darwin. "Oecologie" encompassed all that pertains to *der Wissenshaft von der Oeconomie, von der Lebensweise, von der äusseren Lebensziehungen der organismen zu einander.* Haeckel's translator rendered this as "the science of the relations of living organisms to the external world, their habitat, customs, energies, parasites, etc.," but he might just as well have said (with Donald Worster, a current student of the subject) that ecology is "the study of all the environmental conditions of existence."

We allude to the vastness of our topic less to excuse a certain arbitrariness that is an inevitable characteristic of a book like this than to suggest the extraordinary importance and compelling scope of an area of inquiry that encompasses virtually all fields of human concern and endeavor. For less abstract proof of the immediacy and pervasiveness of environmental concerns, we could ask the reader merely to open his newspaper, turn on her television, look out the window or drive down the freeway. But we'll invite the reader to look instead at a scene—an imagined scene—from the past.

In 1823, James Fenimore Cooper published *The Pioneers*, first of his five Leatherstocking Tales, which together unfold in narrative a vision of the "settlement" of America, the advance of white settlement (which Cooper and his contemporaries deemed synonymous with civilization), the recession of the wilderness, the displacement of one world by another. Chapter 22 opens with a picture of an imaginary New York village called Templeton in 1794: "The snow . . . finally disappeared, and the green wheat fields were seen in every direction, spotted with the dark and charred stumps that had, the preceding season, supported some of the proudest trees in the forest." For the process of settlement customarily began, in those days, with the chopping of trees, which were left to dry during the summer, and then burned, leaving only blackened logs and stumps. Nothing was salvaged, save for ashes used as the basis of potash and soap. Cooper's fictional frontiersman hero, Natty Bumppo, better known as Leatherstocking, or Pathfinder, or Deerslayer, or Hawkeye, would call this wanton destruction an example of the "wasty ways" of men. Others would argue that it was the inevitable price of "civilization." In this, we have the essence of all environmental dispute.

But Natty Bumppo was about to witness a display of "wasty ways" much harder to explain, let alone rationalize, and far more profound in its implications.

As a beautiful spring morning broke over Lake Otsego, Elizabeth Temple, daughter of Judge Marmaduke Temple, the founder of Templeton, was

awakened by the exhilarating sounds of the martins, who were quarrelling and chattering around the little boxes which were suspended above her windows, and the cries of Richard, who was calling, in tones as animating as the signs of the season itself—

"Awake! awake! my lady fair! the gulls are hovering over the lake already, and the heavens are alive with the pigeons. You may look an hour before you can find a hole, through which, to get a peep at the sun. Awake! awake! lazy ones! Benjamin is overhauling the ammunition, and we only wait for our breakfasts, and away for the mountains and pigeon-shooting.". . .

"See, cousin Bess! . . . the pigeon-roosts of the south have broken up! They are growing more thick every instant. Here is a flock that the eye cannot see the end of. There is food enough in it to keep the army of Xerxes for a month, and feathers enough to make beds for the whole country. Xerxes . . . was a

Grecian king, who—no, he was a Turk, or a Persian, who wanted to conquer Greece, just the same as these rascals will overrun our wheat-fields, when they come back in the fall.—Away! away! Bess; I long to pepper them from the mountain." . . .

If the heavens were alive with pigeons, the whole village seemed equally in motion, with men, women, and children. Every species of fire-arms, from the French ducking-gun, with its barrel of near six feet in length, to the common horseman's pistol, was to be seen in the hands of men and boys; while bows and arrows, some made of the simple stick of a walnut sapling, and others in a rude imitation of the ancient cross-bows, were carried by many of the latter. . . .

We have already said, that across the inclined plane which fell from the steep ascent of the mountain to the banks of the Susquehanna, ran the highway, on either side of which a clearing of many acres had been made, at a very early day. Over those clearings, and up the eastern mountain, and along the dangerous path that was cut into its side, the different individuals posted themselves, as suited their inclinations; and in a few moments the attack commenced. . . .

The reports of the fire-arms became rapid, whole volleys rising from the plain, as flocks of more than ordinary numbers darted over the opening, covering the field with darkness, like an interposing cloud; and then the light smoke of a single piece would issue from among the leafless bushes on the mountain, as death was hurled on the retreat of the affrighted birds, who would rise from a volley, for many feet into the air, in a vain effort to escape the attacks of man. Arrows, and missiles of every kind, were seen in the midst of the flocks; and so numerous were the birds, and so low did they take their flight, that even long poles, in the hands of those on the sides of the mountain, were used to strike them to earth.

During all this time, Mr. [Richard] Jones, who disdained the humble and ordinary means of destruction used by his companions, was busily occupied . . . in making arrangements for an assault of more than ordinarily fatal character. Among the relics of the old military excursions, that occasionally are discovered throughout the different districts of the western part of New-York, there had been found in Templeton, at its settlement, a small swivel [cannon], which would carry a ball of a pound weight. . . . The grand conceptions of Richard had suggested the importance of such an instrument, in hurling death at his nimble enemies. . . .

So prodigious was the number of the birds, that the scattering fire of the guns, with the hurling of missiles, and the cries of boys, had no other effect than to break off the small flocks from the immense masses that continued to dart along the valley, as if the whole creation of the feathered tribe were pouring through that one pass. None pretended to collect the game, which lay scattered over the fields in such profusion, as to cover the very ground with the fluttering victims. . . .

"Victory!" shouted Richard, "victory! we have driven the enemy from the field."

Ectopistes migratorius, the passenger pigeon, presented a spectacle of nature's abundance to 18- and early 19th-century Americans, who witnessed seemingly endless flocks of the bird in great seasonal migrations. By the close of the 19th century, the species was extinct, the victim of hunting carried out on a scale amounting to extermination.

Thus, on its surface, Cooper's passage is an early chapter in the long and dreary book of endangered species. But it takes very little probing to find much more in this episode. Cooper's Templeton is a settlement that literally burned its niche into the wilderness, and its inhabitants see themselves engaged in a war against the very representatives of the natural world, the pigeons, which they call enemy and against which they train an array of weaponry ranging from clubs, to bows, to firearms of every description, including a small cannon. Nor is this orgy of bloodlust a mere figment of Cooper's literary imagination, peculiar to Richard Jones and the other fictive citizens of Templeton. Cooper's scene is the product of his civilization as well as of his time and place.

Since at least the introduction of Christianity, Western culture has been largely and essentially antinatural. "Christianity," ecological historian Donald Worster observes, "has maintained a calculated indifference, if not antagonism, toward nature." At best, according to our cultural tradition, nature's chief function is to serve humankind. At worst, nature is an enemy, harboring demons, dark appetites and brutal instincts that must be slain. Pope Pius IX, for example, refused to allow the establishment of a society in Rome to protest the slaughter of bulls for sport and amusement. The pope declared that, since a bull has no soul, it can lay no claim on man's moral sympathies. Nature, from which man is separated by his divine soul, is either to be conquered and used or conquered and defeated.

Little wonder that contempt and hostility toward the natural realm simmer just beneath the surface of our civilization. This is in sharp contrast to most Eastern systems of belief, which invest nature and its creatures with the very divinity in which humankind is presumed to participate. Likewise, most American Indian cultures make no sharp distinction between man and nature. A "great spirit" animates and unites all of creation. To be sure, Native American peoples traditionally made extensive use of the products of nature—flesh, fowl and vegetable—but the notion of defeating nature as an enemy, of conquering and dividing it into the exclusive property of this individual or that, was largely foreign to their imagination. The peoples of the East and the Native peoples of the New World had no need for a science of ecology; for woven into the fabric of their cultures and religions was an unself-conscious understanding of a seamless symbiosis among plants, animals, the elements and humankind.

Western culture, in contrast, amputated human existence from the natural realm. By the mid 18th century, this mechanistic view of man and nature resulted in an ideal of science founded on rationality and in an unstoppable drive to channel natural energies into thousands of "useful" machines to produce tens of thousands of "useful" products. It is at the doorstep of the Industrial Revolution that the origins of ecology or environmentalism can be found. The early naturalists characteristically wrote of "nature's economy." For example, in his 1789 *Natural History of Selbourne,* the Englishman Gilbert White observed, "Nature is such an economist, that the most incongruous animals can avail themselves of each other!" In an age torn by strife, by increasingly mechanized forms of warfare and by the class warfare triggered by the economics of manufacture, the prototypes of ecology emerged as anodynes and antidotes, sweet visions of natural harmony from which humankind might not only learn, but into which, from time to time at least, it could retreat for respite and refreshment of spirit.

Existing side by side with this view—which Donald Worster calls the arcadian tradition—was an emerging system of ecology that partook wholly of the rational vision we most frequently associate with the 18th century. Naturalists such as Carolus Linnaeus and, later, Alexander von Humboldt saw in (or imposed on) the natural world new patterns of economy. Worster has dubbed this rational approach the "imperial tradition," because it sought to make of nature an empire ruled by reason—wholly intelligible to humankind and, therefore, subject to human domination.

The reader will find in the pages that follow vestiges of both the "arcadian" and the "imperial" traditions even as ecology developed into an increasingly sophisticated science through such landmark 19th- and early 20th-century figures as Charles Darwin, Ernst Haeckel, Lester Ward, August Grisebach, C. Hart Merriam, Eugenius Warming, A. G. Tansley, Frederic Clements and a profusion of later 20th-century figures. The reader will also discover that at no time in the history of its development was ecology confined exclusively to the realm of science. This, in fact, is the great challenge for anyone writing a guidebook to the topic. "Ecologists" include scientists, world leaders, government officials and administrators, politicians and policymakers, lobbyists and social activists, industrialists and industry consultants, geographers, writers, photographers, artists, explorers, clergy, social workers, communications specialists, conservatives, radicals, outlaws and law enforcement officials. Ecology, after all, is not merely science. It is life.

Consider, once again, Cooper's pigeon slaughter scene. The biologist, the historian, the psychologist, the moralist, the theologian, the geographer might each find in it rich occasion for diverse comment, *all* of which, nevertheless, would bear on ecology. By what criteria, then, have we decided whom to include in this book?

In fact, we have found it impossible to enforce rigid rules. In the main, two principles have guided us. To be included here, an individual must either be significantly representative of a significant point of view or methodology or must have exercised significant influence on the study of ecology or on environmental policy. This allows us potentially to include individuals from virtually every field of human endeavor—though the majority of figures actually included are scientists, activists, government administrators and ecologically minded creative writers. Our broad criteria also allow for the representation of many points of view, including some that are distinctly hostile to much of what most acknowledged or self-proclaimed environmentalists profess in common. Thus, for example, our book includes entries on pioneering naturalist John Muir, scientist-activist Barry Commoner and ecological essayist Barry Lopez as well as Ronald Reagan's provocative secretary of the interior James Watt, Exxon *Valdez* Captain Joseph Hazelwood and ecological terrorist Saddam Hussein—all of whom have had significant impact on the environment.

For historical personalities, 17th-, 18th-, 19th- and *early* 20th-century figures, we have sharpened our criteria somewhat, confining ourselves to individuals whose contributions to ecological study constitute generally acknowledged landmarks in the development of this most comprehensive field.

Finally, we recognized early on that much contemporary activity in ecology and the environmental movement is less the work of individuals than it is of certain vital organizations. Our conservative estimate is that some 1,600 U.S. government departments and agencies; international, national and regional commissions; state and territorial agencies and citizens' groups; and international, national and regional organizations are currently active and influential in creating or influencing environmental thought and action. From these, we have chosen a relatively small number of key government bodies and private organizations as most crucial to the field and most representative of its varied facets.

The environment is, of course, global, and, therefore, the scope of this book is international. However, we have concentrated most of our attention on the United States. In part, this is the result of our own nationality and of the nationality of our projected audience. But, no less significantly, our focus reflects the extraordinary degree of environmental activism and activity—political, social, scientific and governmental—in this country. What accounts for this national wealth of ecological enterprise? We believe that, yet again, a reading of James Fenimore Cooper suggests an answer as plausible as anyone else has offered.

The Templeton pigeon shoot is only one of Cooper's many remarkable images of man confronting the New World. Cooper's characters are quintessentially American in that they are repeatedly presented with the opportunity and the necessity of creating an environment, of establishing a relationship between the "virgin land" and themselves. A later American author put the situation this way: Standing in the shadow of the Long Island mansion of Jay Gatsby, F. Scott Fitzgerald's Nick Carraway gradually "became aware of the old island here that flowered once for Dutch sailors' eyes—a fresh, green breast of the new world. Its vanished trees, the trees that had made way for Gatsby's house, had once pandered in whispers to the last and greatest of all human dreams; for a transitory enchanted moment man must have held his breath in the presence of this continent, compelled into an aesthetic contemplation he neither understood nor desired, face to face for the last time in history with something commensurate to his capacity for wonder." Americans are burdened by a vague awareness of having inherited a continent of dreams and imagination compromised by the realities of exploitation and spoliation. Often restless, reckless and thoughtless, driven by greed and bound by the cheapest of short-term goals, Americans are nevertheless blessed and afflicted with an ecological conscience, which, try as they might, they can never wholly submerge. It comes, we believe, with the territory, and it is, therefore, properly and inevitably reflected in this book.

A

Abbey, Edward (January 29, 1927–March 14, 1989)

Novelist, magazine journalist, lecturer and university professor Edward ("Cactus Ed") Abbey wrote extensively about the American West and the environmental problems created by human society. In seven novels and 13 works of nonfiction, he focused on the themes of confinement versus space and corruption versus salvation, often calling for radical methods to heal environmental ills.

Abbey worked for 15 years as a NATIONAL PARK SERVICE ranger and fire lookout while he struggled to get his writing career started. Hardly a compliant civil servant, he criticized park service policies that called for building roads through wilderness areas and for other disruptions, and whenever he could he attempted to sabotage those efforts. In *The Monkey Wrench Gang,* his 1975 novel, George Haycraft and his followers become environmental vigilantes whose outrageous activities—spiking trees, pouring sand in bulldozer gas tanks and the like—undermined the construction of dams, roads, bridges and other "improvements" in Arizona park lands. The book was a national bestseller and inspired the EARTH FIRST! organization.

Abbey's *Desert Solitaire,* a nonfiction account of a park ranger's work over a single season in the West, makes a strong plea for the preservation of the wilderness and accurately and lovingly describes the ranger's encounters with the natural environment.

The winner of a Fulbright Fellowship (1951–52) and a Guggenheim Fellowship (1973), Abbey wrote for several magazines and journals, including *Audubon, National Geographic, Outside* and *Rocky Mountain Magazine* as well as for more general-interest publications. His novels include *Jonathan Troy* (1954), *The Brave Cowboy* (1956), *Fire on the Mountain* (1962), *Black Sun* (1971), *The Monkey Wrench Gang* (1975), *Good News*

(1980) and *The Fool's Progress* (1988). His nonfiction works include *Desert Solitaire: A Season in the Wilderness* (1968), *Appalachian Wilderness: The Great Smoky Mountains* (1970), *Slickrock: The Canyon Country of Southeast Utah* (1971, with Philip Hyde), *Cactus Country* (1973), *The Hidden Canyon* (1977), *The Journey Home: Some Words in Defense of the American West* (1977), *Desert Images: An American Landscape* (1978), *Back Roads of Arizona* (1978), *Abbey's Road: Take the Other* (1979), *Down the River* (1982), *Beyond the Wall* (1984) and *Slumgullion Stew: An Edward Abbey Reader* (1984). Born in Home, Pennsylvania, Abbey died in Oracle, Arizona.

Further reading: Garth McCann, *Edward Abbey* (Boise: Boise State University Press, 1977).

Abernathy, William Jackson (November 21, 1933–December 29, 1983)

Harvard Business School Professor William Jackson Abernathy was the author of *The Productivity Dilemma: Roadblock to Innovation in the Automobile Industry* (1978) and other books analyzing America's corporate management of technology. An influential consultant to government and industry, the writer and educator criticized the nation's major auto manufacturers—and other large-scale public and private enterprises—for their insular adherence to an obsolete corporate philosophy, one characterized by short-sighted profit-seeking, rigid overinstitutionalization, adversarial relations with labor and stagnant technology. Abernathy espoused a more fluid and inventive collaboration between workers and management as the key to improving products, revolutionizing manufacturing methods and ensuring long-term competitiveness in world markets.

Born in Columbia, Tennessee, Abernathy studied electrical engineering at the University of Tennessee (B.S., 1955) and worked for a year in the Columbia-based film division of E. I. Du Pont. After serving as a first lieutenant in the U.S. Air Force, he moved to Rochester, New York, where he was a project engineer in the electronic systems division of General Dynamics from 1959 to 1962. Abernathy's firsthand observation of technology mismanagement prompted him to seek graduate training in business administration at Harvard University. After earning his master's degree (1964) and doctorate (1967), he accepted an assistant professorship at the University of California, Los Angeles. The following year he began teaching at Stanford University, and in 1972, he returned to Harvard Business School as an associate professor. He was made full professor in 1977, and in 1982, he was named the first William Barclay Harding Professor of the Management of Technology. A member of the National Academy of Sciences and the American Association for the Advancement of Science, Abernathy received the *Harvard Business Review*'s McKinzie Award in 1980. He succumbed to cancer at 50, while organizing his second major Harvard colloquium on productivity and technology, and shortly after beginning work on another book intended to popularize his management recommendations.

Adams, Ansel (February 20, 1902–April 22, 1984)

At the age of 14, during a family vacation in Yosemite Valley, San Francisco-born Ansel Adams began his lifelong dual love affair with the camera and with the rugged beauty of the American West. Not until he was 28, however, did he decide to turn that love into a career.

In 1934, Adams was appointed to the board of directors of the SIERRA CLUB, a post he held until 1971. He continued his service to the club as honorary vice-president from 1978 until his death in 1984 at his home in Carmel, California.

Adams's first photographic portfolio, *Parmelian Prints of the High Sierra*, was published in 1927. Eleven years later he released *Sierra Nevada: The John Muir Trail*. During World War II, he worked as a photomuralist for the U.S. Department of the INTERIOR.

In 1946, 1948 and 1959, Adams was awarded Guggenheim Fellowships to photograph national parks and monuments. Meanwhile, he worked with Nancy Newhall on an exhibition and book entitled *This Is the American Earth*, published by the Sierra Club in 1955. His other publications include *The Camera* (1980), *The Negative* (1982) and *The Print* (1983), three technical works that were originally published in five volumes in 1948. Among the many pictorial books he produced are *My Camera in Yosemite Valley* (1949), *My Camera in the National Parks* (1950), *Illustrated Guide*

Virginia and Ansel Adams in Yosemite National Park about 1974. *Photo by Mishi Kamiya, courtesy of the National Park Service*

to Yosemite Valley (revised 1963), *The Portfolios of Ansel Adams* (1977) and *Yosemite and the Range of Light* (1979). His last book, *Examples: The Making of Forty Photographs,* was released in 1983, a year before his death.

Adams's many honors include the Sierra Club's John Muir Award in 1963, the U.S. Department of the Interior's Conservation Service Award in 1968, the Photographic Society of America's Progress Medal in 1969, the Presidential Medal of Freedom in 1980 and the National Wildlife Federation's Special Achievement Award in 1983. His stunning photographs have done much to engage the public in battles to save the wilderness and to protect public lands from encroachment.

Further reading: Nancy Newhall, *The Eloquent Light* (New York: Aperture Foundation, 1963).

Adams, Charles Christopher (July 23, 1873– May 22, 1955)

An early advocate of the necessity of relating human ecology to land use, Charles Christopher Adams was educated at Illinois Wesleyan University (B.S., 1895), Harvard University (M.S., 1899) and the University of Chicago (Ph.D., 1908). Illinois Wesleyan awarded him a Sc.D. in 1920. Adams served as an assistant in biology at Illinois Wesleyan University from 1895 to 1896; assistant entomologist at the Illinois State Laboratory of Natural History, 1896 to 1898; curator of the University of Michigan Museum, 1903 to 1906; director of the Cincinnati Society of Natural History, 1906 to 1907; and associate professor of animal ecology at the University of Illinois State Laboratory of Natural History, 1908 to 1914. In 1914, Adams left his native Illinois (he was born in Clinton) to become professor of forest zoology at the New York State College of Forestry in Syracuse until 1926. During his tenure there, Adams also directed the Roosevelt Wildlife Forest Experiment Station. From 1926 to 1943, he served as director of the New York State Museum in Albany.

The author of more than 150 journal articles and a book, *Guide to the Study of Animal Ecology* (1913), Adams was a stern critic of the Bureau of BIOLOGICAL SURVEY during the 1920s and 1930s because of its policy of exterminating predator animals in the country's parks and nature reserves. In 1924, he spoke at the annual meeting of the American Society of Mammalogists, an organization whose members were highly critical of the bureau's use of poison gas to kill predator animals, and over the next several years he wrote extensively on the subject of conserving predator mammals. Adams even advocated using a portion of the national forest and park lands specifically to sustain populations of predators. Partly owing to Adams's tireless efforts the official policy was changed by 1936, and all extermination programs in the National Parks System were discontinued.

Adams, Charles Francis Jr. (May 27, 1835– March 20, 1915)

Historian and lawyer Charles Francis Adams Jr. first entered conservation work as chairman of the executive committee of the Merry-Mount Park Association. This organization established Merrymount Park in Quincy, Massachusetts, in 1885, when Adams donated 83 acres of land. He next combined his organizational skills with those of landscape architect Charles Eliot to create in 1891 a metropolitan park commission in Boston, called the Trustees of Public Reservations. Adams served as chairman of the commission from 1892 to 1895, and during his tenure, the organization established the Blue Hills Reservation, Middlesex Fells Reservation and Stony Brook Reservation.

Further reading: Adams, *Autobiography* (Boston: Houghton Mifflin, 1916); Edward Chase Kirkland, *Charles Francis Adams, Jr., 1835–1915: The Patrician at Bay* (Cambridge: Harvard University Press, 1965).

Adams, John Hamilton (February 15, 1936–)

The founder and executive director of the NATURAL RESOURCES DEFENSE COUNCIL, John Adams helped launch and lead a program of strategic legal actions that have won precedent-setting court decisions safeguarding the environment and the public health. Assembling a team of scientific researchers and expert attorneys, Adams and his organization have

John Adams, head of the Natural Resources Defense Council. *Dan Gelbwaks/NRDC*

undertaken public interest litigation to protect air and water quality, preserve wilderness areas and spur the creation and enforcement of regulations affecting industrial pollution, wilderness development, nuclear waste disposal, commercial pesticide use and other environmental concerns.

Born in New York City, Adams attended Michigan State University (B.A., 1959) and Duke University Law School (LL.B., 1962). After graduation, he joined the Wall Street firm of Cadwalader, Wickersham, and Taft, and in 1963, he was admitted to the New York State Bar. Two years later he was named assistant U.S. attorney for the Southern District of New York, a position he held until 1969. Adams's growing involvement with environmental issues led him to inaugurate the Natural Resources Defense Council in 1970, and he has served as its executive director since then. Today, Adams heads a permanent staff of over 150 attorneys, researchers, planners, policy specialists and other professionals dedicated to resource protection.

One of 10 environmental leaders to collaborate on a 1985 report titled *An Environmental Agenda for the Future*, Adams has been an adjunct professor of law at New York University since 1974 and is chairman of the board of the Open Space Institute. He is also a board director with the American Conservation Association, the Catskill Center for Conservation, the Hudson River Foundation for Science and Environmental Research, the Institute for Resource Management, the New York Lawyers Alliance for Nuclear Arms Control, the Winston Foundation for World Peace and the WORLD RESOURCES INSTITUTE. He serves on the Board of Advisors of the Environmental Media Association and on New York Governor Mario Cuomo's Environmental Advisory Board, and he was recently appointed to the Service Policy Advisory Committee of the U.S. Trade Representative.

In 1990 Adams was honored with the first annual "As They Grow" Award from *Parents* magazine and a Frances K. Hutchinson Conservation Award from the Garden Club of America; in 1991, he received an honorary doctorate of laws from Knox College and a Distinguished Alumni Award from Duke University.

Adirondack Mountain Club (Founded: 1922)

RR. 3 Box 3055t,
Lake George, New York 12845;
(518) 668-4447

The Adirondack Mountain Club was founded to promote outings, appreciation and conservation activities in mountain areas, especially New York's Adirondacks, one of the natural areas that first came to the attention of early preservationists. The club maintains various portions of the Adirondack trail system and operates two lodges. The club also publishes literature relating to the Adirondacks and the mountains of the Northeast. Its membership numbers about 11,000.

Robert J. Ringlee serves as president of the Adirondack Mountain Club, and Walter M. Medwid is executive director.

Agassiz, Jean Louis Rodolphe (May 28, 1807–December 14, 1873)

Born in Metier, Switzerland, Agassiz was a professor at Neufchâtel, where he pioneered the classification of fossil fishes and glacial deposits. Agassiz immigrated to America in 1846, becoming professor of natural history in the Lawrence Scientific School of Harvard University, where he founded the Harvard Museum of Comparative Zoology.

Agassiz's principal contributions to the fields of ecology and environmentalism were his establishment of a museum of comparative zoology at Harvard and his radical teaching methods, which stressed contact with nature and revolutionized the teaching of natural science in the United States. Agassiz's legacy was profound: All of the notable teachers of natural history during the second half of the 19th century were either his students or students of his students. Agassiz's writings include *A Journey to Brazil* (1868), based on a scientific expedition, and the

Louis Agassiz. *Courtesy of the Burndy Library, Norwalk, Connecticut*

four-volume *Contributions to the Natural History of the United States* (1857–62).

Further reading: J. Marcou, *Life, Letters and Works of Louis Agassiz* (Farnborough, Hampshire, England: Gregg International, 1972).

Agricultural Stabilization and Conservation Service (Established: 1961)

P.O. Box 2415,
Washington, D.C. 20013; (202) 447-5237

This branch of the U.S. Department of AGRICULTURE is responsible for the administration of commodity, land-use and resource-conservation programs, including the Agriculture Conservation Program, a federal grant program to encourage farmers to practice conservation and environmental protection by underwriting up to 75% of the cost of these measures.

The service also has responsibility for the Forestry Incentive Program, the Water Bank Program and the Experimental Rural Clean Water Program. In cooperation with the Extension Service of the USDA and with state and county extension services, the Agricultural Stabilization and Conservation Service works to educate farmers and other land users in methods of practicing ecologically sound agriculture.

Agriculture, U.S. Department of (USDA)
(Established: 1862)
14th Street and Independence Avenue SW,
Washington, D.C. 20250; (202) 447-2791

Established on May 15, 1862, as an executive commission, the department was upgraded to a cabinet post by an act of February 9, 1889. The mandate of the Department of Agriculture is to improve and maintain farm income and to develop and expand markets abroad for agricultural products; to help to curb and to cure poverty, hunger and malnutrition; and to "enhance the environment and to maintain our production capacity by helping landowners protect the soil, water, forests, and other natural resources." The department also has the responsibility for inspecting agricultural products to ensure standards of safety and quality for consumers.

Department of Agriculture programs that directly bear upon environmental issues include: soil and water conservation loans, watershed protection and flood prevention loans and resource conservation and development loans, administered by the Farmers Home Administration; marketing and inspection services, including a Plant Variety Protection Program, Animal and Plant Health Inspection Service (which includes the regulation of genetically engineered organisms) and food inspection programs; international affairs and commodity programs, including the Agricultural Stabilization and Conservation Service; science and education programs, which include a wide variety of research and education efforts and the maintenance of a National Agricultural Library; the U.S. FOREST SERVICE, transferred from the U.S. Department of the INTERIOR by act of February 1, 1905, which has a wide range of environmental responsibilities; and the Soil Conservation Service. Established by the Soil Conservation Act of 1935, this administrative body has responsibility for developing and carrying out a national soil and water conservation program in cooperation with landowners and operators and other land users. The service assists in agricultural pollution control, environmental improvement and rural community development. Such Soil Conservation Service programs as Conservation Operations, River Basin Surveys and Investigations, Watershed Planning, Watershed and Flood Prevention Operations, Great Plains Conservation Program, Resource Conservation and Development Program and the Rural Abandoned Mine Program have a

profound effect on the environment. The Department of Agriculture also includes its own Office of Energy and a Graduate School, which is a self-supporting, nonprofit school for adults that draws upon government professionals and specialists as well as the community at large to provide continuing education in agriculturally related subjects.

Ahern, George Patrick (December 29, 1859–May 13, 1942)
George Patrick Ahern, born in New York City, served in the U.S. Infantry in the Dakota Territory, Minnesota and Montana, gaining firsthand knowledge of the region. After leaving the Army, Ahern became a forest advisor to the General Land Office and in 1896 led Gifford PINCHOT and Henry GRAVES through Montana and Idaho in an expedition to identify land the Bureau of Forestry would set aside as forest reserves. The following year, Ahern put his expertise to work at the Montana Agricultural College, where he taught forestry courses.

Ahern turned next to the international scene. After returning to military service in Cuba and the Philippines during the Spanish-American War, he remained in the Philippines to establish and direct the Philippine School of Forestry. He left the islands in 1914 for China, where he was instrumental in the creation of the Chinese Forest Service and a school of forestry at Nanking University.

Throughout his long, varied and adventurous career, Ahern fought for strict regulations to curtail timber cutting on private lands. He was the author of two books, *Deforested America* and *Forest Bankruptcy in America*.

Air and Waste Management Association
(Founded: 1907)
P. O. Box 2861, Pittsburgh, Pennsylvania 15230;
(412) 232-3444

Formerly called the Air Pollution Control Association and the Smoke Prevention Association of America, the Air and Waste Management Association seeks ways to control air pollution and hazardous wastes and solve problems caused by them. Originally dedicated exclusively to air pollution problems, the organization expanded its mission in 1986 to cover waste management as well. The organization's 11,000 members in 50 countries include industrialists, researchers, educators, meteorologists, personnel of government pollution control agencies and equipment manufacturers. Programs offered by the group include continuing education courses, library offerings, awards and annual meetings. The organization publishes the annual *Air & Waste Management Association Directory and Resource Book* and the monthly *Journal of the Air and Waste Management Association*, which includes a calendar of events, computer software reviews, new product information, bibliographies and news on legislative action. In addition, the association publishes a bimonthly newsletter, *News and Views*, with reports from the organization's 21 regional groups and 46 local groups. Other publications include the *Summary of Government Affairs Seminar*, a five-year *Cumulative Index to JAPCA*, technical manuals and other educational materials. Several standing committees are devoted to biomedical and ecological concerns, mobile combustion, particulates, gases and odors, continuing education, economics and risk assessment. These committees work with the 32-member staff, which is organized in three major divisions: Air, Environmental Management and Waste. Martin Rivers serves as executive vice-president of the organization, which operates with an annual budget of $4 million.

Albright, Horace Marden (January 6, 1890– March 28, 1987)

A founding father of the NATIONAL PARK SERVICE, Horace Albright was for two-thirds of a century the voice of compromise between the warring factions of "utilitarians" and "preservationists" within the American conservation movement. A vigorous champion of preserving vast tracts of unspoiled natural beauty, he nevertheless stressed the "practical" values of a national park system, such as the economic advantages of tourism, in order to gain the broadest possible political support for conservation goals.

Born in Bishop, California, in the Owens Valley, Albright developed a reverence for nature early on. He graduated from the University of California in 1912 and joined the staff of Franklin K. Lane, U.S. secretary of the interior. Stephen T. MATHER, a wealthy businessman and conservationist who volunteered to work with Secretary Lane on the administration of a national park system, chose Albright as his special assistant in 1915. Together, Mather and Albright presided over the founding of the National Park Service and drafted the National Park Service Act of 1916, which stressed so-called preservationist values in saving grand examples of natural beauty.

Albright served as assistant director of the National Park Service until 1919 and as superintendent of Yellowstone National Park during the 1920s. He succeeded Mather as director of the park service in 1929. During the administrations of Mather and Albright, a rivalry developed between the National Park Service, which mainly embodied "preservationist" principles, and the Forest Service, which tended to support

Horace M. Albright after receiving the Presidential Medal of Freedom at a December 1980 ceremony in Santa Monica, California. *Photo by Dick Frear, courtesy of the National Park Service*

"utilitarian" values—including a policy of developing areas for "multiple use," encompassing aesthetics, recreation and the exploitation of natural resources. While Albright never abandoned the preservationist inclination of his agency, he made many compromises with the utilitarian view. This won political and legislative support for the National Park Service, but alienated radical preservationists such as Robert Sterling YARD, who not only wanted to protect national park lands from any industrial or commercial development, but also from extensive recreational use.

As superintendent of Yellowstone, Albright set the standard for park administration. As director of the park service, he made his agency a strong and enduring political force. He established Grand Teton National Park, Carlsbad Cavern National Park, Great Smoky Mountains National Park and the Death Valley and Colonial national monuments. During the first term of Franklin D. Roosevelt, Albright worked closely with Interior Secretary Harold ICKES in the creation of the CIVILIAN CONSERVATION CORPS (CCC) and related programs. He extended NPS jurisdiction over parks and monuments in Washington, D.C., and over Civil War battlefields and burial grounds. Albright also established a historic preservation program to restore and preserve historic structures and sites and to interpret them to the public. Indeed, under Albright's direction, interpretive and educational programs were created throughout the national park system.

In August 1933, Albright stepped down as director of the NPS to become vice-president and general manager of the United States Potash Company. He remained in the private sector until his retirement in 1956, but he never abandoned the cause of conservation. He served in various capacities with many conservation organizations, which frequently drew on his political connections and expertise. With John D. Rockefeller Jr., he successfully lobbied to make Jackson Hole a national park. He also worked with Rockefeller to create the Colonial Williamsburg restoration and served as the first president of RESOURCES FOR THE FUTURE.

Albright received the Interior Department's Conservation Service Award (1953) and the SIERRA CLUB'S John Muir Award (1986). In 1980, President Jimmy Carter presented him with the Presidential Medal of Freedom. Albright is the author of *The Birth of the National Park Service*.

Further reading: Robert Shankland, *Steve Mather of the National Parks* (New York: Tudor, 1951); Donald C. Swain, *Wilderness Defender: Horace M. Albright and Conservation* (Chicago: University of Chicago Press, 1970).

Allee, Warder Clyde (June 5, 1885–March 18, 1955)

Born to a Quaker family in rural Parke County, Indiana, Warder Clyde Allee graduated from Earlham College in Richmond, Indiana, in 1905. After teaching high school in Hammond from 1907 to 1910, he entered the University of Chicago's graduate program, receiving a Ph.D. in biology in 1912. From 1912 to 1915, he held a series of positions, teaching at the University of Illinois, Williams College and the University of Oklahoma. From 1915 to 1921, he was professor of biology at Lake Forest College, north of Chicago. In 1921, Allee was named assistant professor of zoology at the University of Chicago, where he remained until his retirement in 1950. From then until his death in 1955, he was head of the department of biology at the University of Florida, Gainesville.

Throughout his long career, Allee's research focused on mass physiology and animal aggregations. At the University of Chicago, he was at the center of a circle of scientists who gathered for weekly meetings in his home. Among them were Thomas Park, Alfred Emerson, Karl Schmidt, and Orland Park, the four scientists who collaborated with Allee on *Principles of Animal Ecology* (1949), commonly known as "AEPPS," after the authors' initials. In this work, these pioneers of the organismic-community concept of ecology hold that the individual is of little importance in the natural order, but that the social group is crucial to survival. The authors and other scientists who gathered around them—known as the Ecology Group—had spent years working together to develop their concepts before publishing AEPPS, but upon Allee's retirement in 1950, the group disbanded.

Allee and his circle studied how, through evolution, new entities emerged whose characteristics could not be analyzed in terms of their predecessors. For Allee, emergent evolution took the form of increasingly complex levels of cooperation in social patterns, and he believed that animal aggregations were primitive stages of sociality. In addition, he found that cooperation was one of the two principles underlying all social structure. The other was competition. While Charles DARWIN had already been credited with identifying the competition principle, the principle of cooperation and Allee's research into the harmful effects of underpopulation became known as "Allee's principle." Many of these ideas were first presented in Allee's *Animal Aggregations* (1931).

In the mid-1930s, Allee turned to an examination of dominance-subdominance, leadership and territoriality, and in 1934, he and coauthor Ralph Masure introduced the term "peck-dominance" into their description of pigeon behavior. Ten years later, Allee and Alpheus Guhl studied two flocks of hens—one with a discernible dominance hierarchy that had been determined by one-on-one confrontation, and another with no discernible social order. Allee and Guhl concluded that the flock characterized by a dominance hierarchy was better suited to compete or cooperate with other flocks than the flock with no social order.

Among Allee's other publications are *Animal Life and Social Growth* (1932), *Handbook of Social Psychology* (1935), *The Social Life of Animals* (1938) and *Cooperation Among Animals, with Human Implications* (1951). He was the coauthor of *Jungle Island* (1925), *Nature of the World and of Man* (1926), *Ecological Animal Geography* (1937) and *A Laboratory Introduction to Animal Ecology and Taxonomy* (1939). From 1930 until his death, Allee served as managing editor of *Physiological Zoology*. He was a trustee of the Marine Biology Laboratory at Woods Hole, Massachusetts, from 1932 until 1955.

Allee's notion of cooperation as an evolutionary principle has led to an ethical vision of the environment in which each part is dependent on all others.

In addition, his work is viewed as the primary impetus behind the creation of the "Chicago School" of animal behavior during the 1940s and 1950s.

Allen, Arthur Augustus (December 28, 1885–January 17, 1964)

The first full professor of ornithology in the United States, Arthur Augustus Allen was a native of Buffalo, New York, who worked at Cornell University during his entire professional career. At the university, he created an ornithological laboratory, which was the first in the United States to be designated a university department. In addition to teaching at the university level, Allen spread his message about the importance of studying and preserving bird species by documenting them through color photography and sound recording. Among his nine popular book-length works are *The Book of Bird Life* (1930), *American Bird Biographies* (1934) and *Stalking Birds with a Color Camera* (1951). He served as chairman of Cornell University's Commission on Wildlife Conservation and president of the Eastern Bird Banding Association. In addition, he was a founding member of the WILDLIFE SOCIETY and the American Society of Mammalogists and was a trustee of the American Wildlife Institute.

Allen, Robert Porter (April 24, 1905–June 18, 1963

For 30 years, Robert Porter Allen worked for the NATIONAL AUDUBON SOCIETY, first serving as research associate and sanctuary director and later as research director. He is best known for his efforts to save the whooping crane. (He located the nesting grounds of a wild flock near the Arctic Circle and preserved habitat areas in Texas and Canada.) Allen also devised a plan to protect flamingos and roseate spoonbills, and his monographs on those species as well as the whooping crane remain the standard references. Among his writings are *The Flame Birds* (1947), *On Vanishing Wildlife* (1957), *On the Trail of Vanishing Birds* (1957) and *Birds of the Caribbean* (1961). At the time of his death, he was planning a 16-volume work on the birds of North America. Robert Porter Allen was born in South Williamsport, Pennsylvania.

Alliance for Clean Energy (Founded: 1983)
1901 N. Fort Myer Drive, 12th floor, Rosslyn, Virginia 22209; (703) 841-1781

This industry-sponsored organization was founded to promote the use of low-sulphur coals as a measure to abate acid rain. The organization, which mounts publicity and educational campaigns, is primarily a lobbying group that favors local rather than federal regulation on sulphur emissions. The organization favors legislation that will permit coal-burning industries to choose among an array of options to meet clean-air goals. The alliance actively lobbies against a national clean-air tax. Its membership consists chiefly of coal producers and coal haulers.

Alliance for Environmental Education (Founded: 1972)
10751 Ambassador Drive, No. 201, Manassas, Virginia 22110; (703) 335-1025

The Alliance for Environmental Education, under the direction of Steven C. Kussmann, chairman, has 150 members, including organizations, corporations and government agencies. The alliance promotes formal and informal educational programs intended to create a citizenry better informed about environmental issues and more committed to resolving environmental problems. The group publishes an Annual Report, the *Center Directory* and a semiannual *Membership Directory*, and holds an annual conference. Its major program is the Network for Environmental Education, and its annual budget is $550,000.

American Forest Council (Founded: 1926)
1250 Connecticut Avenue NW, Suite 320, Washington, D.C. 20036; (202) 463-2455

The American Forest Council promotes the timber industry's positions on environmental issues, publishes a periodical poster entitled "GreenAmerica"; disseminates information through paid advertising, public service announcements and news bureaus; and sponsors educational programs for elementary and secondary school students. The group evolved from a 1926 program of the National Lumber Manufacturers Association to raise funds to be used in expanding lumber markets. In 1936, the NLMA formalized the program by creating a subsidiary group, American Forest Products Industries Inc., of which the former American Forest Institute and the current American Forest Council are direct descendants. The organization sponsors the American Tree Farm System, which includes nearly 40,000 tree farms comprising 80 million acres of forest land. For the owners of land in the system, the group publishes the *American Tree Farmer: The Official Magazine of the American Tree Farm System*.

American Forestry Association. See AMERICAN FORESTS

American Forests (Founded: 1875)
1516 P Street NW, Washington, D.C. 20005; (202) 667-3300

In March 1992, the American Forestry Association was renamed American Forests. It has a membership of 60,000, a staff of 21 and, currently, an annual budget of $2 million. The organization was created by 25 horticulturalists and nurserymen attending the 1875 annual meeting of the American Pomological Society in Chicago. John Aston Warder, a former medical doctor from Ohio, served as the group's first president from 1875 to 1882, years during which the association was primarily concerned with tree culture and planting. In 1882, the last year of Warder's presidency, the group merged with the newly formed American Forestry Congress, an organization Warder and others had created to foster a national policy on forest conservation. Fifteen years later, the organization created out of that merger reincorporated as the American Forestry Association.

During the 1905 AFA-sponsored American Forest Congress in Washington, D.C., President THEODORE ROOSEVELT delivered the keynote address, "The Forest in the Life of a Nation." Meeting participants passed resolutions calling for the federal government to enact a series of reforms, most notably the consolidation of federal forest programs under the U.S. Department of AGRICULTURE. A bill transferring the Bureau of Forestry to the department passed Congress later in 1905.

The association also sponsored the Weeks Act of 1911, which permitted the federal government to purchase forest land for watershed protection, and the McNary-Woodruff Act of 1928, which increased federal appropriations for the purchase of forest land. The forests of the southern Appalachians and the White Mountains in New Hampshire were protected by these laws.

Today, the association is primarily an educational organization with a magazine and book-publishing program. The monthly journal, first called *The Forester* and renamed *American Forests* in 1931, has been published continuously since 1898. In addition, the *National Register of Champion Big Trees and Famous Historical Trees*, published since 1940, encourages the general public to locate and measure the country's largest native trees. This program has resulted in the listing of more than 650 specimens.

Further reading: Henry Clepper, "Crusade for Conservation: The Centennial History of the American Forestry Association," *American Forests* 81 (October 1975), pp. 19–113.

American Nature Association (Founded: 1922; disbanded: 1959)

A spin-off from the American Forestry Association (now AMERICAN FORESTS), the American Nature Association first engaged in a program to promote the planting of trees along the nation's highways and at roadside stops. The group published a monthly magazine entitled *Nature* and grew to include a member-ship of 60,000 by the 1940s. With the success of other similar groups, such as the IZAAK WALTON LEAGUE OF AMERICA and the AMERICAN TREE ASSOCIATION, membership in the American Nature Association decreased, and the organization was dissolved in 1959. The American Museum of Natural History absorbed *Nature* into its publication *Natural History*.

American Nature Study Society (Founded: 1908)
c/o John A. Gustafson, 5881 Cold Brook Road, Homer, New York 13077; (607) 749-3655

Approximately 1,000 professional and amateur naturalists, conservationists and teachers make up the membership of the American Nature Study Society, founded by the editorial board of the *Nature-Study Review*. Dedicated to improving science education in elementary schools, the group awards an annual Eva L. Gordon prize for outstanding science publications for children and conducts educational programs, such as the Wild Foods Weekends. The group is the oldest environmental education association in the United States and is affiliated with the ALLIANCE FOR ENVIRONMENTAL EDUCATION and the INTERNATIONAL UNION FOR CONSERVATION OF NATURE AND NATURAL RESOURCES. It publishes *Nature Magazine*, a quarterly for children, and the *ANSS Newsletter*.

American Rivers Inc. (Founded: 1973)
801 Pennsylvania Avenue SE, Suite 400, Washington, D.C. 20003; (202) 547-6900, Fax (202) 543-6142

Dedicated to the preservation and restoration of U.S. rivers and their adjacent landscapes, the Washington, D.C.–based group American Rivers conducts a variety of programs for riparian conservation. The organization lobbies government to secure wilderness protection for rivers flowing through federal lands and seeks to expand the number and mileage of significant waterways included in the National Wild and Scenic Rivers System, which was created by Congress in 1968.

AR advocates the reform of hydropower siting and operations policies in order to prevent, minimize and repair harmful disruption of important ecosystems by damming, and the group pursues measures to protect aquatic and river-dependent species endangered by such development. The group's Western Water Allocation and Instream Flow Protection program urges greater ecological consideration in the management of federal reserved water rights and Bureau of RECLAMATION activities, and its Clean Water Protection initiative emphasizes a systemic approach to water quality issues, including increased attention to the maintenance of biological integrity in river

Jacks Fork River near Current River, Missouri. *Photo by Tim Palmer, courtesy of American Rivers*

and extension, and to increase appreciation of forests as natural resources essential to the sound economic future of the country." The ATA was not a membership organization as such, but recruited what it called its "Tree Planting Army" from among elementary school students. By 1929, the ATA mustered 129,000 "troops."

The ATA produced educational materials for schools, including the *Forestry Primer,* of which some 4 million copies were distributed. The organization also engaged in legislative lobbying, helping to secure passage of the Clarke-McNary Act of 1924, which laid the basis for U.S. FOREST SERVICE cooperative programs and expanded the authority of the U.S. Department of AGRICULTURE to buy lands. During the George Washington Bicentennial year of 1932, the ATA was responsible for planting more than 27 million trees nationwide.

The American Tree Association became inactive in the 1950s.

American Wildlands (Founded: 1977)
7500 East Arapahoe Road, Suite 355, Englewood, Colorado 80112; (303) 771-0380

American Wildlands, an organization with 4,000 members, works to protect and ensure the appropriate and effective management of wildland resources in the United States. Focusing on wilderness, watersheds, wetlands, free-flowing rivers, fisheries and wildlife, the group engages in scientific and economic research, always making its findings available to the public. The group identifies wildland regions in need of protection. Once an area is identified, the group organizes public support committees through its Wildland Resource Conservation Program and helps them prepare proposals for adding the identified area to the National Wilderness System, the National Wild and Scenic River System or other land management systems. Through public forums, institutes and other programs, the organization promotes responsible use of soil, water, plants, animals and other resources. The group's River Defense Fund is dedicated solely to the protection of river resources.

American Wildlands also sponsors American Wilderness Adventures, a program that offers wild country and river trips, including rafting, canoeing, sailing, horseback riding, photography, backpacking and adventure study in more than 80 different regions.

Formerly called the American Wilderness Alliance, the organization is headed by Clifton R. Merritt, executive director. It operates on an annual budget of $300,000 and has a staff of nine.

habitats and stricter scrutiny of the environmental impact of flow regimes in diverted water systems. The organization endeavors to raise public awareness and improve municipal stewardship of America's outstanding urban rivers, provides technical and legal support for other conservation organizations and citizen coalitions involved in regional, state or local river preservation efforts, and compiles an annual list of rivers most endangered by damming, mining, timber cutting and other commercial activities. The publisher of *America's Rivers: An Assessment of State River Conservation Programs* and the *Guide to Wild and Scenic Designation,* the organization also produces the quarterly periodical *American Rivers.*

American Tree Association (Founded: 1922)
Closely associated with the activities of Charles Lathrop PACK, the American Tree Association was one of the leading promoters of the revival of the Arbor Day tradition in America during the 1920s and 1930s. Its avowed purpose was "to further forest protection

Sally A. G. Ranney, president of American Wildlands.
American Wildlands

American Wildlands publishes the annual *American Wilderness Adventures*, a listing and description of the wilderness adventure trips it sponsors. Other publications include *It's Time to Go Wild*, a bimonthly newsletter; *On the Wild Side Bulletin*, a quarterly; the annual *Wild America Magazine*; and the *Wildland Resource Economic Report*.

Andrus, Cecil Dale (August 25, 1931–   )

The governor of Idaho from 1971 to 1977 and from 1987 to the present, Cecil Dale Andrus was secretary of the interior under President Jimmy Carter from 1977 to 1981 and was instrumental in securing passage of the Alaska National Interest Lands Conservation Act. After President Carter was defeated in his reelection bid, Andrus worked from 1981 to 1986 with the WILDERNESS SOCIETY and the NATIONAL WILDLIFE FEDERATION in addition to representing mineral interests. As governor, Andrus has taken a strong position against the federal government's proposal to store nuclear waste materials in the state of Idaho and two other western states.

Andrus was born in Hood River, Oregon.

Animal Liberation Front (Founded [U.S.]: 1979)

An underground organization, the Animal Liberation Front was formed in England with the goal of ending the exploitation of animals. In 1979, the group also became active in the United States, where its members have raided and broken into government and university laboratories, medical research facilities, slaughterhouses, hatcheries, furriers and other organizations and businesses that use animal products. The group has claimed responsibility for setting fires, defacing property, destroying equipment, stealing research materials and freeing animals housed in laboratories for research purposes. It is estimated that the group has approximately 100 members in the United States.

In November 1991, the British soft drink and drug manufacturer Smith-Kline Beecham P.L.C. was forced to ask retailers to pull 3 million bottles of a soft-drink product from store shelves when police announced their discovery of an Animal Liberation Front plot to contaminate the beverage in a protest against the company's use of animals in drug testing. A spokesman for the organization disclaimed Animal Liberation Front involvement in the plot. He pointed out that organizational policy prohibits any action that would "endanger life of any kind."

The driving principle behind the Animal Liberation Front was expressed by two members interviewed in 1988 for the *Sacramento Bee*. Justifying the group's sometimes violent methods, the members explained, "What's violent is animal experimentation. It must be stopped, even if laws must be broken."

Animal Welfare Institute (Founded: 1951)

P.O. Box 3650, Washington, D.C. 20007;
(202) 337-2333

The Animal Welfare Institute was founded to "reduce the sum total of pain and fear inflicted on animals by man." It works toward achieving the humane treatment of laboratory animals and the development and use of non-animal testing methods. It encourages the humane teaching of science and the prevention of painful experiments on animals by high school students. The institute promotes reform of cruel methods of animal trapping and seeks a ban on the importation and sale of wild-caught exotic birds. It works toward the regulation of shipping conditions for all animals. The institute promotes the preservation of species threatened by extinction and the abatement of cruel treatment of food animals, including excessive confinement on factory farms and inhumane slaughtering methods.

The institute maintains programs specifically targeting the treatment of laboratory animals, the wildlife trade, trapping and the treatment of farm animals. In 1971, it launched the Save the Whales Campaign and is now the parent organization of SAVE THE WHALES, which monitors the actions of whaling nations and promotes a boycott of the products of commercial whaling.

AWI provides representation, speakers and exhibits at relevant conferences worldwide, such as the Convention on International Trade in Endangered Species and the INTERNATIONAL WHALING COMMISSION. The institute is also a founding member of Monitor, a consortium of animal welfare and conservation organizations.

AWI conducts public education and publishing programs. It issues *The Animal Welfare Institute Quarterly* and offers free or inexpensive books and videos, including *Facts About Furs* and *The Endangered Species Handbook*. In 1951, Dr. Albert Schweitzer granted AWI permission to issue a medal in his honor to be presented annually for outstanding achievement in the field of animal welfare.

Christine Gesell STEVENS is the institute's founder and president.

Appalachian Trail Conference (Founded: 1925)
P. O. Box 807, Harpers Ferry, West Virginia 25425; (304) 535-6331

The Appalachian Trail Conference is a federation of trail and hiking clubs as well as individuals interested in using and preserving the Appalachian Trail. The organization manages the trail, a 2,100-mile foot path that runs, for the most part, along the crest of the Appalachian Mountains from Maine to Georgia. In addition, the group is dedicated to protecting nearly 100,000 acres of federally owned land surrounding the trail. The group publishes *Appalachian Trailway News* five times a year; a bimonthly newsletter, *The Register*; the semiannual *Trail Lands*, which includes information on the organization's conservation programs; and trail guidebooks, maps and other materials designed for use by trail hikers. In addition, the group holds a biennial conference. David N. STARTZELL serves as executive director of the Appalachian Trail Conference, which has 24,000 members, a permanent staff of 29 and an annual budget of $1.8 million.

Archibald, George William (July 13, 1946–   )
Cofounder and director of the INTERNATIONAL CRANE FUNDATION in Baraboo, Wisconsin, George W. Archibald is a world-recognized authority on crane species. He is chairman of the INTERNATIONAL COUNCIL FOR BIRD PRESERVATION's World Working Group on Cranes, based in Cambridge, England, and a member

International Crane Foundation director George Archibald dances with a seven-year-old whooping crane named Gee Whiz in the foundation's Johnson Exhibit Pod. *Photo by David Thompson, International Crane Foundation*

of the U.S. Whooping Crane Recovery Team and the Species Survival Commission of the INTERNATIONAL UNION FOR THE CONSERVATION OF NATURAL RESOURCES.

Born in New Glasgow, Nova Scotia, Archibald received his bachelor of science from Dalhousie University in Halifax in 1968. He traveled to Hokkaido, Japan, in 1972 and spent a year engaged in field research and conservation initiatives to safeguard breeding sites of the red-crowned crane in a project underwritten by the New York Zoological Society. Cofounding the International Crane Foundation in 1973, Archibald continued his research and habitat protection work in Australia and Korea over the next two years and earned his doctorate in ornithology from Cornell University in 1976. A celebrated expert in the captive breeding of rare crane species, he has served as an advisor to the Zhalong Nature Reserve in Qigihar, China, since 1987 and to the Tram Chim Nature Reserve of Tam Nong, Vietnam, since 1989. He has been honored with the Netherlands' Order of the Golden Ark (1982), the WORLD WILDLIFE FUND Gold Medal (1985), the MacArthur Award (1984) and the UNITED NATIONS ENVIRONMENT PROGRAMME Global 500 Roll of Honor for Environmental Achievement (1987). Archibald is a member of numerous national and international ornithological and wildlife conservation organizations.

Army Corps of Engineers (Established: 1802)
(202) 272-0001

Although the Army Corps of Engineers was officially established in 1802, it may be dated to 1775, when

Hikers on the Appalachian Trail. *Appalachian Trail Conference*

engineers assigned to the Continental Army built the fortifications at Bunker Hill during the first days of the Revolution. The corps undertook its first civil works project in 1824.

Today, the status of the corps is unique in national government. It is part of the U.S. Army and, therefore, technically under the jurisdiction of the Department of Defense. However, it is primarily a civilian agency with some 40,000 civilian employees supervised by a staff of about 200 Army officers. Its principal mandate is to facilitate safe navigation of the nation's inland waterways and to manage flood-control projects. The corps also supervises many dredge-and-fill operations and regulates some pollutant discharges into navigable waters. The corps also has had responsibility for certain non-water-related construction projects, including the building of the Alaska Highway, the Washington Monument, the U.S. Capitol and all Veterans Administration hospitals across the country, which it also maintains.

The Rivers and Harbors Act of 1899 assigned environmental regulatory functions to the corps, which were expanded by the Clean Water Act of 1972. Most projects the Army Corps of Engineers undertakes are contracted to private firms, which corps officials supervise.

Arnold, Richard Keith (November 17, 1913–   )
A long-time employee of the U.S. FOREST SERVICE, this native of Long Beach, California, first worked as a fire research officer for the California (Pacific Southwest) Forest and Range Experiment Station at Berkeley and as a member of the forestry faculty at the University of California. He managed Operation Fire-stop, a program developed by the U.S. Forest Service, the Civil Defense Administration, the California Division of Forestry, the universities of California and Southern California and various forest industries to research and develop fire prevention and control techniques. In 1963, he transferred from the Pacific Southwest Forest and Range Experiment Station to the Washington, D.C., headquarters of the Forest Service, where he served as director of the Division of Forest Protection Research until 1966. Between 1966 and 1969, he was dean of the School of Natural Resources at the University of Michigan, but he returned to the Forest Service to become deputy chief in charge of research, a post he held until 1972.

Arnold returned to the academic world in 1972 as a professor at the University of Texas. While there, he also served as director of the Marine Science Institute and associate dean of the Lyndon Johnson School of Public Affairs.

Arnold was associate editor of the *Journal of Forestry* from 1956 to 1958 and served on the council of the SOCIETY OF AMERICAN FORESTERS from 1964 to 1969. He was also chairman of the United Nations Forest Fire Working Group for the North American Forestry Commission, Food and Agriculture Organization.

Asia-Pacific People's Environment Network
(Founded: 1982)
c/o Sahabat Alam Malaysia, 43 Salween Road, 10050 Penang, Malaysia; (4) 375705

The Asia-Pacific People's Environment Network (APPEN), coordinated by David Heah, was founded to serve the environmental interests of organizations in 25 countries in the Asia-Pacific region. Focusing on the depletion of natural resources and the degradation of the environment, the organization gathers and distributes information and research reports on environmental issues. Its reports and books include *The Bhopal Tragedy: One Year After; Damming the Narmada; Decimation of World Wildlife; Japan as Number One: Environment, Development and Natural Resource Crisis in Asia and the Pacific; Environmental Crisis in Asia-Pacific; Forest Resources Crisis in the Third World;* and *Global Development and Environmental Crisis: Has Humankind a Future?* In addition to book publishing, the organization offers educational programs for its 350 institutional and individual members, maintains a library and publishes the biweekly *APPEN Features,* the quarterly *Asian-Pacific Environment Newsletter,* a *Directory of Environmental NGOs in the Asia-Pacific Region* and the bimonthly *Environmental News Digest.*

Aspinall, Wayne N(orviel) (April 3, 1896– October 9, 1983)
Wayne N. Aspinall was elected to Congress as Democratic representative from Colorado in 1949 and served until 1973, suffering a defeat in large part due to the pressure of environmental groups, which objected to his continued advocacy of land reclamation projects and "multiple use"—policies that combine recreational, wilderness and commercial uses of public lands.

Aspinall was chairman of the powerful House Interior and Insular Affairs Committee from 1959 until 1973. He therefore played a key role in all natural resources legislation during these years and was a formidable opponent of what he characterized as "environmental extremists." During the administrations of John F. Kennedy and Lyndon JOHNSON, he worked to delay and weaken what finally became the Wilderness Act of 1964. At Aspinall's insistence, the act included numerous multiple-use provisions.

Aspinall advocated many water projects of the Bureau of RECLAMATION that were vigorously opposed by environmentalists. One of the most extensive of these was the Central Arizona Project of the mid-1960s, which proposed diverting Colorado River water to cities and farmlands in Arizona. Environmental activists opposed the bill, and even the administration's own Budget Bureau recommended against it; Aspinall nevertheless engineered its passage with the addition of five irrigation projects that would directly benefit agricultural interests in Colorado.

The policies and projects of this representative did not always prevail, however. Measures to augment the flow of the Colorado River by tapping the river basins of the Pacific Northwest were defeated in the 1960s, as was legislation to build two dams and a hydroelectric station in the Grand Canyon section of the Colorado River. This fell victim to a massive lobbying campaign mounted by David BROWER and the SIERRA CLUB in 1967.

Aspinall was a native of Middleburg, Ohio, and was educated at the University of Denver (A.B., 1919) and the Denver Law School (LL.B., 1925). He practiced law in Colorado and engaged in peach orchard farming. Aspinall was elected to the Colorado House of Representatives in 1931, serving until 1938 (he was speaker from 1937 to 1938). From 1939 to 1949, he served as state senator.

In addition to the Interior and Insular Affairs Committee, Aspinall served on the Public Land Law Review Commission and the Joint Committee on Atomic Energy.

AuCoin, Les (October 21, 1942–   )
A native of Redmond, Oregon, Les AuCoin was Democratic representative from Oregon's First District from 1974 to 1992. A liberal, AuCoin vigorously supported environmental issues, perhaps most notably during 1991, when he successfully managed conflicts between enforcement of the Endangered Species Act and Oregon lumber interests and when he was instrumental in engineering legislation to protect Columbia and Snake river salmon populations from proposed dredging operations.

AuCoin was educated at Pacific University, where he earned a B.A. in journalism in 1969. He worked as a newsman with the *Redmond Spokesman* in 1960, volunteered for service with the U.S. Army infantry from 1961 to 1964, returned briefly to the *Spokesman* and then moved to the *Portland Oregonian*, working as a newsman from 1965 to 1966. In 1966, he became director of public information at Pacific University. AuCoin held this position from 1966 to 1973, then served as an administrator with the architectural firm of Skidmore, Owings, and Merrill in 1973 and 1974.

From 1971 to 1975, AuCoin served as state representative from Washington County, becoming majority leader of the Oregon House of Representatives in 1973. He left the state House in 1975 when he was elected to his first term in Congress.

AuCoin has served on the House Committee on Banking, Finance, and Urban Affairs; Committee on Merchant Marine and Fisheries; the House Task Force on Home Ownership; the House Committee on Appropriations; and the Select Committee on Hunger. In 1992 he ran unsuccessfully for the Senate, losing to Robert Packwood. Democrat Elizabeth Purse won election to AuCoin's former House seat.

Audubon, John James (April 26, 1785–January 27, 1851)

John James Audubon, who was born in Santo Domingo (Haiti) and lived for a time in France, immigrated to the United States in 1803. Although he engaged in a variety of business ventures from 1803 to 1819, studying and drawing birds were his true passions. After abandoning his business career, he produced a portfolio of watercolors of American birds and traveled to England to publish the paintings in book form. *The Birds of America*, a sumptuous four-volume work, was published between 1827 and 1838, and an accompanying text was issued as *Ornithological Biography* in five volumes from 1831 to 1838.

In the 1840s, Audubon turned his attention to American mammals, a study later completed by his sons. Other published works of Audubon are *A Synopsis of the Birds of North America* (1839) and *The Viviparous Quadrupeds of North America* (1845–48). Audubon was among the first Americans to receive international recognition for cultural and scientific achievements.

Further reading: Alice Ford, *John James Audubon: A Biography* (New York: Abbeville Press, 1986); Francis Hobart Herrick, *Audubon the Naturalist*, 2 vols. (New York: Dover Publications, 1968).

Ayres, Richard Edward (February 2, 1942–   )

When the NATURAL RESOURCES DEFENSE COUNCIL was incorporated in 1970, Richard Edward Ayres, named

John James Audubon, as depicted in an engraving by Alonzo Chappel. *National Audubon Society*

senior staff attorney, began work on strengthening and enforcing the country's air pollution control laws. Born in Salem, New Jersey, Ayres took his B.A. at Princeton University, an LL.B. at Yale University Law School and an M.A. at Yale University Graduate School of Political Science. He has participated in several environmentally related lawsuits, including a case against the TENNESSEE VALLEY AUTHORITY, which resulted in a mandated reduction of sulphur dioxide pollution. During the Carter administration, he served on the National Commission on Air Quality and the Steel Tri-Partite Commission. In addition, Ayres has chaired the National Clean Air Coalition and has served as a member of the board of the LEAGUE OF CONSERVATION VOTERS. In 1987, he coauthored an article with Donald N. Strait entitled "High Noon for Smog Control" for *Environment* magazine, a stern and influential criticism of the federal government's failure to confront the ozone problem.

B

Bahouth, Peter (August 26, 1953–   )
Executive director of GREENPEACE U.S.A., Peter Bahouth holds a B.A. from the University of Rochester and a J.D. from the Northeast School of Law. Beginning in 1979, he volunteered his legal services to Greenpeace while he was working as a trial attorney in Boston. In 1982, he was elected to the board of directors of Greenpeace, and was named chairman in 1984. After the *Rainbow Warrior*, a flagship of GREENPEACE INTERNATIONAL, was sunk by French secret service agents in 1985 while it was in a New Zealand port preparing to protest French nuclear testing in the South Pacific, Bahouth negotiated damages to be paid to the organization and to the estate of a Greenpeace photographer killed in the incident.

Peter Bahouth, former executive director of Greenpeace USA and now regional trustee for Greenpeace International. © *Townsend/Greenpeace*

In 1987, Bahouth coordinated the production of a Greenpeace-sponsored record album called *Breakthrough*, which included performances by Peter Gabriel, the Talking Heads, R.E.M., the Grateful Dead, U2, Belinda Carlisle, John Cougar Mellencamp and many other recording artists. The album debuted in the Soviet Union, where it enjoyed monumental sales.

Bailes, Kendall Eugene (June 9, 1940–March 28, 1988)
A California-based historian, educator and author, Kendall Bailes was editor of the book *Environmental History: Critical Issues in Comparative Perspective* (1985).

Born in Fort Morgan, Colorado, Bailes studied at Dartmouth College (B.A., 1963) before earning his master's degree (1966) and doctorate (1971) in history and Russian area studies at Columbia University in New York. Bailes began his teaching career at Kansas State University (1970–71), then became an assistant professor (1971) and associate professor (1977) of history at the University of California, Irvine. In 1981 he was made full professor, and the following year he was appointed dean of humanities. He also taught courses at the University of California, Los Angeles, and joined the faculty there in 1987, the year before he died.

Bailes contributed essays to a number of scholarly publications, and his first book, *Technology and Society under Lenin and Stalin: Origins of the Soviet Technical Intelligentsia, 1917–1941* (1978) won the Herbert Baxter Adams Prize of the American Historical Association. He was a member of the A.H.A. and of the American Association of Advanced Slavic Studies.

Baker, John Hopkinson (June 30, 1894–September 21, 1973)
John Hopkinson Baker abandoned his career as a Wall Street broker in 1934 to take up conservation work full time. At the NATIONAL AUDUBON SOCIETY,

where he served as executive director from 1934 to 1944 and president from 1944 to 1959, Baker developed the Audubon Camps, which provided natural history and ecological instruction to teachers and other adults, established nature centers for children and initiated the "Audubon Screen Tours" series of annual lectures held across the country. He was active in the campaign to establish Everglades National Park and spearheaded the Audubon Society's research and scientific monograph programs. From 1948 to 1953, he was chairman of the Fish and Wildlife Advisory Committee of the U.S. Department of the INTERIOR, and from 1957 to 1960 served as a member of that committee. He was also a member of the board of the NATIONAL PARKS AND CONSERVATION ASSOCIATION and the NATURAL RESOURCES COUNCIL OF AMERICA. To commemorate his activities in conservation, the National Audubon Society created the John H. Baker Scholarship Fund for Conservation Education in 1969.

Ballinger, Richard Achilles (July 9, 1858–June 6, 1922)

Appointed secretary of the interior by President William Howard Taft in March 1909, Richard Achilles Ballinger is best known for his involvement in the Ballinger-Pinchot controversy. The problem began when Gifford PINCHOT, chief forester in the Bureau of Forestry (now the U. S. FOREST SERVICE), criticized Ballinger's stand on various water-power sites and other conservation matters, but especially his position on coal claims in Alaska. Acting on behalf of 33 claimants, well-known western mining and sawmill entrepreneur Clarence Cunningham entered claims to vast tracts of Alaskan land, and Ballinger ordered Louis R. Glavis of the General Land Office in Oregon to expedite processing the claims. When Glavis asked for more time, Ballinger, bent on hurrying the claims through, refused to grant an extension. Pinchot and Fred Dennett, assistant commissioner of the General Land Office, discovered that the claimants planned to sign their claims over to a company backed by J. P. Morgan and a group of wealthy industrialists, bankers and investors, despite a federal law prohibiting such consolidation. With the help of Pinchot, Glavis prepared a report to President Taft, who summarily referred the matter back to Ballinger and issued a statement exonerating Ballinger of any blame in handling the Cunningham claims. He also instructed Ballinger to fire Glavis.

A few months later, in November 1909, Glavis wrote and published in *Collier's Weekly* an article entitled "The White-Washing of Ballinger." In it, Glavis fully explained Ballinger's role in the fraudulent Cunningham claims. Congress then began investigating the affair, but not soon enough to keep Pinchot from being fired. Thus the man responsible for building the U. S. Forest Service from a small division with five employees to a huge agency with more than 2,000 employees was no longer at the helm of the nation's forestry program.

Ballinger was born in Boonesboro, Iowa, and died in Seattle, Washington.

Further reading: James L. Penick, *Progressive Politics and Conservation: The Ballinger-Pinchot Affair* (Chicago: University of Chicago Press, 1968).

Bari, Judi (November 7, 1949–   )

A radical environmentalist member of EARTH FIRST!, Judi Bari is a native of Baltimore, Maryland. She attended the University of Maryland but became involved during the Vietnam War era in radical politics. When she dropped out of college, she went to work in a grocery store and became active in the Retail Clerks Union, helping to lead a strike of 17,000 grocery clerks. During the strike she participated in such activities as sealing locks with liquid steel and deflating the tires of managers' cars. Later, Bari left the grocery store and took a job as a postal worker. Finding that none of the three unions involved in the U.S. Post Office Bulk Mail Center in which she worked did anything to protect employees from long hours and dangerous conditions, Bari formed a rank-and-file group and led a successful wildcat strike to gain a 40-hour workweek.

Early in 1979, Bari left the post office and moved to Northern California, where she married and had two children. During this period she became active in the Central America peace movement, serving as regional coordinator for Pledge of Resistance, a group that used mass nonviolent civil disobedience to protest U.S. involvement in Nicaragua and El Salvador.

In 1988, while working as a carpenter building luxury homes out of old-growth redwood, Bari became concerned about the future of the redwood forest and joined Earth First! Based on her labor experience and her own position as a blue-collar worker, she acted to build a coalition with the loggers to oppose the corporations' overcutting. In addition to organizing Earth First! "tree-sits" and log road blockades, Bari formed a union, IWW Local #1, and represented timber workers in their struggle for safe working conditions and their opposition to irresponsible logging practices.

Bari's attempt to approach an environmental problem by enlisting the cooperation of labor put her at odds with some other Earth First!ers, who advocated tree spiking as a method of stopping timber cutting. They drove long spikes into trees, believing that the danger this practice posed to loggers and millworkers would stop the timber companies from cutting the trees. But after a millworker was severely injured when a spiked tree was run through a mill in Bari's neighborhood, breaking a huge sawblade, she publicly repudiated the practice of tree spiking.

In the spring of 1990, Bari organized "Redwood Summer," calling on college students and others to come to Northern California to engage in mass non-violent civil disobedience to protest the redwood overcut. At the same time, she went public with the worker coalition, appearing before her county's governing board with loggers, millworkers and environmentalists. They demanded that the county use its power of eminent domain to seize the corporate timberlands and protect them from destruction by out-of-town corporations. As a result of her activism, Bari became the target of a campaign of death threats, intimidation and forged press releases and other faked documents designed to portray Earth First! as a terrorist group.

In May 1990, shortly before Redwood Summer began, Bari and fellow organizer Darryl Cherney were driving in Bari's car toward Santa Cruz when a pipe bomb exploded beneath the car seat. Bari was severely injured and nearly killed, while Cherney suffered lesser injuries. Oakland police and FBI officials arrested Bari and Cherney for the bombing, alleging that it was their bomb and that they had knowingly carried it. For eight weeks the two were declared guilty in the press, before police finally conceded that they had no evidence against them. No charges were filed, but, Bari contends, the police failed to conduct a serious investigation of the bombing. The bomber remains at large. (Bari and Cherney filed a civil rights lawsuit against the FBI and Oakland police for their handling of the bombing case.)

Despite the assassination attempt and smear campaign, Redwood Summer went on as planned. Three thousand people came to Northern California and, at Bari's urging from her hospital bed, maintained their nonviolence throughout the summer's protests. As a partial result of Redwood Summer, Headwaters Forest, the last unprotected redwood wilderness, was preserved, and some of the timber corporations backed off from their practice of redwood clearcutting.

Judi Bari was permanently disabled by the bombing, suffering spinal dislocation, paralysis of one foot, pelvic instability and partial paralysis of the colon. Nevertheless, she continues to work as an activist in the redwood region. In 1992, she was a principal organizer of the Albion Uprising, in which a rural community successfully banded together for nine weeks of nonviolent direct action to block a timber corporation's plan to cut the redwoods in their neighborhood. Bari has also helped to organize the Men-

docino Real Wood Co-Op, an association of timber workers and landowners who want to engage in nondestructive logging practices. Her 1992 book, *Timber Wars and Other Writings*, details the struggles of the Earth First! movement in the redwood region.

Bean, Michael J. (July 3, 1949–   )
Environmental lawyer Michael J. Bean holds a B.S. in political science from the University of Iowa (he was born in Fort Madison, Iowa) and a J.D. from Yale University Law School. In 1976, he was named director of the Wildlife Program of the ENVIRONMENTAL LAW INSTITUTE and the following year was appointed to his present post as chairman of the Wildlife Program of the ENVIRONMENTAL DEFENSE FUND, where he has worked to strengthen the Endangered Species Act and Marine Mammal Protection Act and has participated in lawsuits involving the National Wildlife Refuge System, the TENNESSEE VALLEY AUTHORITY and the U. S. ARMY CORPS OF ENGINEERS. He is a member of the International Council on Environmental Law and serves on the Commission on Environmental Policy, Law, and Administration of the INTERNATIONAL UNION FOR CONSERVATION OF NATURE AND NATURAL RESOURCES. Bean was a consultant to the U.S. FISH AND WILDLIFE SERVICE on legislative implementation of the 1976 Migratory Bird Treaty with the Soviet Union, and a nongovernmental organization observer at the Second, Third, Fourth and Sixth Conferences of the Parties to the Convention on International Trade in Endangered Species of Wild Fauna and Flora in 1979, 1981, 1983 and 1987. He was a nongovernmental organization observer at the plenipotentiary meeting to negotiate a Convention for the Conservation of Migratory Animals held in Bonn, Germany, in 1979; participated in a meeting of legal experts on the implementation of the Convention on Nature Protection and Wildlife Preservation in the Western Hemisphere, sponsored by the Organization of American States in 1979; and served as legal advisor to the delegation of the government of the Seychelles to the INTERNATIONAL WHALING COMMISSION in 1980.

He is the author of *The Evolution of Natural Wildlife Law* (1977) and has published articles in *Quarterly Review of Biology, Natural History, Defenders, National Parks, Atlantic Naturalist,* and elsewhere.

Becker, Daniel Frome (August 12, 1955–   )
The director of the SIERRA CLUB's Global Warming and Energy Campaign, New York-born attorney Daniel F. Becker also serves on the board of directors of Americans for the Environment and the National Clean Air Coalition, all of Washington, D.C.

A graduate of Hamilton College (B.A., 1977) and Northeastern University (J.D., 1983), Becker was admitted to the Massachusetts Bar in 1983. From 1978 to 1980, he was director of research for Ralph Nader's Congress Watch, then served as campaign coordinator for New York City Commissioner of Consumer Affairs Mark Green in his unsuccessful run for the U. S. House of Representatives. In 1983, he joined the Massachusetts Public Interest Research Group as chief lobbyist and staff attorney, and in 1985, he became legal counsel for ENVIRONMENTAL ACTION in Washington, D.C. The author of numerous magazine and newspaper articles, Becker was editor of *Making Polluters Pay: A Citizen's Guide to Legal Action and Organizing*, published in 1987. He was named to his current position with the Sierra Club in 1989.

Bennett, Hugh Hammond (April 15, 1881–July 7, 1960)
Born in Wadesboro, North Carolina, Bennett graduated from the University of North Carolina in 1903 and joined the staff of the Bureau of Soils of the U. S. Department of AGRICULTURE. Early in his career, he became interested in soil erosion and in 1909 was given responsibility for nationwide soil surveys. His research on the topic took him not only across the United States but also to Central and South America. He worked in Cuba from 1925 to 1926 and again in 1928 to survey soil conditions and recommend changes in sugar production methods. Based on his research on the island, he wrote (with Robert V. Allison) *The Soils of Cuba*.

In 1928, Bennett and William R. Chapline issued *Soil Erosion: A National Menace*, a landmark publication of the Department of Agriculture and a work that helped to persuade Congress of the need for federal appropriations for an erosion control program. The resulting legislation appropriated $160,000 to set up stations across the country where soil agents could study conditions. Bennett was named director of the Soil Erosion Service of the U. S. Department of the INTERIOR in the Dust Bowl year of 1933. His testimony before Congress in 1935 coincided with a freak dust storm in Washington, and congressmen passed Public Law 46, the first soil conservation act. Bennett then became head of the SOIL CONSERVATION SERVICE in the Department of Agriculture.

By 1946, Bennett's agency had 1,700 soil conservation districts set up across the country, helping farmers adopt new, more effective agricultural methods, including contour tillage and the use of stubble mulch. Bennett remained head of the Soil Conservation Service until his retirement at the age of 70 in 1951. In addition to *The Soils of Cuba* and *Soil Erosion: A National Menace*, he also wrote *The Soils and Agriculture of the Southern States* (1921), *Soil Conservation* (1939), *Elements of Soil Conservation* (1947) and *This*

Land We Defend (with William C. Pryor, 1942). He received numerous awards, including the Audubon Medal from the NATIONAL AUDUBON SOCIETY, the Cullum Medal from the American Geographical Society and the John Deere Gold Medal from the American Society of Agricultural Engineers.

Bennett died in Falls Church, Virginia.

Berg, Peter (October 1, 1937–   )
Peter Berg is the founder and director of Planet Drum Foundation, a San Francisco-based ecological research and education organization established in 1974. Coauthor of the book *A Green City Program for the San Francisco Bay Area and Beyond* (with Beryl Magilavy and Seth Zuckerman, 1989, 1990), a pioneering blueprint for urban sustainability, Berg helped develop the concepts of bioregions and reinhabitation and has cosponsored the annual North American Bioregional Congress since 1984. He was also sponsor of the Shasta Bioregion Gathering in 1991. A contributing editor of *Raise the Stakes: The Planet Drum Review*, Berg has written articles for *CoEvolution Quarterly*, *Whole Earth Review*, *Environmental Action*, *The Ecologist*, *Futures* and other periodicals, and has lectured on city ecology in the United States, Canada, Mexico, Australia, and Russia. Berg was born in Jamaica, Queens, New York, and received his A.A. at the University of Florida in 1959.

Further reading: Berg, *Figures of Regulation: Guides for Rebalancing Society with the Biosphere* (San Francisco: Planet Drum Foundation, 1982); Berg (ed.), *Reinhabiting a Separate Country: A Bioregional Anthology of Northern California* (San Francisco: Planet Drum Foundation, 1978).

Berger, John J(oseph) (May 8, 1945–   )
John J. Berger was born in New York City and was educated at Stanford University, receiving his B.A. in 1966. He served as a writer and reporter with the Fremont, California, *News Observer* from 1969 to 1970 and then as managing editor of Alternative Features Service, Berkeley, California, from 1970 to 1973. He was an editorial specialist with the Far West Laboratory for Educational Research and Development in San Francisco from 1973 to 1975, then joined FRIENDS OF THE EARTH in 1976 as energy products director. He published *Nuclear Power, the Unviable Option: A Critical Look at Our Energy Alternatives* that same year.

Since 1976, Berger has continued to research and to write on energy and the environment under the auspices of Friends of the Earth. In addition to his critical analysis of nuclear power, he has written *Restoring the Earth: How Americans Are Working to Renew Our Damaged Environment* (1985) and is the editor of *Environmental Restoration: Science and Strategies for Restoring the Earth* (1989).

Bergson, Henri (October 12, 1859–January 3, 1941)

An extraordinarily influential French philosopher, Henri Bergson is best known for his epistemological theories—which stress the dominance of direct intuition in acquiring knowledge and understanding—and those concerning the nature of time.

Bergson was also interested in biological evolution and formulated the concept of *élan vital,* the idea that a vital spirit, force or energy is present in, pervades and animates all living things. This mysterious, deep spirit, according to Bergson, cannot be analyzed through physics or chemistry; nor, indeed, can the core reality of nature be understood through the intellect. In 1907, he published his theory of *élan vital* in *L'Evolution créatrice,* translated into English in 1913 as *Creative Evolution.* Bergson's "vitalism," as it was called, influenced a number of naturalists, particularly those with mystic or romantic tendencies, most notably the American John BURROUGHS.

Bergson was awarded the Nobel Prize for literature in 1927.

Further reading: Anthony E. Pilkington, *Bergson and His Influence: A Reassessment* (Cambridge: Cambridge University Press, 1976).

Berle, Peter Adolf Augustus (December 8, 1937–   )

Lawyer and executive Peter Adolf Augustus Berle worked as the New York state commissioner of environmental conservation from 1976 to 1979. His commission, employing a staff of 5,000, discovered and disposed of the hazardous waste in the upstate Love Canal. From 1971 to 1985, Berle was a partner in Berle, Kass & Case, a law firm specializing in environmental litigation. He was the chairman of the New York State Governor's Transition Task Force on the Environment from 1974 to 1975, and has served since 1989 as chairman of the Commission on the Adirondacks in the 21st Century.

In 1985, Berle became president of the NATIONAL AUDUBON SOCIETY and the following year accepted a position as visiting professor of environmental science and forestry at the State University of New York. At the Audubon Society, he enlarged the organization's educational program, "Audubon Adventures," which in 1985 reached 48,000 students and now reaches more than 500,000. He redesigned the society's ornithological journal, *American Birds,* in order to attract a broader audience. Under his direction, the society's annual budget has grown from $25 million to $43 million.

Berle serves on the ENVIRONMENTAL PROTECTION AGENCY's Clean Air Act Advisory Committee and the

Peter A. A. Berle, president of the National Audubon Society. *National Audubon Society*

Science Advisory Commission on Biotechnology. In addition, he is a member of the National Commission on the Environment, an organization formed in 1991 to address global environmental issues. Building on experience gained in the Love Canal disaster, Berle founded and is the director of Clean Sites Inc., an organization that promotes the clean-up of hazardous waste sites across the country.

Berry, Thomas (November 9, 1914–   )

Thomas Berry is an "eco-theologian," an ordained Catholic priest who believes that modern man needs a new, ecologically based myth of cosmic origins to give new life to a shattered and alienated civilization that is currently at tragically destructive odds with the environment. Berry's evolving eco-theology is founded as much in contemporary particle physics as it is in traditional religious teaching. As modern physics has revealed the universe as a dynamic, fluid, living system rather than a static order, so Berry hopes to convey a vision of a universe that is alive and interconnected—to use his word, "enchanted"—a universe in which man feels himself not an alienated observer or participant, but an organic part of an organic whole. The attainment of such a vision, Berry believes, requires nothing less than an empirically based yet religiously inspiring story of creation itself.

Berry was born in Greensboro, North Carolina, and educated at St. Michael's Monastery in Union City, New Jersey, and at the Catholic University of America, which awarded him a Ph.D. in 1949. He was ordained a Roman Catholic priest of the Passionist Congregation in 1942 and has taught the history of religions at Fordham University since 1966. In 1970 he founded the Riverdale Center for Religious Research, which he has directed since its founding. Berry is also associated with the Teilhard Association for the Future of Man.

His early books include *The Historical Theory of Giambattista Vico* (1959), *Buddhism* (1967) and *Religions of India: Hinduism, Yoga, Buddhism* (1971). His more recent books reflect his research and thought in ecotheology and include *Management: The Managerial Ethos and the Future of Planet Earth* (1980), *Teilhard in the Ecological Age* (1982), *Technology and the Healing of the Earth* (1985), *The Dream of the Earth* (1990) and *Befriending the Earth: A Theology of Reconciliation between Humans and the Earth* (1991).

Berry, Wendell (Erdman) (August 5, 1934–)

Wendell Berry is among the most distinguished contemporary writers of poetry and prose. His work calls to mind that of two earlier writers, Henry David THOREAU and William Faulkner. Like Thoreau, Berry's outlook is intensely environmental, and he draws his larger conclusions about the relation among humankind, nature, and culture from specific instances and particular places. Like Faulkner, Berry has taken a real place—his native Henry County, Kentucky—and elevated it to a kind of mythic-fictive environment called Port William, akin to Faulkner's Yoknapatawpha County.

Berry's poetry and fiction focus thematically on the despoliation of Kentucky, which the author reveals as a microcosm of the modern American's increasing alienation from nature in general. Berry emphasizes the healing virtues of achieving a harmony with nature. He does not limit the expression of his ideas to verse or fiction, but is also the author of several volumes of essays concerning, for the most part, the role of traditional agriculture in American history and life. These works include *A Continuous Harmony: Essays Cultural and Agricultural* (1972), *The Unsettling of America: Culture and Agriculture* (1977), *The Agricultural Crisis: A Crisis of Culture* (1977), *The Gift of God Land: Further Essays Cultural and Agricultural* (1981),

Recollected Essays: Nineteen Sixty-Five to Nineteen Eighty (1981), and *Home Economics: Fourteen Essays* (1987).

Berry does not content himself with expressing his ideas on paper. He is a working farmer who eschews modern methods and farm machinery in favor of the traditional procedures employed by the previous five generations of his farming family. Berry was educated at the University of Kentucky (A.B., 1956; M.A., 1957), and, before returning to the farm, taught English at the university.

Berry's audience goes well beyond a literary coterie on the one hand and environmentalists on the other. His work appeared during the 1960s in such publications as *The Whole Earth Catalogue* and *Mother Earth News*, and he has contributed to the likes of *Hudson Review*, *Harper's* and the *Nation*, as well as *Organic Gardening* and *Blair and Ketchum's Country Journal*.

Berry has been the recipient of Guggenheim and Rockefeller foundation grants, and received the National Institute of Arts and Letters Literary Award in 1971.

Bertrand, Gerald Adrian (July 7, 1943–)

An environmental lawyer who holds a B.S. in zoology (University of New Hampshire), an M.S. in biology (Florida State University), a Ph.D. in biological oceanography (Oregon State University) and a J.D. in environmental law (University of Wisconsin), Boston-born Gerald Adrian Bertrand served as an ecological advisor to the chief of the U.S. ARMY CORPS OF ENGINEERS. In that capacity, he helped develop corps policies, which called for redesigning several water projects, including the Cross Florida Barge Canal Project. Under presidents Nixon, Ford and Carter, Bertrand worked as senior scientist for the President's COUNCIL ON ENVIRONMENTAL QUALITY. In 1977, he was employed by the U.S. FISH AND WILDLIFE SERVICE as chief of international affairs. In this capacity he worked on conservation programs for more than 50 different countries. Since 1980, he has served as president of the Massachusetts Audubon Society and has been a board member of the American Committee for International Conservation, the Ocean Research and Education Society, the ANIMAL WELFARE INSTITUTE and the Fauna and Flora Preservation Society.

Bessey, Charles Edwin (May 21, 1845– February 25, 1915)

Teacher, writer and scientist, Charles Edwin Bessey was a graduate of the "scientific course" of Michigan Agricultural College (1869) and remained at the school for a short time as an assistant in horticulture. He moved next to Ames, Iowa, where he established courses in botany and horticulture at the Iowa Agri-

Charles Bessey. *Courtesy of the New York Botanical Garden*

cultural College (present-day Iowa State University). In 1872, Bessey went to Harvard University to study under Asa GRAY and William Farlow, and in 1880, he completed *Botany for High Schools and Colleges*, a textbook that was widely used until 1910. After completing another successful textbook, *Essentials of Botany*, in 1884, he moved to the University of Nebraska as a professor of botany. Bessey served as associate editor of the journals *American Naturalist* and *Science*.

Bessey's contributions to the study of botany are many, but he is best known for devising an effective system of teaching the subject by combining two systems of angiosperm classification, one by Engler and Prantl and the other by Bentham and Hooker, to produce a rearranged system of plant families based on 28 "dicta."

A native of Milton Township, Ohio, Bessey died in Lincoln, Nebraska.

Beston, Henry (June 1, 1888–April 15, 1968)

Praised by literary critics as a latter-day Henry David THOREAU, Henry Beston built a diminutive two-room cabin at Eastham, Cape Cod, Massachusetts, as a weekend retreat. From this vacation shelter, which soon became Beston's home for a full year, the writer-naturalist observed the changing seasons at Cape Cod, recording his observations, as Thoreau did, in a journal. Beston published his work in 1928 as *The Outmost House*, which many still consider a supreme model of understated, graceful, meticulously observed nature writing.

A native of Quincy, Massachusetts, Beston was educated at Harvard University (B.A., 1909; M.A., 1911). He served in the American Field Service and the U.S. Navy during World War I, then returned to Massachusetts, where he became a full-time editor and writer.

Beston's later books include *Northern Farm* (1948) and *White Pine and Blue Water* (1950), both widely admired—although *The Outmost House* remains Beston's classic work. On October 11, 1964, four years before his death (at Nobleboro, Maine), Beston was present at ceremonies proclaiming his Cape Cod cabin a National Literary Landmark.

Bingham, Eula (July 9, 1929–   )

A native of Covington, Kentucky, Eula Bingham was educated at Eastern Kentucky University, earning an M.S. in 1954. She received her Ph.D. from the University of Cincinnati in 1958. Bingham was assistant professor of chemistry at the College of Medicine, University of Cincinnati, from 1961 to 1970, when she was promoted to associate professor, serving in that capacity until 1977. Since 1981, she has been professor of environmental health (and from 1981 to 1990, dean of graduate studies and research).

Bingham served as assistant secretary for occupational safety and health in the U.S. Department of Labor from 1977 to 1981 and has been active with many agencies and on numerous commissions, including the study section on safety and occupational health of the National Institute for Occupational Safety and Health (1972–76); the Food and Drug Advisory Commission of the FOOD AND DRUG ADMINISTRATION as well as the administration's Environmental Health Advisory Commission; the science advisory board of the ENVIRONMENTAL PROTECTION AGENCY; the National Air Quality Criteria Advisory Commission; the ad hoc Lead in Paint Commission of the National Academy of Sciences; the Department of Labor's Standards Advisory Commission on Coke Oven Emissions, on which she served as chairman; the National Academy of Sciences-NUCLEAR REGULATORY COMMISSION Committee on Ground Water Protection; and the committee on methods for *in vivo* toxicity testing of the Committee on Life Sciences and Technology of the National Academy of Science.

Bingham has been a trustee of the NATURAL RESOURCES DEFENSE COUNCIL since 1983 and a director of the Ohio Hazardous Substance Institute since 1990.

A member of the Institute of Medicine, she is a recipient of the Rockefeller Foundation's Public Service Award (1980) and the Alice Hamilton Award of the American Public Health Association (1984).

Biological Survey (Established: 1885)

Created as an economic ornithology section of the U.S. Department of AGRICULTURE's Division of Entomology, the Biological Survey became the Division of Ornithology and Mammalogy in 1886, and the Division of Biological Survey in 1896. It was given full bureau status in 1905, until it was transferred to the Department of the INTERIOR in 1939 and, the following year, consolidated with the Bureau of Fisheries as the FISH AND WILDLIFE SERVICE. Originally established to carry out scientific research, the survey took on an increasing number of regulatory and administrative functions with the passage of the Lacey Game and Wild Birds Preservation and Disposition Act of 1900 and a series of regulatory acts that followed it through the 1930s.

Further reading: Jenks, Cameron, *History of the Biological Survey* (1929: reprint ed., New York: Da Capo, 1973).

Block, John Rusling (February 15, 1935–   )

Currently president of the National-American Wholesale Grocers Association, John R. Block was secretary of agriculture from 1981 to 1986, during the administration of Ronald REAGAN. As a key member of Reagan's overwhelmingly anti-environmentalist administration, Block was posted as one of "The Reagan Dirty Dozen" by ENVIRONMENTAL ACTION in 1984. While it is true that Block was never aggressive in developing or supporting programs that address a key element of the U.S. Department of AGRICULTURE mandate—"to enhance the environment and to . . . [help] landowners protect the soil, water, forests, and other natural resources"—neither did Block take the kind of antagonistic hard line on environmental issues that was characteristically adopted by Interior Secretary James WATT, for example. Environmentalists nevertheless criticized Block for maintaining USDA farm policies that consistently favored big farmers at the expense of small; for maintaining or increasing agribusiness subsidies; for reducing support for food stamp and other government nutrition programs; for dismantling many of the food safety and nutrition programs initiated during the Carter administration; and especially for increasing federal funding for agricultural research aimed at developing techniques to increase use of the nation's fragile topsoil and water resources even as the USDA was reducing federal funding to support conservation measures.

Most distressing to environmentalists was Block's reduction of federal funding for soil-erosion programs. As Illinois director of agriculture (1977–81), Block had been praised as a conservation-minded administrator, especially because of his concern over the issue of erosion prevention. (As a farmer, however, he had turned part of his land over to soybeans, a quick-profit crop that is among the most soil-erosive.)

Block resigned as secretary of agriculture early in 1986, yielding not to the pressure of environmentalists, but to what *U.S. News and World Report* (January 20, 1986) called "the frustration and anger of 2.3 million financially pinched farmers."

A native of Galesburg, Illinois, Block studied vocational agriculture before earning his B.S. at the U.S. Military Academy at West Point in 1957. He joined the 101st Airborne Division, serving as an officer for three years until he returned to Illinois in 1960 to become a partner in his father's corn, soybean and hog farm. Over the next two decades, John Block built the family operation into a 3,000-acre, multi-million-dollar business that earned him the American Jaycees' Outstanding Farmer Award for 1969.

In 1977, Illinois Governor James R. Thompson Jr. appointed Block director of the state department of agriculture. In this post, Block succeeded in getting state vehicles converted to gasohol and protected prime farmland from the ravages of strip mining by carefully, thoroughly and systematically enforcing regulations. Block was instrumental in creating financial incentives encouraging farmers to prevent soil erosion, and he was effective in promoting Illinois agricultural exports. Governor Thompson presented Block with the state's Outstanding Achievement Award.

Blumberg, Louis (May 13, 1948–   )

An assistant regional director of the WILDERNESS SOCIETY and director of the organization's California Ancient Forest Campaign, Louis Blumberg is the coauthor (with Robert Gottlieb) of the book *War on Waste: Can America Win Its Battle with Garbage?* (Island Press, 1989).

Born in Waukegan, Illinois, Blumberg received a B.A. in cultural anthropology from the University of California, Santa Barbara (1971), and a master's degree from the Graduate School of Architecture and Urban Planning at the University of California, Los Angeles (1987). A professional percussionist for over 20 years, Blumberg first became active in environmental work in 1985, when he was a coordinator for Santa Monica Recycle and the Coalition for Clean Air and a member of the Citizen's Advisory Council to the Southern California Hazardous Waste Management Authority.

In 1986, Blumberg interned as an assistant deputy of planning and environment in the office of Los Angeles City Councilman Michael Woo, and in the same year, he also served as a UCLA research associate with the John R. Haynes and Dora Haynes Foundation's Prospects for Accountability and Innovation in Public Waste Agencies. He was also a board member of the Los Angeles Citizens for Safe Drinking Water. Working with the Sierra Club, the Environmental Defense Fund and the Natural Resources Defense Council in the winter of 1987–88, Blumberg planned and coordinated a statewide attorney's conference on the enforcement of California's Proposition 65, a toxics initiative. He continued to work as an independent consultant for the next two years, providing technical assistance on the impact of hazardous waste incineration and directing the Utah Incinerator Project for the Tides Foundation in San Francisco (1987–89), and preparing an environmental policy white paper for the Los Angeles 2000 Committee (1988). During this period, Blumberg was also active in the Southern California Association of Governments' Air Quality Management Plan Community Work Group, and in 1987, he was an airport commissioner with the City of Santa Monica.

Blumberg joined the U.S. ENVIRONMENTAL PROTECTION AGENCY, Region IX, in 1989, and he was a management analyst there for one year. In 1990, he became assistant director of the Wilderness Society's California-Nevada Regional Office, and he continues to serve there as lead staff member in forest issues. Since 1991, Blumberg has also lectured on integrated waste management at San Francisco State University. He is a member of the California State Board of Forestry Best Management Practices Committee, the Oversight Committee of the California Industrial Forest Landowners' Timber Inventory (University of California, Berkeley) and the Planning and Implementation Team of the California Spotted Owl Interagency Taskforce.

Blumberg and Gottlieb's *War on Waste* was well received as a thoroughly researched and exceptionally literate study of America's garbage dilemmas. Blumberg has written other articles and reports on waste management and environmental policy, and these have appeared in the *San Francisco Chronicle, the Nation, Environmental Action* and *LA Weekly Magazine*. Blumberg lives in San Francisco.

Bookchin, Murray (January 14, 1921–   )

New York-born Murray Bookchin is America's leading anarchist theorist and radical analyst of what he has called the "almost apocalyptic clash between humanity and the natural world." During the 1960s, he was active in several anarchist organizations, including the Radical Decentralist Project, a faction of Students for a Democratic Society (SDS). By the 1970s, he was concentrating on writing, teaching and directing the newly formed Institute for Social Ecology at Goddard College in Plainfield, Vermont.

Using the pseudonym of Lewis Herber, Bookchin wrote *Our Synthetic Environment* in 1962, which he revised under his own name in 1974. The book addresses problems of environmental pollution from herbicides, pesticides and food additives. It also examines human stress caused by the conditions of urbanization, and it studies the deterioration of human physical abilities caused by dependence on machines. Under the Herber pseudonym, Bookchin also wrote *Crisis in Our Cities* (1965), which describes the pollution and stress that plague urban dwellers, calling metropolitan planning "probably the most serious single problem faced by man in the second half of the twentieth century." Under his own name, Bookchin coauthored *Hip Culture: Six Essays on Its Revolutionary Potential* (1971) and wrote *Post-Scarcity Anarchism* (1971), *Spanish Anarchists* (1978), *Toward an Ecological Society* (1980) and *The Ecology of Freedom* (1982). Bookchin's *The Rise of Urbanization and the Decline of Citizenship* was published by the SIERRA CLUB in 1987. In 1990, he wrote *Remaking Society: Pathways to a Green Future,* and the following year he wrote (with Dave FOREMAN, founder of EARTH FIRST!) *Defending the Earth: A Dialogue Between Murray Bookchin and Dave Foreman.*

In a 1989 article for *The Progressive,* Bookchin wrote that "the global crisis is the result of our social and economic arrangements, not simply the product of random mishaps." He views such occurrences as the oil spill of the Exxon *Valdez* and the nuclear disasters at Chernobyl and Three Mile Island not as "accidents" but as "inevitable outcomes of our society." According to Bookchin, growth, overpopulation and the proliferation of the industrial society are only partly to blame for ecological disasters. Of far greater consequence is what Bookchin calls the "privatization of the environmental crisis." Declaring that "if 'simple living' and militant recycling are our only responses to the environmental crisis, the crisis will certainly intensify," Bookchin urges the development of an "ecological society and sensibility." The first step toward this is to convince the public and policy makers that our major ecological problems are rooted in social problems—the "profligate waste of resources in the interests of the few," the curse of a "grow-or-die" economy and the reliance on competition in a capitalist system.

Boone and Crockett Club (Founded: 1888)
241 South Fraley Boulevard, Dumfries, Virginia 22026; (703) 221-1888

Begun in 1888 by a group of wealthy New York hunting enthusiasts, including THEODORE ROOSEVELT, the Boone and Crockett Club was created "to promote manly sport with the rifle, . . . to promote travel and exploration in the wild and unknown, . . . to work for preservation of the large game of this country, . . . to promote inquiry into, and to record observations on the habits and natural history of, the various wild animals, [and] to bring about among the members the interchange of opinions and ideas on hunting, travel, and exploration; on the various kinds of hunting rifles; on the haunts of game animals, etc."

Among its first conservation activities was support for the passage of the Yellowstone Park Protection Act in 1894 and passage of the Forest Reserve Act of 1891. As a member of the Boone and Crockett Club and coeditor with George Bird GRINNELL of the club's books, Theodore Roosevelt developed many of the conservation concepts that he would later implement as president of the United States.

Some of the group's publications include *Boone and Crockett Club News Journal*, *Records of North American Big Game* (9th ed., 1988), *Measuring and Scoring North American Big Game Trophies* (1985) and *Records of North American Whitetail Deer* (2nd ed., 1991).

Further reading: John F. Reiger, *American Sportsmen and the Origins of Conservation* (New York: Winchester Press, 1975).

Borgstrom, Georg Arne (April 5, 1912– February 7, 1990)
A Swedish-born food scientist and internationally recognized expert in world hunger, Georg Borgstrom was the author of *The Hungry Planet: The Modern World at the Edge of Famine* (1965; 1972) and many other books emphasizing the urgent need for better management of the earth's resources to feed its ever-growing population.

Born in Gustav Adolf, Sweden, Borgstrom was educated at the University of Lund (B.S., 1932; M.S., 1933; Dr. Sci., 1939), where he then taught plant physiology for three years. From 1941 to 1948, he directed the Institute of Plant Research and Food Storage at Nynashamn, Sweden, then moved to Goteborg as head of the Swedish Institute of Food Preservation Research (1948–56), where he also taught food technology (1953–56). Borgstrom came to the United States in 1956, accepting a post as professor of food science (1956) and, eventually, geography (1966) at Michigan State University in East Lansing.

He taught there for 25 years, becoming an American citizen in 1962.

Author or editor of more than 30 books on food science and global hunger, Borgstrom was fluent in many languages and lectured throughout the world. He was honored with several awards, including the International Socrates Prize (1968), the J. A. Wahlberg Gold Medal (1974), the Literary Merit Prize of the Swedish Authors Foundation (1973) and the International Award of the Institute of Food Technologists (1975). Borgstrom was a fellow of the World Academy of Arts and Sciences, the American Institute of Nutrition and the Royal Swedish Academies of Agricultural and Engineering Sciences. In 1988, Borgstrom returned to Goteborg, and he died there at the age of 77.

Borgstrom's publications include *Focal Points: A Food Strategy for the Seventies* (1973), *The Food and People Dilemma* (1973), *Harvesting the Earth* (1973), *Too Many: A Study of Earth's Ecological Limitations* (1969, rev. 1971), *Principles of Food Science* (1968; 1976) and *Japan's World Success in Fishing* (1964).

Botkin, Daniel Benjamin (August 19, 1937–)
Professor in the Department of Biology and the Environmental Studies Program at the University of California, Santa Barbara, Daniel Benjamin Botkin has conducted research in mineral cycling and energy flow in ecosystems, ecosystems theory and models, interactions among plants and animals and population dynamics of long-lived and endangered species.

Born in Oklahoma City, Botkin earned an A.B. degree from the University of Rochester, an M.S. from the University of Wisconsin, Madison, and a Ph.D. in biology from Rutgers University. He worked as assistant professor of ecology at the School of Forestry and Environmental Studies at Yale University from 1968 to 1974 and as associate professor at the Ecosystems Center of the Marine Biology Laboratory at Woods Hole, Massachusetts, from 1975 to 1978. He has received research grants from the National Science Foundation, the WORLD WILDLIFE FUND and the CONSERVATION FOUNDATION, the National Oceanic and Atmospheric Administration, NASA and the Andrew J. Mellon Foundation, and has served on the boards of various scientific organizations, including the Space Science Board of the National Academy of Sciences and the Science Advisory Board of the U.S. Marine Mammal Commission.

Botkin is the author of *Discordant Harmonies: A New Ecology for the Twenty-first Century* (1990), in which he developed an innovative view of nature that stresses flux rather than balance. Policies formulated to deal with the environment must take the ever-changing condition of nature into account, rather than harking back to a notion of ideal balance that never, in fact, existed.

Brand, Stewart (December 14, 1938–   )
Author, publisher, computer expert and founder of the educational and ecological Point Foundation of Sausalito, California, Stewart Brand was the creator and editor of *The Last Whole Earth Catalog: Access to Tools and Ideas* (1968–71), a pioneering compendium of alternative resources for natural and self-sufficient living.

Born in Rockford, Illinois, Brand earned a B.S. at Stanford University (1960) and studied design and photography at San Francisco Art Institute College and San Francisco State College. After two years' service in the U.S. Army infantry, where he was made first lieutenant, Brand became a multimedia performance artist from 1962 to 1968 and was a founding artist of San Francisco's "America Needs Indians" performance events (1963–66). Joining novelist Ken Kesey and his band of Merry Pranksters from 1964 to 1969, Brand participated in the psychedelic bus journey made famous by Tom Wolfe's 1968

Stewart Brand. © *Thomas Victor, 1986, courtesy of Stewart Brand*

chronicle *The Electric Kool-Aid Acid Test*. Brand organized the San Francisco Trips Festival of 1966 and, later, the city's New Games Tournament (1973).

The Last Whole Earth Catalog first appeared in 1968, and its unique presentation of mail-order resources, countercultural bibliography, practical advice and philosophical commentary made it a bible of the back-to-nature movement, as well as a critical success. The *Catalog* was issued for three years and won the National Book Award in Contemporary Affairs in 1972; revised and updated versions of the unorthodox compendium have followed since. In 1973, Brand founded the nonprofit Point Foundation, contributed $1 million to ecology groups and launched the magazine *CoEvolution Quarterly*, which continues publication today as *The Whole Earth Review: Access to Tools and Ideas*. A Lindisfarne fellow since 1975, Brand was a special consultant to California Governor Jerry Brown from 1976 to 1979. From 1980 to 1981 he edited and published *The Next Whole Earth Catalog*, and in 1982 founded Uncommon Courtesy: School of Compassionate Skills, which gave classes on such subjects as Creative Philanthropy, Business as Service and Street Saint Skills. From 1982 to 1983, Brand was on the faculty of the School of Management and Strategic Studies of the Western Behavioral Science Institute in La Jolla, California.

Brand's interest in the creative, culturally transformative possibilities of emerging computer technologies resulted in his 1974 book *Two Cybernetic Frontiers*, and the writer has continued to document the field's potential in numerous books and articles. From 1983 to 1985, he was editor-in-chief of a *Whole Earth Software Catalog;* in 1984, he established The WELL (Whole Earth Lectronic Link), a Point Foundation teleconferencing system; and in 1988 he cofounded the Global Business Network. His 1987 book, *The Media Lab: Inventing the Future at M.I.T.*, explored the leading edge of communications research. Brand continues to write articles for *Whole Earth Review* and other publications and has participated in several high-level roundtable discussions on the future of computer technology. He lives in a renovated tugboat in Sausalito, California.

Further reading: Brand (ed.), *Whole Earth Epilog* (New York: Penguin Books, 1974); *Space Colonies* (New York: Penguin Books, 1977); *The Next Whole Earth Catalog* (Nashville: Alternatives, 1980–81); Brand (ed., with J. Baldwin), *Soft Tech* (New York: Penguin Books, 1978).

Briggs, Shirley Ann (May 12, 1918–   )
Born in Iowa City, Briggs graduated from the University of Iowa with a B.A. in art and botany and an M.A. in art. She put her talents to work for the U.S. Bureau of RECLAMATION as chief of the graphics sec-

tion from 1948 to 1953, then worked for the Smithsonian Institution and the NATIONAL PARK SERVICE, where she produced dioramas of habitat groups. In 1946, Briggs founded *Atlantic Naturalist* magazine for the Audubon Naturalist Society of Central Atlantic States and served as editor until 1969. She was a founder of the RACHEL CARSON COUNCIL and since 1970 has served as executive director of the organization, which is devoted to disseminating information on toxic contaminants. The ENVIRONMENTAL PROTECTION AGENCY benefited from her expertise when she served on the agency's Pesticide Policy Advisory Committee from 1975 to 1977. Other committees and commissions on which she was active include the Advisory Panel on Monitoring Environmental Contaminants in Food (for the Office of Technology Assessment) and the Advisory Committee for the Conference on Pesticides and Human Health of the Society for Occupational and Environmental Health. She also served as a member of the executive committee of the NATURAL RESOURCES COUNCIL OF AMERICA.

Among the books Briggs has illustrated are *The Pronghorn Antelope* (1948), *The Wonders of Seeds* (1956), *The Trumpeter Swan* (1960), *Insects and Plants* (1963) and *Landscaping for Birds* (1973). Since 1962, she has worked as an instructor of conservation philosophy in the Graduate School of the U.S. Department of AGRICULTURE.

British Ecological Society (Founded: 1913)
Burlington House, Piccadilly; London W1V 0LQ, England; (71) 4342641

The British Ecological Society is a coalition of scientists and ecologists devoted to the application of ecological knowledge to environmental management. The group offers seminars and annual symposia in which such issues as the ecological consequences of nuclear war, the management of uplands and habitat restoration are explored, discussed and debated. The society's 4,700 members participate in committees devoted to ecological genetics, forest ecology, freshwater ecology, industrial ecology, mathematical ecology, bog research, production and decomposition ecology, tropical ecology, education and careers and teaching. Members receive four periodical publications, *Functional Ecology*, *Journal of Animal Ecology*, *Journal of Applied Ecology* and *Journal of Ecology*. The society also devotes a portion of its budget to funding grants to researchers of ecological topics.

Broome, Harvey (July 15, 1902–March 9, 1968)
Conservationist, attorney and author Harvey Broome was a founder of the WILDERNESS SOCIETY in 1935 and the organization's president from 1957 until 1968.

A native of Knoxville, Tennessee, Broome graduated from the University of Tennessee in 1923 and earned his LL.B. from Harvard Law School in 1926. Student secretary of the YMCA at Wayne University in Detroit (1929–30), he served as a law clerk at the U.S. Court of Appeals, 6th Circuit, from 1930 to 1949, then joined the Knoxville law practice of Kramer, Dyle, McNabb & Greenwood, where he remained until 1958. For the following 10 years, while presiding over the Wilderness Society, he also served as law clerk at the U.S. District Court in Knoxville.

A close friend and frequent hiking companion of Supreme Court Justice William O. DOUGLAS, Broome was trustee of the Robert Marshall Wilderness Fund and a member of the IZAAK WALTON LEAGUE, the NATIONAL PARKS AND CONSERVATION ASSOCIATION, the Outdoor Writers Association (honorary life member), the SIERRA CLUB and the East Tennessee Historical Society. Among his writings are *Harvey Broome, Earth Man: Some Miscellaneous Writings* (1970), *Faces of the Wilderness* (1972) and *Out Under the Sky of the Great Smokies: A Personal Journal* (1975).

Browder, Joseph (April 10, 1938–   )
A native of Amarillo, Texas, Joseph Browder began his career in environmental politics in the 1960s, when he was active in the leadership of the NATIONAL AUDUBON SOCIETY, serving as an officer of the Miami, Florida, Audubon chapter and then as southeastern representative for the society from 1968 to 1970. During the 1960s and 1970s, Browder worked with the Audubon Society and other national environmental organizations in campaigns to protect Everglades National Park, including efforts to secure a permanent water supply for the park, to prevent development of a commercial airport in the Everglades and to preserve more than 500,000 acres of Everglades Big Cypress land. In 1975, Tropical Audubon Society named Browder conservationist of the year for his efforts in behalf of Everglades National Park.

From 1970 to 1972, Browder was conservation director of FRIENDS OF THE EARTH, responsible for the organization's work in Washington, D.C. From 1970 to 1976, he was treasurer of the LEAGUE OF CONSERVATION VOTERS. In 1972, he became a cofounder and chief executive officer of the Environmental Policy Center (after 1982 called the ENVIRONMENTAL POLICY INSTITUTE). From 1974 to 1976, Browder helped coordinate preparation of energy and environmental issue papers for the Democratic National Campaign Committee, and in 1976, presidential candidate Jimmy Carter appointed Browder to coordinate energy and natural resources transition planning for the Carter-Mondale presidential campaign. Browder served the Democratic National Committee from 1982 to 1984 as

The Ten Thousand Islands area of Everglades National Park. *U.S. Department of the Interior, National Park Service photo by Richard Frear*

a volunteer staff director of the Democratic National Advisory Panel on Promoting Energy Security and Protecting the Environment. He was senior advisor to the 1984 Democratic National Convention Platform Committee and an advisor in preparation of energy and natural resources materials for the 1986 Democratic congressional campaign. In 1988, he served as a member of the Finance Committee of the Democratic National Committee.

From 1977 to 1981, Browder was an advisor to the U.S. Department of the INTERIOR, with responsibility for developing the federal coal-leasing program and developing programs for coordinating with state governments in planning the use of federal lands as sites for energy facilities.

With his wife, Louise Cecil DUNLAP, Browder is a partner in Dunlap & Browder, Inc., an environmental and public policy consulting and lobbying firm. Browder is also a director of the Florida Audubon Society, an advisory board member of Citizens for a Better South Florida and an advisor to the Everglades Coalition, a consortium of national and Florida environmental groups working to protect the Ever-

glades. He is also a director of CUBA/USA Venture Enterprises Inc. and La Habana Investments Corp.

Browder has been guest lecturer at Harvard University's John F. Kennedy School of Politics, the Amos Tuck School of Business at Dartmouth College, the University of Michigan Graduate School of Natural Resources, the University of California and other schools. He served on the Energy Study Committee of the National Council of Churches, and as a policy expert for the American Energy Assurance Council 1988 crisis simulation. He has published widely in public policy and environmental journals and has contributed to such books as *Nixon and the Environment* (1972), *An Environmental Agenda for the Future* (1985) and *Public Interest in the Use of Private Lands* (1989). In 1987, he was honored by the Friends of the United Nations Environment Programme for promoting improved natural resource management and energy utilization.

Brower, David Ross (July 1, 1912–   )

A native of Berkeley, California, David Ross Brower first became interested in environmental issues in the

David R. Brower, founder and chairman of Earth Island Institute. © *Alan Blaustein, courtesy of Earth Island Institute*

1930s as a Sierra Nevada mountain climber and a member of the SIERRA CLUB. He turned his interest into a profession when he took on editorial work for the *Sierra Club Bulletin* in 1935. In 1941, he joined the staff of the University of California Press and began developing his skills in photography and writing for environmental publications.

After leaving the University of California Press in 1952, Brower became the executive director of the Sierra Club, a position he held until 1969. In that role he led campaigns to preserve Dinosaur National Monument during the 1950s, North Cascades National Park during the mid-1950s to 1968 and Redwood National Park from 1963 to 1968. In addition, he fought against the proposed building of dams in the Grand Canyon, an environmental battle that spanned 1952 to 1968. Throughout these campaigns and others, Brower effectively used aggressive publicity campaigns to sway opinion, and the Sierra Club gained a reputation for effective militancy.

During the 1960s, Brower implemented his plans for the Sierra Club's Exhibit Format book series. Many of the 20 volumes in the series were direct outgrowths of the club's battles to save specific scenic areas. In addition, Brower edited *On the Loose*, a highly popular book by Terry and Renny Russell in 1967.

Brower fell victim to political turmoil within the Sierra Club in the 1960s. Many of the club's board members were angered by Brower's stance against the construction of a nuclear power plant in California's Diablo Canyon. Like many other environmentalists of the decade, they saw nuclear power as a valid source of nonpolluting energy, and they asked Brower to resign in 1969 on the grounds of "general intransigence," a disregard for the board's direction and financial irresponsibility.

Brower then created a new environmental group, FRIENDS OF THE EARTH, with headquarters in San Francisco. Serving as its president from 1969 to 1979, Brower led the group to even more militant stances than had been possible at the Sierra Club, but despite their differences, especially over nuclear power, the two organizations cooperated on environmental campaigns in Alaska and the California redwood forests. In addition to these campaigns, the Friends of the Earth battled against acid rain, nuclear power (especially the Clinch River breeder reactor in Tennessee), the U.S. supersonic transport (SST) program and the leasing of coal and oil fields on public lands.

Publications Brower directed during the 1970s while he was president of Friends of the Earth include the 10-volume *The Earth's Wild Places*, the *Celebrating the Earth* series and other books and films.

In 1979, Brower resigned as president of the board of Friends of the Earth but remained active as a board member. A string of executive directors then resigned, citing Brower's interference as a cause. Still, the group continued to grow, particularly during the early REAGAN years, when James WATT, as secretary of the interior, stirred up controversy over environmental issues at every turn. By 1983, Friends of the Earth claimed 30,000 members and had a staff of 60—which Friends director Rafe POMERANCE considered excessive. He undertook a series of staff cuts, thereby angering Brower, who took out an ad in the Friends news magazine, *No Man Apart*, encouraging members to "save the team." Pomerance dumped the issue into the recycling bin before copies were distributed, and the board of directors removed Brower from service. Undaunted, Brower took the club to court and regained his seat.

After 1983, membership in Friends of the Earth dwindled—reaching a low of 16,000 in 1986——and the organization's deficit had skyrocketed to $700,000 by 1984. In 1985, the board voted to close the San Francisco office and relocate in Washington, D.C.—a move, in part, against Brower, whose home was California and whose supporters filled the San Francisco office.

While the board in-fighting was at its peak, Brower returned to the Sierra Club as director. There he continued to work against nuclear power as well as nuclear arms, but the club's board set other priorities. Brower's supporters then circulated a petition calling for the board to reconsider the exclusion of nuclear power from its priorities. The board responded by adding the issue to its "hit list," but categorized it as an "unfunded" item. Despite the efforts of the Nuclear Concerns Coalition of the Sierra Club, the nuclear issue remains, even at present, peripheral for the club, whose leaders are concerned that focusing on the matter will alienate members and donors.

Brower resigned from the board of directors of the Friends of the Earth in 1979. In 1982, he founded yet another organization, the EARTH ISLAND INSTITUTE, which focuses on preservation of the rain forests, pesticide education and other issues to which (as Brower saw it) the Sierra Club and the Friends of the Earth were not sufficiently committed.

Brower has received many honors and awards, including honorary degrees from Hobart and William Smith College and the University of Maryland, awards from the California Conservation Council (1953), NATIONAL PARKS ASSOCIATION (1956) and the Brooklyn College Library Association (1970), the Carey-Thomas Award (1964), the Paul Bartsch Award of the National Audubon Society of the Central Atlantic States (1967), the Golden Ark from the Prince of the Netherlands (1979), the Rose Award of the World Environment Festival (1986) and others. Named an honorary fellow of John Muir College, University of California, San Diego (1986), Brower has twice been nominated for a Nobel Peace Prize (1978 and 1979). As director of the Earth Island Institute, he remains a powerful voice in the environmental arena.

Further reading: Brower, *For Earth's Sake: The Life and Times of David Brower* (New York: Peregrine Smith Books, 1990); John McPhee, *Encounters with the Archdruid* (New York: Farrar, Straus and Giroux, 1971).

Brown, Janet Welsh (September 20, 1931–   )
Senior associate of the WORLD RESOURCES INSTITUTE and executive director of the ENVIRONMENTAL DEFENSE FUND, Janet Welsh Brown coedited with Andrew Maguire *Bordering on Trouble: Resources and Politics in Latin America* (1986). The anthology describes the major environmental issues in Latin America and argues that poverty and the destruction of natural resources are at the root of the region's political difficulties.

Born in Albany, New York, Brown was a professor at Sarah Lawrence College (1956–58), the University of the District of Columbia (1958–73) and Howard University (1964–68). She served as executive director of the ENVIRONMENTAL DEFENSE FUND from 1979 to 1984 and has worked on several projects of the National Science Foundation and the National Institutes of Health. From 1975 to 1976, she was president of the Scientific Manpower Commission and has served on the boards of the Federation of Organizations of Professional Women, the Independent Sector of Urban Environment Conference, and the LEAGUE OF CONSERVATION VOTERS. She currently serves as director of the Office of Opportunities in Science, American Association for the Advancement of Science, and is professor of political science and international relations at the University of the District of Columbia, Howard University and Sarah Lawrence College.

Brown, Lester Russell (March 28, 1934–   )
President and senior researcher of the WORLDWATCH INSTITUTE since 1974, Lester Russell Brown is the author of *Man, Land and Food* (1963), *Increasing World Food Output* (1965), *Seeds of Change* (1970), *World Without Borders* (1972), *In the Human Interest* (1974), *By Bread Alone* (1974), *The Twenty-Ninth Day* (1978), *Building a Sustainable Society* (1981) and several Worldwatch reports. Before joining the staff of Worldwatch, Brown, a native of Bridgeton, New Jersey, worked for the U.S. Department of AGRICULTURE as an agricultural analyst and was the secretary of agriculture's advisor on agricultural policy in foreign countries. From 1966 to 1969, Brown was the administrator of the International Agricultural Development Service, and from 1969 to 1974, he was a senior fellow with the Overseas Development Council.

In 1989, Brown was awarded the Sasaka International Environmental Prize of $50,000. Other awards he has received include the Special Conservation Award from the NATIONAL WILDLIFE FEDERATION, the U.S. Department of Agriculture's Senior Service Award, the Lorax Award of the Global Tomorrow Coalition and a fellowship from the MacArthur Foundation.

At the Worldwatch Institute, Brown issues annual State of the World reports, which are available in several different languages and which sell nearly a quarter of a million copies a year. In addition, the institute publishes periodic reports on global environmental issues.

Brown serves on several boards of environmental organizations, including the Planning Commission for New Directions, the Overseas Development

Council, Better World Society, Renew America and the Global Studies Center.

Brown, Quincalee (November 9, 1939–   )

A native of Wichita, Kansas, Quincalee Brown was educated at Wichita State University (B.A., speech communications, 1961), the University of Pittsburgh (M.A., speech communications, 1963) and the University of Kansas (Ph.D., speech communications and human relations, 1975). She is currently executive director of the Water Environment Federation and the Water Environment Research Foundation, a 38,000-member international not-for-profit organization dedicated to the preservation and enhancement of water quality worldwide.

Brown directs programs that encourage sound national water pollution control policies and promote public understanding of water quality issues. WEF operates on a $12 million budget with a staff of 103, produces a variety of publications and holds an annual conference attended by more than 13,000. Brown is also active on the National Advisory Council for Environmental Policy and Technology of the ENVIRONMENTAL PROTECTION AGENCY and is a member of the board of directors of the Lake Superior Center, an international scientific and educational organization for the study of freshwater bodies.

Before she joined WEF, Brown was executive director of the American Association of University Women and its Educational Foundation (1980–85) and executive director of the Montgomery County (Maryland) Commission for Women (1975–80). From 1974 to 1975, she was manager of the U.S. Government Printing Office's federal women's program, and she serves on the boards of the General Federation of Women's Clubs and the Water Pollution Control Federation. She was assistant professor of speech communications and director of debate at Wichita State University (1963–69) and Ottawa University (1970–73).

Brown, William Yancey (August 13, 1948–   )

William Yancey Brown is the director of environmental affairs for Waste Management Inc., an international company employing 62,000. A native of Artesia, California, Brown holds an undergraduate degree in biology from the University of Virginia, an M.A.T. from Johns Hopkins University, a Ph.D. in zoology from the University of Hawaii and a J.D. degree from Harvard Law School.

Brown was an assistant professor of biological sciences at Mount Holyoke College, Massachusetts, from 1973 to 1974, and he was employed part-time by the ENVIRONMENTAL PROTECTION AGENCY while he was a

law student. After graduating from law school in 1977, Brown was named director of the Endangered Species Scientific Authority, a government agency created by President Jimmy Carter to oversee the United States' compliance with international treaties governing endangered species conservation. In 1979, he was named director of the International Convention Advisory Commission, an agency created under the Endangered Species Act. In 1981 he went to work for the ENVIRONMENTAL DEFENSE FUND as senior scientist, attorney and, later, acting director.

Between 1987 and 1991, Brown was chairman of the board of the CENTER FOR MARINE CONSERVATION.

Bruckner, John (December 31, 1726–May 12, 1804)

A preacher in Norwich, England, for more than 50 years, John Bruckner was the author of *A Philosophical Survey of the Animal Creation* (1768), an essay in justification of the apparent violence of nature. In his attempt to reconcile nature's predatory system with "the felicity of the universe," Bruckner used not only the mechanistic model of nature popular in the 18th century, but also the innovative organic concept of a "continued web of life" in which "life may be considered as an impetuous torrent." The life forces of the various species, Bruckner explained, were constantly preying upon each other. He stated that although the violence was sometimes ugly, it was the very force that sustained nature.

Bruckner observed that for every species helped by clearing the forests in what was then wilderness America, 10 species were threatened. Questioning whether human beings have the right to exploit other species, Bruckner concluded that all species have an equal right to existence.

Bryan, Richard H. (July 16, 1937–   )

Despite heavy opposition from automobile manufacturers and their political allies, United States Senator Richard H. Bryan (D, Nevada) has championed legislation to make all cars more fuel-efficient by the turn of the century, increasing the Corporate Average Fuel Economy (CAFE) standards 20% by 1995 and 40% by 2001. A former state senator, state attorney general and governor of Nevada, Bryan serves on the Senate Commerce, Science and Transportation Committee; the Banking, Housing and Urban Affairs Committee; the Joint Economic Committee; and the Select Committee on Ethics.

Born in Washington, D.C., Bryan attended the University of Nevada (B.A., 1959) before earning his LL.B. at the University of California's Hastings College of Law (1963). Bryan's public career began in Clark County, Nevada, where he was deputy district attorney (1964–66), public defender (1966–68) and then counsel for the Clark County Juvenile Court (1968–69). Elected to the Nevada House of Representatives in 1969, he served until 1971; in 1973, he won a seat in the Nevada Senate. From 1979 to 1982, Bryan held the office of state attorney general, and in 1982, he was voted governor of Nevada, an office he held until his election to the U.S. Senate in 1988.

Originally written as an amendment to the 1990 Clean Air Act, Bryan's CAFE bill was struck down in a 1990 Senate floor vote, but the senator has continued to battle auto industry objections and political foes in his ongoing fight for passage of the fuel-efficiency legislation. As a member of the Commerce Committee, Bryan has also supported more aggressive consumer protection regulation by the Consumer Product Safety Commission.

Buffon, Comte Georges-Louis Leclerc de
(September 7, 1707–April 16, 1788)

Born in Montbard, Comte Georges-Louis Leclerc de Buffon was a leading scientist and encyclopedist of 18th-century France. A proponent of the catastrophe theory of the earth's creation, he believed that the earth had been formed over several epochs, each of which was characterized by a major catastrophe, such as an all-engulfing flood (Noah's flood, for example), volcanic eruption and so on. Between these catastrophes were long periods of calm. With the emergence of modern man, the catastrophes ended and human beings took responsibility for the direction of the earth's progress.

Buffon was curator of the Jardin du Roi (now Jardin des Plantes) and author of *Histoire naturelle, génèrale et particulière*. Thirty-six volumes of *Natural History* (as the title was translated) appeared during his lifetime, and eight additional volumes were completed by E. de Lacépède after Buffon's death. In two volumes of *Natural History—Theory of the Earth* and *Epochs of Nature*—Buffon presented his theory of creation. In other volumes he discussed the evolution of species by examining how some animals have retained vestigial parts that no longer serve a useful purpose. The excitement his works generated did much to promote the study of natural history during the 18th century and early 19th century.

Burford, Anne McGill (Gorsuch) (April 21, 1942–   )

In February 1981, Anne Gorsuch was named administrator of the ENVIRONMENTAL PROTECTION AGENCY. (In 1983 she married ROBERT BURFORD, director of the Bureau of LAND MANAGEMENT from 1981 to 1989.) A native of Casper, Wyoming, and a former corporate lawyer and member of the Colorado state legislature, Anne Burford was a controversial appointee. Conservationists and environmentalists claimed that her official actions, undertaken in the cause of antibureaucratic reform, nearly destroyed the EPA. In a reorganization of the agency in the summer of 1981, Burford eliminated the Office of Enforcement and divided its duties among four other divisions. Then her agency submitted proposals for amendments to the Clean Air Act that, according to congressional researchers, radically abridged the intent of the law. Burford again tangled with conservationists and environmentalists when she submitted the EPA's proposed budget for 1983, which called for a 20% reduction in funding—down to $975 million—and a staff cut to 8,000. When President Reagan first took office, the EPA budget was $1.356 billion, and the permanent staff numbered 11,404.

Critics next attacked Burford's record on prosecuting violations of environmental laws. In 1980, the EPA referred 230 cases to the Justice Department, whereas during the first eight months of Burford's tenure at the EPA, the number of cases sent to Justice dwindled to 42. The final battle Burford waged was over the Superfund, the fund maintained to identify and clean up the nation's worst environmental hazards. In 1982, the Superfund account contained approximately $180 million—money that, by federal law, was to be spent only for cleaning up waste sites. An EPA inspector general released information in 1983 indicating that as much as $53 million of Superfund money had been misappropriated, some of it by the administration of the EPA itself. When Congress asked for documentation on how the Superfund monies had been spent, Burford refused to release the information. Charged with contempt of Congress and abandoned by the administration, Burford resigned on March 9, 1983.

Burford did not stay out of the environmental field for long. In July 1984, President Reagan appointed her to chair the National Advisory Council on Oceans and the Atmosphere.

Burford, Robert (February 5, 1923–   )

A former member of the Colorado House of Representatives (1975–81) and speaker of the house (1979–81), Robert Burford was named director of the Bureau of LAND MANAGEMENT of the Department of the INTERIOR in 1981. He held this post through considerable controversy until 1989, when he founded a natural resources consulting service.

In his native Grand Junction, Colorado, Burford is the co-owner and operator of a cattle ranch that for many years has used some 32,000 acres of public lands for grazing his livestock. When he was appointed director of the Bureau of Land Management, Burford obtained a waiver from the secretary of the interior, allowing him to retain at least partial ownership of his family's ranch. In addition, he signed a document stating that he would remove himself from any decision affecting grazing permits that his ranch owns. Nevertheless, Burford came under fire in 1982 when he approved a Grazing Management Policy that altered the BLM's method of categorizing allotments of acreage. In addition, Burford was criticized when his ranching operation, along with three others, enjoyed extraordinarily rapid BLM approval of an application for water rights to a well on public land. At a December 1985 hearing of the Subcommittee on Environment, Energy and Natural Resources, Burford was questioned about his policies at the BLM and was unable to provide a single example of his having withdrawn from the decision-making process because of potential impact on his own property.

Under Burford's leadership, the BLM relaxed many of its policies governing public lands. As a result, conservationists and environmentalists sneeringly dubbed the BLM the "Bureau of Livestock and Mining."

Burroughs, John (April 3, 1837–March 29, 1921)

The author of 27 books on the flora and fauna of the Hudson River Valley and the Catskill Mountains, John Burroughs worked in the U.S. Department of the Treasury from 1863 to 1873, moving the next year to a farm at Esopus, New York, not far from Roxbury, where he was born. Among his many nature books, noted for their rare combination of lyrical language and scientific accuracy, are *Wake Robin* (1871), *Winter Sunshine* (1875), *Birds and Poets* (1877), *Locusts and Wild Honey* (1879), *John James Audubon* (1902), *Ways of Nature* (1905), *Camping and Tramping with Roosevelt* (1907) and *The Summit of the Years* (1913). A close friend of Walt Whitman, Burroughs wrote the first biography of the great American poet, *Notes on Walt Whitman, As Poet and Person* (1867).

Five years after Burroughs's death, the American Museum of Natural History (New York City) created a medal in his honor to be awarded periodically for outstanding achievement in nature study conservation and natural history.

Further reading: Charles F. Davis, *Harvest of a Quiet Eye: The Natural World of John Burroughs* (Madison, Wisc.: Tamarack Press, 1976); Perry D. Westbrook, *John Burroughs* (Boston: Twayne, 1974).

John Burroughs

Butcher, Devereux (September 24, 1906–May 22, 1991)

A prolific writer on conservation topics, Devereux Butcher, born in Devon, Pennsylvania, headed various conservation groups during his long career. From 1942 to 1957, he served as founding editor of the National Parks magazine and from 1942 to 1950 as director of the National Parks Association, which is now the NATIONAL PARKS AND CONSERVATION ASSOCIATION. While campaigning against proposed hydroelectric power dams at Dinosaur National Monument in Utah and Colorado and against logging in the Olympic National Park in Washington State, he and his wife, Mary Taft Butcher, published *National Wildlands News*, an environmental newspaper.

Butcher was the author of *Exploring Our National Parks and Monuments* and *Knowing Your Trees*, an American Forestry Association (now AMERICAN FORESTS) publication. He was a member of the board of directors of Defenders of Furbearers (renamed DEFENDERS OF WILDLIFE) and the Hawk Mountain Sanctuary in Pennsylvania. He also served on the advisory committee on conservation of the U.S. Department of the INTERIOR.

Butcher died in Gladwin, Pennsylvania, near Philadelphia.

Butcher, Russell Devereux (February 8, 1938–   )

Son of the late environmentalist and author DEVEREUX BUTCHER, Russell Devereux Butcher is Pacific Southwest Regional Director of the NATIONAL PARKS AND CONSERVATION ASSOCIATION, whose 300,000 members work to promote the protection, enhancement and public understanding of the national parks system. Butcher's father served as founding director of the National Parks Association, which later became the National Parks and Conservation Association.

Russell Devereux Butcher is the author of *Maine Paradise* (1973), which is about Acadia National Park; *New Mexico: Gift of the Earth* (1975); *The Desert* (1976); and *Field Guide to Acadia National Park, Maine* (1977). He was research editor for SIERRA CLUB Books from 1962 to 1964; chief of media relations for the SAVE-THE-REDWOODS LEAGUE from 1963 to 1965; conservation specialist with the NATIONAL AUDUBON SOCIETY from 1965 to 1966; chief of public relations and publications for the Museum of New Mexico from 1967 to 1969; and a fulltime writer during much of the 1970s. Butcher assumed his post with the National Parks and Conservation Association in 1980. He is a graduate of the University of Colorado at Boulder (B.A., political science, 1959) and attended University of Michigan Law School from 1960 to 1961.

Butler, Ovid McQuat (July 14, 1880–February 20, 1960)

Born in Indianapolis and a graduate of Butler University, Ovid McQuat Butler worked briefly as a newspaperman before entering the Yale Forest School and graduating with an M.F. degree in 1907. After his graduation, he went to work for the U.S. FOREST SERVICE and was stationed first at the Boise National Forest in Idaho. Transferred to the district office at Ogden, Utah, he was named chief of the Division of Forest Management. In this position, he was engaged in research that culminated in Department of Agriculture reports 115 and 116, published as *The Distribution of Softwood Lumber in the Middle West*. He also worked at the Forest Service office in Albuquerque, New Mexico, and at the Forest Products Laboratory in Madison, Wisconsin.

In 1922, Butler was hired by the American Forestry Association (now AMERICAN FORESTS) and within a year was named executive secretary and editor. Working in these roles until his retirement in 1948, he was recognized as a leading authority on forest policies, both public and private. At the AFA, he also joined forces with William B. GREELEY, chief of the Forest Service, to develop and promote the passage of the Clarke-McNary Act of 1924, a law that called for cooperative federal, state and private efforts in reforestation and fire control. During the Depression of the 1930s, he encouraged President Franklin D. ROOSEVELT to develop a program to put unemployed men to work in the nation's forest programs. Out of his discussions with the president, the CIVILIAN CONSERVATION CORPS (CCC) evolved.

After World War II, Butler directed an American Forestry Association program to survey the nation's forests and report on their condition after war industries had taken their toll.

Butler served as president of the SOCIETY OF AMERICAN FORESTERS from 1927 to 1928 and was a delegate to the World Forest Congress in Budapest in 1936. In 1952, he was given the American Forestry Association's Distinguished Service Award.

C

Cahn, Robert (March 9, 1917–   )
A Seattle-born journalist with the *Seattle Star*, the *Pasadena Star-News*, *Life* magazine, *Collier's* magazine, *The Saturday Evening Post*, the *Christian Science Monitor* and the United States Information Agency, Robert Cahn became interested in environmental issues while researching articles on the national parks. He received a Pulitzer Prize in 1969 for the resulting series of 16 articles, entitled "Will Success Spoil the National Parks," published in the *Christian Science Monitor*, and in 1988 was awarded the Marjory Stoneman Douglas Award by the NATIONAL PARKS AND CONSERVATION ASSOCIATION.

From 1970 to 1972, Cahn served on the President's COUNCIL ON ENVIRONMENTAL QUALITY, and from 1974 to 1977, he was writer-in-residence at the CONSERVATION FOUNDATION.

His writings include *Footprints on the Planet: A Search for an Environmental Ethic* (1978), *Global 2000 Report to the President* (1980), *American Photographers and the National Parks* (1981; with Robert Glenn Ketchum), *The Fight to Save Wild Alaska* (1982) and *The Birth of the National Park Service: The Founding Years, 1913–1933* (1985; with Horace M. Albright). He was editor of the 1985 publication *An Environmental Agenda for the Future*.

Cahn has served on the Citizens Advisory Committee on Environmental Quality and the Coastal Zone Management Advisory Committee. He has been a board member of the Trust for Public Land, the Bolton Institute for a Sustainable Future, the John Muir Institute for Environmental Studies and the Global Tomorrow Coalition.

Cain, Stanley Adair (June 19, 1902–   )
Born in Jefferson County, Indiana, Cain earned his B.S. at Butler University and his Ph.D. in plant ecology at the University of Chicago. He taught at Butler and at Indiana University and the University of Tennessee and was a Guggenheim fellow in 1940. In 1945, he was appointed chief of the science section at the U.S. Army University in France. He was a botanist at the Cranbrook Institute of Science from 1946 to 1950 and professor of conservation and chairman of the Department of Conservation at the University of Michigan from 1950 to 1961.

From 1965 to 1968, Cain served as assistant secretary of the U.S. Department of the INTERIOR, with primary responsibility for wildlife and national parks. After his government service, he returned to academic life as a professor in the department of applied biology at the University of California, Santa Cruz.

Cain has served on the boards of the ECOLOGICAL SOCIETY OF AMERICA, the CONSERVATION FOUNDATION, the International Botany Congress, the Michigan Conservatory and the American Association for the Advancement of Science. In 1955, he worked as an ecological expert on a UNESCO Technical Assistance Mission to Brazil, and a year later chaired an environmental biology panel for the National Science Foundation. He has worked on various advisory boards, including those for National Parks, Historical Sites, Buildings and Monuments; the Department of the Interior; and the International Biological Program of the National Academy of Science. Among his many publications are *A Manual of Vegetation Analysis* and *Plant Geography*, and he is the recipient of the Botanical Society of America's certificate of merit (1956).

Callison, Charles Hugh (November 6, 1913–   )
A native of Alberta, Canada, Callison was a newspaperman in Kansas and Missouri before the Missouri Conservation Commission hired him in 1941 as an education and information specialist. In this ca-

pacity, he established and edited the commission's magazine, *Missouri Conservationist*. In 1946, he became executive secretary of the Conservation Federation of Missouri and editor of *Missouri Wildlife*. Five years later, he began his work for the NATIONAL WILDLIFE FEDERATION in Washington, D.C., where he was director of conservation. He edited *Legislative News Service*, a bulletin issued by the NATURAL RESOURCES COUNCIL OF AMERICA, and served as chairman of the council from 1957 to 1959. In 1960, he moved to New York City to work as assistant to the president of the NATIONAL AUDUBON SOCIETY, and from 1966 until his retirement in 1978, he was the organization's executive vice-president. Continuing his work in conservation, Callison founded the Public Lands Institute in 1978, and when the organization was incorporated into the NATURAL RESOURCES DEFENSE COUNCIL as a separate division, he became division director.

Callison has served with numerous conservation organizations, including the Advisory Committee on Fish and Wildlife of the U.S. Department of the INTERIOR; the Legislative Committee of the International Association of Game, Fish, and Conservation Commissioners; the Federal Water Pollution Control Advisory Board; and President Nixon's Task Force on Natural Resources and the Environment. He has been honored with awards from the National Audubon Society, the U.S. Department of the Interior, the American Forestry Association (now AMERICAN FORESTS) and the Garden Club of America. The author of *Man and Wildlife in Missouri*, he was also editor of the 1967 edition of *America's Natural Resources*.

Canada-United States Environmental Council
(Founded: 1974)
1244 19th Street NW, Washington, D.C. 20036;
(202) 659-9510

Primarily a coordinating coalition of several United States and Canadian environmental advocacy groups, the council works mainly to develop and lobby for legislation and regulation to combat acid rain. The organization is also committed to protecting the Great Lakes and aspects of the Arctic environment.

The council is led by two coordinating committee co-chairmen, James T. Deane, of DEFENDERS OF WILDLIFE, from the United States, and Paul Griss, of the Canadian Nature Federation, representing Canada.

Carhart, Arthur Hawthorne (September 28, 1892–November 30, 1978)
After serving in the U.S. Army during World War I, Arthur Hawthorne Carhart, a native of Mapleton, Iowa, joined the staff of the U.S. Forest Service as a

landscape engineer. Assigned to the Rocky Mountain District, he was responsible for conducting land-use studies and creating management plans for national forests in Colorado, Minnesota and elsewhere in the West. In this role he developed pioneering plans for Forest Service lands, which included substantial provisions for recreation. Indeed, his 1920 plan for the San Isabel National Forest in Colorado was the first Forest Service plan to propose recreation activities. The San Isabel plan also called for a halt to grazing and timber cutting and was given the endorsement of the San Isabel Public Recreation Association, which raised funds to finance recreational improvements in the forest and constructed a community lodge at Squirrel Creek, the first campground ever constructed in a national forest. Among cattle grazers and timber cutters, Carhart's recreational plans were anything but popular, and Carhart was also opposed by the director of the National Park Service, Stephen MATHER, who argued that the national forests should not be used for recreation because the national parks were already set up to fill that need. Forests, he argued, should be set aside for commercial development.

Discouraged by the lack of administrative and congressional commitment to the national forest program, Carhart resigned from the Forest Service in 1922 to work as a landscape architect and city planner. In his absence, however, support for his earlier proposals gradually mounted, and in 1929, Congress passed Land Use Regulation L-20, which provided for the protection of wilderness areas in the national forests. The first such land to be protected under the new law was the Flat Tops Primitive Area surrounding Trappers Lake, Colorado.

Carhart was honored by the IZAAK WALTON LEAGUE in 1956 for his efforts to preserve national forests. He was the author of more than 5,000 articles and 25 books on conservation, including *Water in Your Life*, *Timber in Your Life*, *The National Forests*, *Planning for Wild Land Management*, *Fresh Water Fishing* and *Hunting North American Deer*. He was honored with the Jade of Chiefs Award of the Outdoor Writers Association of America.

Carson, Rachel (May 27, 1907–April 14, 1964)
Carson's *Silent Spring* (1962), a dramatic indictment of the widespread overuse and abuse of chemical pesticides, is frequently cited as the popular manifesto that launched the environmental movement. Born in Springdale, Pennsylvania, Carson graduated from Pennsylvania College for Women in 1929 and received a graduate degree in biology from Johns Hopkins University in 1932. In 1931, she served as

staff biologist at the University of Maryland, and in 1936 worked as an aquatic biologist for the U.S. Bureau of Fisheries. In 1949, she became editor-in-chief for the FISH AND WILDLIFE SERVICE, the U.S. Department of the INTERIOR agency that was formed by the merger of the Bureau of Fisheries and the Biological Survey. She left this position in 1952 to become a full-time writer.

Carson's four major works, *Under the Sea Wind* (1941), *The Sea Around Us* (1951), *The Edge of the Sea* (1956) and *Silent Spring* (1962), have enjoyed a wide popular audience. Beautifully written, they served to raise public awareness of environmental issues. While many specialists were critical of *Silent Spring*, and governmental agencies as well as private industry strongly resisted its message, President John F. Kennedy made no secret of his admiration for the book. Federal restrictions on DDT and other environmentally hazardous pesticides may be traced to the influence of the volume.

The NATIONAL WILDLIFE FEDERATION presented her with its Conservationist of the Year award in 1963, and the Department of the Interior renamed the Coastal Maine Refuge the Rachel Carson National Wildlife Refuge in 1969.

Further reading: Philip Sterling, *Sea and Earth: The Life of Rachel Carson* (New York, Dell Publishing Co., Inc., 1970).

Carter, Jimmy (James Earl) (October 1, 1924–   )

Jimmy Carter became the nation's 38th president in 1977. His administration continued and even expanded the policies of Richard NIXON and Gerald Ford, bringing the "environmental decade" of the 1970s to its climax.

The Carter years were marked by two major environmental crises, which raised public awareness of environmental issues. In 1978, President Carter declared upstate New York's Love Canal, which had been polluted by toxic waste, a federal disaster area, and in 1980, he authorized the immediate evacuation of 719 families from the area. Then, on March 28, 1979, the nuclear reactor at the Three Mile Island electric power plant near Harrisburg, Pennsylvania, approached meltdown, releasing some radioactive

Crop dusting with chemical pesticides. *U.S. Environmental Protection Agency photo by S. C. Delaney*

gases into the air. Although disaster was narrowly averted, Americans were forced to rethink their assumptions about energy, big business and government regulation.

These crises were played out against a background of economic recession and an ongoing "energy crisis" that had first become apparent to most Americans in October 1973, during the administration of Richard M. Nixon, when the Organization of Petroleum Exporting Countries (OPEC) enacted an embargo on oil exports to nations, including the United States, that had supported Israel in its war with Egypt. Gasoline prices shot up dramatically as a result of the embargo, and long filling-station lines and fuel shortages became commonplace for several months. In December 1978, OPEC raised oil prices sharply, and by June 1979, gasoline shortages once again spread throughout the country. On August 4, 1977, the Carter administration created a new department, the U.S. Department of ENERGY, to oversee and regulate what had come to be recognized as a crucial resource and a key to national security. Controversy quickly engulfed the administration's management of the department, however. President Carter nominated Lynn R. Coleman, a long-time oil company lawyer-lobbyist, as general counsel for the department, raising protests of conflict of interest. He also nominated Omi G. Warren, a 30-year-old University of Georgia journalism school graduate, to the important post of assistant secretary of energy for conservation and solar application. Her major qualification was apparently nothing more than her service in Georgia state government under Governor Carter.

Despite such controversies and a growing perception that President Carter, in contrast to candidate Carter, too often sided with big business against environmentalists, the Carter administration was characterized by active federal involvement in environmental issues. Almost immediately after he took office in 1977, Carter addressed a strong message to Congress on making the environment a top national priority. Early in his administration, President Carter requested $100 million in additional funding to develop solar and other alternative sources of energy, and in addition to extensive energy legislation and regulation, the Carter administration commissioned the *Global 2000 Report,* a massive attempt to define energy, environmental, population and other issues for the immediate future and the coming century. The creation of the EPA Superfund for identifying and cleaning up the nation's worst toxic-waste sites was largely the work of the Carter administration. A policy of preserving the nation's endangered wetlands was developed during the Carter years, and the administration also created the Young Adult Conservation Corps (see YOUTH CONSERVATION CORPS), which was terminated a few years later by President Ronald REAGAN.

President Carter signed into law the Federal Water Pollution Control Act of 1977, which required most cities to build sewage treatment plants and offered federal grants for construction. This was certainly one of the administration's most successful pieces of environmental legislation. In December 1980, Carter signed into law the great Alaska Lands Act, which added almost 104 million acres of land to the nation's system of national parks, monuments, preserves, wildlife refuges, forests and wild and scenic rivers.

James Earl Carter was born in the little town of Plains, Georgia. Although he served as governor of Georgia from 1971 to 1975, Carter was a relative unknown to most of the American public when the Democrats nominated him as their presidential candidate in 1976. In his 1975 book *Why Not the Best?,* Carter described himself as "a Southerner and an American, I am a farmer, an engineer, a father and a husband, a Christian, a politician and former governor, a planner, a businessman, a nuclear physicist, a naval officer, canoeist, and among other things a lover of Bob Dylan's songs and Dylan Thomas's poetry." He attended Georgia Southwestern University from 1941 to 1942 and Georgia Institute of Technology from 1942 to 1943, before entering the United States Naval Academy. He graduated from the academy in 1946 with a B.S. degree and a naval commission, and served as a lieutenant commander from 1946 to 1953, including a stint under Admiral Hyman Rickover, working on the nuclear submarine program. In 1952, Carter studied nuclear physics at Union College, Schenectady, New York, earning a postgraduate degree. He resigned from the Navy in 1953 to run his family's peanut farm and warehouse business.

After serving two terms in the state senate, from 1963 to 1966, Carter was defeated in the Georgia gubernatorial primary of 1966, but was elected governor on a second try in 1970.

While the Carter presidency was marked by much goodwill and many advances on the environmental front, the nation was beset by the energy crisis and "stagflation"—simultaneous inflation and recession. Perhaps even worse, his administration had failed to liberate 90 Americans held hostage in Iran since they had been seized at the U.S. Embassy in Tehran on November 4, 1979. Carter was soundly defeated by Ronald Reagan in his bid for reelection.

Cary, Austin (July 31, 1865–April 28, 1936)
Cary devoted his long career as a forester to convincing the commercial lumber industry to adopt

responsible long-range planning of cutting and planting.

A native of East Machias, Maine, and graduate of Bowdoin College (A.B., 1887; M.A., 1890) who majored in botany and entomology, Cary worked as a timber cruiser in northern New England and published observations on the life cycles of northern Maine trees. After European study in the Black Forest of Germany, he worked for the New Hampshire-based Berlin Mills Company as the nation's first company-employed forester. He taught at the Yale Forest School (1904–05) and Harvard (1905–09) and wrote *A Manual for Northern Woodsmen* (1909). After a brief term as superintendent of forestry for the state of New York (1909–10), Cary joined the U.S. FOREST SERVICE as a kind of forester at large, advising landowners and private industry on forest resource management. Although he had begun his forestry career in northern New England, his efforts in the American South earned him the title of "Father of Southern Forestry."

Further reading: Roy R. White, "Austin Cary, the Father of Southern Forestry," *Forest History* 5 (Spring 1961): 2–5.

Cellarius, Richard A. (July 28, 1937–   )

A current director and past president of the SIERRA CLUB, conservationist Richard Cellarius is a professor of biology and environmental studies at Evergreen State College in Olympia, Washington. Since 1986, he has also been research cooperator for the U.S. Forest Service, Pacific Northwest Research Station.

A Sierra Club member since 1950, the Oakland, California-born scientist received his B.A. in physics from Reed College, Portland, Oregon, in 1958 and his Ph.D. in biological science at New York City's Rockefeller University in 1965. After postdoctoral study at the University of Chicago and the University of Michigan, Ann Arbor, Cellarius was an assistant research biophysicist with the Mental Health Research Institute, University of Michigan (1966–68), and taught botany at Ann Arbor from 1966 until 1972, when he joined the faculty of Evergreen State College.

Cellarius was first elected to the Sierra Club's board of directors in 1974, and he has held a number of titles within the organization, including vice-president for science and research (1974–76), secretary (1976–77, 1979–80, 1981–82, 1986–88), vice-president (1977–78) and president (1988–90). He was also chairman of the Publications Committee (1976–79, 1983–85) and the International Committee (1985–86).

A member of the Global Tomorrow Coalition, the American Institute of Biological Sciences, the Northwest Association for Environmental Studies and other academic societies, Cellarius has written or coauthored numerous scientific articles and government reports on the subjects of photobiology, forest science and management and environmental issues.

Center for Clean Air Policy (Founded: 1985)

444 North Capitol Street, Suite 526, Washington, D.C. 20001; (202) 624-7709

The Center for Clean Air Policy, along with its participating state governors and leaders in the corporate, academic and public interest fields, is dedicated to resolving problems caused by air pollution. The organization, formerly called the Center for Acid Rain and Clean Air Policy Analysis, disseminates to the public information about the economic and environmental benefits of air pollution controls and carries out research on acid rain control, energy conservation and waste management. Currently, the group is assessing the air quality in the western United States.

In 1987, the center, which characterizes itself as a mediation organization, published *Acid Rain: Road to a Middleground Solution*. Based on 16 months of dialogue among environmental groups, coal companies, governors, utilities and consumer groups, the report outlined specific strategies for industry and government to control acid rain. Other organization publications include *The Untold Story: The Silver Lining for West Virginia in Acid Rain Control, Healing the Environment Part One: State Options for Addressing Global Warming, Midwest Coal by Wire: Addressing Regional Acid Rain and Energy Problems* and *Air Pollution Control and the German Experience: Lessons for the United States*. Edward A. Helme serves as executive director.

Center for the Defense of Free Enterprise (Founded: 1976)

Liberty Park, 12500 NE 10th Place, Bellevue, Washington 98005; (206) 455-5038

According to the group's vice-president, Ron Arnold, the Center for the Defense of Free Enterprise has 125,000 members (as of October 1992) and gains 200 to 300 members per month. It operates on a budget of $300,000 per year.

The organization focuses on alleviating a "multitude of restrictions that are placed on America's free enterprise system" and engages in programs to defend the right of individual Americans and American businesses to participate in the free market without government hindrance.

Much of the group's activity is, in Arnold's words, "about counterbalancing the excesses of the environmental movement," which is seen as having sometimes brought about economically crippling restrictions on free enterprise. The center considers itself a key part of the counter-environmentalist "wise use movement," advocating a philosophy of living in productive harmony with nature—with the emphasis on "productive."

The center is made up mostly of individual property rights groups and a wide variety of single-issue groups that represent mining, grazing, logging, light manufacturing and other interests. The center administers a Free Enterprise Legal Defense Fund, which supports litigation against environmental regulation and, when necessary, against environmental organizations.

The center maintains the American Press Syndicate, which distributes materials to some 400 newspapers nationwide; the Free Enterprise Press; and a Portland, Oregon, radio station. In addition, its American Broadcasting Network furnishes programming to some 52 radio stations nationwide. The center offers assistance in community organizing and conducts a "direct attack program" against selected environmental organizations. This, the most controversial of the organization's methods, involves lawsuits, media campaigns and direct mail campaigns to the target group's membership aimed at undermining support for the organization.

Alan Gottlieb is president of the Center for the Defense of Free Enterprise.

Center for Law in the Public Interest
(Founded: 1971)
11835 West Olympic Boulevard, Suite 1155, Los Angeles, California 90064; (213) 470-3000

The 1,500-member Center for Law in the Public Interest represents groups in selected legal cases important to the general public. Cases undertaken by the center include class-action suits involving environmental land-use issues as well as criminal justice reform, consumer fraud, civil rights and corporate and governmental responsibility. In addition to its litigation work, the center operates the People for Parks Charitable Fund, a program designed to disseminate information on park issues and to aid community groups in establishing parks. Jack Nicholl serves as executive secretary of the organization. Members receive *Public Interest Briefs*, a quarterly newsletter focusing on public policy and reporting on cases undertaken by the center.

Center for Marine Conservation (Founded: 1972)
1725 DeSales Street NW, Suite 500, Washington, D.C. 20036; (202) 429-5609

The center is dedicated to the conservation and protection of ocean habitats and marine animals, especially whales and turtles. The center encourages, supports and conducts science and policy research, and promotes public awareness and education. It seeks to institute correct management of habitats and to ensure that human activity will not lead to the extinction of marine species.

CMC activities have included beach clean-ups, efforts to abate marine debris, the establishment of a sanctuary for the endangered humpback whale, programs to prevent entanglement in commercial fishing gear and programs to stop the international trade in turtle products. The center publishes a quarterly, *Marine Conservation News,* and issues periodic reports on marine conservation issues. Roger E. McManus is president of the organization.

Center for Short Lived Phenomena (Founded: 1968)
P. O. Box 199, Harvard Square Station, Cambridge, Massachusetts 02238; (617) 492-3310

Founded by the Smithsonian Institution, the Center for Short Lived Phenomena was reorganized as a private body in 1975. The group collects information on the effects of oil spills, clean-up efforts and related lawsuits. It distributes statistical information compiled annually on spills worldwide. Richard Golob is director of the center.

Chafee, John H. (October 22, 1922–   )
The junior senator from Rhode Island, John H. Chafee is the ranking Republican on the Senate Environment and Public Works Committee. He played a crucial role in the 101st Congress (1990) in securing the reauthorization of the Clean Air Act.

Although he was a Republican serving in the era of Ronald REAGAN, Chafee incorporated into the Clean Air Act reauthorization a tough position on acid rain and smog reduction, which put him at odds with many other Republicans. However, in the Environmental Protection Subcommittee, where Chafee is also the ranking Republican, he parted company with Democratic pro-environment legislators by weakening restrictions on tailpipe emissions. Chafee favored emphasis on programs mandating cleaner fuels rather than restrictions on auto manufacturers.

Chafee introduced into the Clean Air Act an amendment to ban the use of ozone-layer-depleting chlorofluorocarbons by the year 2000. The amendment would phase out CFCs even sooner than mandated by an international agreement signed by the United States.

Chafee has always been a strong advocate of the environment. He successfully guided the reauthorization of the 1973 Endangered Species Act in 1988, and he was coauthor of a bill banning the dumping of sludge in the Atlantic Ocean. He introduced a bill in the 101st Congress to expand waste reduction and recycling activities as part of the reauthorization of the Resource Conservation and Recovery Act.

A native of Providence, Rhode Island, Chafee was educated at Yale University (B.A., 1947) and Harvard (LL.B., 1950). He served in the Marine Corps during World War II and returned to service during the Korean War. Chafee served in the Rhode Island House of Representatives from 1957 to 1963 and was minority leader from 1959 to 1963. He was Rhode Island's governor from 1963 to 1969, but was defeated for reelection. President Richard M. NIXON appointed Chafee secretary of the navy in 1969, and he served until 1972. Unsuccessful in his first bid for the U.S. Senate in 1972, he was elected in 1976 and has served since.

Chapman, Herbert Haupt (October 8, 1874– July 13, 1963)

Chapman's series of forestry texts—*Forest Valuation* (1915), *Forest Mensuration* (1921), *Forest Finance* (1926) and *Forest Management* (1931)—served for many years as standards in the field. Awarded a bachelor of science degree (1896) and a bachelor of agriculture degree (1899) from the University of Minnesota, he was superintendent of the Minnesota Agricultural Experiment Station (1898–1903) and worked for the establishment of national forests in Minnesota. After receiving a master of forestry degree from Yale in 1904, he worked for the U.S. FOREST SERVICE and taught at Yale as an instructor from 1906 to 1911, when he was named Harriman Professor of Forest Management.

During his long tenure at Yale (he retired in 1943), Chapman wrote his texts and served in varying capacities with the Forest Service. He was an important early advocate of controlled burning of ground cover for fire protection and to encourage vigorous reproduction.

Chapman worked with the Society of American Foresters to develop a system of accrediting schools of forestry and was director of the American Forestry Association (renamed AMERICAN FORESTS). Chapman was born in Cambridge, Massachusetts.

Charles Darwin Foundation for the Galapagos Isles (Founded: 1959)

c/o Craig MacFarland, National Zoological Park, Washington, D.C. 20008; (202) 673-4705

The Charles Darwin Foundation for the Galapagos Isles supports and administers scientific and conservation research at a work station in Ecuador. Primar-ily engaged in the protection of wildlife on the Galapagos, the organization publishes its research findings, operates a museum of biological specimens from the Galapagos Islands, maintains a library of scientific papers related to the Galapagos and offers scholarships to science students from Ecuador for work at the research station. Craig MacFarland serves as president of the foundation, which has an annual budget of $650,000.

Church, Frank (July 25, 1924–April 7, 1984)

Best known as a foreign relations expert who led a Senate probe of CIA covert activities, Frank Church also shaped domestic conservation policy by balancing the economic interests of his resource-rich state of Idaho with environmental concerns. In 1956, by championing public ownership and development of power facilities, Church defeated an incumbent senator who was supported by the private utilities and lumber and mining interests. During his first term in office, Church won a post on the Interior Committee, which has jurisdiction over federal lands, mining, water policy and other issues vital to Idaho. He later chaired the Subcommittee on Energy Research and Water Resources. He built one of the most liberal voting records in the Senate.

Church was born in Boise, Idaho. He graduated from Stanford University in 1950, and served in the Senate from 1957 to 1981. He was an early and outspoken opponent of President Johnson's escalation of U.S. involvement in Vietnam. His work on the Foreign Relations Committee and, especially, as chair of the Select Committee on Intelligence gained him national recognition in the mid-1970s, which led to an unsuccessful bid for the Democratic presidential nomination in 1976. A target of the National Conservative Political Action Committee, Church was defeated in his Senate reelection bid in 1980.

Citizen's Clearinghouse for Hazardous Waste (Founded: 1981)

P. O. Box 926, Arlington, Virginia; (703) 276-7070

The Citizen's Clearinghouse for Hazardous Waste has a membership of 19,000 and an annual budget of $650,000. The organization grew from the grassroots efforts of Lois GIBBS and others living in upstate New York's Love Canal area, when they were confronted by the nation's worst and most notorious instance of hazardous waste pollution.

Under Gibbs's leadership, the organization promotes community action against toxic dumps and has assisted more than 7,000 local organizations across the country through conferences, publications, training seminars and technical support.

WILLIAM WOODS UNIVERSITY LIBRARY

Among the organization's most visible successes was a program called "McToxics Campaign," which brought public pressure to bear on the McDonald's fast-food corporation to force it to stop using polystyrene packaging.

Citizen's Clearinghouse publishes two newsletters, *Everyone's Backyard* and *Environmental Health Monthly*, and has produced more than 40 guidebooks and "fact packs" for use by community groups.

Citizens for a Better Environment (Founded: 1971)
407 South Dearborn Street, Suite 1775, Chicago, Illinois 60605; (312) 939-1530

Citizens for a Better Environment, a membership organization with 70,000 contributors nationwide, focuses on ways to reduce human exposure to pollutants and toxic substances. The organization conducts research, publishes its findings and supports an advocacy program at the state, regional and national levels. Staff members provide testimony at administrative hearings and undertake litigation on behalf of communities. In addition, the organization sponsors public education programs and provides technical assistance to citizen groups interested in controlling pollution and toxic substances in their communities. The national organization is headed by William Davis, president.

Citizens for a Better Environment supports five state groups and one regional group. The California state group—an independent affiliate since 1987—recently won a lawsuit against air quality agencies in the San Francisco Bay area for failing to comply with health standards for ozone and carbon monoxide. The state group also drafted a large portion of the 1990 California Environmental Protection Initiative and supported a requirement that oil refineries and terminals operating in San Francisco Bay must recover vapors released during the loading of petrochemicals on tankers and barges.

Members of the national organization and its state and regional groups receive a quarterly journal, *Environmental Review*, which reports on public health issues related to toxic substances and on the organization's activities. In addition to the journal, the organization also publishes research reports and fact sheets.

Citizens for Sensible Control of Acid Rain (Founded: 1983)
1301 Connecticut Avenue NW, Suite 700, Washington, D.C. 20036; (202) 659-0330

Citizens for Sensible Control of Acid Rain disseminates information to its 135,000 members and the general public about acid rain and clean coal technologies. The organization is funded by electric utilities, coal suppliers and manufacturing companies interested in forwarding initiatives for clean air policies.

Civilian Conservation Corps (CCC)
Created by federal legislation in 1933 only a month after President Franklin D. ROOSEVELT took office, the Civilian Conservation Corps hired thousands of young men, World War I veterans, Native Americans and woodsmen who had lost their jobs during the Great Depression. Corps employees engaged in reforestation, timber-stand improvement, soil conservation, wildlife restoration, land reclamation, park development, flood control and fire fighting. By October 1935, 560,000 men had been hired by the program, but enrollment dwindled to 300,000 as economic conditions in the country improved and CCC members found jobs elsewhere. The corps was officially disbanded in June 1942.

Among the many accomplishments of the CCC were planting 2.25 billion trees, building 6 million dams to control erosion, improving forest-stands on 4 million acres, building 122,000 miles of truck trails and responding to a variety of emergency situations, including fires and floods.

The CCC was also a model of interdepartmental cooperation at the federal level. The Department of Labor, the Department of AGRICULTURE, the Department of the INTERIOR, the ARMY CORPS OF ENGINEERS, the U.S. Army and the Office of Education all had a hand in the work of the Corps.

Further reading: John A. Salmond, *The Civilian Conservation Corps, 1933–1942: A New Deal Case Study* (Durham, N.C.: Duke University Press, 1967).

Clapp, Earle Hart (October 15, 1877–July 2, 1970)
After graduating from the University of Michigan School of Forestry (1905), Clapp, a native of North Rush, New York, joined the U.S. FOREST SERVICE, specializing in the development of techniques for pricing timber on government land. In 1915, he was made chief of the Forest Service's newly established research branch, and in the 1920s, he played a major role in the advancement of federal forestry programs. *Report on Senate Resolution 311* (1920), for which Clapp was largely responsible, brought to legislative attention the problem of forest depletion. His *Forest Experiment Stations* (1921) presented a plan for a system of 10 regional research stations and one central laboratory, and he was instrumental in the passage of the McSweeney-McNary Act of 1928, which funded

Civilian Conservation Corps team at Leigh Lake, Grand Teton National Park, Wyoming, 1933. *Courtesy of the National Park Service*

forestry research. Clapp and his research branch staff contributed to the *National Plan for American Forestry: Report on Senate Resolution 175* ("Copeland Report," 1933), which set forth a federal-state cooperative plan to reserve as public land large tracts for the growth of timber.

Clark, William Cummin (December 20, 1948–   )

Born in Greenwich, Connecticut, and educated at Yale University and the University of British Columbia, William Cummin Clark was a scientist with the Institute of Energy Analysis at Oak Ridge from 1981 to 1984. In 1987, he was named senior research associate at Harvard University's Kennedy School of Government.

Clark has been a member of the National Academy of Sciences' Committee on Global Change and has directed studies on the sustainable development of the biosphere at the International Institute of Applied Systems Analysis in Austria. He is an executive editor

of *Environment* magazine, published by a division of the Helen Dwight Reid Educational Foundation.

Among Clark's research interests are the stability and resilience of ecosystems, policy analysis for the management of resources, third world development strategies, local climate and sustainable development.

Clausen, Peter A. (September 24, 1944–June 24, 1991)

A former college professor, Central Intelligence Agency political analyst and nuclear policy specialist with the U.S. Department of ENERGY, Peter A. Clausen joined the staff of the Union of Concerned Scientists in 1983 as a senior analyst of nuclear arms control and nonproliferation. A year later he was named research director at the union. A strong advocate of nuclear disarmament, he coauthored two union books: *The Fallacy of Star Wars* (1984) and *Empty Promise: The Growing Case Against Star Wars* (1986). He also wrote *Nonproliferation and National Interest: America's Re-*

sponse to the Spread of Nuclear Weapons (1991). In addition to his work at the union, he served as an adjunct research fellow in the Center for Science and International Affairs at the John F. Kennedy School of Government, Harvard University.

Clean Water Action (Founded: 1971)
c/o David Zwick, 1320 18th Street NW, Washington, D.C. 20003; (202) 457-1286

Operating with an annual budget of $11 million, Clean Water Action is a citizens' organization working to provide clean, safe water to communities across the country. The organization carries out a lobbying program and organizes grass-roots campaigns through its 28 regional offices. Focusing on the protection of groundwater resources, the organization researches and advocates programs to prevent pollution and promotes the passage of laws mandating the clean-up of toxic waste sites. The organization also works to protect and preserve coastal and inland waters, with grass-roots campaigns focused on the Chesapeake Bay, the Atlantic shore, the New England coast, the Great Lakes and inland lakes, rivers and streams throughout the country. Another program, Home Safe Home, promotes the use of environmentally safe products in homes and businesses in order to prevent dangerous chemicals from entering the nation's water supply.

The organization was instrumental in securing passage of the Clean Water Act of 1972, the Safe Drinking Water Act of 1974, the Superfund law of 1986 and the Clean Air Act of 1990.

In 1989, after the Exxon *Valdez* oil spill off the coast of Alaska, Clean Water Action, along with five other environmental organizations, called for the public to boycott Exxon products and return credit cards to the company. Some 10,000 cards were returned. In addition, the groups called on Exxon to deposit $1 billion a year into a trust fund for the environment (one-fifth of the company's 1988 profits). While the campaign against Exxon raised public consciousness of the dangers of oil transport, no real environmental gains were scored—except, perhaps, in expediting Exxon's clean-up of the oil spill area.

The 400,000 members of Clean Water Action receive a subscription to *Clean Water Action News*, a 12-page quarterly newsletter reporting on the organization's current campaigns and scheduled events, such as Clean Water Day activities in communities throughout the country. The group was formerly called Fishermen's Clean Water Action until 1975 and the Clean Water Action Project until 1989. David Zwick is the organization's director.

Clements, Frederic Edward (September 16, 1874–July 26, 1945)
Born in Lincoln and educated at the University of Nebraska, Frederic Edward Clements became an assistant in botany at the university while completing his doctoral studies. From 1907 until 1917, he was head of the Botany Department at the University of Minnesota. He then moved to the Carnegie Institution, where he remained until his retirement in 1941.

While working at the Carnegie Institution, Clements devised new ecological theories that not only profoundly changed the field, but gradually gained the attention of the lay public as well. Clements offered two theories: first, that the ecology of any given region was constantly in a state of evolution until it reached what he called a "climax community," and, second, that any given community of plants in a region was essentially organismic.

In his pioneering study, *The Development and Structure of Vegetation* (1904), he unfolded the theory of ecological succession. His next major work, *Plant Succession: An Analysis of the Development of Vegetation* (1916), perfected the "climax community" model. According to Clements, all habitats progressed through a "sere," a series of stages beginning with primitive, unbalanced plant groups and ending with an advanced plant system capable of perpetuating itself indefinitely. In its early stages, a habitat is controlled by soil composition. As the habitat evolves and matures, however, soil conditions become less important than climate, because the plants within the habitat actually transform the composition of the soil in a process of propagation, maturation and death. According to Clements's theory, each different climatic region has only one mature "climax community" into which it can evolve. Grasslands were forever predetermined to become grasslands; forests were forever predetermined to become forests. And the predetermining factor was climate.

Clements's second major theory—the organismic character of a habitat—drew on models of evolution proposed by the 19th-century philosopher Herbert SPENCER. In *Principles of Biology*, Spencer carried over to the plant and animal world his ideas of the evolution of human society, from primitive tribal culture to highly civilized and differentiated modern cultures. Spencer wrote about the interdependence of plants and animals and of the "progressive differentiation" and "progressive integration" that occurs as a region evolves. Building on Spencer, Clements developed his own theories of ecological evolution and began working on *Bio-ecology* (1939), a book written with animal ecologist Victor SHELFORD. Clements and Shelford merged the study of plants and the study of animals by relating both to their "biotic community," or "biome." Despite his belief that the evolution of a particular ecological environment is a result of the presence of both the animals and the plants found there, Clements continued to stress the dominance of plants. For him, it was the plants that determined which animals lived in the environment.

Of particular interest to Clements, a child of the American Midwest, was the biome of the grasslands. He noted the different grasses that grow in the region—buffalo grass and blue grama grass in the semiarid western region; little bluestem, western wheatgrass and needlegrass in central Nebraska, Kansas and Oklahoma as well as in the Dakotas, where annual rainfall reached only 20 inches; tall bluestem and switchgrass in the humus-rich soil of the eastern part of the region. In this environment, pronghorns, rattlesnakes, prairie dogs, meadowlarks, grasshoppers, coyotes, jackrabbits and bison had thrived over millions of years. In addition, beginning 40,000 years ago, there were human hunters who had migrated across the Bering Strait, worked their way down into grasslands and became yet another component of the climax community. Then, the eons-old environment was suddenly destroyed. White hunters nearly wiped out the buffalo, and white settlement overran the Indian. In the wake of that destruction came farmers who plowed up the grassland and began building towns and cities. According to Clements, a highly developed human civilization could not exist in a climax community without changing or even destroying it. What Clements (and others) saw in the 1930s Dust Bowl was a demonstration of precisely this. Among the lessons of the Dust Bowl was the vital necessity of recognizing the inextricable bonds between the study of human and the study of natural ecology.

Clepper, Henry Edward (March 21, 1901– March 26, 1987)

Author, forester, and historian Henry Edward Clepper graduated in 1921 from the Pennsylvania State Forest Academy in Mont Alto. His first professional position was with the Pennsylvania Department of Forests and Waters, a government agency he served as field forester and as assistant chief of the Bureau of Research and Education. After spending a year with the U.S. FOREST SERVICE in Washington, D.C., he was named executive secretary of the SOCIETY OF AMERICAN FORESTERS in 1937. For all but two years (when he worked for the War Production Board) of the next 28, he edited the society's *Journal of Forestry*, oversaw publication of the quarterly journal *Forest Science* and the research series "Forest Sciences Monographs" and directed the society's other activities. In addition, he was consulting editor and acting

secretary of the American Fisheries Society and a consulting editor of the Sport Fishing Institute.

Clepper was the editor, author or coauthor of more than 100 articles, bulletins and books, including *America's Natural Resources* (1967), *American Forestry— Six Decades of Growth* (1960), *Careers in Conservation* (1963, 1979), *Origins of American Conservation* (1966), *The World of the Forest* (1965), *Leaders in American Conservation* (1971), *Professional Forestry in the United States* (1971), *Crusade for Conservation* (1975) and *Famous and Historic Trees* (1976). He was awarded the Gifford Pinchot Medal from the Society of American Foresters, the John Astor Warder Medal of the American Forestry Association (now AMERICAN FORESTS) and the distinguished service award from American Forest Products Industries Inc.

Henry Clepper was born in Columbia, Pennsylvania, and died in Washington, D.C.

Cliff, Edward Parley (September 3, 1909–July 18, 1987)

A native of Heber City, Utah, Edward P. Cliff was educated at Utah State University, earning his B.A. in 1931. He became an assistant district ranger at the Wenatchee National Forest in Washington State and was transferred to the Portland, Oregon, office of the U.S FOREST SERVICE in 1934. After coauthoring the *Range Plant Handbook*, he was promoted to supervisor of the Siskiyou National Forest in 1939 and the Fremont National Forest in 1942.

Following additional promotions, Cliff returned to Washington, D.C., as assistant chief of the Forest Service and was promoted to chief in 1962. He served until 1972, a decade that saw greatly increased public interest in environmentalism and the national forests. Under Cliff's leadership, forestry recreation and research programs were significantly expanded, and cooperation between federal and state authorities was increased. Cliff was criticized by some environmentalists for allowing too much commercial timber activity in the national forests, although he tightened policy on these uses toward the end of his tenure as chief.

After leaving the Forest Service, Cliff became a private forestry consultant, working with national and international agencies and corporations. Cliff received many honors during his career, including the Utah State University Distinguished Service Award (1958) and an honorary doctorate of science (1965) from that institution; the U.S. Department of AGRICULTURE Distinguished Service Award (1962); the National Civil Service League Career Service Award (1968); the Tuskegee Institute Distinguished Service Award (1970); and the International Association of Game, Fish and Conservation Commissioners' Award for Outstanding Achievement in Wildlife Habitat Management (1972). The SOCIETY OF AMERICAN FORESTERS presented him with its Gifford Pinchot Medal for 1973.

Clifton, Merritt (September 18, 1953–)

An award-winning investigative journalist specializing in environmental and animal protection issues, Merritt Clifton is editor of *Animal People: News for People Who Care about Animals*, a monthly newspaper based in Shushan, New York.

An Oakland, California, native, Clifton studied creative writing at San Jose State University in California. Since receiving his B.A. in 1974, he has been a lead feature writer, environmental correspondent, columnist, art critic and sports reporter for a number of daily, weekly and monthly newspapers, including *The County Courier* of Enosburg Falls, Vermont (1979–89), *The Townships Sun* of Lennoxville, Quebec (1977–1984), *The Record* of Sherbrooke, Quebec (1978–86) and *Vanguard Press* of Burlington, Vermont (1980–1990). From 1973 to 1992, he was also editor and publisher of *Samisdat*, an alternative literary and environmental journal, and from 1987 to 1992, he was chief writer and news editor of *The Animals' Agenda*, a nonprofit newsmagazine about animals and ecology.

Clifton's free-lance articles have appeared in *The New York Times*, *Greenpeace*, *Environmental Action*, *American Forests*, *Mother Earth News*, *Harrowsmith*, *At the Centre* (the magazine of the Canadian Centre for Occupational Health and Safety), *Snowy Egret* and many other consumer, environmental, literary, art-related and sports-oriented publications. The author of *The Samisdat Method: A Do-It-Yourself Guide to Printing* (1979) and the editor of *Those Who Were There* (1984), an annotated bibliography of works about the Vietnam War by Vietnam veterans, Clifton has also written monographs and commentary for CBC radio and television, CTV, Environment Canada, Friends of Animals, the International Wildlife Coalition, the Humane Society of the United States and the American Humane Association. His published works include three nonfiction books on baseball and two novels—*24X12* (1975, 1980) and *A Baseball Classic* (1978, 1984)—as well as several collaborative series and anthologies.

For his reporting of "canned hunts" (1991) and the human health aspects of acid rain (1988), Clifton has twice won the Project Censored award for exemplary investigative journalism. His writings on animal protection, deforestation, soil erosion, farm bankruptcies and other environmental and public interest issues have also earned awards and honors from the New York State Humane Association (1991), Environment

Quebec (1984), the Association of Quebec Regional English Media (1983) and the Centre for Investigative Journalism (1980).

As a citizen activist, Clifton has helped organize and lead several regional and community anti-pollution and recycling campaigns, and in 1989, he was a founder of the Canada-U.S. Study Group on Animal Protection.

Further reading: Clifton, *Legislative Approaches to Pet Overpopulation* (Englewood, Colo.: American Humane Association, 1992); *North American Fur Sources and Trade in the 1980s* (Washington, D.C.: Humane Society of the United States, 1988).

Clusen, Charles M. (October 11, 1946–)

Born in Manitowoc, Wisconsin, Charles M. Clusen was educated at the University of Michigan, from which he received a B.S. degree in conservation in 1969. He undertook graduate study from 1969 to 1970 at the Racham School of Graduate Studies of the University of Michigan.

From 1970 to 1971, Clusen served as director of the Division of Environment and Population of the Institute for the Study of Health and Society, Washington, D.C. From 1971 to 1979, he worked for the SIERRA CLUB, serving as associate director of the Washington office, as Washington representative and as assistant conservation director. During this period, he led a conservation coalition that was instrumental in gaining passage of the Federal Land Policy Management Act (BLM Organic Act); he led successful campaigns to add Mineral King Valley to Sequoia National Park and to pass the Endangered American Wilderness Act, the National Park Mining Act and the "Game Range" Act; and he managed the Sierra Club's campaign to gain passage of California's Proposition #20, the California Coastal Zone Conservation Initiative.

From 1977 to 1980, Clusen served as chairman of the Washington, D.C.-based Alaska Coalition, which consists of more than 60 national conservation, sportsmen's, labor and civic groups formed to secure the passage of a sound Alaska Lands Act. Clusen spearheaded the nation's largest single conservation campaign, which resulted in the passage of an act designating over 103 million acres of Alaska as national parks, wildlife refuges and wild and scenic rivers. Fifty-six million acres of this land were declared protected wilderness.

Clusen left his Sierra Club post in 1979 to become vice-president in charge of conservation for the WILDERNESS SOCIETY, developing a campaign to block federal oil and gas leasing of wild areas and successfully managing a campaign to designate more than 10 million acres of national forest land as wilderness.

Clusen left this position in 1987 to serve as executive director of the Adirondack Council. He developed and launched the Campaign to Save the Adirondack Park, securing New York Governor Mario Cuomo's support for the campaign, persuading the state of New York to purchase additional park lands and lobbying Congress to include the Adirondacks in the Northern Forest Lands Study conducted by the U.S. FOREST SERVICE. Under Clusen's leadership, the Adirondack Council grew from a membership of 3,000 to 13,000.

Clusen's current positions, which he assumed in 1989, are as senior associate with the NATURAL RESOURCES DEFENSE COUNCIL and special assistant to the chairman of the American Conservation Association. For the council, he developed and conducted a campaign to include Puerto Rico and the U.S. Virgin Islands in the Barrier Resource System, thereby protecting critical mangrove swamps and other sensitive ecological resources. He also successfully lobbied Congress for increased funding of the federal endangered species program and National Parks and Wildlife Refuges in Hawaii. For the American Conservation Association, he conceived and organized the Environment/Population Working Group, consisting of the National Wildlife Foundation, the NATIONAL AUDUBON SOCIETY, the Sierra Club, the Planned Parenthood Federation and the Population Crisis Committee, to collaborate on a campaign to increase funding for international family planning. He also organized "Celebrate Wild Alaska!" a series of events from December 1990 to February 1991 promoting Alaska land conservation.

Clusen serves on the boards of directors of numerous associations and official bodies, including the American Conservation Association, the University of Michigan School of Natural Resources, AMERICAN RIVERS, LEAGUE OF CONSERVATION VOTERS, Adirondack Conservancy/Adirondack Land Trust and Americans for the Environment. He has been honored with the Outstanding Conservation Campaign Award of the Natural Resources Council of America.

Clusen, Ruth Chickering (June 11, 1922–   )

Ruth Chickering Clusen served as a delegate to the U.S.–U.S.S.R. Joint Committee on Environmental Protection in Moscow in 1974 and participated in the 1972 U.S. Conference on the Human Environment in Stockholm, the meeting at which the UNITED NATIONS' ENVIRONMENT PROGRAMME was initiated.

Born in Bruce, Wisconsin, Clusen has worked as an environmental consultant to several governmental agencies and private organizations, including the U.S. Department of State, the U.S. Department of the INTERIOR, the CONSERVATION FOUNDATION and the

U.S. Chamber of Commerce. She chaired the Environmental Quality Committee of the LEAGUE OF WOMEN VOTERS OF THE UNITED STATES, and from 1974 to 1978 served as the league's president. In 1978, she was named assistant secretary for environment at the U.S. Department of ENERGY.

The NATIONAL WILDLIFE FEDERATION named her International Conservationist of 1977, and she became an honorary vice-president of the American Forestry Association (now AMERICAN FORESTS) in 1978.

Coastal Conservation Association (Founded: 1977)

4801 Woodway, Suite 220W, Houston, Texas 77056; (713) 626-4222

Originally named the Gulf Coast Conservation Association, the Coastal Conservation Association was formed in Texas by recreational anglers concerned about declining Gulf Coast fish populations. Dedicated to conserving and enhancing marine life through programs of education, legislation and rehabilitation, the Houston-based national association now includes chapters in nine Gulf and Atlantic states: Alabama, Florida, Georgia, Louisiana, Mississippi, North Carolina, South Carolina, Texas and Virginia. CCA monitors commercial and sport fishing pressure in coastal areas, works with state wildlife and fisheries agencies to develop new programs and enact conservation measures that prevent overharvesting of threatened species and operates New Tide, a youth association. In addition to the individual preservation and restoration projects of state chapters and 54 local groups, the Coastal Conservation Association manages the GCCA/John Wilson Hatchery near Corpus Christi, Texas, to augment the region's redfish population. CCA publishes *Tide,* a bimonthly magazine, and *Rising Tide,* a newsletter for New Tide members.

Colby, William Edward (May 28, 1875– November 9, 1964)

A specialist in mining and forest law, William Edward Colby engaged in several battles to preserve wilderness areas, including the fight to prohibit the building of Hetch Hetchy Dam in Yosemite Valley. In 1901, this native of Benicia, California, established the SIERRA CLUB's high trips program, and over the next 28 years led expeditions into various wilderness areas.

From 1927 to 1937, Colby served as the first chairman of the California State Park Commission, a position in which he supervised the addition of more than 50 new parks to the state's system, including Point Lobos Reserve, Calaveras Big Trees and Bull Creek Flat. He is credited with the idea of establishing the John Muir Trail, a wilderness trail running from the crest of the Sierra Nevada to the top of Mount Whitney.

Colby served on the board of the Sierra Club for 49 years and was the winner of the club's first John Muir Award, bestowed in 1961. After his retirement from active service, the Sierra Club established the Colby Award in his honor.

Cole, Henry S. (May 22, 1943–   )

Henry S. Cole is the science and policy director of CLEAN WATER ACTION, and president of Henry S. Cole and Associates, both of Washington, D.C. He is also a private consultant in environmental sciences.

Cole graduated from Rutgers University College of Agriculture in New Brunswick, New Jersey, with a B.S. in soil science and meteorology in 1965. Four years later, he earned his Ph.D. in atmospheric sciences from the University of Wisconsin, Madison. After gaining his doctorate, Cole taught at the University of Wisconsin, Parkside, as an associate professor of environmental earth sciences for 11 years. At Parkside, Cole also served as a member of the Wisconsin State Air Pollution Advisory Board and as a scientific advisor to Racine Citizens for the Environment. In 1974, he was a research associate in energy and nuclear power issues for U.S. Congressman Les Aspin.

In 1977, Cole became a staff scientist for the Office of Air Quality, Planning and Standards at the ENVIRONMENTAL PROTECTION AGENCY in Washington, D.C. For the next two years his work entailed air pollution meteorology, dispersion modeling and other research related to federal air quality regulations. Cole resumed teaching in 1979 as a professor of environmental science at the School of Human Ecology at Howard University. The following year, he returned to the EPA Office of Air Quality, Planning and Standards as chief of the model application section, Monitoring and Data Analysis Division. During his three years' service, Cole supervised the implementation of air quality studies in the development of Clean Air Act regulations and the formulation of other government policies concerning power plants, hazardous emissions and urban and regional emissions. He also directed the Northeast Corridor Regional Modeling Program, a joint effort by the EPA and the northeastern states to develop regional strategies for the reduction of photochemical smog concentrations. Cole accepted his current position with Clean Water Action in May 1983. Since then, he has also served as a member of the U.S. Office of Technology Assessment (OTA) Panel on Industrial Waste Reduction

(1986) and the OTA Advisory Panel on Superfund Implementation (1988–89).

As director of research for Clean Water Action's national, state and local programs, and as a professional consultant to citizen groups and Superfund-site municipalities, Cole has frequently testified before congressional committees and other government bodies on mercury contamination, hazardous waste site clean-up, solid waste disposal and air pollution meteorology. A chapter contributor to *The Citizens' Toxic Prevention Manual*, produced by the National Campaign Against Toxic Hazards in 1988, Cole has written a wide variety of policy studies, reports and articles for *Clean Water Action News*, the *Journal of Public Health Policy*, the *Journal of Applied Meteorology*, the *Bulletin of Atomic Scientists* and many other educational, technical and government publications.

Cole, Hugh Samuel David (July 6, 1943–   )

Educated in England at the Imperial College of Science and Technology and the University of Sussex, Sam Cole was named codirector of the Project on Technology, Domestic Distribution and North-South Relations of the United Nations Institute for Training and Research in New York City in 1978. From 1981 to 1983, he was senior economist and planner at the Institute of Applied Economic Analysis for the Island Government of Aruba, Netherlands Antilles. Since 1983, he has been professor of environmental design and planning at the State University of New York at Buffalo. Concurrently, since 1988, he has been director of the Center for Regional Studies at the university.

Cole served as a coeditor of *Models of Doom: A Critique of The Limits to Growth* (1973). In 1975 he edited and contributed to *Global Simulation Models: A Comparative Study*, and he is the author of *Global Models and the International Economic Order* (1977), *Worlds Apart: The Future of Global Inequality* (1984) and *Global Models in Future Studies: The New Agenda* (1987). In 1985, he wrote (with John Bessant) *Stacking the Chips: Information Technology and the Distribution of Income*.

Since 1975, Cole has been a member of the executive committee of the World Future Studies Federation.

Commoner, Barry (May 28, 1917–   )

Director of the Center for the Biology of Natural Systems at Queens College in his native New York, Barry Commoner has focused his attention not on simply controlling pollution, but on stopping pollutants from entering the environment to begin with.

This, he recognizes, will require a profound shift in society and its values. As an environmentalist, Commoner is of necessity an intense political and social activist, who argues that the main source of pollutants is the technology of production and that, therefore, the principal polluters are corporate directors who make production decisions based on immediate profits rather than their impact on the environment.

Commoner received an A.B. degree from Columbia University in 1937, and an M.A. (1938) and Ph.D. (1941) in biology from Harvard University. He worked as an assistant biologist at Harvard from 1938 to 1940 and as an associate editor of *Science Illustrated* from 1946 to 1947, when he turned to teaching, becoming a professor of plant physiology at Washington University in St. Louis. In 1981, Commoner moved to his present post, where he addresses such environmental issues as nuclear power, organic farming, pesticides and waste disposal.

Commoner first came to the forefront of the environmental movement as a member of the Greater St. Louis Committee for Nuclear Information. This committee disseminated information about nuclear fallout generated in tests conducted in Nevada. In part due to the efforts of the scientists on the committee, the United States signed an international agreement in 1963 to ban above-ground nuclear testing. Once the threat of nuclear fallout lessened, Commoner turned his attention to pesticides. He found that while new synthetic pesticides on the market were less dangerous to the person applying them, they were much more threatening to the environment because they remained, undegraded, in soil and water and could be carried over long distances through the air.

Commoner's most eloquent presentation of the threats to the environment are found in his *Making Peace with the Planet* (1990). "To what extent should the choice of production technologies be governed by private, generally short-term economic considerations such as profit maximization, and to what extent by long-term social concerns such as environmental quality?" he asks. Many pollutants, he argues, come from new technologies that replaced older, safer production methods—for example, plastic soda bottles instead of glass, and chlorofluorocarbon aerosol propellants instead of atomizer-type sprays. Most significantly, Commoner argues that these technologies were developed from motives of corporate profit rather than in response to genuine consumer demand.

In a March 1990 interview published in *Mother Earth News*, Commoner pointed out that, since the passage of the 1970 Clean Air Act Amendment, which

Barry Commoner, director of the Center for the Biology of Natural Systems. *Courtesy of the Center for the Biology of Natural Systems, Queens College, CUNY*

mandated a 90% reduction in levels of carbon monoxide, hydrocarbon and ozone in urban areas by 1977, little has actually been done to carry out the mandate. When the deadline lapsed unmet in 1977, it was pushed back to the end of 1982. When that year saw only a 14% improvement, the government proposed pushing the deadline for compliance back to 2015. Virtually no gains have been reported since 1982. This, Commoner argues, is a glaring indictment of the government's reliance on controls and restrictions rather than on elimination of pollutants. "Environmental illness is simply an incurable disease," Commoner has said. "There is no cure. It can only be prevented."

In addition to *Making Peace with the Planet*, Commoner's works include *Science and Survival* (1966), *The Closing Circle* (1971), *The Poverty of Power* (1976) and *The Politics of Energy* (1979). He serves on the board of consulting experts of the Rachel Carson COUNCIL. In 1980, he ran for the United States presidency as the candidate of the Citizens Party. Commoner has received many honors, including the Newcomb Cleveland Prize (1953), the First International Humanist Award of the International Humanist and Ethical Union (1970), the Phi Beta Kappa Award for *The Closing Circle* (1972) and many honorary degrees.

Commonwealth Human Ecology Council
(Founded: 1969)
57/58 Stanhope Gardens, London, England SW7 5RL; (71) 373-6761; Fax (71) 244-7470

The Commonwealth Human Ecology Council brings together organizations and individuals in 41 nations, from the fields of government, education and ecology, to promote greater consideration and sociopolitical application of the principles of human ecology. Examining the interrelationship of humans in the overall environment, the group conducts programs in curriculum development, education, research and rural and urban self-reliance. The council holds international and regional conferences, offers workshops and seminars, maintains a library of related reference volumes and publishes books, bibliographies and the periodic bulletins *CHEC Journal, CHEC Points* and *Report Series.*

Connell, James Roger (October 25, 1929–   )
Atmospheric scientist James Roger Connell has conducted research on modeling atmospheric turbulence and fluid flow in relation to aerodynamics and wind turbine rotor response, wind turbine wake properties, turbulence measure and theory and wind turbine rotor aerodynamics. A native of Rolla, Kansas, he holds a B.S. from the University of Illinois, Urbana, and an M.S. and Ph.D. in atmospheric science from Colorado State University.

From 1960 to 1962, Connell was a physicist with the National Bureau of Standards. He then joined the faculty of Colorado State University as an instructor in aerodynamics. In 1969, he moved to St. Louis University as assistant professor of atmospheric science and then taught at the University of Wyoming, Colorado State University, and the Space Institute of the University of Tennessee. Since 1978, he has been staff research scientist of atmospheric fluid dynamics at Northwestern Labs, Battelle Memorial Institute, in Columbus, Ohio.

In the field of ecology, Connell has consistently advocated alternatives to modern society's seemingly unalterable belief in progress and growth. In 1970, he wrote with William MURDOCH an article entitled "All About Ecology" for *The Center Magazine*, a publication of the Center for the Study of Democratic

Institutions in Santa Barbara, California. The authors refute the notion that "the answer to most of our problems is technology. . . . One job of the ecologist is to dispel this faith in technology." Connell and Murdoch claim that technological solutions to environmental problems only create new problems. As an example, they cite the "clean" energy source of nuclear power, which produces radioactive wastes. They conclude that "the ecologist must convince the population that the only solution to the problem of growth is not to grow." Connell's work with wind-driven turbines is one way in which he has sought to return to and modify an earlier technology to create energy without consuming nonrenewable resources or creating pollution. Connell was awarded the Gold Medal of the U.S. Department of ENERGY in 1984.

Connolly, Matthew Bernard, Jr. (July 28, 1941–   )
Ornithologist and wildlife conservationist Matthew Connolly Jr. is the executive vice-president and chief operating officer of the waterfowl and wetlands preservation group DUCKS UNLIMITED. Born in Norwood, Massachusetts, Connolly earned degrees from the Stockbridge School of Agriculture in Amherst, Massachusetts (A.S., 1964), and the University of Massachusetts (B.S., 1968). After graduation, Connolly moved to Boston and served as a state ornithologist with the Massachusetts divisions of Fish and Game (1968–71), Conservation (director, 1971–73), Coastal Zone Management (1973–76) and Fisheries and Wildlife (1976–79). Connolly joined the staff of Ducks Unlimited in 1979, working as a group manager in Long Grove, Illinois. In 1985, he was named execu-

Matthew B. Connolly, Jr., executive vice-president of Ducks Unlimited, Inc. *Ducks Unlimited, Inc.*

tive vice-president of the NORTH AMERICAN WILDLIFE FOUNDATION, and in 1987, he assumed his current post at Ducks Unlimited.

Connolly has consulted on numerous regional and government committees, including the New England River Basins Commission (1973–77), the National Outer Continental Shelf advisory board to the U.S. Department of the INTERIOR (1974–76), the Northeast Association of Fisheries and Wildlife Agencies (president, 1978) and the North American Waterfowl Management Plan Implementation Board (chairman, 1988–90). Active in many conservation organizations, Connolly is chairman of the North American Wetlands Council, governor of America's Clean Water Federation and a member of the migratory bird committee of the International Wildlife Agencies.

Conservation Foundation (Founded: 1948; merged 1985 with WORLD WILDLIFE FUND)

Founded by Fairfield OSBORN, George E. Brewer and Samuel H. Ordway Jr., the Conservation Foundation was not a membership organization, but a research and communications foundation dedicated to promoting knowledge about the earth's resources and their wise management. The foundation conducted programs in land use, water resources, the resolution of environmental disputes, pollution and toxic substances control and other environmental issues. It worked with other agencies and individuals to fund environmental projects, grant fellowships and prepare educational materials, which included the landmark *The Living Earth* and *Living Forest* film series coproduced with Encyclopedia Britannica Films in 1948 and 1949. In 1977, the foundation issued *The Lands Nobody Wanted*, a seminal report on 24 million acres of national forest lands in the eastern U.S. The organization publishes the bimonthly *Conservation Foundation Newsletter* and periodically issues *Resolve*, a journal devoted to reporting environmental disputes.

Parent organization of the ENVIRONMENTAL LAW INSTITUTE, the Conservation Foundation merged with the World Wildlife Fund in 1985.

Conservation International (Founded: 1987)

1015 18th Street NW, Suite 1000, Washington, D.C. 20036; (202) 429-5660

With headquarters in Washington, D.C., and locally run projects in 20 countries around the world, Conservation International works to preserve tropical and temperate rain forests and other threatened ecosystems while assisting related communities to develop sustainable, conservation-based economies. The group arranged the world's first "debt-for-nature" swap in

A section of the Amazon rainforest being cleared for agricultural use by the traditional slash-and-burn method. *AP/ Wide World Photos.*

1987 when it purchased and forgave part of Bolivia's national debt in exchange for permanent protection of Amazonian wilderness tracts. CI was honored for this innovation with the UNITED NATIONS ENVIRONMENT PROGRAMME's Global 500 Award, and since then, conservation organizations have finalized similar transactions with at least seven other nations. CI has helped establish several Biosphere Reserves—protected land parcels that surround core forest preserves with buffer zones of benign human settlement and activity—as well as three binational "peace parks" to safeguard sensitive ecosystems that overlap troubled political borders in Central America.

CI's urgent, nontraditional scientific approach is exemplified by its Rapid Assessment Program, which assigns expert field specialists to swiftly evaluate the conditions of endangered habitats and their resident species in order to determine sites of greatest conservation priority. The group then works with governments and other environmental organizations to save these "hot spots" from destruction or further harmful development. CI initiates plant and animal species recovery projects, supports research in ethnobotany and builds local capacity for conservation by helping communities identify and market non-timber rain forest products that may be renewably harvested without damaging the environment. The organization also promotes ecotourism by fostering small-scale nature tours that nourish local economies while increasing international awareness of biological diversity and its importance to the global environment.

In 1990, Conservation International produced *The Rain Forest Imperative: A Ten-Year Strategy to Save Earth's Most Threatened Ecosystems*; the group also publishes the newsletter *Tropicus* and (in conjunction with the Myrin Institute) the *Orion Nature Quarterly*. CI maintains an international user network for its multilingual Geographic Information System (GIS), a computer database instrumental in environmental planning.

Cooper, Toby (October 8, 1944–   )

Toby Cooper's first professional work in environmental preservation was as a member of the steering committee of the Teach-In on the Environment at the University of Michigan in 1970. Having graduated from the University of Michigan in 1966 with a degree in biology and zoology, the Los Angeles native enrolled in graduate school at the university and received an M.S. in zoology in 1969 and undertook doctoral studies in wildlife management. From 1971 to 1972, he was an instructor in biology and environmental studies at Principia College. He next worked with the University of California, Santa Cruz, project on organic farming. Between 1973 and 1975 he served on the staff of the NATIONAL PARKS AND CONSERVATION ASSOCIATION and then moved to DEFENDERS OF WILDLIFE, where he worked as wildlife programs coordinator, programs director and director of national issues. His articles on environmental issues have appeared in several magazines and journals, including *National Parks, Defenders, Frontiers* and *Backpacker*.

Cooper, William Skinner (August 25, 1884– October 8, 1978)

American botanist, geomorphologist and educator William Skinner Cooper was an important figure in the development of early 20th-century plant ecology.

A native of Detroit, Cooper earned his B.S. in botany and ecology at Michigan's Alma College (1906), his S.D. from Johns Hopkins University (1907) and his Ph.D. from the University of Chicago (1911). After an academic year as ecology lecturer at Stanford University, Cooper became an instructor of botany at the University of Minnesota in 1915, and he taught there for 36 years, retiring as emeritus professor in 1951. Skinner was awarded honorary doctorates in science from Alma College (1930) and the University of Colorado (1961).

A participant in several scientific expeditions to southern Alaska and a member of the National Research Council's Committee on Preservation of Natural Conditions, Cooper was a key campaigner for the designation of Glacier Bay as a national monument. He served as vice-president (1927) and president (1936) of the ECOLOGICAL SOCIETY OF AMERICA, and the society honored him as eminent ecologist in 1963. In 1956, he was awarded the Certificate of Merit by the Botanical Society of America.

Cooper wrote extensively in botany and geomorphology, and his influential 1926 paper *Fundamentals of Vegetational Change* outlined principles of vegetation dynamics that remain basic to ecology today. Among his other research subjects were the glacial geology and forests of Alaska and the sand dunes of Pacific North America. A fellow of the American Geographical Society, the Geological Society of America and the Arctic Institute of North America, Cooper died in Boulder, Colorado, at the age of 94.

Corn, Morton (October 18, 1933–   )

Environmental engineer and occupational health specialist Morton Corn served as director of the Occupational Safety and Health Agency (OSHA) during President Richard Nixon's second term. Corn, a native New Yorker, was a professor at the Graduate School of Public Health and the School of Engineering of the University of Pittsburgh from 1967 to 1979. In 1977, he started his own engineering practice, Morton Corn Associates, and in 1980, he joined the faculty of Johns Hopkins University as professor and head of the division of environmental and health engineering, School of Hygiene and Public Health.

Corn has served as a consultant to the Health Physics Division at the Oak Ridge National Laboratory, to the Division of Biology and Medicine of the U.S. Atomic Energy Commission, to the Los Alamos Scientific Laboratory and to the National Academy of Sciences-Natural Resources Council Committee on the Biological Effects of Air Pollution. From 1978 to 1981, he served on the scientific advisory board of the ENVIRONMENTAL PROTECTION AGENCY.

Corn's research has focused on aerosol physics, air pollution and industrial hygiene and ventilation.

Costle, Douglas Michael (July 27, 1939–   )

Administrator of the ENVIRONMENTAL PROTECTION AGENCY from 1977 to 1981, Douglas Michael Costle has been dean of the Vermont Law School in South Royalton since 1987. Before joining the staff of the EPA, Costle, a native of Long Beach, California, worked in private law firms until 1969, when he was named senior staff associate for environment and natural resources of the President's Advisory Council on Executive Organization, known as the Ash Commission. In this capacity, he recommended the formation of the EPA. Costle worked as a consultant for the EPA and as deputy commissioner and commissioner of the Connecticut Department of Environmental Protection. While heading the state agency, he developed the "Connecticut Plan," which fines industries for noncompliance with state environmental regulations at a rate equal to the amount of money the industry saves by noncompliance.

Costle returned to Washington in 1975 as assistant director of the Congressional Budget Office, with particular responsibility for natural resources and commerce. After President Jimmy Carter's election, Costle joined Carter's transition team on government organization and then, in February 1977, was named head of the EPA. Amid criticism that the EPA's regulations were incompatible with the economic goals of the country, Costle developed programs to demonstrate the cost-effectiveness of pollution control. He argued, for example, that the regulations calling for a reduction in air particulates each year saved American businesses $8 billion by reducing workers' health-related absences and increasing productivity. In 1979, Costle reached an accord with United States Steel, which agreed to spend $400 million over three years to reduce air pollution in nine Pittsburgh facilities. In working with other industries, however, Costle was sometimes criticized as being too willing to compromise.

After leaving the EPA, Costle founded Environmental Testing and Certification, an Edison, New Jersey, company that provides pollution testing for private industries.

Council on Environmental Quality, U.S.
(Established: 1969)
722 Jackson Place NW, Washington, D.C. 20006;
(202) 395-5750

Created by the National Environmental Policy Act of 1969, among the epoch-making pieces of environmental legislation enacted during the administration of Richard M. NIXON, the Council on Environmental Quality is an executive agency charged with overseeing and coordinating all federal policy decisions with respect to the environment. The council sets federal environmental policy, monitors the compliance of other federal agencies, and adjudicates disputes among federal agencies and between federal agencies and state authorities over environmental matters.

One of the council's most vital, demanding and controversial functions is in the area of environmental impact statements. All federal agencies are required to prepare such statements before undertaking any actions or projects that have significant impact on the environment. The council establishes guidelines for the statements and reviews any cases in which the impact is of national scope or where controversy exists. The Council on Environmental Quality also collects and publishes data and information on problems and trends in the nation's environmental quality. The council prepares the annual State of the Environment Report, which the president is obliged to deliver to Congress.

The Council on Environmental Quality has no regulatory authority in the private sector (that is the province of the ENVIRONMENTAL PROTECTION AGENCY) and President Bill Clinton has proposed dismantling the council.

Cousteau, Jacques-Yves (June 11, 1910–)
The celebrated oceanographer, underwater photographer, cinematographer, writer and television personality Jacques-Yves Cousteau was born in St. André de Cubzac, France, and was educated at Stanislas Academy in Paris, from which he received a B.S. degree in 1927. He entered the French Naval Academy in 1930 and was a midshipman aboard the *Jeanne d'Arc* in 1932. During 1933–35, he served aboard the cruiser *Primauquet*, was chief of the French naval base at Shanghai and was trained as a naval aviator. A serious accident ended his flying career, and he became a gunnery officer, using his free time to conduct a series of diving experiments. Beginning in 1936, he experimented with developing prototypes of underwater breathing apparatus, and in 1943, he and Émile Gagnan designed and built the Aqualung, the invention that made scuba diving possible.

During World War II, Cousteau was active in the Free French resistance movement, operating mainly in the south of France. Following the war, he returned to diving and established, with Commander Phillipe Taillez, the Experimental Diving Unit based in Toulon, Sète and the Lion Gulf. Cousteau commanded the navy tender *Ingénieur Élie Monnier* and headed the Undersea Research Group of the French navy from 1946 to 1956.

In 1950, Cousteau acquired the *Calypso*, an American minesweeper retired from service. Under his direction, the *Calypso* was transformed into an oceanographic research vessel, and Cousteau was launched upon his career as the world's most famous oceanographer.

Cousteau had originally set out to observe and record the living sea, commenting only occasionally on man's relation to it, but in the course of a half-century, he became increasingly aware of the ecological dangers to which human activity has exposed the sea, and his activities became more focused on the relation of humankind not only to the ocean, but to the entire planet.

Cousteau founded the Campagnes Océanographiques Françaises, headquartered in Marseilles, in 1950, and the Centre d'Études Marines Avancées in 1952. He is president of both organizations. He was elected director of the Oceanographic Institute and Museum in Monaco, resigning the position in 1988. In 1972, along with his son Jean-Michel COUSTEAU, he founded the COUSTEAU SOCIETY. In the United States he serves as president of the society, directing

Jacques-Yves Cousteau, founder of the Cousteau Society. © *The Cousteau Society, 1986*

its activities. A sister organization in France, L'Équipe Cousteau, was created in 1981.

Cousteau has always directed his efforts toward public education, producing books, films and many television documentaries on underwater life. To facilitate diving and filming, he worked with André Laban in 1951 to develop the first underwater camera equipment for television transmisson. He was also instrumental in the development of such devices as the diving saucer, the Bathygraf cinecamera, deep-sea camera sleds and mini-submarines. During the 1960s, Cousteau was active in research on saturation diving, which permits long-term work and study at great depths. In the Conshelf III project of 1965, six men breathing a helium-oxygen mixture lived and worked at a depth of 100 meters for three weeks.

Through the years, numerous research institutes, broadcasting companies, foundations and universi-ties have provided support for Cousteau's expeditions aboard the *Calypso*, which has taken him—and an international audience of book readers, filmgoers and televiewers—to seas across the globe. Cousteau is a prolific writer and filmmaker. His work has been repeatedly honored, earning prizes that include Cannes Film Festival awards, Academy Awards, Emmys and the Gold Medal of the National Geographic Society. Among his most notable films are *Épaves* (1945), *The Silent World* (1956), *The Golden Fish* (1959), *World Without Sun* (1964), *The Desert Whales* (1969) and perennially popular television films. His books, illustrated with his own photography, include *Sixty Feet Down: The Story of a Film* (1946), *SCUBA Diving* (1950), *The Silent World* (1953), *The Cousteau Almanac* (1981), *Jacques Cousteau's Calypso* (1983), *Jacques Cousteau's Amazon Journey* (1984) and *Jacques Cousteau/Whales* (1988).

Through the Cousteau Society, Cousteau has been directly active in environmental issues ranging from nuclear disarmament to preventing marine pollution. In 1980, with Professor Lucien Malavard and Bertrand Charrier, he began studying wind-propulsion systems for ships, helping to develop the Turbosail system in 1982. *Moulin à Vent,* an experimental Turbosail-equipped vessel, was launched in 1983, and two years later, the wind-propelled *Alcyone* was built.

For his World War II service in the resistance, Cousteau was named Chevalier de la Légion d'Honneur, and he was subsequently promoted to "Officer" and "Commander" of the Légion in recognition of his scientific accomplishments. One of a select few foreign members of the National Academy of Sciences (U.S.), Cousteau received a United Nations International Environmental Prize in 1977. He was awarded the U.S. Presidential Medal of Freedom in 1985. In 1987, he was inducted into the Television Academy of Fame (U.S.), and he received the Founders Award of the International Council of the National Academy of Television Arts and Sciences. Cousteau was placed on the UNITED NATIONS ENVIRONMENT PROGRAMME's Global 500 Roll of Honor for Environmental Achievement in 1988. He has also received a National Geographic Centennial Award and numerous honorary degrees from various universities. He was inducted into the Académie Française in 1989, and he received the Third International Catalan Prize from the Catalan Institute of Mediterranean Studies, Barcelona, Spain, in 1991.

Further reading: Paul Westman, *Jacques Cousteau: Free Flight Undersea* (Minneapolis: Dillon Press, 1980).

Cousteau, Jean-Michel (May 6, 1938–   )

Son of ocean explorer, filmmaker and environmentalist JACQUES-YVES COUSTEAU, Jean-Michel Cousteau, who was born in Toulon, France, is a founding director of the COUSTEAU SOCIETY and has been executive vice-president since 1979. He is also a founding member and vice-president of L'Équipe Cousteau, created in 1981 as the the society's sister organization in France.

Jean-Michel Cousteau is a spokesman for the marine environment, communicating directly with the public through popular lectures, films and an educational field study program called Project Ocean Search. Since 1973, this program has offered the public the opportunity to explore pristine marine environments. Jean-Michel Cousteau believes that public education is a key factor in protecting and preserving the environment. He was awarded an honorary Ph.D. in Humane Letters from Pepperdine University in recognition of his contributions to education.

Cousteau Society executive vice president Jean-Michel Cousteau. © *The Cousteau Society, 1985*

Cousteau has spent his life researching and exploring the oceans of the world aboard the Cousteau Society research vessels *Calypso* and *Alcyone.* He leads the expeditions for "Cousteau's Rediscovery of the World," an extensive television series and writes a bimonthly column on the environment that is syndicated worldwide.

A graduate of the Paris School of Architecture, Cousteau is a member of the Ordre National des Architectes. He has collaborated on the design of artificial floating islands, six schools, a residential and recreational complex in Madagascar and the headquarters of an advanced marine studies center in Marseilles. Cousteau also headed the team that converted the *Queen Mary* into the Living Sea Museum in Long Beach, California.

Cousteau was a member of the selection committee for the National NASA/AIA (National Aeronautics and Space Administration/American Institute of Architects) Space Station design competition in 1972.

In addition to his work with the Cousteau Society, he is also a member of the advisory boards of *Outside Magazine,* John Denver's Windstar Foundation and the International Advisory Board of PADI (Professional Association of Diving Instructors).

Among his notable film ventures, Cousteau served as executive producer of "Jacques Cousteau: The First 75 Years," which documents the long career of his father. His film "Cousteau/Mississippi" received an Emmy award, and his "Snowstorm in the Jungle," a film on the drug trade along the Amazon, was nominated for an Emmy.

The Cousteau Society Inc. (Founded: 1973)
870 Greenbrier Circle, Suite 402, Chesapeake, Virginia 23320; (804) 523-9335

Best known for its work in the exploration of the oceans, The Cousteau Society documents the ways in which human and marine environments are interrelated. The Cousteau Society is a nonprofit, membership-supported organization dedicated to the protection and improvement of the quality of life for present and future generations. The organization has produced some 40 books, eight sets of film strips, four feature films and more than 75 television documentary films about the marine environment, and it has researched and documented the effects of growing human populations on ecosystems.

Created in 1973, the society now has over 300,000 members worldwide. Its president, JACQUES-YVES COUSTEAU, is an internationally recognized filmmaker, explorer and environmentalist. He and his son, JEAN-MICHEL COUSTEAU, direct the activities of the veteran research vessel, *Calypso,* and the new windship, *Alcyone.* The Cousteaus and their teams have explored the water system throughout the world for over 40 years.

The society believes that only an informed and alerted public can best make the choices to ensure a healthy and more productive world. In addition to television films broadcast worldwide, the society's books, filmstrips, teachers' guides, articles and public appearances heighten awareness of environmental issues. Lecturers give an insider's look at society projects and history. Publications include the bimonthly membership magazines, *Calypso Log* for adults and *Dolphin Log* for children.

In the tradition of the Aqualung, co-invented by Captain Cousteau, the society develops research equipment, such as the "Sea Spider," a miniature surface-temperature probe; a system to measure marine photosynthesis for the *Calypso;* and a revolutionary wind-propulsion system of Turbosail cylinders that help power the *Alcyone.* Through cooperation with independent scientists, teams have been using energy analysis to evaluate ecosystems and sustainable resource-use strategies.

The society is sponsoring a nine-year, 35-part "Rediscovery of the World" international television series, filmed by crews on its two oceanographic vessels, which are circumnavigating the globe to take a fresh look at the planet. Two full teams of crew members, divers, cinematographers and others support this massive undertaking.

The Cousteau Society examines the vital links between humanity and nature, evaluating the benefits and liabilities of their interaction. The society speaks in testimony and counsel to governing bodies and leaders on issues of global concern. It cooperates with scientists from many nations on expeditionary projects and extends its support to other environmental protection efforts, such as the Marine Mammal Stranding Network. In addition to these activities, the society is working toward United Nations adoption, as part of its charter, of an environmental "Bill of Rights for Future Generations."

The society has a staff of 125, and operates on an annual budget of $13 million.

Cowles, Henry Chandler (February 27, 1869–September 12, 1939)

Henry Chandler Cowles was a pioneer ecologist who gained for the emerging field the respect of biologists, geologists and geographers. His Ph.D. dissertation, "The Ecological Relations of the Vegetation of the Sand Dunes of Lake Michigan," was published in the *Botanical Gazette* (1899), as was "The Physiographic Ecology of Chicago and Vicinity" (1901). These two early works firmly established Cowles's reputation as a leading ecologist. In them he examined the spatiotemporal links among ecological succession, geomorphology and climate change, and he determined the interaction of the geomorphological process and biological succession.

Cowles, born in Kensington, Connecticut, was educated at Oberlin College, from which he received an A.B. degree in 1893. He moved to Nebraska in 1894 and took a job as an instructor in natural science at Gates College. The next year, he accepted a fellowship at the University of Chicago to study in the geology department under T. C. Chamberlain. After a short time, he moved to the botany department headed by John M. Coulter and received his Ph.D. in 1898.

Over the next 36 years, Cowles taught plant ecology at the university and was named chairman of the botany department in 1925. Cowles served as editor of the *Botanical Gazette* as well as a reviewer for the journal. He was a member of the organizing committee and president (1910) of the Association of American Geographers. In 1930, he became president of the Botanical Society of America and president of the phytogeography and ecology section of the International Botanical Congress.

In his research, Cowles developed a causal classification of succession. Succession, he argued, could be caused by climatic changes (chorographic succession), geomorphological processes (physiographic succession) and by interactions of organisms (biotic succession). In contrast to Frederic CLEMENTS, who adopted a more holistic approach to succession, Cowles remained firm in his emphasis on the individual plant's response to external stimuli. In addition, he believed that succession could be progressive or retrogressive, while Clements theorized that succession was always progressive.

Coyle, Kevin J. (December 8, 1950–   )
Appointed president of the country's most effective national river organization, AMERICAN RIVERS Inc. in

Kevin Coyle, president of American Rivers. *American Rivers*

the spring of 1990, Kevin Coyle, who earned his law degree in 1978 from Temple University, served as assistant regional director of the NATIONAL PARK SERVICE for the Mid-Atlantic Region from 1979 to 1982. He administered the service's Land and Water Conservation Fund and the Wild and Scenic Rivers planning program. Coyle was twice honored for meritorious service by the U.S. Department of the INTERIOR.

In 1982, Coyle became the first president of the American Land Resource Association and organized a 3,000-member network of land resource professionals. He founded the association's quarterly, *American Land Forum*.

Calling rivers the "heart of the ecosystem," Coyle believes that the river conservation movement has nevertheless traditionally lagged behind other aspects of environmental activism, especially those involving such land issues as wilderness parks and refuges. "When you're conserving a river area, you're conserving a source of life," he said in a 1990 interview with *Canoe* magazine.

In addition to developing grass-roots programs to help protect and clean up rivers, Coyle is leading his organization toward a 50-year goal of securing state or federally protected status for 10% of the nation's river miles. It is a formidable objective, representing some 360,000 miles of river nationwide, of which only 60,000 miles qualify for federal protection under the Wild and Scenic Rivers program—though a mere 9,000 river miles are currently protected. Coyle sees action at the state level as the best chance for achieving his organization's 10% goal.

Crowell, John B., Jr. (March 18, 1930–   )
When, in 1981, the Reagan administration called Harvard-trained attorney John Crowell Jr. to join the U.S. Department of AGRICULTURE as assistant secretary of Natural Resources and Environment, the vice-president and general counsel of Louisiana Pacific Corporation, one of the nation's largest timber companies, became head of the U.S. Forest Service. Asserting that "the national forests haven't contributed a fair share of the wood we need for commercial use," Crowell reprioritized Forest Service and SOIL CONSERVATION SERVICE activities by reducing funds for land acquisition, reforestation, soil and water protection and wildlife preservation while simultaneously increasing budgets for tree-cutting, road-building and minerals management. Crowell's stated goal of doubling timber sales from federal forests was impeded by the agriculture agency's formidable existing backlog of uncut and unpaid timber contracts, and the assistant secretary's policies—including recommendations to sell outright some government-

owned wilderness parcels—inspired such strong resistance from conservationists of all political persuasions that lawsuits opposing Forest Service activities doubled instead.

Throughout his tenure, Crowell's longstanding affiliation with the timber industry caused critics to question his aggressive marketing and low pricing of federally owned forest resources, particularly when his proposals were seen to benefit the interests of his former employer. Crowell's reputation was further challenged after Louisiana Pacific's 1982 conviction on charges of fraud, stock market manipulation and misrepresentation in its takeover of a fiberboard company, a deal that took place during Crowell's years as general counsel with the timber giant. One U.S. senator requested a White House inquiry into Crowell's involvement with the transaction.

Born in Elizabeth, New Jersey, Crowell earned his bachelor of arts at Dartmouth College in 1952 and graduated from Harvard Law School in 1957. He worked as an attorney for the Georgia Pacific Corporation from 1959 to 1972, and moved to the Louisiana Pacific Corporation the following year. After leaving his government office in 1985, Crowell joined the Portland, Oregon, law firm of Lubersky, Campbell, Bledsoe, Anderson and Young.

Culver, John (August 8, 1932–   )

John Culver's mastery of the art of mediating between opposing interest groups won him a reputation as one of the most effective advocates of environmental legislation in the U.S. Senate. A member of the Environment and Public Works Committee from 1975 to 1981, Culver served on the Environmental Pollution and Nuclear Regulation subcommittees. As chairman of the Resource Protection Subcommittee in 1978, he was caught in a dispute between environmentalists and developers that threatened continuation of the development-checking Endangered Species Act. Culver's compromise was to create an Endangered Species Committee, which had the power to continue challenged development projects with a vote of at least 5–2. Conservatives were thus unable to prevent renewal of the Endangered Species Act, and adequate environmental safeguards were maintained. Culver also led the anti-noise Quiet Communities Act through the Senate in 1978, supported wetlands protection and opposed nuclear breeder reactors.

Culver was born in Rochester, Minnesota, and raised in Cedar Rapids, Iowa. He developed an impressive early resume that included degrees from Harvard (1954), Harvard Law (1962) and service in the Marine Corps (1955–58). He was U.S. representative from Iowa (Democrat) from 1965 to 1975 before gaining his Senate seat. Throughout his career, Culver had one of the most liberal voting records in Congress and was, in addition to his environmental stands, an important advocate of arms control. He was targeted in 1980 by the National Conservative Political Action Committee and lost his Senate re-election bid. Since then he has been a member of the law firm of Arent, Fox, Kintner, Plotkin and Kahn.

Cutler, Malcolm Rupert (October 28, 1933–   )

An environmental administrator for over 30 years, Malcolm Rupert Cutler is the founding director of the Environmental Education Center of Virginia in Roanoke.

Born in Plymouth, Michigan, Cutler received his bachelor of science in wildlife management from Michigan State University in 1955. After brief stints as a consumer publications writer for Argus Cameras and as editor of The Winslow Mail of Arizona, he began his environmental career in 1957 as executive secretary of Wildlife Conservation, Inc., of Boston. The following year Cutler was named chief of the education division of the Virginia Commission of Game and Inland Fisheries, and he served there until 1962, when he moved to the NATIONAL WILDLIFE FEDERATION as assistant head of the education division (1962–63) and then chief staff writer and managing editor of National Wildlife magazine (1963–65). He joined the WILDERNESS SOCIETY in Washington, D.C., in 1965, and was assistant executive director there for the next four years. Returning to Michigan State University in East Lansing in 1969, Cutler undertook a graduate fellowship in resource development and earned his M.S. in 1971 and his Ph.D. in 1972. At Michigan State he went on to develop and teach courses in environmental policy and law as assistant professor of resource development and extension specialist in natural resources policy (1972–77).

In 1977, President Jimmy Carter appointed Cutler to the U.S. Department of AGRICULTURE as assistant secretary for conservation, research and education. During his tenure, Cutler initiated and supervised the creation of the Science and Education Administration and the Office of Environmental Quality, and conducted the Roadless Area Review of the National Forest System (RARE II).

In 1980, Cutler left government office and became senior vice-president for programs and chapter relations at the NATIONAL AUDUBON SOCIETY in New York. Three years later he accepted the executive directorship of the Washington, D.C.-based Environmental Fund, and during his administration, the private foundation became Population-Environment Balance

Inc., a nonprofit educational organization, and established the William Vogt Center for U.S. Population Studies. Cutler served next with the DEFENDERS OF WILDLIFE, where he was president from 1988 to 1990, and in January 1991, he founded the Environmental Education Center of Virginia, the natural and cultural history interpretation and environmental mediation program of Virginia's Explore Park, a 2,000-acre state park overseen by The River Foundation for the Virginia Recreational Facilities Authority. A member of the Society of American Foresters and the Wilderness Society, Cutler continues as the Environmental Education Center's director today.

D

Dadd, Debra Lynn (June 18, 1955–   )
A California-based environmental consumer advocate and writer, Debra Lynn Dadd is the author of *The Nontoxic Home and Office* (1992), *Nontoxic, Natural & Earthwise: How to Protect Yourself from Harmful Products and Live in Harmony with the Earth* (1990) and *Healthful Houses: How to Design and Build Your Own* (with Clint Good, 1988), among other books.

Educated at California State University at Hayward and San Francisco (1972–76), Lynn has contributed articles to *Vegetarian Times, New Age Journal, East West* and other periodicals. She wrote the column "Earthwise" for *Environmental Action* magazine from 1986 to 1990, and was editor and publisher of *The Earthwise Consumer* newsletter from 1989 to 1991. A consulting editor with *Greenkeeping* magazine, Dadd recently cofounded WorldWise, Inc., a wholesale distributor of natural and environmentally friendly products; she is vice-president for product research and development. She is the author of *Nontoxic and Natural: How to Avoid Dangerous Everyday Products and Buy or Make Safe Ones* (1984).

Dana, Samuel Trask (April 21,1883–May 8, 1978)
Educated at Bowdoin College (B.A., 1904) and Yale University, from which he received a Master of Forestry degree in 1907, Samuel T. Dana joined the U.S. FOREST SERVICE's Office of Silvics as a researcher the same year. Over the next decade, Dana conducted forest research, leaving the service temporarily during World War I to join the U.S. Army as an expert on military requirements for wood products. Rejoining the Forest Service after the war, he became assistant chief of the Branch of Research.

Dana left the Forest Service in 1921 to become forest commissioner of Maine, then returned in 1923 as director of the newly established Northeastern Forest Experiment Station. In 1927, Dana became the first dean of the University of Michigan School of Forestry and Conservation (after 1950 called the School of Natural Resources). Dana served until 1953, having created many programs at Michigan and having earned a reputation as the doyen of education in natural resources and conservation.

After retiring from the university, Dana produced the seminal *Forest and Range Policy: Its Development in the United States* (1956) and two studies for the American Forestry Association (now AMERICAN FORESTS), *California Lands* (1958) and *Minnesota Lands* (1960). He was senior author of *Forestry Education in America: Today and Tomorrow* (1963), produced for the SOCIETY OF AMERICAN FORESTERS.

Dana was president of the Society of American Foresters from 1935 to 1936 and editor of its *Journal of Forestry* from 1928 to 1930 and 1942 to 1945. He was adviser to various government agencies, including the U.S. Department of AGRICULTURE and the Bureau of OUTDOOR RECREATION. The Society of American Foresters presented Dana with its Sir William Schlich Memorial Medal, and the American Forestry Association bestowed its John Aston Warder Medal. American Forest Products Industries (now called American Forest Council) presented him with a Distinguished Service Award. The World Forestry Congress recognized his achievements in 1966.

Dannemeyer, William E. (September 22, 1929–   )
William E. Dannemeyer, conservative Republican congressman from California's Orange County (39th Congressional District), held the ranking spot on Energy and Commerce's Health and the Environment Subcommittee. From this influential platform,

Dannemeyer has directed an outspoken campaign against "liberal" environmental and health-related issues. While his right-wing positions tend to be so extreme as to garner relatively little support, even his severest critics concede that he argues his case from principle, with "utter consistency" and with considerable forensic skill. At the core of Dannemeyer's anti-environmentalist sentiments is a fundamentalist Christian belief that the environmental movement is at best God-denying materialism and at worst a form of quasi-pagan nature worship.

Dannemeyer cast the lone vote in committee against the Clean Air Act and has consistently supported offshore oil drilling. *The Nation* (December 9, 1991) reported a November 1991 speech Dannemeyer made in Eureka, California, heartland of the state's timber industry, during a campaign for the U.S. Senate. Dannemeyer warned his listeners of the existence of a political party "in some ways more powerful than the combined clout of the Democratic Party and the Republican Party"—the "environmental party."

> We should understand that this environmental party has as its objective a mission to change this society, to worship creation instead of the creator. You have to understand their theology. I can't prove this by empirical analysis, but my gut reaction to their thought is simply this: If you go through life and you don't believe in a hereafter and all you see before you today are trees, birds . . . if anybody begins to consume those things, you can get excited about that because it's your whole world. And this is where the militancy comes.

Dannemeyer went on to note that the Supreme Court's decision in *Roe* v. *Wade*, guaranteeing at the federal level the right of a woman to seek an abortion, was handed down in 1973, the same year that Congress passed the Endangered Species Act: "It's an interesting paradox in American politics," Dannemeyer declared. "As a people, we are [witnessing] the death of a million and a half humans at a time when we are protecting the critters of our society."

William E. Dannemeyer is a native of Los Angeles and was educated at Santa Maria Junior College (1946–47), Valparaiso University (B.A., 1950) and the Hastings College of Law of the University of California, from which he received his law degree in 1952. After a stint in the army from 1952 to 1954, Dannemeyer practiced as an attorney and then served in the California State Assembly, as a Democrat from 1963 to 1967 and as a Republican from 1977 to 1979. He was elected to the U.S. House of Representatives in 1978. In 1992, he was defeated in a Senate primary bid. His former House seat was won by Republican Ed Royce.

Darling, Frank Fraser (June 23, 1903–October 22, 1979)

A graduate of the University of Edinburgh, Frank Fraser Darling worked on the agricultural staff of the Bucks County (Scotland) Council from 1924 to 1927. The following year, he enrolled in the Institute of Animal Genetics at the University of Edinburgh, and from 1930 to 1934, he served as chief officer of the Imperial Bureau of Animal Genetics. After completing two fellowships, he directed the West Highland Survey from 1944 to 1950 and became senior lecturer in ecology and conservation at the University of Edinburgh. In 1959, he became vice-president of the CONSERVATION FOUNDATION in New York.

In 1969, Fraser Darling presented the influential Reith lectures over the BBC. The following year, the lectures were published as *Wilderness and Plenty*, and their immediate popularity brought Fraser Darling fame as an ecological prophet. His other works include *Wild Life Conservation* (1934), *Wild Country* (1938), *The Seasons and the Farmer* (1939), *Wild Life of Britain* (1943), *Natural History in the Highlands and Islands* (1947), *Alaska: An Ecological Reconnaissance* (1953), *The Unity of Ecology* (1963), *Impacts of Man on the Biosphere* (1969) and many research papers.

Darling, Jay Norwood ("Ding") (October 21, 1876–February 12, 1962)

A celebrated political cartoonist, "Ding" Darling also had a long and distinguished career as Iowa's Fish and Game Commissioner and as a conservationist. A prime mover in founding the NATIONAL WILDLIFE FEDERATION, he was that group's first president.

Although he was born in Norwood, Michigan, Darling grew up in Sioux City, Iowa, and, from an early age, learned to love the outdoors. He graduated from Beloit College (Wisconsin) in 1900, having majored in biology but having also developed a career as a political cartoonist, first for the *Sioux City Journal* and then for the *Des Moines Register and Leader* (later called the *Register and Tribune*). Except for a brief stint at the *New York Globe* (1911–13), he worked for the *Register* as a nationally syndicated cartoonist until 1949.

In 1931, Darling helped persuade the Iowa legislature to create a State Fish and Game Commission. In 1932, as commissioner, Darling secured funding for a Cooperative Wildlife Research Unit at Iowa State College (later Iowa State University), which set the pattern for 50 such units at land-grant universities in 29 states. Darling oversaw the consolidation of the Fish and Game Commission and the Park Commission into a State Conservation Commission (1935) and promoted Aldo LEOPOLD's state biological survey, which resulted in a "Twenty-Five Year Plan" for conservation in Iowa. The plan served as a model for similar programs in numerous states.

Darling created the first federal duck stamp in 1934, sales of which enabled the purchase of 2 million acres of waterfowl habitat. In that year, Franklin D. ROOSEVELT appointed him chief of the Bureau of BIOLOGICAL SURVEY—precursor of the FISH AND WILDLIFE SERVICE—and Darling launched a program of reform that included stricter game regulation and a broader, more effective system of wildlife refuges and wildlife protection. The flying goose insignia that marks all federal refuges was his design. Darling resigned from the survey in 1935 to lead in the creation of the National Wildlife Federation.

In addition to two Pulitzers earned by his cartooning, Darling was awarded the Audubon Medal and the Roosevelt Medal. Active in conservation to the very end of his life, he was named co-chairman (with Walt Disney) of National Wildlife Week in 1962. He died shortly before the week's observance. Jay N. "Ding" Darling National Wildlife Refuge, which he helped create on Sanibel Island, Florida, is named in his honor.

Further reading: Darling, *Ding's Half Century* (New York: Duell, 1962); David L. Lendt, *Ding: The Life of Jay Norwood Darling* (Ames: Iowa State University Press, 1979).

Darwin, Charles Robert (February 12, 1809–April 19, 1882)

Darwin was born in Shrewsbury, England, the son of a prominent physician and the grandson of Erasmus Darwin, a famous naturalist. He enrolled in Edinburgh University in 1825 with the intention of studying medicine, but decided on the ministry instead and entered Cambridge University in 1828. In 1831, the year in which Darwin took his Cambridge degree, the botanist Stevens Henslow arranged for the young man to sail to South America and the Pacific as an unpaid naturalist aboard a Royal Navy exploration ship, H.M.S. *Beagle*. The expedition consumed five years and convinced Darwin to undertake a career in science.

On his return to England in 1836, he began organizing his research, publishing *Journal of Researches into the Geology and Natural History of Various Countries Visited During the Voyage of H. M. S. Beagle Round the World* (1839) and two other works: *Structure and Distribution of Coral Reefs* (1842) and *Geological Observations* (1844–46).

Two years after his return from South America, Darwin read Thomas MALTHUS's *Essay on Population*, a book that was ultimately to have a profound influence on his interpretation of the data he had gathered in the course of the *Beagle* voyage. Darwin began to develop new theories of evolution that would forever change scientific thought.

Essay on Population is a depressing account of the cycle of overpopulation, disease and famine and retrenchment. Malthus explores how man had advanced through civilization only because of the threat of hunger. Yet, despite this advancement, the same terrible, inevitable cycle sustained itself because, as Malthus saw it, food supply increases arithmetically while population increases geometrically. Each species, according to Malthus, has a fixed rate of fertility, and only intervention by predators or starvation keeps any one species from total domination of the earth. Darwin adhered to Malthus's account of fertility, but he added a new element: natural selection. For Darwin, species that were most suited to their environment survived the cycle, forcing less well-adapted species into extinction. Darwin based his theory on ecology rather than genetics. He saw nature as a "web of complex relations" and each species as occupying a particular place (Darwin often called it an "office") in the grand scheme. By *place* (or *office*), Darwin meant the source of food or one species' own role as food for another. Unlike other scientists of his day, Darwin did not see a particular place as the immutable province of a species. Migrations, climate changes and other factors could cause a species to change "offices." In addition, he incorporated into his theory the findings of geologist Charles LYELL, who argued that the earth itself had evolved over millions of years in a slow, but steady process. (Darwin became closely acquainted with Lyell through the Geological Society, of which Darwin served as secretary from 1838 to 1844.)

Darwin's theory is best known for its explanation of genetic variation. Darwin postulated that, during times of climatic or geologic change, species were affected by new conditions that brought about changes in their offspring. The parents and offspring then struggled for primacy, with the variation most fitted to the environment winning out. The variant offspring forced the parent to extinction, unless there happened to be an "office" for the offspring to seize.

Another key aspect of Darwin's complex theory is the principle of divergence. Darwin believed that variant offspring could sometimes devise new "offices" to occupy. He saw as nature's goal an ever-increasing diversity of species within a given area. Each species and variant has a particular role to play, and the existence of countless roles is nature's way of limiting the struggle for scarce resources. For him, each species occupies a position of extreme importance in relation to other species: one species is food for another; one species keeps the population of another in check.

Darwin published nothing of his theory for two decades, discussing it with only a handful of trusted colleagues. In 1858, he was finally compelled to reveal his work when Alfred Russel Wallace sent him a letter in which he proposed a theory of natural selection similar to Darwin's own. Within a year, Darwin completed writing *On the Origin of Species by Means of Natural Selection,* which appeared in bookshops in 1859. The book created a worldwide sensation, touching off a debate among scientists and between scientists and religious thinkers that has yet to reach a conclusion.

In the years following publication of *Origin of Species,* Darwin—always in ill health, and now a semi-invalid—defended his theories and refined them further in *The Descent of Man* (1871), which examined sexual selection and presented an epoch-making and still-controversial case for the evolution of man from higher primates.

Further reading: Darwin, *Autobiography and Selected Letters* (New York: Dover, 1958); Gertrude Himmelfarb, *Darwin and the Darwinian Revolution* (Garden City, N.Y.: Doubleday, 1959).

Dasmann, Raymond Frederic (May 27, 1919–)

Born in San Francisco, Raymond Frederic Dasmann began his career in conservation as a forest guard for the U.S. FOREST SERVICE and the California Division of Forestry in 1939. After World War II, he worked as a research assistant and associate at the Museum of Vertebrate Zoology and the School of Forestry at the University of California. He taught biology at the University of Minnesota, Duluth, from 1953 to 1954 and then joined the faculty of Humboldt State College in California as an assistant professor. He was subsequently promoted to associate professor and head of game management.

Dasmann was a Fulbright research biologist at the National Museums of Southern Rhodesia from 1959 to 1961 and a lecturer in zoology at the University of California, Berkeley, in 1961, before he returned to Humboldt State College as professor of wildlife management and chairman of the Division of Natural Resources.

Dasmann has written several books, including *Pacific Coastal Wildlife* (1957), *Environmental Conservation* (1959, 1976), *Wildlife Biology* (1964, 1981), *African Game Ranching* (1963), *The Last Horizon* (1963), *No Further Retreat* (1971), *Planet in Peril* (1972), *The Conservation Alternative* (1975) and *California's Changing Environment* (1981).

From 1966 to 1970, he served as the director of environmental studies of the CONSERVATION FOUNDATION. Next he was named senior ecologist for the INTERNATIONAL UNION FOR CONSERVATION OF NATURE AND NATURAL RESOURCES. In 1977, he returned to teaching at the University of California, Santa Cruz, as professor and board chairman of environmental studies.

He has served as president of the WILDLIFE SOCIETY and as a consultant to UNESCO.

Davies, Tudor Thomas (September 3, 1938–)

Director of the Office of Science and Technology at the ENVIRONMENTAL PROTECTION AGENCY in Washington, D.C., Tudor T. Davies has been an administrator with the EPA for 20 years.

Born in Bridgend, Glamorgan, Wales, Thomas earned a bachelor of science and a doctorate in geology at the University of Wales in Swansea. He came to the United States in 1966, after pursuing a postdoctoral fellowship at Dalhousie University in Halifax, Nova Scotia (1964–66). He was assistant and then associate professor of geology at the University of South Carolina, Columbia, from 1966 until 1973. Davies joined the EPA's Office of Research and Development in 1972 and directed its Great Lakes Program until 1975, when he became deputy director of the Gulf Breeze Environmental Research Laboratory in Florida (1975–79). He went on to head the agency's Chesapeake Bay Program (1977–83) and the Narragansett Environmental Research Laboratory in Rhode Island (1979–83). In 1984, he was appointed head of the Office of Marine and Estuarine Protection in Washington, D.C., and he served there for seven years, assuming his current post in 1991.

de Bary, (Heinrich) Anton (January 26, 1831– January 19, 1888)

Anton de Bary, a native of Frankfurt-am-Main, Germany, is best remembered as one of the most influential of 19th-century botanists and one of the earliest bacteriologists, the author of more than 100 papers on subjects ranging from apogamy in ferns to insect-killing plants. He is generally recognized as the founder of mycology, the study of fungi, and his work on rusts, smuts and other fungal infestations had immediate practical impact on the struggle against the potato blight that swept Europe in the mid-19th century. De Bary's research also provided an important corroboration of Louis Pasteur's epoch-making attack on the theory of spontaneous generation.

Anton de Bary's most important contribution to the field of ecology proper was his coining of the term and concept of "symbiosis" in his 1879 *Die Erscheinung der Symbiose*. Using the term to signify "the living together of unlike organisms," de Bary described a broad range of relationships, ranging from absolute mutual dependencies to partial and periodic dependencies. The Danish scientist Eugenius WARMING elaborated de Bary's concept of symbiosis into an important part of his pioneering study in "ecological plant geography," *Plantesamfund* (1895), revised and translated into English in 1909 as *The Oecology of Plants: An Introduction to the Study of Plant Communities*. In this way, de Bary's symbiosis became an important element in the foundation of ecological theory.

De Bary was one of 10 children born to August Theodor de Bary, a physician, and Emilie Meyer de Bary. Both parents encouraged the boy's early scientific bent, and the young de Bary frequently joined in botanical excursions conducted by a local group of amateur naturalists. Georg Fresenius, a physician and teacher of botany, provided early guidance, especially in the study of fungi and algae. De Bary graduated from the Frankfurt Gymnasium in 1848 and studied medicine at Heidelberg, Marburg, and Berlin. He received his degree in medicine in 1853, having written a doctoral dissertation on a botanical subject. Although de Bary practiced medicine briefly in Frankfurt, he soon abandoned it for the full-time study of botany.

De Bary established a botanical laboratory in Freiburg during the late 1850s, and in 1867, he established another at the University of Halle. Following the Franco-Prussian War, de Bary was appointed professor of botany at the University of Strassburg, which quickly became an international center for botanical study.

De Bary died in Strassburg at 57.

Defenders of Wildlife (Founded [as Defenders of Furbearers]: 1947)

1244 19th Street NW, Washington, D.C. 20036; (202) 659-9510

Education programs, litigation, research and advocacy are the tools the Defenders of Wildlife use to promote the preservation and protection of wildlife and wildlife habitats. Since its founding in 1947, the organization has grown to a membership of 80,000, including 8,000 volunteer activists. It maintains field offices in Oregon, Montana and California. The group focuses on the promotion of biological diversity, the prevention of species endangerment, the protection

The gray wolf, an endangered species that Defenders of Wildlife is working to restore to Yellowstone Park and the American West. *Courtesy of Defenders of Wildlife*

of key habitats and movement corridors, the improvement of wildlife protection on public lands and the reduction of losses of marine species to drift nets and plastics.

The organization issues a bimonthly magazine, *Defenders*, which publishes articles on wildlife issues in a four-color format, a quarterly *Activist Newsletter* and an annual *Endangered Species Report*.

Deland, Michael R. (December 13, 1941–   )

Chairman of the COUNCIL ON ENVIRONMENTAL QUALITY under George Bush, Michael R. Deland directed the Office of Environmental Quality in Washington, D.C. In this capacity, he oversaw the development of environmental policy, the interagency coordination of environmental quality programs and environmental data acquisition and assessment, and served as environmental advisor to the president. Deland is also responsible for overseeing implementation of the National Environmental Policy Act, and each year his office produced a book-length report on the nation's environmental quality.

The Boston-born administrator received his bachelor of arts from Harvard College in 1963 and served as an officer in the U.S. Navy (1963–65) before earning his juris doctor from Boston College in 1969. He worked for a year as staff assistant and legal counsel to the president of the University of Massachusetts, then joined the ENVIRONMENTAL PROTECTION AGENCY's Regional Office (Region I) in New England, where he was staff attorney (1971–72), chief of the Legal Review Section (1972–73) and then chief of the Enforcement Branch (1973–76). In 1976, Deland became environmental counsel and consultant for Environmental Research and Technology Inc., a national firm based in Concord, Massachusetts, and over the

Michael R. Deland, former chairman of the Council on Environmental Quality. *Courtesy of the Council on Environmental Quality*

next seven years, he also wrote numerous articles and papers for publication, including the monthly "Regulatory Focus" column in *Environment, Science, and Technology.*

Deland was named New England regional administrator for the Environmental Protection Agency (Region I) in 1983, and during his tenure there, he received several awards and citations, including the Massachusetts Audubon Society Award and the New England Environment Leadership Award of the New England Environmental Network. In 1987, Deland was honored as Environmentalist of the Year by the Massachusetts Conservation Commissions, and two years later, he was given the NATIONAL WILDLIFE FEDERATION's Special Achievement Award for his role in the clean-up of Boston Harbor and the protection of valuable fishing grounds from offshore oil drilling. (Also in 1987, Deland—who is an avid sailor and onetime America's Cup competitor—won the U.S. National Championship, Shields Class.)

Unanimously confirmed by the U.S. Senate, Deland accepted appointment to the council on August 1, 1989. His appointment ended on January 20, 1993, after President Clinton took office. Dinah Bear, gen-

eral counsel for the Council on Environmental Quality, became acting chair.

DeVoto, Bernard Augustine (January 11, 1897–November 13, 1955)

A novelist, historian, critic, journalist, editor and teacher, Bernard Augustine DeVoto, born in Ogden, Utah, is best known for his historical trilogy written between 1943 and 1952, *Year of Decision: 1846* (an examination of Manifest Destiny), *Across the Wide Missouri* (a study of the fur trade in the old West) and *The Course of Empire* (a National Book Award-winning history of the West). From 1935 to 1955, DeVoto contributed a monthly column to *Harper's Magazine*, "The Easy Chair," in which he began serving as a watchdog for the western lands. Between 1948 and 1954, he was a member of the Advisory Board on National Parks, Historic Sites, Buildings and Monuments.

Further reading: DeVoto, *The Easy Chair* (Boston: Houghton Mifflin, 1955); Wallace Stegner, *The Uneasy Chair: The Life of Bernard DeVoto* (Garden City, N.Y.: Doubleday, 1974).

Dewitt, John Belton (January 13, 1937–   )

Executive director of the SAVE-THE-REDWOODS LEAGUE, Oakland-born John Dewitt has been active in forestry and wilderness preservation for over 35 years.

Dewitt began his career with the U.S. Forest Service and the National Park Service, working as a forest ranger and naturalist at El Dorado National Forest and Yosemite and Mount Rainer national parks between 1955 and 1959, when he graduated from the University of California at Berkeley with a B.A. in wildlife conservation. After another brief park service posting at Death Valley National Monument, Dewitt joined the Bureau of LAND MANAGEMENT in 1960 and served as a Land Law examiner, information officer and appraiser for the next four years. In 1964, he became assistant secretary to the Save-the-Redwoods League, and he was promoted to secretary and executive director of the San Francisco-based preservation group in 1971.

As a consultant to the U.S. Department of the INTERIOR from 1964 to 1990, Dewitt offered recommendations on conservation policy to four presidential administrations. He worked on the advisory council of the Trust for Public Land from 1975 to 1978, and directed both the northern California chapter of the NATURE CONSERVANCY (1976–77) and the Tuolumne River Preservation Trust (1981–85). He has served on the advisory council of the Anza Borrego Desert Commission since 1983. A member of numerous conservation groups and the author of *California Redwood*

John B. Dewitt, secretary and executive director of Save-the-Redwoods League, June 11, 1981, at Jedediah Smith Redwoods State Park. *Photo by David Swanlund, courtesy of the Save-the-Redwoods League*

Parks and Preserves (1982), Dewitt has been honored with several state and national awards for his efforts to preserve America's majestic old-growth forests and other wilderness areas.

Dickenson, Russell Errett (April 12, 1923–)

Director of the NATIONAL PARK SERVICE from 1980 to 1986, Texas-born Russell Errett Dickenson went to work for the agency in 1946 as a seasonal employee at Grand Canyon National Park. He later served as ranger, chief ranger and superintendent at Chiricahua National Monument in Arizona, Big Bend National Park in Texas, Glacier National Park in Montana, Grand Teton National Park in Wyoming, Zion National Park in Utah and Flaming Gorge National Recreation Area in Utah. He moved up to management within the park service, working as director of the Pacific Northwest Region, deputy director of the National Park Service and director of the National Capital Region.

Dickenson was the first American to receive Germany's Golden Flower of Rheydt Award for environmental preservation on the national and international level. He also received the Cornelius Amory Pugsley Gold Medal Award of the American Scenic and Historic Preservation Society, the Award for Excellence of the National Society for Park Resources and the George Washington Medal of the U.S. Capitol Historical Society.

Dilg, Will H. (1867–March 27, 1927)

A writer for outdoor magazines and a founder of the IZAAK WALTON LEAGUE OF AMERICA in 1922, Will H. Dilg served as the group's first president from 1922 to 1926. He led the league's battle to save wilderness lands now included in the Boundary Waters Canoe Area, planned the Upper Mississippi Wildlife and Game Refuge and established a fund to save the elk in Jackson Hole, Wyoming.

Dingell, John D. (July 8, 1926–)

Democratic representative from industrial Trenton, Michigan (Sixteenth District), John Dingell was first sent to Congress in 1955 following a special election to fill the seat left vacant by his late father, John D. Dingell Sr. Dingell has been reelected ever since, making him the senior House Democrat.

Representative Dingell has earned a reputation as an ardent conservationist and served for many years on the Merchant Marine and Fisheries Committee, doing much to advance the cause of environmentalism through the committee. An avid outdoorsman himself, having worked as a U.S. FOREST SERVICE park ranger from 1948 to 1952 (he is also a hunter and an opponent of gun control), Dingell was active in working to maintain natural habitats years before doing so became fashionable.

During the period of the administration of Ronald REAGAN, Dingell was among the chief congressional adversaries of former ENVIRONMENTAL PROTECTION AGENCY administrator ANNE GORSUCH BURFORD. It was Dingell's Oversight and Investigations Subcommittee that investigated Burford's stewardship and helped promote the highly publicized controversy over her refusal to surrender subpoenaed documents to Congress. In the end, Burford stepped down as EPA administrator.

Dingell is on the Migratory Bird Conservation Commission and the Technology Assessment Board of the Office of Technology Assessment, and has chaired the powerful House Energy and Commerce Committee since 1981. As a representative from Michigan, the economy of which is heavily dependent on a beleaguered auto industry, Dingell has taken some positions that have offended orthodox environmentalists. During the early 1980s, he sought to revise the Clean Air Act because he believed that it set too stringent limitations on exhaust emissions and would therefore contribute to the collapse of the

Glacier National Park. *U.S. Department of the Interior, National Park Service photo*

U.S. auto industry. He also worked unsuccessfully to deregulate the oil and natural gas industry during the late 1970s and early 1980s.

John Dingell was educated at Georgetown University (B.S., 1949) and Georgetown University Law School (J.D., 1952). He served in World War II and from 1953 to 1955 was assistant Wayne County prosecutor.

Dominy, Floyd E. (December 24, 1909–   )
Floyd E. Dominy was born in Hastings, Nebraska, and educated at Hastings College and at the University of Wyoming, from which he received a B.A. in 1932. He did postgraduate work at Wyoming (1932–33) and Columbia University (1944). Dominy was a high school instructor in vocational agriculture from 1933 to 1934 and a county agricultural agent for Campbell County, Wyoming, from 1934 to 1938. From 1938 to 1942, he was field representative for the western division of the American Agricultural Association, and in 1942, he became assistant director of the food supply division of the Office of the Coordinator of Inter-American Affairs, Washington, D.C.

He left this post in 1944 to become chief of the allocation and repayment bureau of the Bureau of RECLAMATION, U.S. Department of the INTERIOR. In 1946, he was promoted to assistant director of the division of irrigation, serving until 1953, when he became chief of the division. In 1957, Dominy was promoted to associate commissioner of the Bureau of Reclamation, and in 1959 became commissioner, serving until October 31, 1969.

Floyd Dominy's tenure as commissioner spanned a period of sharply changing public views of the environment. The bureau had been founded by supporters of a utilitarian philosophy calling for the wholesale development of natural resources to benefit the greatest number of people. By the 1960s, environmentalists—and much of the general public—were vigorously questioning the soundness of many of the bureau's dam operations and other water projects. Dominy had grown up believing in the absolute good of harnessing and taming nature. As a county agent, he once helped ranchers build a thousand dams in the space of a single year. Often, he worked side by side with ranchers, building the dams by

Lake Powell, created by the Glen Canyon Dam. *U.S. Department of the Interior, Bureau of Reclamation, courtesy of the National Park Service*

hand. He brought the same zeal to the Bureau of Reclamation—and then ran up against environmentalists led by the SIERRA CLUB's David BROWER.

The bureau proposed building the Echo Park Dam in Dinosaur National Monument in the early 1950s, touching off the five-year "Dinosaur Battle" that pitted Brower and the Sierra Club against the Bureau of Reclamation. The proposal was finally defeated, but in January 1963, another battle erupted over an even more threatening dam project, which would plug the Colorado River in the Grand Canyon at two places. Brower and the Sierra Club waged a 10-month campaign, employing magazine ads and lobbying efforts to quash the proposal. The dam was indeed defeated, but the price was an Internal Revenue Service decision to revoke the Sierra Club's tax-exempt status.

Brower did offer Dominy a compromise in the battle over the Grand Canyon projects, yielding to a proposal to build a dam in Glen Canyon on the Colorado River just south of the Utah border. While Dominy counted the building of the dam a victory for the Bureau of Reclamation, environmentalists retaliated symbolically in 1979. EARTH FIRST! founder Dave FOREMAN and a small group of "eco-warriors" went to Glen Canyon Dam and unfurled a 100-yard-long black plastic streamer down the face of the dam to simulate the appearance of a huge crack. The gesture further galvanized the environmental movement against Bureau of Reclamation projects.

Douglas, David (1798–July 12, 1834)

Born in Scone, Perthshire, Scotland, David Douglas was a self-taught botanist who had gained his basic

David Douglas. *Courtesy of* American Forests, *Washington, D.C.*

knowledge of plant life working as a gardener's apprentice. Despite his lack of formal training, Douglas became assistant to the prominent academic botanist William Jackson Hooker at Glasgow University in 1820. It was Hooker who recommended young Douglas to the post of plant collector for the Horticultural Society of London. In this position, Douglas traveled extensively in North America and Hawaii (then called the Sandwich Islands), where he discovered, named and collected more than a thousand different plants, including 650 in California alone. Among Douglas's discoveries are the Monterey cypress, the California poppy and seven of America's native pines. The Douglas fir is named for him.

Douglas was an unpleasant man, depressed, sour, puritanical and apparently emotionally unstable. Nevertheless, his contribution to the botany of the New World is enormous, and the number of species he identified endures as a record for the work of a single researcher. Of particular interest to historians of the environmental movement are his journals, in which he recorded not only botanical data, but observations and commentary on man's wasteful ways and needless spoliation of a then-pristine nature.

Douglas was killed in Hawaii when he was trampled by a wild bull. Some believe the melancholy Douglas deliberately provoked the animal in a successful effort to bring about his own death.

Further reading: William Morewood, *Traveler in a Vanished Landscape* (New York: Potter, 1973).

Douglas, Marjory Stoneman (April 7, 1890–   )

Born in Minneapolis, Douglas worked as a newspaper reporter and editor, wrote short stories and was an English instructor. She began her work in conservation in 1927 as a member of the committee formed to encourage the inclusion of the Everglades in the National Park system. In the 1940s, she began writing novels and regional histories, and her first book, *The Everglades: River of Grass,* appeared in 1947. She founded the FRIENDS OF THE EVERGLADES and served as the group's president from 1970 to the present. Her work in conservation, especially to preserve the Everglades, is described in *Voice of the River,* a 1988 book she wrote with John Rothchild.

Douglas was named Conservationist of the Year by the Florida Audubon Society in 1975 and Conservationist of the Year by the Florida Wildlife Federation in 1976 and was given the Nash Conservation Award by the American Motors Corporation in 1977.

Douglas, William Orville (October 16, 1898– January 19, 1980)

William Orville Douglas was named a Supreme Court justice in 1939, a post he held until his retirement in 1976. In 1972, he wrote *The Three Hundred Year War: A Chronicle of Ecological Disaster,* in which he examined the assault of white settlers on the continent of North America in blind service to the "Twin Gods" of "Materialism and Technology." Douglas lamented Americans' historical lack of an "ecological ethic" and complained that "our efforts on the environmental front have been largely public relations gestures." He called for a national spiritual reawakening among American citizens, who, he declared, needed to become activists for the environment.

In 1975, Douglas was presented with the John Muir Award from the SIERRA CLUB.

Born in Maine, Minnesota, Justice Douglas died in Washington, D.C.

Drude, (Carl Georg) Oscar (June 5, 1852– February 1, 1933)

A professor of botany and a longtime director of the Botanic Garden in Dresden, Germany, Oscar Drude was one of the founders of modern plant ecology.

U.S. Supreme Court Justice William O. Douglas on the annual 10-mile C & O Canal walk, 1970. *Courtesy of the National Park Service*

Drury, Newton B. (April 19, 1889–December 14, 1978)

In the early 1920s, the SAVE-THE-REDWOODS LEAGUE solicited the aid of Newton Drury's public relations and advertising firm in managing its programs; throughout the decade, on behalf of the league, Drury, a native of San Francisco, campaigned for the creation of a California State Park Commission, a park site survey and a park development bond issue. When the bond referendum passed in 1928, Drury raised matching private donations, including $3 million from the Rockefellers. The newly formed State Park Commission subsequently hired Drury as land acquisition officer, an appointment that led to Secretary of the Interior Harold L. ICKES's offering him the position of director of the NATIONAL PARK SERVICE in 1933. He declined, but accepted when Ickes offered him the post again in 1940. For the next 11 years, Drury navigated a compromise course between the demands of preservationists on the one hand and advocates of multiple use on the other.

Leaving the park service in 1951, he was appointed by California Governor Earl Warren as chief of the State Division of Beaches and Parks. In 1959, he returned to the Save-the-Redwoods League (as executive secretary, 1959–71, and president, 1971–75) and worked to establish a Redwood National Park. Although Drury's moderate approach brought him and the league into sharp conflict with the SIERRA CLUB, which was also campaigning for the national park, both organizations joined forces in urging its expansion after Redwood National Park was finally established.

Dubos, René (Jules) (February 20, 1901– February 20, 1982)

A native of Saint Brice, France, René Dubos came to the United States in 1924 and was naturalized in 1938. He was educated at the College Chaptal, Paris (1915–19), and the Institut National Agronomique (1919–21). In 1927, he received a Ph.D. degree from Rutgers University.

A microbiologist and ecologist, Dubos first gained recognition in 1939 for research that led to the commercial production of antibiotics. A prolific author, Dubos wrote more than 20 books on science and the environment, including works intended for scientists and medical professionals and books intended for a general audience, including *Only One Earth: The Care and Maintenance of a Small Planet*, which was adopted as the platform for the United Nations Conference on the Human Environment in 1972. His *So Human an Animal* won the 1969 Pulitzer Prize for nonfiction.

Dubos was assistant editor at the International Institute of Agriculture in Rome (1922–24); a research

Born in Braunschweig, Germany, Drude studied natural sciences and chemistry at the Collegium Carolinum, Braunschweig, and at Göttingen University, where he received his doctorate in 1873. After working as a herbarium assistant to F. G. Bartling at Göttingen, Drude became a lecturer there in 1876. In 1879, he was named director of the Dresden Botanic Garden and a professor of botany at Dresden Polytechnikum, where he taught until his retirement as emeritus in 1920.

In 1890 Drude published his *Handbuch der Pflanzengeographie*, which outlined a new system of plant geography based on physical formations, climate and other environmental and biological relationships; the scientist illustrated these ecological groups in the planting arrangements at the Botanic Garden. In 1913, he published *Oekologie der pflanzen*, a further extension and refinement of his taxonomic theories. With the celebrated phytogeographer Adolf Engler of Berlin, Drude collaborated on *Die Vegetation der Erde*, a multivolume collection of monographs on the flora of the world, but the series, begun in 1910, was never completed. Drude died in Dresden in 1933.

assistant in soil microbiology and an instructor in bacteriology at the New Jersey Experimental Station of Rutgers University (1924–27); a fellow of the Rockefeller Institute (1927–28), assistant at the institute (1928–30), associate (1930–38), associate member (1938–41) and full member (1941–42); George Fabyan Professor of Comparative Pathology and professor of tropical medicine at the Harvard University Medical School (1942–44); a member of the Rockefeller Institute (1944–82) and professor there from 1957.

In addition to the 1969 Pulitzer Prize, Dubos was honored by a wide array of professional organizations, including the American College of Physicians, the American Academy of Pediatrics, the American Clinical and Climatological Association, the Public Health Association, the National Tuberculosis Association, the Pharmaceutical Industries, Massachusetts General Hospital, the University of California, the University of Chicago, the Robert Koch Institute, the Passano Foundation, *Modern Medicine* and Phi Beta Kappa. Rochester University, Harvard, Rutgers, University of Paris, the New School for Social Research, University College of Dublin, Yeshiva University, University of Liège, University of Rio de Janeiro, University of Alberta, University of Pennsylvania, University of California, L'Académie de Lille and Carleton College all conferred honorary degrees on Dubos.

Ducks Unlimited, Inc. (Founded: 1937)
One Waterfowl Way, Memphis, Tennessee 38120; (901) 758-3825

With 50 state offices, 4,400 regional groups, and over half a million individual members, Ducks Unlimited is the largest private-sector waterfowl conservation organization in the world. Founded by North American sportsmen during the drought-ridden 1930s, the group works to preserve and restore existing wetlands and to create new habitats for ducks, geese and other wildlife, especially in Canada's prairie provinces, where 70% of the continent's waterfowl population originates. During the last 18 years, Ducks Unlimited has undertaken wetlands projects throughout the birds' migration corridors, protecting and expanding stopping places and wintering grounds in the United States and Mexico as well as safeguarding the crucial nesting and brood-rearing sites of the north. These conservation and rehabilitation activities are financed primarily by thousands of outings, shooting and fishing tournaments and other fundraising events held locally each year by the regional Ducks Unlimited groups. The organization publishes the bimonthly *Ducks Unlimited Magazine* and, periodically, a report titled *International Waterfowl Symposium*

Transactions. Ducks Unlimited was an influential proponent of the North American Waterfowl Management Plan, an international agreement preserving some 6 million acres of prime waterfowl habitat.

Dunkle, Frank H. (October 12, 1924–   )
A past director of the U.S. FISH AND WILDLIFE SERVICE and a former Wyoming state legislator, Frank Dunkle is a special assistant to the director of the Bureau of MINES in Denver, Colorado, and a visiting professor at the Colorado School of Mines.

Born in Oakmount, Pennsylvania, Dunkle served with the U.S. Navy during World War II (1943–46) and the Korean War (1950–52). While earning his B.S. in wildlife management (1950) at Montana State University in Bozeman, he worked as a special warden with the Montana Fish and Game Department. He joined the NATIONAL PARK SERVICE as a ranger at Yellowstone National Park, returning to Montana State University in 1954 for his master's degree in wildlife management and wildlife education (1955). Dunkle became education assistant with the Montana Fish and Game Department (1955–1957), then conservation supervisor with the Montana Department of Public Instruction. Two years later, he rejoined Montana's Fish and Game Department as head of its information and education division, a position he held until 1963, when he was promoted to state director.

During his nine-year tenure as Fish and Game chief, Dunkle instituted many conservation programs, for which he was honored with the Sears Foundation Water Conservation Award for Montana (1968), the Nature Conservancy's Green Leaf Award (1969), the Rocky Mountain Center for the Environment's Award for Outstanding Environmental Achievement (1970) and the American Motors National Conservation Award (1971).

Dunkle was defeated in a bid for Montana governor in 1972. He established his own company, the Ecological Consulting Service, then was elected to the Montana State Senate in 1975. He sponsored and supported a wide range of legislation to facilitate resource development while safeguarding the environment. In 1977, he was named Outstanding State Legislator of the Year by the National Association of State and Federal Employees.

Dunkle founded Resources Education Foundation in 1975, serving as its executive secretary until 1977. He also founded another consulting firm, Research Associates (1977–80). Dunkle served as executive director of the Montana Mining Association (1978–80) and the Montana Republican State Central Committee (1980–81). In 1981, he became staff director of the Mountain Plains Regional Council of the U.S. Department of the INTERIOR in Denver. When the council was abolished in 1983, Dunkle entered the U.S. Fish and Wildlife Service as coordinator of the Colorado River Endangered Fishes Project, also in Denver. In 1986, President Ronald Reagan appointed him director of the U.S. Fish and Wildlife Service. He was also named to the Mount St. Helens' Scientific Advisory Board, and in 1987, Dunkle's alma mater, Montana State University at Bozeman, granted him an honorary doctor of science. Interior Department head Donald P. HODEL commended the conservation administrator with the Secretary's Award for Exceptional Service in 1988, the same year Dunkle was honored with the International Wild Waterfowl Association's Conservation Award, the Minnesota Waterfowl Association's Award for Efforts to Preserve and Protect the Nation's Waterfowl and Wetland, the Sport Fishing Institute's Sports Fisherman of the Year award and the American Fishing Tackle Manufacturers Association's Award of Merit. In 1989, Dunkle was succeeded at the Fish and Wildlife Service by John F. TURNER. Dunkle then served for a year as director of the U.S. Fish and Wildlife Service's National Ecology Research Center in Fort Collins, Colorado, and in 1990, he received his present intergovernmental personnel appointment to the School of Mines in Golden, Colorado.

Dunlap, Louise Cecil (February 7, 1946–   )

Born in Lancaster, Pennsylvania, Louise Cecil Dunlap was educated at Duke University, from which she received a B.A. in political science in 1968. From 1968 to 1970, she served as an intern in the Department of Housing and Urban Development, becoming legislative assistant to the president of the NATIONAL PARKS AND CONSERVATION ASSOCIATION in 1970. In this position, she worked on energy and environmental policy issues before Congress and the executive branch. From 1971 until she joined in founding the ENVIRONMENTAL POLICY INSTITUTE in 1972, she was assistant legislative director of FRIENDS OF THE EARTH and was instrumental in that organization's campaign to stop the supersonic transport (SST).

In 1972, Dunlap became a cofounder of the Environmental Policy Center (called since 1982 the Environmental Policy Institute). From 1976 to 1986, Dunlap served as president of the group, the first woman to become chief executive of a major national environmental organization. With the largest staff of environmental lobbyists in Washington, D.C., she led EPI in directing national citizen lobbying efforts on coal surface mining, federal coal leasing, energy facility siting, energy conservation, outer continental shelf oil and gas leasing, water pollution control, water resources, biotechnology and nuclear power. Under Dunlap's leadership, EPI conducted research on energy and other resource policy issues for the National Academy of Sciences, COUNCIL ON ENVIRONMENTAL QUALITY, Federal Energy Administration and the National Academy of Administration.

For her efforts in organizing a nationwide citizens' coalition to bring about the enactment of the first federal law to regulate the strip mining of coal, Dunlap was accorded national recognition by President Jimmy Carter in 1977. In 1987, she was recognized by the Citizens Mining Coalition and the Environmental Policy Institute for her work to regulate strip mining.

Dunlap and her husband, Joseph BROWDER, are partners in Dunlap & Browder, Inc., a Washington, D.C., firm specializing in legislative and regulatory strategies; in planning to minimize the delay and cost associated with conflicts about the social, economic and environmental consequences of development; analysis of public policy impact on business opportunities; and environmental and public policy lobbying. Dunlap was the principal lobbyist working on behalf of the Alternative Motor Fuels Act of 1988 and is a central figure in the development of national strategies for alternative transportation fuels. She is a member of Senator JAY ROCKEFELLER's National Alternative Fuels Task Force.

Dunlap, who served as an alternate delegate from Maryland to the 1984 Democratic National Convention, is a member of the boards of SCENIC AMERICA and the Clean Water Fund. She has also served on the boards of the LEAGUE OF CONSERVATION VOTERS, Coast Alliance, Environmental Policy Institute and the NATIONAL CLEAN AIR COALITION. She has been honored by the Friends of the United Nations Programme as an environmental leader, and in 1990 was recognized by the SIERRA CLUB.

Dunlap is a founding member of the Democratic Senatorial Campaign Committee Women's Council and of Duke University's Women's Studies Council.

E

Earthcare Network (Founded: 1981)

408 C Street NE, Washington, D.C. 20002;
(202) 547-1141

This coalition of 16 environmental advocacy groups works to protect the global environment. The organization focuses on tropical deforestation, desertification, sea law, Antarctic protection, global warming and preservation of the ozone layer. Earthcare Network acts as a liaison between its member organizations and various national and international administrative and regulatory bodies. It concentrates on the environmental impact of multinational treaties, trade agreements and the financial programs of multilateral organizations. John Michael MCCLOSKEY is chairman of the organization, which publishes *Earthcare Appeals*, a quarterly.

Earth First! (Founded: 1980)

P.O. Box 5176, Missoula, Montana 59806

Earth First! is certainly the most controversial and radical of currently active environmental organizations. It was founded by a loosely constituted group of environmental activists—some have called them "eco-warriors"—led by Dave FOREMAN and Mike Roselle. Foreman was an environmental lobbyist working for the WILDERNESS SOCIETY. Frustrated by the wrangling and compromising necessary to promote environmental legislation, he reached the climax of disillusionment in 1979, when the U.S. FOREST SERVICE evaluated the 62 million acres under its jurisdiction and decided to ban timber, mining and tourism interests from only 15 million acres of the land. With four like-minded activists, a disgusted Foreman retreated to Mexico's Pinacate Desert. The group discussed Edward ABBEY's novel *The Monkey Wrench Gang*, which is about a group of ecological saboteurs—"ecoteurs"—who "ecotaged" road-building

equipment by pouring sand into the vehicles' gas tanks and mused over dynamiting the Glen Canyon Dam. The novel's characters called such activity "monkey wrenching." Thus inspired, Foreman and the others decided to become environmental radicals, and Earth First! was born.

The group's early activities were largely symbolic—ecological versions of "guerrilla theater." In the early 1980s, a group of Earth Firsters rappelled down the

Lake Powell, *U.S. Department of the Interior, Bureau of Reclamation*

face of Elwha Dam in Washington, painting a "crack" down the dam's face, along with the words "Elwha be free." But by mid-decade, Earth First! was engaging in deliberately provocative, confrontational and potentially deadly acts of ecotage, most notoriously driving metal spikes into redwoods slated for logging. A hand-held chain saw or a mill saw blade coming into contact with one of these spikes could easily injure, mutilate or kill a logger. (Actually, only one such injury is recorded, and it is by no means certain that this instance of spiking was the work of the organization.)

As Earth First! acquired an increasingly notorious reputation for outlawry, authorities responded with arrests (Foreman was charged in June 1989 with conspiring to disable three nuclear facilities), while loggers sometimes responded with violence, including fistfights, general harassment and threats. Sometimes it was worse. In August 1989, the car of Earth Firster Judi BARI was rammed by a logging truck. Officials determined that it was an accident, but the Earth First! people were unconvinced. Nine months later, Bari and another organizer, Darryl Cherney, were injured when a pipe bomb exploded in Bari's car. Various anti-environmental extremists claimed responsibility for the bomb. Police officials and the FBI theorized that Bari planted the bomb herself, intending only to fake an attack. Bari's own remark concerning the incident suggests the self-perception of a typical Earth Firster as belonging to an officially despised—and even hunted—organization: "I want the FBI to find the bomber," she said, "and fire him."

By the early 1990s, Earth First! seemed to be in decline, at least as an organization in the traditional sense. At its height, it had counted some 10,000 members and operated on a budget of $100,000. Today, it is staffed wholly by volunteers, has no director and lists no budget. It does continue to publish *Earth First! The Radical Journal* and offers such products as bumper stickers, tee-shirts and the like. Some 25 local chapters also issue their own newsletters. But founder Dave Foreman left the group in August 1990. *U.S. News & World Report* (September 17, 1990) quoted his parting observation: "I don't believe that muddying the issues with a lot of class-struggle rhetoric or weird lifestyle stuff works."

Whatever the political effectiveness of the group may have been or may yet prove to be, Earth First! stands as an important expression of so-called Deep Ecology—a radical environmentalism advocating the proposition that all living organisms are created equal. John Davis, former editor of *Earth First! The Radical Journal*, has gone so far as to declare: "I suspect that eradicating smallpox was wrong. It played an important part in balancing ecosystems." Other Earth First-

ers seem to look forward with notable glee to the collapse of modern civilization and a return to the Pleistocene epoch.

While Earth First! has provoked much hostility from the outside, internal strife generated by the uneasy coexistence of a variety of extreme points of view has recently been on the increase. Foreman, for example, once suggested that famine should be allowed to take its course in Ethiopia, and that immigration from Mexico and Central America should be curbed because it threatened the American wilderness. An anonymous *Earth First!* columnist—whom Judi Bari later identified as radical environmentalist Christopher MANES—welcomed AIDS as ecologically necessary population control. Such extreme and distasteful positions have put great strain on an already very loosely constituted organization and have brought disclaimers from other members, who want to maintain Earth First! as a viable force for eco-political—albeit radical—action.

Further reading: John Davis, *Earth First! Reader: Ten Years of Radical Environmentalism* (Layton, Utah: Gibbs Smith, 1991).

Earth Island Institute (Founded: 1985)
300 Broadway, Suite 28, San Francisco, California 94133; (415) 788-3666

The Earth Island Institute, founded by David BROWER, former executive director of the SIERRA CLUB and founder of FRIENDS OF THE EARTH, FRIENDS OF THE EARTH INTERNATIONAL and the LEAGUE OF CONSERVATION VOTERS, supports more than 20 projects focused on environmental issues and related concerns, such as human rights, economic development in third-world countries and economic conditions in inner cities. The organization sponsors a series of Conferences on the Fate of the Earth, which explore the interrelationship of environmental protection, economic development, human rights and world peace. The institute's Environmental Litigation Fund assists individuals and community groups to compel businesses and government agencies to comply with environmental laws. The institute produces educational programs for the Green political movement in the United States and other countries and publishes research on agricultural issues, global climatic conditions and old-growth forests. Its Sacred Land Film Project has produced films about energy and resource development in the American West. The Urban Habitat Program organizes grass-roots campaigns to restore urban neighborhoods and preserve public spaces. The Environmental Project on Central America supports the environmental movement in that region through publications, videos and fund-raising cam-

A sea turtle "participant" in the Sea Turtle Restoration Project of Earth Island Institute. *Photo by Michael Kuehn, courtesy of Earth Island Institute*

paigns. The International Marine Mammal Project focuses on preventing the slaughter of dolphins by the U.S. tuna industry and promoting a worldwide ban on the use of drift nets. In this project, the Earth Island Institute joined with the SEA SHEPHERD CONSERVATION SOCIETY in calling for a boycott of tuna canned in the United States, an action that resulted in the American tuna industry's adoption of "dolphin-safe" fishing methods.

Earth Island Institute supports the Earth Island Action Group, a lobbying and advocacy organization. In addition, it offers a speakers' bureau and maintains a library of 2,000 volumes.

The 33,000 members of Earth Island Institute receive the *Earth Island Journal*, a 46-page quarterly magazine that reports on the institute's programs, environmental news and volunteer opportunities.

East African Wild Life Society (Founded: 1956)
P. O. Box 20110, Nairobi, Kenya; (2) 748170

The East African Wild Life Society, directed by Nehemiah K. Arap Rotich, works to preserve the wildlife and wildlife habitats of East Africa. Among the organization's active programs are animal rescue and relocation and the prevention of poaching. The society also conducts environmental education and research and publishes the quarterly *African Journal of Ecology* and *SWARA*, a bimonthly journal. The group has 12,000 members, a staff of 25 and an annual budget of $500,000.

Ecological Society of America (Founded: 1915)
Center for Environmental Studies, Arizona State University, Tempe, Arizona 85287; (602) 965-3000

From its beginnings as a small association of academics and ecologists, the Ecological Society of America

has grown to an organization with 6,100 members (in 1991) as the public has become more aware of the importance of environmental issues. Its scholarly journals, *Ecology* and *Ecological Monographs,* and the *Bulletin of the Ecological Society of America,* a quarterly newsletter, reach an audience of professional ecologists, educators, scientists and lay enthusiasts. Articles in these publications are aimed at increasing understanding of the relationships among fisheries, industry, public health and conservation. The society's Ecological Information Network, based in Washington, D.C., consists of a computerized data bank of more than 750 ecologists who may be called on to provide ecological information to lawmakers at both the state and national level and to industrial and business decision-makers. In 1980, the society began a certification program for ecologists.

Edge, Mabel Rosalie (November 3, 1877–November 30, 1962)
New York-born Mabel Edge used her inherited fortune to finance the Emergency Conservation Committee, a radical, uncompromising preservationist organization she founded (with journalist Irving Brant) in 1929. The ECC's first victory was to reform the NATIONAL AUDUBON SOCIETY, which had "entangling alliances" with firearms manufacturers. Next, the ECC—for all practical purposes synonymous with Mrs. Edge—successfully campaigned for the creation of the Hawk Mountain Wildlife Sanctuary in Pennsylvania, a refuge for birds of prey.

Mrs. Edge battled lumber interests in Washington State and succeeded in bringing about the creation of Olympic National Park. Her efforts also aided in the addition of 6,000 acres of old-growth sugar pine forest to Yosemite National Park and the establishment of Kings Canyon National Park. While her contribution to the national parks movement was great, Mabel Edge was contentious beyond possibility of compromise, often deliberately alienating fellow conservationists. As a result, the ECC died with her in 1962.

Further reading: Maurice Broun, *Hawks Aloft: The Story of Hawk Mountain* (New York: Dodd, Mead Co., 1949); Stephen Fox, *John Muir and His Legacy* (Boston: Little, Brown, 1981).

Ehrlich, Anne Howland (November 17, 1933–   )
California-based writer and researcher Anne Ehrlich is the coauthor of numerous nonfiction books on contemporary issues in the fields of environmental science and human ecology. Among her best-known works are *The Population Explosion* (with PAUL R. EHR-

Olympic National Park. *U.S. Department of the Interior, National Park Service photo*

LICH, 1991), *Healing the Planet: Strategies for Solving the Environmental Crisis* (with P. R. Ehrlich, 1990), *Hidden Dangers: Environmental Consequences of Preparing for War* (with John Birks, 1990) and *Extinction: The Causes and Consequences of the Disappearance of Species* (with P. R. Ehrlich, 1981).

Born in Des Moines, Iowa, Anne Howland attended the University of Kansas from 1952 to 1955. In 1954, she married population biologist and writer Paul R. Ehrlich, with whom she has collaborated on many books. She began work as a research assistant and biological illustrator at Stanford University in 1959, and she continues to serve there as a senior research associate in biological sciences. From 1977 to 1980, she was consultant to the COUNCIL ON ENVIRONMENTAL QUALITY, and from 1984 to 1986, she was a commissioner with the Greater London Area War Risks Study. In addition to her book-length works, Ehrlich has contributed articles to a number of scientific journals and popular periodicals. She is a recipient of the American Humanists Society Distinguished Service Award.

Ehrlich, Paul Ralph (May 29, 1932–)
The author of more than 650 books, articles and papers, Paul Ralph Ehrlich has devoted his career to the study of population growth and its negative impact on the environment. Born in Philadelphia, Ehrlich took his B.A. in zoology at the University of Pennsylvania, and an M.A. and Ph.D. from the University of Kansas. As Bing Professor of Population Studies at Stanford University, Ehrlich received the Crafoord Prize in Population Biology and the Conservation of Biological Diversity in 1990. The award, presented by the Royal Swedish Academy of Sciences, cited his research on the dynamics and genetics of fragmented populations and the effect of population patterns on survival.

Among Ehrlich's many other honors are membership in the National Academy of Sciences, the American Academy of Arts and Sciences and the American Philosophical Society. He received the John Muir Award of the SIERRA CLUB in 1980, the gold medal of the WORLD WILDLIFE FUND in 1987, the Humanists Distinguished Service Award of the American Hu-

Yosemite National Park. *U.S. Department of the Interior, National Park Service photo by Richard Frear*

manists Association in 1985 and the first Distinguished Achievement Award of the Society for Conservation Biology in 1987.

Ehrlich served as president of ZERO POPULATION GROWTH from 1969 to 1970, was named honorary president in 1970, and was elected president of the Conservation Society in 1972. He was the recipient of a 1990 MacArthur Foundation Fellowship.

Ehrlich's best-selling *The Population Bomb*, published in 1968 and revised and reprinted in 1971, was instrumental in the growth of the ecological movement during the early 1970s. Written in collaboration with his wife, ANNE HOWLAND EHRLICH, senior research associate in biological sciences at Stanford University, *The Population Bomb* paints a dire picture of the future of the planet. The authors argue that, given the growth of the human population, civilization is doomed to collapse unless world governments institute policies to control the expansion of human numbers. Among the early signs of environmental failure the authors have cited in their publications are global warming, acid rain, soil erosion, groundwater depletion, destruction of the ozone layer, desertification and deforestation. The Ehrlichs do not place total blame for the pending disaster on Third World countries, although their rates of population

growth have skyrocketed. According to them, wealthy nations are at fault as well. Although population growth rates have stabilized in these countries, their citizens use more natural resources per capita than those in poorer countries and are more dependent on technologies that harm the environment. According to the Ehrlichs, population, affluence, and environmentally damaging technologies have formed a tripartite destructive force that may be remedied only by strong interventionist policies, especially using market mechanisms.

Ehrlich's other books include *The End of Affluence* (1974), *The Golden Door* (1979), *EcoScience* (1977), *Extinction* (1981), *The Population Explosion* (1990) and *Healing the Planet* (1992); the last two were written in collaboration with Anne Howland Ehrlich. The Ehrlichs have criticized the liberal immigration policies of the United States, asserting that 25% of the growth in America's population results from immigration, and they call for a plan to balance births against immigration. "If the United States is going to avoid even more serious problems of overpopulation, its people are inevitably trapped in a zero-sum game; every immigrant admitted must be compensated for by a birth foregone. This will require either a further lowering of American birthrates (which are already low enough to bring an end to natural increase even-

Paul Ehrlich. *Photo courtesy of Paul Ehrlich*

tually) or much more attention to the problems of restricting immigration in the future."

Eichbaum, William M. (December 24, 1941–   )

William Eichbaum is the vice-president for environmental quality at the WORLD WILDLIFE FUND in Washington, D.C. An active member of the environmental community since 1969, Eichbaum has consulted on numerous national and regional advisory panels and currently serves on the National Research Council's Committee on Wastewater Management for Coastal Urban Areas, the Marine Board and the Advisory Board of the ENVIRONMENTAL LAW INSTITUTE.

Born in Knoxville, Tennessee, Eichbaum studied international relations at Dartmouth College (B.A., 1963) and the Graduate Institute of International Studies in Geneva, Switzerland (1961–62). After earning his bachelor of laws degree at Harvard Law School in 1966, he joined the Philadelphia practice of Pepper, Hamilton & Scheetz. Two years later Eich-

baum became the Pennsylvania staff attorney chief of the Police Law Reform Unit at Community Legal Services Inc. From 1970 to 1971, he was director of the Environmental Pollution Strike Force and special assistant attorney general for the commonwealth of Pennsylvania, then he moved to Pennsylvania's Department of Environmental Resources, where he was deputy secretary for enforcement and general counsel for the next six years. In 1977, Eichbaum was named associate solicitor for surface mining at the U.S. Department of the INTERIOR, a position he held until 1979. After an academic year as guest scholar at the Woodrow Wilson Center of the Smithsonian Institution, in 1980 Eichbaum accepted the post of assistant secretary of environmental programs with the state of Maryland's Department of Health and Mental Hygiene. In 1987, he became under secretary of the Executive Office of Environmental Affairs for the Commonwealth of Massachusetts, and in 1989, he joined the World Wildlife Fund. An adjunct associate professor of environmental law at the State University of New York at Stony Brook, he has also taught at the University of Maryland Law School (1990), the Free Law School of Philadelphia (cofounder, 1970) and Drexel University, Philadelphia (1970).

Eichbaum has written numerous articles on environmental law and planning for a variety of legal journals and other publications and was coauthor, with Tom Horton, of the book *Turning the Tide: Saving the Chesapeake Bay* (1991). He has served as an advisor to the Coastal Seas Governance Project (1985–90), the Environmental Law Institute Board (1980–87), Maryland Sea Grant College (1981–87), the National Environmental Enforcement Council for the U.S. Department of Justice (1985–87) and the Chesapeake Critical Area Commission (1984–87), among other projects and panels. He is the recipient of several awards and commendations.

Elton, Charles Sutherland (March 29, 1900–   )

One of the first scientists in the world to study animals in relation to their environment, Charles Sutherland Elton founded the Bureau of Animal Population at Oxford University and served as its director from 1932 to 1967. A native of Liverpool, England, he was an ecologist on Oxford University's expeditions to Spitzbergen in 1921, to the Arctic in 1924, to Lapland in 1930 and on Merton College's expedition to the Arctic in 1923.

Elton published *Animal Ecology* in 1927, calling it a treatment of the "sociology and economics of animals." He compiled existing ecological knowledge into a new model of a natural "community" and proposed new principles to describe the economy of nature. The food chain became a system in which all animals were producers and consumers, and Elton demonstrated a direct link between the size of the producer and the size of the consumer. For example, elephants cannot sustain themselves on insects; they need a food that is more stationary and substantial. Elton then discussed how the size of animal-producer populations could affect the food chain. Whales, for example, are able to live off small crustaceans because they are so numerous and so easy to catch. Elton found that the smaller an animal is, the more common it is in nature, and that larger animals are distributed more sparsely. This concept he called the "pyramid of numbers," which he used to show how various species of animals interact. Elton also proposed that each animal fills a particular "niche," a place in the food chain Charles DARWIN had called an "office." To Elton, the niche determined not only what an animal looked like, but also what it did and what it ate.

In the mid-1940s, Elton went to work for the Department of Zoological Field Studies at Oxford University, studying the natural history of Wytham Woods, an estate owned by the university. He was determined to gain an understanding of the dynamics of a single plot of acreage, so that, as he wrote in *The Pattern of Animal Communities* (1966), "we will be able to face conservation problems and understand what goes wrong in our artificially simplified croplands and planted forests." Although he continued to describe animals and plant life in terms of consumers and producers, he called for humankind to develop a relationship with nature less dominated by economics. He wrote that, "in giving priority to economic productivity, especially in regard to the production of large cash crops from the land, the human environment itself may gradually become dull, unvaried, charmless and treated like a factory rather than a place to live in."

Between his 1927 *Animal Ecology* and his 1966 *The Pattern of Animal Communities*, Elton wrote *Animal Ecology and Evolution* (1933), *The Ecology of Animals* (1933), *Exploring the Animal World* (1933), *Voles, Mice, and Lemmings: Problems in Population Dynamics* (1942), *The Control of Rats and Mice* (1954) and *The Ecology of Invasions by Animals and Plants* (1958).

Elton was a founding member of Oxford University's Exploration Club and was a member of the NATURE CONSERVANCY from 1949 to 1956. He has won numerous awards for his ecology work, including the Eminent Ecologist Award from the ECOLOGICAL SOCIETY OF AMERICA in 1961, the Gold Medal from the Linnaean Society in 1967 and the Darwin Medal from the Royal Society in 1970.

Emerson, George Barrell (September 12, 1797–March 4, 1881)

Appointed chairman of the commission for the Zoological and Botanical Survey of Massachusetts in 1837, educator and botanist George Barrell Emerson spent nine summers traveling across the state examining trees and shrubs. In 1846, he completed one of the reports developed from the survey, *Report on the Trees and Shrubs Growing Naturally in the Forests of Massachusetts*, which has been called a classic in New England botany. In this work, Emerson chronicled the destruction of the state's wooded regions. "The cunning foresight of the Yankee seems to desert him when he takes the axe in hand," he observed.

Emerson also served as president of the Boston Society of Natural History from 1837 to 1843. He was the principal of two private schools in the state before founding a private school for girls in 1823. After retiring from teaching in 1855, he wrote, with Charles L. Flint, *Manual of Agriculture for the School, the Farm, and the Fireside* (1862). A native of Wells, Maine, Emerson died in Newton, Massachusetts.

Further reading: Robert C. Waterston, *Memoir of George Barrell Emerson* (Boston: Houghton, Mifflin, 1884).

Emerson, Ralph Waldo (May 25, 1803–April 27, 1882)

"There are days which occur in this climate, at almost any season of the year, wherein the world reaches its perfection," Ralph Waldo Emerson began his celebrated essay *Nature* (1836). This philosopher, poet and lecturer, one of the giants of 19th-century American literature, was a proponent of Transcendentalism, a Neo-Platonic philosophy that celebrates nature as a reflection or incarnation of the divine "Oversoul" in mankind while seeking to transcend or dominate nature in search of a higher order.

Emerson graduated from Harvard University (1821), where he studied theology, and, after teaching school (1821–26), became pastor in the Old Second Church, a Unitarian congregation in Boston. Following the death of his first wife in 1831, Emerson resigned his pastorate in 1832 and traveled to Europe, where he met some of the leading minds of the 19th century, including Samuel Taylor Coleridge, William Wordsworth and Thomas Carlyle. When he returned to the United States, he took up a career as a lecturer and was much in demand.

In *Nature*, published anonymously in 1836, Emerson outlined his philosophy of Transcendentalism,

Ralph Waldo Emerson

which greatly influenced American thought, literature and attitude toward the natural world. Throughout his work, Emerson taught that nature has more value than a mere examination of its beauty or "economy" can reveal. Nature can serve as a resource for the human imagination and as a reflection of man's inner spiritual life. For Emerson, whose Transcendentalism was strongly flavored with Neo-Platonism, it was the mind that gave nature its beauty and significance.

Emerson was born in Boston and died in Concord, Massachusetts.

Further reading: Gay Wilson Allen, *Waldo Emerson: A Biography* (New York: Viking, 1981); Ralph L. Rusk, *The Life of Ralph Waldo Emerson* (New York: Scribner's, 1949).

Energy, U.S. Department of (Established: 1977)
1000 Independence Avenue SW, Washington, D.C. 20585; (202) 586-5000

The Department of Energy was created when President Jimmy CARTER merged many of the federal government's energy agencies into a single cabinet-level body. The new department drew its programs and staff from the U.S. Department of the INTERIOR, the Federal Power Commission, the Atomic Energy Commission, the Energy Research and Development Administration and the Federal Energy Administration. James Schlesinger, former head of the Atomic Energy Commission, spearheaded the reorganization of the government's energy programs and became the first secretary of energy. Although the reorganization did centralize much of the government's energy-related activites, a move deemed necessary by the government and the public alike because of the energy crisis of the 1970s, some crucial functions were left out of the mix. The department had no control over the licensing and inspection of nuclear power plants, a job that remained with the NUCLEAR REGULATORY COMMISSION. Environmental questions relating to energy development were left to the ENVIRONMENTAL PROTECTION AGENCY. The Department of the Interior, through its Bureau of LAND MANAGEMENT, continued to be responsible for leasing public lands for mineral exploration. In addition, the new department had no authority over government programs designed to increase the gasoline mileage of American cars, a function that stayed with the Department of Transportation.

While these important activities remained the responsibility of other agencies, the Department of Energy did play several crucial roles. The new department, having taken over the duties of the Energy Research and Development Administration, had authority to direct research and administration of new sources of energy. Among these programs was a nuclear-weapons project originally begun by the Atomic Energy Commission. The department had authority to regulate and allocate crude oil and to manage four power boards: the Southeastern Power Administration, the Southwestern Power Administration, the Alaska Power Administration and the Bonneville Power Administration. The department also took over the management of naval oil and shale oil reserves, a job formerly managed by the Department of Defense, and the research and statistical programs related to oil and coal mining, formerly carried out by the Department of the Interior's Bureau of MINES.

When President Ronald REAGAN assumed office in 1981, he revealed his intention to abolish the Department of Energy. While some of the department's programs were phased out through budget cuts, others continued in full force. The pro-nuclear administration was at last unable to dismantle the department completely, and today the department remains fully funded. James D. WATKINS, secretary of energy under President George Bush, was replaced by Hazel R. O'Leary in the administration of President Bill Clinton.

Energy Foundation (Founded: 1991)
75 Federal Street, San Francisco, California 94107;
(415) 546-7400

The Energy Foundation was created by the John D. and Catherine T. MacArthur Foundation, the Pew Charitable Trusts and the Rockefeller Foundation in consultation with a group of scientists, policy makers, business leaders and analysts to assist in the nation's transition to a sustainable energy future by promoting energy efficiency and renewable energy.

The foundation functions in two ways. Its primary mission is to make grants to individuals and organizations with projects that will contribute to America's energy future. The foundation also has the option, when it determines that an unmet need exists in the field, to convene workshops, commission papers or take other direct initiatives as required.

Its initial budget is $20 million over three years.

Environmental Action (Founded: 1970)
1525 New Hampshire Avenue NW, Washington, D.C. 20036; (202) 745-4870

With more than 20,000 members, Environmental Action lobbies elected officials on policy issues involving solid wastes, toxic substances, drinking water, recycling, global warming, plutonium production, utility policies, the ozone and acid rain. Affiliated with the Environmental Action Foundation, the group publishes a bimonthly magazine, *Environmental Action*, on the environmental movement and its goals.

Asserting that "a clean, unpolluted environment is a fundamental human right," the organization was instrumental in securing passage of the Superfund law, which identifies the nation's major areas of toxic contamination and funds their clean-up. Environmental Action's political action committee, EnAct/PAC, supports pro-environment candidates, monitors the voting records of congressmen on environmental issues and conducts a "Dirty Dozen Campaign" to identify each year the 12 most anti-environmental legislators in Congress. Ruth Caplan is the director of Environmental Action.

Environmental Action Coalition (Founded: 1970)
625 Broadway, New York, New York 10012; (212) 677-1601

The Environmental Action Coalition specializes in environmental education and in grass-roots projects aimed at protecting the environment. The EAC has focused primarily on the New York City metropolitan area, but is active throughout New York state and the mid-Atlantic region, and is influential in creating national environmental policy.

EAC's major area of concentration is recycling. EAC provided the organization and financing for New York City's first voluntary recycling network in the early 1970s and, since that time, has worked for the establishment of an integrated waste management program, urging cooperation between public and private sectors. The coalition provides a national information service on all environmental issues and maintains a comprehensive environmental library.

Nancy Wolf is executive director of the coalition.

Environmental Defense Fund (Founded: 1967)
257 Park Avenue South, New York, New York 10010; (212) 505-2100

The Environmental Defense Fund has a staff of 133 and a membership of over 2,000,000. Dedicated to the protection and improvement of the environment, it employs lawyers, scientists and economists to reform public policy on toxic chemicals, toxicology, radiation, air quality, energy, water resources, agriculture, ozone depletion and the greenhouse effect, wildlife and the environment worldwide. Staff lawyers take legal action against environmental abusers, and scientists undertake studies of environmental pollutants. When the organization was first formed, it tackled the problem of DDT by showing how the pesticide moved through the food chain and was eventually consumed by human beings. This study led to a ban on the use of DDT in the United States.

The Environmental Defense Fund publishes an *Annual Report* and a bimonthly *EDF Letter* for its members. Fred KRUPP currently serves as executive director.

Environmental Law Institute (Founded: 1969)
1616 P Street NW, Suite 200, Washington, D.C. 20036; (202) 328-5150

Founded by the Public Law Education Institute and the CONSERVATION FOUNDATION, the Environmental Law Institute conducts and sponsors research on environmental law and policy, serves as a clearinghouse for environmental law information and conducts educational programs, including conferences, seminars and workshops. The institute has offered courses in environmental law with law schools, governmental agencies and nonprofit organizations and is cosponsor of conferences with the American Bar Association, the American Law Institute and the Smithsonian Institution.

The institute maintains an environmental law library of 20,000 volumes and publishes *Environmental Law Reporter*, *Environmental Forum* and *Law of Environmental Protection*. Affiliated with the National Wetlands Technical Council, the institute also publishes

Osprey and two chicks. In 1967, Environmental Defense Fund founders secured a ban on DDT spraying in Suffolk County, Long Island, New York. This and other EDF actions helped restore the declining osprey population on Long Island. *Photo by Michael Mael, courtesy of the Environmental Defense Fund*

the *National Wetlands Newsletter*. Its book publication program has issued *The Regulation of Toxic and Oxidant Air Pollutants in North America*, *Superfund Deskbook*, *Community Action to Prevent Chemical Accidents: A Handbook for Ohio Citizens*, *Citizen Suits: Private Enforcement of Federal Pollution Control Laws*, *Hazardous Wastes: Confronting the Challenge*, *Wetlands of the Chesapeake*, *Superfund: A Legislative History*, *Directory of State Environmental Agencies*, *Groundwater: Strategies for State Action* and *Our National Wetland Heritage*. J. William Futrell is president of the Environmental Law Institute.

Environmental Policy Institute (Founded: 1974)
Executive Offices, 218 D Street SE, Washington, D.C. 20003; (202) 544-2600

Based in Washington, D.C., the Environmental Policy Institute conducts research, disseminates information and actively lobbies for the conservation and protection of natural resources, both in the U.S. and around the globe. A division of FRIENDS OF THE EARTH

since 1990, EPI focuses particular attention on energy issues, vigorously advocating the domestic development and safe, efficient utilization of renewable, non-nuclear energy sources. The *EPI Quarterly Report* monitors current progress and ongoing challenges in environmental protection, and the organization's individual programs and publications—on water and energy conservation, agricultural and chemical safety, transportation of hazardous materials, nuclear power and waste disposal and other subjects—provide independent research and reference information to government, corporations and the media, as well as to private citizens.

A watchdog of U.S. executive branch enforcement of environmental regulations, the public interest group has also been effective in its campaigns to strengthen the language of new legislation.

Environmental Protection Agency (Established: 1970)
Washington, D.C. 20640; (202) 260-2090

Created during a government reorganization ordered by President Richard NIXON, the Environmental Protection Agency began operations on December 2, 1970, with 6,000 employees gathered from 15 government programs. Most of the personnel came from the U.S. Department of the INTERIOR's Federal Water Quality Administration and from the Department of Health, Education, and Welfare's National Air Pollution Control Administration. Smaller numbers came from the Bureau of Water Hygiene, the Bureau of Solid Waste Management, the Office of Pesticides and the Pesticides, Wildlife, and Fish Office, among other offices. President Nixon appointed William RUCKELSHAUS director of the new agency, charged immediately with solving the nation's waste management problems. Throughout the 1970s, this initial mission was expanded to cover pesticides, noise control, drinking water and toxic substance control.

In his role as EPA's administrator, Ruckelshaus hired a large corps of attorneys to work in the enforcement area and immediately set out to bring criminal charges against corporations that violated environmental laws. Court cases were lengthy, however, and the courts usually acted on a case-by-case basis, interpreting environmental laws differently each time. Throughout the 1970s, the EPA met with relatively little success in enforcing federal laws. Five years after its creation, the EPA reported that only 70% of the nation's 247 air quality regions had met basic health standards. One-fifth of the nation's industrial polluters still had not complied with EPA requirements. In addition, a tenth of the nation's industrial water polluters had not yet installed the mandated new nonpolluting technology.

The EPA's record did not improve during the 1980s. This was due in part to the nature of the agency's mission. Created to enforce laws passed by Congress, the EPA staff tended to view each environmental problem separately. Those working on water pollution, for example, paid little attention to air pollution or ecosystems. In addition, the EPA did not set priorities that encompassed the total environment. To begin developing a more holistic view, the EPA undertook a study in 1986 and 1987 of the relative risks posed by environmental problems. The risks were divided into four major categories: human cancer risk, human non-cancer health risk, ecological risk and welfare risk. The resulting report, *Unfinished Business: A Comparative Assessment of Environmental Problems*, pointed out discrepancies between the major risks identified and the resources allocated to the EPA by Congress to address them.

In 1989, William K. REILLY, who had been recently appointed administrator of the EPA, asked the Science Advisory Board to undertake a study of EPA's *Unfinished Business*. The board's study, published in September 1990, characterized the EPA's stance over its first 20 years as "reactive." The agency worked to control pollution or abate other environmental problems only when called upon to enforce new environmental laws passed by Congress. In an attempt to redress the fragmented nature of past EPA action, the Science Advisory Board created the Relative Risk Reduction Strategies Committee, which soon made a series of recommendations intended to improve the EPA's ability to respond to current problems and to avoid future ones. One of the recommendations was that the EPA devote as much of its resources to ecological problems as it does to human health problems. The report stated that "human health and welfare ultimately rely upon the life support systems and natural resources provided by health ecosystems" and criticized the EPA's dedication to human health issues at the expense of natural ecosystems. In addition, the report called on the EPA to develop ways to "influence and shape individual, community, and business choices" of products that are nonpolluting and environmentally safe.

Throughout its troubled history, the EPA has been caught between environmentalists' demands for stricter enforcement of laws and the administration's call for a pro-economy and pro-industry stance. The recommendations by the Science Advisory Board, if undertaken by the EPA, would radically alter the daily operations of the agency and change its philosophy from reaction to advocacy.

European Environmental Bureau (Founded: 1974)
20, rue du Luxembourg, B-1040 Brussels, Belgium; (2) 5141250

The international European Environmental Bureau is a coalition of environmental organizations in the European Economic Community. The organization promotes environmental conservation and the restoration and efficient use of human and natural resources. Working to increase public awareness of environmental issues, the organization carries out lobbying programs, conducts annual conferences and publishes the *RISED Bulletin* and the *RISED Newsletter* through its Regular Information System on Environment and Development program. The organization is headed by Raymond Van Ermen, secretary general, and has 95 members, a staff of two and a $300,000 annual budget.

Evans, Michael Brock (May 24, 1937–   )
A former environmental lawyer in private practice from 1963 to 1967, Michael Brock Evans was named northwest conservation representative for the SIERRA CLUB and the FEDERATION OF WESTERN OUTDOOR CLUBS in 1967. In this role, he spearheaded the creation of nearly 30 new environmental organizations and

councils in the northwestern states, northwest Canada and Alaska.

In 1973, Evans, a native of Columbus, Ohio, became the director of the Sierra Club's offices in Washington, D.C., where he was instrumental in club activities relating to the Alaska oil pipeline, the Big Cypress Swamp Preserve in Florida, the Boundary Waters Canoe Area in Minnesota, the Congaree Swamp in South Carolina, the Clean Air Act, the Forest Management Act and other programs and campaigns. In 1980, he was promoted to associate director of the club, and a year later he became vice-president for national issues of the NATIONAL AUDUBON SOCIETY.

Evans has contributed numerous articles and columns to *Sierra* and *Audubon* magazines in addition to writing an article on nuclear power issues for the *Oregon Law Review* and, for the *Idaho Law Review,* an article on the wilderness as part of cultural history.

Evelyn, John (October 31, 1620–February 3, 1706)

A charter member of the Royal Society, John Evelyn wrote scientific treatises and dozens of political and aesthetic essays and books. *Fumigugium* (1661) focused on the problem of smog in London and proposed ways to abate the pollution. Evelyn suggested that certain industries should be banned from the city and that a greenbelt of trees and shrubs should be planted around London. *Sylva,* the first book published by order of the Royal Society (1664), focused on the conservation of trees. After selling more than 1,000 copies, the first edition was amended with the addition of chapters on the cultivation of fruit trees and the production of cider, a gardener's almanac and other horticultural studies. In addition to his own works, Evelyn translated books from other languages, including *The Compleat Gard'ner; or, Directions for Cultivating and Right Ordering of Fruit-Gardens and Kitchen-Gardens; With Divers Reflections on Several Parts of Husbandry* (1719).

Evelyn was born and died in Wotton, Surrey.

Further reading: Arthur Ponsonby, *John Evelyn* (London: Heinemann, 1933).

Evenden, Frederick George (April 11, 1921– February 20, 1982)

Frederick George Evenden, the first full-time executive secretary (1963–68) and executive director (1968–78) of the WILDLIFE SOCIETY in Washington, D.C., began his career in ecology in 1948 as a research biologist in the U.S. FISH AND WILDLIFE SERVICE'S Office of River Basin Studies.

At the Wildlife Society, Evenden oversaw a doubling of membership and spearheaded the campaign to establish the Renewable Natural Resources Foundation, a consortium of professional environmental organizations and ecological think tank in Bethesda, Maryland.

Born in Woodburn, Oregon, Evenden graduated from Oregon State University in 1943 with a degree in wildlife management. After military service as a weather observer with the Army Air Corps during World War II, he returned to his studies and earned a Ph.D. from Oregon State, where he specialized in the habitats of birds in the Willamette Valley. After working for the U.S. Fish and Wildlife Service, he was named executive director of the Sacramento Science Center and Junior Museum in 1953.

Evenden retired from the Wildlife Society in 1978 and worked as a private consultant. Among his commissions was one from the International Association of Fish and Wildlife Agencies to study hunter education programs.

Evenden contributed much time and energy to numerous environmental committees, including the Professional Improvement Committee of the International Association of Fish and Wildlife Agencies (1966–68), the American Ornithologists' Union's Committee on Conservation (1966–69) and the National Conservation Committee of the Boy Scouts (1963–78).

In his private life, Evenden was an avid bird-watcher and researcher, who kept detailed records of sightings. At the time of his death, he had sighted 1,530 different species and was ranked 149th in the world among bird counters.

F

Fall, Albert Bacon (November 26, 1861–
November 30, 1944)
Born in Frankfort, Kentucky, Albert Bacon Fall was
elected senator from New Mexico when that territory
achieved statehood in 1912. In the Senate, Fall was
an outspoken critic of Woodrow Wilson's policies
toward Mexico and was appointed secretary of the
interior by Wilson's successor, President Warren G.
Harding. As secretary, Fall was responsible for oil
lands newly transferred to federal control for the
purposes of securing a steady supply of fuel to the
U.S. Navy. In 1922, Fall negotiated an agreement
with oil baron Harry F. Sinclair for the Teapot Dome
Naval Oil Reserve in Wyoming and another agreement with Edward L. Doheny—a personal friend of
long standing—for a reserve at Elk Hills, California.
The leases were subsequently deemed improper and
created the Teapot Dome Scandal, the most notorious
scandal of Harding's corruption-ridden administration.

Public outcry forced Fall's resignation as secretary
of the interior in 1923, and when a later Senate
investigation disclosed that he had accepted funds
totaling some $400,000 for negotiating the transfers,
Fall's name made headlines for nearly a decade. In
1927, the courts nullified the agreements Fall had
made with Sinclair and Doheny, and in 1929, the
former secretary of the interior was found guilty of
having accepted a bribe. In 1931, at age 69, he was
sent to prison to serve a one-year term—the first U.S.
cabinet member to be convicted of a crime and sentenced to prison.

Fall died in El Paso, Texas.

Further reading: Burl Noggle, *Teapot Dome: Oil and Politics
in the 1920's* (Baton Rouge: Louisiana University Press,
1962); David H. Stratton, "New Mexico Machiavellian? The
Story of Albert B. Fall," *Montana: The Magazine of Western
History*, October 1957, Southwestern Studies 4, no. 3, Monograph no. 15; Stratton (ed.), *The Memoirs of Albert B. Fall*
(El Paso: Texas Western Press, 1966).

Federation of Western Outdoor Clubs
(Founded: 1932)
365 West 29th Street, Eugene, Oregon 97405; (503)
686-1365

The Federation of Western Outdoor Clubs promotes
conservation of forests, wildlife and natural areas
throughout the western United States. Its affiliates
include 45 hiking, camping, climbing and boating
clubs and some local chapters of the NATIONAL AU-
DUBON SOCIETY and the SIERRA CLUB.

The group's publication, *Outdoors West*, issued twice
a year, serves as a forum for the exchange of ideas
on ecological issues and promotes political activism
in the environmental movement.

Fell, George Brady (September 27, 1916–   )
As a founder, vice-president, secretary and executive
director of the NATURE CONSERVANCY during the 1950s,
George Brady Fell led the organization to a position
of strong advocacy of environmental concerns. In
1958, he organized the Natural Land Institute and
became the organization's first director. In the state
of Illinois (Fell was born in Elgin), he initiated legislation to create a natural preserves system and the
Illinois Nature Preserves Commission, an organization he served as secretary from 1964 to 1970 and as
executive secretary from 1970 to 1982. He drafted the
Illinois Conservation District Act, which was passed
in 1963, and the Illinois Natural Areas Preservation
Act, passed in 1981. He was the first secretary-treasurer of the Natural Areas Association from 1978 to
1983.

Before working with the Nature Conservancy, Fell
had worked with the U.S. SOIL CONSERVATION SER-

VICE and with the Conservation Committee of the Illinois State Academy of Science. In 1949, he was named vice-president of the Ecologists Union.

Fernow, Bernhard Eduard (January 7, 1851–February 6, 1923)

A native of Posen, Prussia, Fernow immigrated to the United States in 1876 and was hired by Cooper Hewitt & Co. to manage its 15,000 acres of Pennsylvania woodlands (1878). Fernow was the first professional forester to practice in the U.S. and was a prime mover of the American Forestry Congress (1883–95). In 1886, he was named chief of the Division of Forestry (U.S. Department of AGRICULTURE), which he set about staffing with highly qualified personnel. As chief, he issued some 200 articles, addresses and monographs as well as 50 circulars and bulletins that served as the cornerstone of professional forestry in America.

Fernow started the first four-year forestry school in the United States, at Cornell, in 1898, and in Canada, at the University of Toronto, 1907. He taught and lectured at these and other institutions, was instrumental in establishing the Adirondack Forest Preserve and the New York Forest Commission, and drafted much model forestry legislation. Founder and editor of *Forest Quarterly* (1902), Fernow wrote three standard forestry texts: *The Economics of Forestry* (1902), *A Brief History of Forestry* (1907) and *The Care of Trees in Lawn, Street, and Park* (1910).

Further reading: Charles E. Randall, "Fernow, the Man Who Brought Forestry to America," *American Forests* 70 (April 1964): 14–16, 44, 46.

Finklea, John Furman (August 27, 1933–   )

A native of Florence, South Carolina, Dr. John Finklea specializes in research on occupational health, with emphasis on the epidemiology of chronic diseases, and on the health effects of air pollutants and pesticides. The author of numerous articles on preventive medicine and the environment, Finklea was educated at Davidson College and at the Medical College of South Carolina, from which he received his M.D. in 1958. He received a doctorate in public health from the University of Michigan in 1966 and has served as an associate in medicine at the School of Medicine, Northwestern University, from 1966 to 1967 and as associate professor of pediatrics and preventive medicine at the Medical College of South Carolina from 1966 to 1969.

Finklea was chief of the ecological research branch of the division of health effects research for the National Air Pollution Control Administration from 1969 to 1971 and was promoted to director of the division of health effects research. In 1971, he became director of environmental health of the ENVIRONMENTAL PROTECTION AGENCY's National Environmental Research Center, serving in this capacity until 1975, when he became director of health research at the National Institute of Occupational Safety and Health. Finklea left the institute in 1978 to accept an appointment as professor of public health at the University of Alabama, Birmingham, his present position.

John Finklea has served on many environmentally related committees, boards and official bodies, including the National Center for Health Statistics Advisory Board, the National Air Quality Advisory Committee, the Advisory Committee of the National Academy of Sciences' Atomic Bomb Casualty Commission and the Committee on Hearing, Bioacoustics and Biomechanics. He has served as consultant and scientific advisor to the Environmental Health Program and as a member of the advisory committee on the conservation of energy for the Federal Power Commission's National Power Survey in 1974.

Fischer, Michael Ludwig (May 29, 1940–   )

Executive director of the SIERRA CLUB since 1987, Michael Ludwig was born in Dubuque, Iowa, and was educated at the University of Santa Clara, from which he received a B.A. in political science in 1964; the University of California, Berkeley, from which he earned a master's degree in city and regional planning in 1967; and Harvard University, where he did graduate work in environmental management during 1980.

Most of Fischer's professional career has involved work in urban and regional planning. From 1960 to 1965, he was a planner with the city of Mountain View, California; from 1967 to 1969, he worked for San Mateo County; from 1969 to 1973, he served as associate director of the San Francisco Planning and Urban Research Association; and from 1973 to 1976, he was executive director of the North Central Region of the California Coastal Zone Conservation Commission. Fischer became chief deputy director of the Governor's Office of Planning and Research in 1976, then left in 1978 to take a position as executive director of the California Coastal Commission. He served in this capacity until 1985, when he became senior associate with Sedway Cooke Associates, environmental consultants. In 1987, he left this position to take up the directorship of the Sierra Club.

Fischer is coauthor of the California state plan, *An Urban Strategy for California*, published in 1978.

FishAmerica Foundation (Founded: 1983)
% Sport Fishing Institute, 1010 Massachusetts
Avenue NW, Suite 320, Washington, D.C. 20001;
(202) 898-0869

An organization that offers funding for angling and
conservation group projects and other local initiatives
to protect and enhance North American water and
fishery resources, FishAmerica Foundation has financed over 208 projects in 39 states and seven
Canadian provinces. Among the efforts the foundation has supported are the development of fish
spawning beds and hatcheries, fish stocking, fish egg
plantings and the implementation of water aeration
and weed control measures. In addition, FishAmerica
Foundation promotes public awareness of fishing
and water conservation issues and has helped un-
derwrite acid rain education campaigns and acidic
water reclamation programs. From its office in Washington, D.C., the organization publishes *FishAmerica
Forum* three times a year.

Fish and Wildlife Service, U.S. (Established
[as the Bureau of Fisheries]: 1871)
Department of the Interior, Washington, D.C.
20240; (202) 208-5634

First created as an independent agency, the Bureau
of Fisheries was subsequently placed in the Department of Commerce. In 1885, the Bureau of BIOLOGI-
CAL SURVEY was created as part of the Department of
AGRICULTURE, and in 1939, both bureaus were transferred to the U.S. Department of the INTERIOR. The
following year, the two bureaus were combined within
the department and redesignated as the U.S. Fish
and Wildlife Service. The service was again reorganized in 1956 pursuant to the Fish and Wildlife Act
of that year, but the name remained unchanged.
The 1956 act established two bureaus as constituting
the service, the Bureau of Commercial Fisheries and
the Bureau of Sport Fisheries and Wildlife. In 1970,
the Bureau of Commercial Fisheries was transferred
to the Department of Commerce. The Bureau of Sport
Fisheries and Wildlife, which remained in Interior,
was renamed the U.S. Fish and Wildlife Service in
1974.

The service is charged with conserving and managing the nation's wildlife resources, including migratory birds, endangered species and some marine
mammals. It administers inland sport fisheries and
certain fishery and wildlife research activities. The
service assists in the development of an environmental stewardship ethic for American society based on
ecological principles, scientific knowledge of wildlife
and a sense of moral responsibility. It works cooperatively with the states to improve conservation and

management of fish and wildlife resources, and it
administers a national program of public education.

The U.S. Fish and Wildlife Service provides leadership for the protection and improvement of land
and water environments—habitat preservation—and
carries out such activities as biological monitoring;
surveillance of pesticides, heavy metals and other
environmental pollutants; studying fish and wildlife
populations; studying the ecology of given areas; and
assessing the environmental impact of hydroelectric
dams, nuclear power facilities, stream channeliza-
tion, dredge-and-fill permits and the like. The service
also provides review of environmental impact statements generated by various federal agencies.

A high priority of the service is improving and
maintaining fish and wildlife resources through management of migratory birds and other wildlife. This
includes working to meet public demand for recreational fishing while maintaining fisheries at a sustainable level that will ensure future survival. Programs
in fulfillment of this aspect of the service's mission
include managing wildlife refuges; law enforcement;
such research as bird banding, production and harvest studies; surveying wildlife breeding, migrating
and wintering patterns; and carrying out disease
studies.

The Fish and Wildlife Service maintains cooperative fish and wildlife research units located at universities to conduct research and to supervise graduate
study. It maintains or supervises hatcheries in many
states and on Indian lands. The service also provides
national and international leadership in identifying,
protecting and restoring endangered species of fish,
wildlife and plants. It developed an Endangered and
Threatened Species List, and it works with states and
other nations to prepare recovery plans and to enforce laws designed to protect endangered species.
The Fish and Wildlife Service is responsible for enforcing regulations concerning importation of endangered species.

The service conducts various public education programs and publishes numerous brochures and leaflets. It administers federal aid programs to help fund
projects designed to develop, conserve and enhance
fish and wildlife resources.

Flader, Susan L. (April 29, 1941–   )
A native of Sheboygan, Wisconsin, Susan L. Flader
is an environmental educator and student of the
history of environmental studies. Her principal publications have been devoted to the life and work of
the great pioneering environmentalist ALDO LEOPOLD.

Flader was educated at the University of Wisconsin, Madison, and Stanford University, from which
she received her Ph.D. in history and humanities in

1971. She has served as instructor in environmental studies and a fellow of the Institute for Research in the Humanities at the University of Wisconsin (1970–71), and as a lecturer, then visiting assistant professor at the Institute for Environmental Studies (1970–71). In 1973, she was appointed assistant professor of history at the University of Missouri, Columbia, was promoted to associate professor in 1975, and is now full professor.

Flader's publications include *The Sand Country of Aldo Leopold* (with Charles Steinbacker, 1973); *Thinking Like a Mountain: Aldo Leopold and the Evolution of an Ecological Attitude toward Deer, Wolves, and Forests* (1974) and many articles and reviews in professional journals. With J. Baird Callicott, Flader edited a collection of Leopold's essays under the title *The River of the Mother of God and Other Essays* (1991), which was widely reviewed in the professional as well as popular press.

Flader's honors include the Frederick K. Weyerhaeuser Award (1973), the University of Missouri's Curators' Publication Award (1974) and the Theodore C. Blegen Award (1974).

Florio, James Joseph (August 29, 1937–)

New Jersey's controversial governor (elected 1989) was born in Brooklyn, New York, and, while a congressman from New Jersey's First District, served as chairman of the Energy and Commerce subcommittee that produced the so-called Superfund legislation.

Officially called the Hazardous Substances Response Trust Fund, "Superfund" is part of the Comprehensive Environmental Response, Compensation and Liability Act (CERCLA) of 1980. The Superfund, administered by the ENVIRONMENTAL PROTECTION AGENCY, finances the clean-up of the nation's most critical hazardous waste sites.

Florio, a high school drop-out and onetime boxer, enlisted in the U.S. Navy during the Korean War. He went on to earn his bachelor's degree (Trenton State College, 1962), also attended Columbia University and received his law degree from Rutgers University in 1967. A practicing attorney from 1967 to 1974, Florio served in the New Jersey General Assembly (1970–74) and then as U.S. representative (1974–90).

Narrowly defeated in the New Jersey gubernatorial race of 1985, Florio won election as governor in 1989 by a wide margin, in large part bolstered by his environmental record. Running on an uncompromising reform platform and committed to balancing his state's budget, Florio provoked controversy and even outrage by raising state income and sales taxes almost immediately after taking office.

Food and Agriculture Organization of the United Nations (Established: 1946)

c/o Dr. J. A. Phelan, International Dairy Development Programme, Via delle Terme di Caracalla, I-00100 Rome, Italy; (6) 57971

With 157 member nations and a staff of 6,000, the Food and Agriculture Organization of the United Nations works to raise nutritional levels and living standards of people worldwide through improvements in food and agricultural production and distribution. The organization also promotes the sustainable development of forests and conducts reforestation programs. The organization formulates international policy concerning world trade in food and agricultural commodities and legislation on genetic resources, food standards and the environment.

FAO maintains a vast library of 1 million volumes and important computer databases, including AGRIS (International Information System for the Agricultural Sciences and Technology), CARIS (Current Agricultural Research Information System), ICS (Interlinked Computer Storage and Data Processing System of Food and Agricultural Commodity Data), ASFIS (Aquatic Sciences and Fisheries Information Systems), FISHDAB (Fisheries Data Base) and FORIS (Forest Resources Information System).

The organization encompasses various production and conservation committees and publishes a variety of annuals and bulletins, including *Animal Health Yearbook*, *Ceres* (a bimonthly), *Commodity Review and Outlook*, *Environment and Energy Bulletin*, *FAO Plant Protection Yearbook*, *Unasylva Forestry* and others.

The organization administers an annual budget of $574 million.

Food and Drug Administration (Established: 1907)

5600 Fishers Lane, Rockville, Maryland 20857; (301) 443-2894

Established on January 1, 1907, pursuant to the Food and Drug Act of 1906, the agency was given its present name under the Agriculture Appropriation Act of 1931. The FDA's activities are directed toward protecting the health of the nation against impure and unsafe food, drugs and cosmetics, as well as other potential hazards. From the environmental point of view, the FDA's most important division is the National Center for Toxicological Research, which conducts research programs to study the biological effects of potentially toxic chemical substances found in the environment. Research concentrates on health effects of long-term, low-level exposure to chemical toxicants and the basic biological processes for such toxicants in animal organisms. The center works to develop improved methodologies and test protocols for evaluating the safety of toxicants.

Foreman, Dave (October 18, 1946–   )
Founder of the radical environmental group EARTH FIRST! Dave Foreman has been widely criticized for his unorthodox actions against nuclear power plants, logging companies and other industries. In the summer of 1991, he stood trial for conspiring to sabotage three nuclear plants in Arizona, California and Colorado.

The author of *Confessions of an Eco-Warrior* (1991) and *Ecodefense: A Field Guide to Monkeywrenching* (1985), Foreman advocates the use of violence, when necessary, to protect the environment. The violent methods he subscribes to include tree spiking, which destroys the power equipment loggers use (and, according to logging industry officials as well as some environmentalists, is potentially fatal to the logger or sawmill operator who hits a spike in a tree), and the destruction of offending highways and dams. When Foreman stood in the path of a construction truck driving through Siskiyou National Forest in Oregon, he was knocked to the ground and dragged under the truck for 100 yards, sustaining serious injury.

Despite his willingness to employ violent means, Foreman insists, however, that Earth First! is essentially confrontational rather than violent. After his arrest in 1989, he disassociated himself from the organization because he claimed it had begun attracting people interested in opposing authority rather than protecting the environment, and that the organization was drifting away from environmental protection to other left-wing social causes.

Born in Albuquerque, Foreman graduated from the University of New Mexico and taught school on a Zuni Indian reservation in New Mexico. From 1973 to 1982, he worked for the WILDERNESS SOCIETY as Southwest representative and as lobbying coordinator. A 1979 U.S. FOREST SERVICE decision to allow mining, timbering and tourism on 47 million acres under its control turned Foreman away from lobbying and toward confrontation as a solution to environmental problems. Foreman and four friends went to the desert in Mexico, where they consoled each other over the loss of the wilderness acreage and talked about *The Monkeywrench Gang,* a book by Edward ABBEY that describes the actions of ''ecoteurs'' (pro-environment saboteurs) in the Southwest. It was then that the five decided to form Earth First! as an organization that would make the goals of other environmental groups seem tame. Their first action was to unfurl a 100-yard-long black plastic streamer down the face of Glen Canyon Dam to simulate the appearance of a huge crack.

In a 1990 article for *Mother Jones,* Foreman wrote that he had ''hung up [his] pearl-handled wrenches for good.'' But he went on to provide advice to other would-be monkeywrenchers. Among the 13 points he outlined were recommendations to work alone or with one or two trusted partners only, to avoid affiliation with environmental groups, to camouflage vehicles with American flags and NRA stickers and to hide all copies of *Ecodefense.*

Today, Foreman is chairman of the Wildlands Project, which is developing a comprehensive wilderness recovery plan for North America. He also operates Books of the Big Outside, a mail-order environmental book sales business, and he is executive editor of *Wild Earth* magazine. Foreman is also active as an author on environmental subjects.

Forest Service, U.S. (Established: 1905)
Public Affairs Office, Forest Service, Department of Agriculture, P.O. Box 96090, Washington, D.C. 20090-6090; (202) 447-3760

The U.S. Forest Service was created by the Transfer Act of February 1, 1905, which transferred federal forest reserves and the responsibility for their management from the U.S. Department of the INTERIOR to the U.S. Department of AGRICULTURE. The forest reserves themselves were established from public domain lands by presidential order under authority of the Creative Act of March 3, 1891. Since then, a series of acts have regulated management, use and additional purchase of lands.

The mission of the Forest Service is to supply national leadership in forestry and to provide a continuing flow of natural resource goods and services to meet the needs of the nation and to contribute to the needs of the international community. Specific Forest Service objectives include promoting the sustained flow of renewable resources, such as outdoor recreation, forage, wood, water, wilderness, wildlife and fish, in a combination that best meets the present and future needs of society; administering nonrenewable resources to help meet the nation's needs for energy and mineral resources; promoting a healthy and productive environment for the nation's forests and rangelands; developing science and technology to advance the management and protection of natural resources; and generally furthering the conservation of natural resources through programs of cooperation with other federal as well as state and local agencies.

The U.S. Forest Service manages the National Forest System, consisting of 156 national forests, 19 national grasslands and 15 land utilization projects under principles of multiple use and sustained yield. The service attempts to balance the need for such commodities as wood and paper products with the need for recreation, natural beauty, wildlife habitat, livestock forage and water supplies. The service works to protect lands under its jurisdiction from fire, disease, insect pests and pollution. National forests provide refuge for endangered species of birds, animals and fish.

The Forest Service maintains extensive cooperative programs with states, local agencies and private industry. In cooperation with state agricultural colleges, the service carries out programs of forest research throughout the nation. The service operates human resource programs in forestry, including Volunteers in the National Forests. In cooperation with the U.S. Department of Labor, the Forest Service takes part in Job Corps and Senior Community Service Employment Program projects that provide training and meaningful outdoor experiences for participants while accomplishing significant conservation work.

In addition to its Washington, D.C., headquarters, the U.S. Forest Service maintains nine major regional field offices and nine experiment stations nationwide.

Forrester, Jay W. (July 14, 1918–)

Currently Germeshausen Professor of Management at Massachusetts Institute of Technology, Jay W. Forrester, a native of Climax, Nebraska, is the author of *World Dynamics* (1971), which, in turn, became the basis of Dennis and Donella Meadows's *The Limits of Growth* (1972). A popular application of Forrester's theory of nonrenewable resources, *The Limits of Growth* sold more than 1 million copies in 20 languages. The Meadowses used Forrester's computer models to develop forecasts for the depletion of natural resources, the decrease in food supply, booms in population and the increase in pollution. Both Forrester's and the Meadowses' works were financed in part by the Club of Rome, an international group of businessmen who had undertaken an ambitious "Project on the Predicament of Mankind."

Many of the projections made in *World Dynamics* and *The Limits of Growth* have failed to be realized. The Meadowses predicted that the world's supply of gold would be depleted by 1981, mercury by 1985, tin by 1987, zinc by 1990, petroleum by 1992 and copper, lead and natural gas by 1993. Yet in 1990, the Bureau of MINES estimated that there was enough mercury, tin and zinc in reserve to last at least 20 years, and that there was enough copper to last more than 40. In addition, new estimates of petroleum reserves predict the supply will last 50 years.

Forrester claimed that population growth was so rapid that only famine or a pollution crisis could bring it under control. He was criticized, however, for failing to take into account demographers' findings that population growth had peaked in the 1960s and their assertion that, by 2090, the world's population would be 10 billion, a level they claimed was manageable. Forrester estimated that, in 1970, the world's population density was 69 people per square mile, and that this overcrowding served as a limiting factor in economic growth. In 1989, the population densities in many countries were far higher than Forrester's estimates, with an average of 97 people per square mile. Forrester's critics argued that overcrowding in such countries as the Netherlands (with 1,123 people per square mile), West Germany (with 637 people per square mile) and Japan (with 937 people per square mile) had hardly damaged the economies of those nations. In contrast, it is the poorest countries that usually have the lowest population densities. Forrester's predictions of worldwide food shortages have also failed to come true. During the 1970s and 1980s, food output consistently exceeded demand, according to a report by the WORLD RESOURCES INSTITUTE.

In *World Dynamics*, Forrester focused on "the dynamics of social systems." He attempted to show through computer analysis "how the behavior of world systems results from mutual interplay between its demographic, industrial, and agricultural subsystems." His 1969 work, *Urban Dynamics*, used similar computer modeling techniques to examine the current and future conditions of cities. His other books include *Industrial Dynamics* (1961) and *Principles of Systems* (1968).

Frampton, George Thomas, Jr. (August 24, 1944–)

President of the WILDERNESS SOCIETY since January 1986, George Thomas Frampton Jr. practiced law in his native Washington, D.C., and worked as a fellow with the Center for Law and Social Policy and as an assistant special prosecutor on the Watergate Special Prosecution Force. From 1978 to 1979, he was deputy director of the Nuclear Regulatory Commission's Special Inquiry Group, which investigated the Three Mile Island nuclear accident. Frampton holds degrees from Yale University, the London School of Economics and Harvard Law School.

Franklin, Jerry Forest (October 27, 1936–)

Since 1986 Bloedell Professor of Ecosystems Analysis in the College of Forest Resources, University of Washington, and since 1975 chief plant ecologist,

U.S. FOREST SERVICE Pacific Northwest Research Station, Jerry F. Franklin chairs the Long-Term Ecological Research (LTER) Coordinating Committee of the National Science Foundation.

LTER is a coordinated network of 17 research projects nationwide devoted to studying long-term ecological phenomena, including, for example, gradual changes associated with community succession, soil development and populations of large vertebrates as well as the ecological effects of phenomena that occur rarely or episodically, such as floods, hurricanes, wildfires, volcanic eruptions and the reproduction of long-lived plant species. Long-term studies are essential to the formulation and testing of ecological theories inasmuch as long-term phenomena play a central role in ecological science. The LTER program is particularly important because of the inherent difficulty of conducting vital long-term studies: They require years of continuous financial support and leadership.

Born in Walport, Oregon, Franklin received a B.S. degree in 1959 and an M.S. in 1961 from Oregon State University. He earned a Ph.D. in botany from Washington State University in 1966. With the U.S. Forest Service, Franklin served as research forester from 1959 to 1965, plant ecologist from 1965 to 1968, principal plant ecologist from 1968 to 1973 and deputy director of the coniferous forest biome from 1970 to 1973. In 1973, Franklin became the director of the ecosystem analytical program of the National Science Foundation, serving in that capacity until 1975. He was appointed professor of forest science and botany at Oregon State University in 1976 and served until 1990.

Franklin is a member of the board of governors of the NATURE CONSERVANCY, a nature lecturer for Sigma Xi, and was a Bullard Fellow at Harvard University in 1986. His research specialties include the structure and function of forest ecosystems, forest community ecology and succession, alpine communities and vegetation-soil relationships, especially Abies-Tsuga forest types.

Franklin has been honored with the Arthur S. Fleming Award (1972) and the Barrington Moore Award of the Society of American Foresters (1987).

Freeman, S(imon) David (January 14, 1926–   )

This native of Chattanooga, Tennessee, combined a background in law and engineering to create a nationally significant career in energy policy formulation and administration. Freeman was educated at the Georgia Institute of Technology, receiving his B.A. in engineering in 1948. In 1956, he took a law degree at the University of Tennessee, graduating first in his class.

From 1954 to 1961, Freeman was staff engineer and staff attorney with the TENNESSEE VALLEY AUTHORITY in Knoxville. He left this position in 1961 to serve as assistant to the chairman of the Federal Power Commission in Washington, D.C., then entered private law practice from 1965 to 1967. In 1967, he was appointed energy policy staff director of the Office of Science and Technology in the White House. In this position he coordinated energy matters on a government-wide basis, helping to prepare the president's first national energy message in 1971. He participated in the creation of the ENVIRONMENTAL PROTECTION AGENCY as a separate agency in 1971.

After serving as visiting professor at the University of Pittsburgh (1971–72), Freeman joined the Ford Foundation Energy Policy Project, working to develop a research agenda and recruiting and directing a staff for a major study of United States energy options. This work produced A Time to Choose, a document focusing on energy conservation as a significant source of supply to fuel a growing economy. In 1974, Freeman published Energy: The New Era, which explained how energy conservation measures and the development of renewable energy sources could help move the nation to a more secure future.

From 1974 to 1976, Freeman was a staff member of the Senate Commerce Committee, responsible for advising committee members and other senators on energy legislation. Freeman participated in the enactment of such energy conservation legislation as the Automobile Fuel Economy Act. In 1976, he moved to the White House as a member of the Energy Staff, assisting in the preparation of President Jimmy CARTER's first energy plan, which emphasized a strategy of conservation.

Freeman assumed the leadership of the TVA in 1977, becoming widely known for aggressively promoting energy conservation and environmentally sensitive practices. He left this post in 1984 to become a private consultant in Seattle, Washington, and is currently general manager of the Lower Colorado River Authority, a position he took in 1986. He is responsible for the sale of electricity in central Texas and for water resources and flood control in the area.

Friends of the Earth (Founded: 1972)

218 D Street SE, Washington, D.C. 20003; (202) 544-2600, Fax (202) 543-4710

With programs of research, independent monitoring, public education and litigation, Friends of the Earth seeks to help stop environmental damage from pollution and other destructive human practices, restore the integrity of hurt and threatened ecosystems and establish national and international guidelines for the future preservation and wise stewardship of the world's natural resources. Affiliated with FRIENDS OF THE EARTH INTERNATIONAL, this Washington, D.C.-based organization lobbies for protective legislation and advocates environmentally responsible policies for a wide range of resource issues, including ozone emissions, tropical deforestation, air and water contamination, solid and hazardous waste disposal, nuclear power and weapons production, coal mining operations, toxic chemicals manufacture and handling, agricultural erosion, marine and wilderness development, species endangerment and biotechnology. The organization urges the redirection of federal funding from ecologically hazardous activities to cleanup and resource conservation programs, promotes corporate accountability for environmental impact and exerts pressure on federal agencies and local officials to enforce existing regulations.

Working with sister groups overseas and with other activist organizations, Friends of the Earth supports the creation of international agreements safeguarding the global environment and pushes for the reform of world investment policies, encouraging financial institutions to use lending practices and other economic incentives to inhibit destructive resource exploitation and foster sustainable, renewable enterprises instead. The group publishes fact sheets, research reports, bibliographies and the quarterly ozone-related newsletter *Atmospheres*.

Friends of the Earth International (Founded: 1971)
Postbus 19199, NL-1000 GD Amsterdam, Netherlands; (31) 20 6221369

Friends of the Earth International acts as a federation for 51 national groups—including, in the U.S., FRIENDS OF THE EARTH—dedicated to the protection, restoration and responsible management of world resources. Based in Amsterdam, the Netherlands, the organization conducts and coordinates international campaigns to restrict air and marine pollution, preserve rivers and watersheds, halt the destruction of tropical rainforests and deter global warming. The federation maintains access to a computerized network of environmental information, publishes the English-language monthly *FoE Link* and holds an annual meeting for representatives of member groups. Friends of the Earth International is an affiliate of the INTERNATIONAL UNION FOR CONSERVATION OF NATURE AND NATURAL RESOURCES.

Friends of the Everglades (Founded: 1969)
101 Westward Drive, No. 2, Miami Springs, Florida 33166; (305) 888-1230

With a budget under $25,000 and 5,000 members, the Friends of the Everglades is a grass-roots organization dedicated to fostering and facilitating "through education a harmonious coexistence between human and natural environmental systems as best exemplified by the unique Florida Everglades." The group works to protect and preserve the Everglades, much of which has been drained for agricultural use and residential development. The organization combats the effects of overpopulation, speculation, development, waste and pollution and seeks to enforce stricter adherence to state and federal environmental laws governing the region.

The Friends of the Everglades operates the Environmental Information Service to facilitate communication among various environmental organizations, government agencies and the public. The group also supports environmental education programs in Dade County, Florida; maintains a speakers' bureau; and publishes *EIS Newsletter*, *Environet* and *Everglades Reporter*. In addition, the organization produces the *Florida Evironet Directory*, the *Toxic Substances Report* (an annual) and such miscellaneous publications as *The Dade County Environmental Story*, Conference Proceedings, *Who Knows the Rain?*, *Lake Okeechobee: A Lake in Peril*, *The Nature of Dade County—A Hometown Handbook*, various occasional reports and a resource book for teachers.

Nancy Carroll Brown is president of the organization.

Friends of the River, Inc. (Founded: 1975)
Fort Mason Center, Building C, San Francisco, California 94123; (415) 771-0400

This activist organization engages in lobbying, litigation and other advocacy actions on behalf of the designation and protection of wild rivers. The group was originally formed to oppose construction of the New Melones Dam on California's Stanislaus River, and since then has expanded its mission to protecting rivers throughout the nation—though the focus of most of its activity remains in California.

As an activist group, Friends of the River has on occasion engaged in civil disobedience.

Richard Roos-Collins serves as chairman of the board of Friends of the River, and David Bolling is executive director.

Fritsch, Albert Joseph (September 30, 1933–   )
Born in the small town of Maysville, Kentucky, Albert Fritsch combines the career of environmental

scientist—specializing in alternative energy sources and the conservation of energy resources—with the calling of a Jesuit priest.

Educated at Xavier University in Cincinnati (B.S., 1955; M.S., 1956), he also attended West Baden College (1959–61) and received his Ph.D. from Fordham University in 1964. Fritsch did postdoctoral work at Loyola University of Chicago. Entering the Society of Jesus (Jesuits) in 1956, he was ordained a Roman Catholic priest in 1967. He was a research fellow in chemistry at the University of Texas, Austin (1969–70), and technical consultant to the Center for the Study of Responsive Law, Washington, D.C. (1970–71). In 1972, he became cofounder, in Washington, D.C., of the Center for Science and Public Interest, where he served as director until 1977. In that year, he became executive director of Appalachia-Science in the Public Interest, a nonprofit organization dedicated to making science and technology responsive to the needs of the poor.

Since 1974, Fritsch has served as president of the Technical Information Project; since 1978, he has been president of the Appalachian Coalition; since 1980, he has been president of Sun-Rep, a solar energy organization. In 1980, he also became president of the board of directors of the Solar Lobby. An advocate of alternative energy sources, Fritsch is a formidable opponent of the oil industry.

Albert Fritsch is a prolific writer on environmental subjects. His *A Theology of the Earth* appeared in 1972. Also in that year, he published *Gasoline*, and the following year, *Big Oil: A Citizen's Factbook* (with John W. Egan). Other works include: *How Aerosol Sprays Can Affect Your Safety and Health* (1973; with Barbara Hogan and Susan Guhl), *Asbestos and You* (1973, 1975; with Barry I. Castleman), *The Contrasumers: A Citizen's Guide to Resource Conservation* (1974; with Castleman), *Lifestyle Index* (1974), *Major Oil: What Citizens Should Know About the Eight Major Oil Companies* (1974; with Ralph Gitomer), *Shale Oil: An Environmental Critique* (editor, 1974), *Energy and Food: Energy Used in Production, Processing, Delivery, and Marketing of Selected Food Items* (1975, 1977; with Linda W. Dujack et al), *A Citizen's Oil Factbook: What Every Citizen Should Know About the Eighteen Largest Oil Companies* (editor, 1975), *Solar Energy: One Way to Citizen Control* (editor, 1976), *Ninety-nine Ways to a Simple Lifestyle* (coeditor, 1977), *Strip Mine Blasting* (1977; with Dennis Darcy et al), *Harlan County Flood Reporter* (1978; with Jerome Nardt), *Citizen's Blasting Handbook* (1978; with Mark Morgan), *Citizen's Coal Haul Handbook* (1978; with John Clemens and Francis Kazemek), *Toxic Substances and Trade Secrecy* (1978), *The Household Pollutants Guide* (coeditor, 1978), *Environmental Ethics* (1979; with Elaine Burns et al), *Citizen's Resource Handbook* (1979; with Robert Schemel), *Toxic Substances: Decisions and Values* (1979–80), *Environmental Ethics: Choices for Concerned Citizens* (1980; with Gerald McMahon et al) and *Green Space* (1982).

Frome, Michael (May 25, 1920–   )

Born in New York City, Michael Frome became a newspaper writer and public relations person before he began his career as a free-lance writer in 1958. At first he concentrated on tourist-related articles, but later turned to works on the natural environment. His articles began appearing in *American Forests* and *Field and Stream* in 1967 and 1968. He wrote a weekly column entitled "Environmental Trails" for the *Los Angeles Times*, and in 1983, he was named environmental editor of *Western Outdoors*.

Frome also became a teacher, accepting a position as visiting professor of environmental studies at the Pinchot Institute for Conservation Studies in 1978. Between 1982 and 1984, he was visiting associate professor at the College of Forestry of the University of Idaho.

As a leading critic of natural environmental policies, both on the private and public levels, Frome has written several book-length studies, including *Whose Woods These Are: The Story of the National Forests* (1962), *Strangers in High Places: The Story of the Great Smoky Mountains* (1966), *The Forest Service* (1972), *Battle for the Wilderness* (1974), *The National Parks* (1977 and 1979) and *Promised Land* (1986). He is also the author of Rand-McNally's *Park Guide* (1972).

In 1986 Frome was awarded the NATIONAL PARKS AND CONSERVATION ASSOCIATION's Marjory Stoneman Douglas Award for his commitment to environmental preservation.

Fuller, Kathryn S. (July 8, 1946–   )

Kathryn S. Fuller has been president of the WORLD WILDLIFE FUND since 1989, succeeding William K. REILLY, who was appointed head of the ENVIRONMENTAL PROTECTION AGENCY by President George Bush. The organization Fuller heads studies environmental trends, arbitrates disputes over environmental issues, protects wildlife habitats and supports activities aimed at biodiversity, sustainable development and control of air pollution and toxic substances. The organization was created in 1985 when the World Wildlife Fund and the Conservation Foundation merged.

Fuller worked as a trial lawyer and as chief of the Wildlife and Marine Resources section of the Justice Department before joining the staff of the World Wildlife Fund in 1982 as director of public policy and general counsel.

Kathryn S. Fuller, president of World Wildlife Fund. *Photo by Sam Kittner, Courtesy of World Wildlife Fund*

Fuller, R(ichard) Buckminster (Jr.) (July 12, 1895–July 1, 1983)

R. Buckminster Fuller is best known as the inventor of the geodesic dome, an elegant, multipurpose structural design that was patented in 1953. More than an engineer and inventor, however, Fuller was a popular philosopher, whose enthusiasm reached an eager and fascinated public, including many environmentalists. Fuller's philosophy of engineering and design stressed such ecologically sound principles as appropriate technology, synergistic relationships and the use of renewable resources. He coined the phrase "Spaceship Earth" to suggest the need for a technology on this planet that both is self-contained and avoids waste. Fuller did much to demonstrate how the ideals of environmentalism could be applied in an immediate, practical and yet visionary manner.

Born in Milton, Massachusetts, Fuller attended Harvard University from 1913 to 1914, when he was expelled. He reentered the university and was expelled a second and final time in 1915. He attended the U.S. Naval Academy briefly in 1917. Largely self-educated, Fuller worked at a variety of jobs between 1914 and 1922, ranging from apprentice machine fitter to sales manager for a truck company. In 1922, he became president of Stockade Building System, where he began to develop prefabricated building systems. In 1927, he founded 4-D Co. in Chicago, serving as its president until 1932. In that year he founded the Dymaxion Corporation in Bridgeport, Connecticut, where he developed the visionary prefabricated Dymaxion House, the Dymaxion Car and even the Dymaxion Bathroom. Public acceptance of these innovations was slow in coming, however, but the unveiling of the first geodesic dome in 1947 did win instant acclaim and attention.

Fuller developed his ideas in a large number of books and articles, many of which describe a technological utopia of an "utterly classless, raceless, omnicooperative, omniworld humanity."

In addition to his writing, lecturing and engineering work, Fuller served as an officer of, or consultant to, a bewildering array of corporations and government agencies. From 1956 until his death in 1983, he taught at Southern Illinois University in Carbondale, Illinois, beginning his career there as research professor and achieving the rank of professor emeritus. He was a visiting professor at many institutions, and, most notably, from 1961 to 1962, served as Charles Eliot Norton Professor of Poetry at Harvard University, the institution that had twice expelled him as a student.

Fuller was U.S. representative to the American-Russian Protocol Exchange in the U.S.S.R. in 1959.

Further reading: Fuller, *Critical Path* (New York: St. Martin's, 1981); *Operating Manual for Spaceship Earth* (Carbondale: Southern Illinois University Press, 1969); *Synergetics: Explorations in the Geometry of Thinking* (New York: Macmillan, 1975).

G

Gannett, Henry (August 24, 1846–November 5, 1914)

Henry Gannett, a native of Bath, Maine, joined the U. S. Department of the INTERIOR in 1872 as a topographer on geographical surveys in the West, and in 1882, he was appointed chief geographer for the department. He was named chairman of the newly established U. S. Geographic Board in 1890 and served in that capacity for the next 20 years.

Gannett was a founder of the NATIONAL GEOGRAPHIC SOCIETY, served as the society's first secretary, and was elected its president in 1910. He was also instrumental in founding the Geographical Society of America and was associate editor of the society's *Bulletin*. In 1897, he took on the job of mapping and classifying forest reserves for the U.S. Department of the Interior and later was appointed by President Theodore ROOSEVELT to oversee the first inventory of natural resources in the United States. The resulting report was published in three volumes in 1909. Gannett also wrote the *Manual of Topographic Methods* (1893, 1900, 1906), several geography books and statistical atlases.

Gates, David Murray (May 27, 1921–   )

Botanist and physicist David Murray Gates received his B.S., M.S. and Ph.D. in physics from the University of Michigan. He has served as a research physicist and associate professor at the University of Denver; as science director and liaison officer with the Office of Naval Reserves; as assistant chief of radio propagation, assistant chief of the upper atmosphere and space physics division and consultant to the director at the Physics Division of the National Bureau of Standards; and as professor of natural history at the University of Colorado, where he was also curator of ecology at the university's museum. Gates was professor of biology at Washington University and director of the Missouri Botanical Garden from 1965 to 1971. Since then, he has been a professor of botany at the University of Michigan and director of the university's biological station.

A native of Manhattan, Kansas, Gates has served on the boards of the National Academy of Science, the National Science Board, the WORLD WILDLIFE FUND and the Acid Rain Foundation. His research has focused on infrared spectroscopy of the upper atmosphere, geophysics, energy exchange in plants, transpiration, photosynthesis and the ecological effects of energy use.

Gates's books include *Biophysical Ecology* (1980) and *Energy and Ecology* (1985)—a study of the harmful effects of energy production and use on the environment. His work on energy has made him a leading figure in the "new" ecology, which emphasizes quantification of energy flow and ecological efficiency in nature.

Gauvin, Charles F. (April 27, 1956–   )

President and chief executive officer of Trout Unlimited, Charles F. Gauvin holds an A.B. degree from Brown University (1978) and a degree from the University of Pennsylvania (1985). The organization he heads has 70,000 members and is dedicated to the protection and conservation of trout and salmon and their habitats.

Before joining the staff of Trout Unlimited, Gauvin worked at Beveridge & Diamond, a Washington-based law firm specializing in environmental litigation (1986-91), and Pierce, Atwood, Scribner, Allen, Smith & Lancaster, where he worked in energy and corporate practice groups (1985-86). In 1982, he was a teaching assistant at Brown University, where he taught environmental studies, and from 1980 to 1982, he served as a legislative coordinator for the Rhode Island Statewide Planning Program, with responsibility for drafting legislation on water quality and hazardous waste management.

Geddes, Patrick (October 2, 1854–April 17, 1932)

A sociologist, biologist and educator, Sir Patrick Geddes developed an early interest in the relationship of animals and humans to their environment and became famous as the father of town planning. At the age of 20, this native of Ballater, Scotland, studied zoology under the great Victorian scientist Thomas H. Huxley and undertook a zoological expedition to Mexico. There he was stricken with temporary blindness, and during his gradual recovery, he became less empirically oriented and more theoretical and philosophical in his approach to science.

On his return to Scotland, he was appointed lecturer at Edinburgh University, where he made the revolutionary proposal of applying the concepts and principles of energy and biology to statistics and economics.

In 1888, Geddes was named part-time professor of botany at University College in Dundee, where he founded the Outlook Tower, a sociological laboratory, among other things devoted to town planning and regional surveys. In addition to teaching and conducting research, Geddes worked with the Edinburgh Social Union, an organization dedicated to improving conditions in the slums along Edinburgh's Royal Mile. In 1897, Geddes and his wife, Anna Morton, traveled to Cyprus, where he put to work many of his regional planning concepts by helping residents reclaim their arid farmlands and by starting rural industries.

From 1903 to 1904, Geddes conducted an epoch-making survey of Dunfermline, Scotland, for the Scottish trustees of Andrew Carnegie's $2.5-million gift to his birthplace. Although the trustees ultimately rejected Geddes's plan for the town, Geddes published the book at his own expense, and *Study in City Development* is now considered a seminal essay in urban planning theory.

Between 1914 and 1924, Geddes traveled to India and Palestine, making "diagnosis-and-treatment" surveys of 50 Indian urban areas and making city plans for the military governor of Jerusalem. In 1915, another Geddes classic was published, *Cities in Evolution*, followed by *Town Planning toward City Development* in 1918. These works introduced into the intellectual lexicon of urban planning such terms and concepts as "neotechnics," "biotechnics" and "megalopolis."

Further reading: Philip Boardman, *Patrick Geddes: Maker of the Future* (Chapel Hill: University of North Carolina Press, 1944); Philip Mairet, *Pioneer of Sociology: The Life and Letters of Patrick Geddes* (London: Lund-Humphries, 1957); Marshall Stalley (ed.), *Patrick Geddes: Spokesman for Man and the Environment* (New Brunswick, N.J.: Rutgers University Press, 1972).

Geological Survey, U.S. (Established: 1879)

Public Affairs Officer, U.S. Geological Survey, Department of the Interior, 119 National Center, Reston, Virginia 22092; (703) 648-4460

The U.S. Geological Survey was established under the auspices of the Department of the INTERIOR by act of March 3, 1879, providing for "the classification of the public lands and the examination of the geological structure, mineral resources, and products of the national domain." An act of October 2, 1888, additionally specified topographic mapping and chemical and physical research as elements of the survey's mission, and an act of September 5, 1962, authorized the survey to operate outside of the "national domain" to conduct work on global change.

The Geological Survey investigates and assesses land, water, energy and mineral resources. It investigates such natural hazards as earthquakes, volcanoes, landslides, floods and droughts, and it conducts the National Mapping Program. USGS activities include the preparation of maps and geographical and geological data; the collection and interpretation of data on energy and mineral resources; and the assessment of the quality, quantity and use of the nation's water resources. The USGS performs research to develop and improve the science and technology involved in carrying out its mission, and it publishes the results of its investigations, producing thousands of reports and new maps annually.

Gibbons, Euell (September 8, 1911–December 29, 1975)

A popular proponent of natural wild foods who gained considerable exposure on television and other media, Euell Gibbons published his first book in 1962, *Stalking the Wild Asparagus*, which developed from an interest in wild foods that began when he was a boy in Clarksville, Texas. Gibbons followed the success of his first book with many others, including *Stalking the Blue-Eyed Scallop* (1964), *Stalking the Healthful Herbs* (1966), *Beachcomber's Handbook* (1967), *Feast on a Diabetic Diet* (1969) and *Stalking the Good Life* (1971).

Gibbs, Lois Marie (June 25, 1951–   )

In the spring of 1978, when she was a 27-year-old homemaker in Niagara Falls, New York, Lois Gibbs learned that the school her children were attending had been constructed on top of a dump site containing more than 20,000 tons of hazardous chemicals. She immediately set out to create a grass-roots organization, which became known as the Love Canal Homeowners Association. Over the next two and a half years, members of the organization lobbied the federal government for help in moving their families away from the disastrously polluted Love Canal, demonstrating that the chemicals dumped in their community had caused higher than normal rates of cancer, birth defects, miscarriages and other health problems.

In October 1980, President Jimmy Carter issued an emergency declaration releasing aid to residents near the Love Canal who wished to relocate. But Gibbs's work did not end with this victory. She formed the CITIZENS CLEARINGHOUSE FOR HAZARDOUS WASTES to help communities organize against pollution hazards and polluters.

Gibbs speaks at conferences and seminars across the country and has appeared on hundreds of television and radio shows. She contributed an essay to *Crossroads: Environmental Priorities for the Future* (1989) and, in 1990, won the Goldman Environmental Prize.

In 1981, Gibbs told a *New York Times* reporter: "If there hadn't been trouble at Love Canal, I'd probably be in a homemakers' club now—not the League of Women Voters. . . . But now I have something people need, and I want to give it to them."

Further reading: Gibbs (as told to Murray Levine), *Love Canal: My Story* (New York: Grove Press, 1982); Adeline Levine, *Love Canal: Science, Politics, and People* (New York: Lexington Books, 1982).

Glascock, Hardin Roads, Jr. (November 7, 1921–   )

As chief executive officer of the SOCIETY OF AMERICAN FORESTERS and editor-in-chief of *Journal of Forestry* from 1966 to 1978, Hardin Roads Glascock Jr. oversaw a reorganization of the Society of American Foresters programs; the establishment of departments for science programs, resource policy and public affairs; the

Lois Marie Gibbs, executive director of Citizens Clearinghouse for Hazardous Wastes, is interviewed in action. *Photo by Robbin Lee Zeff, Citizens Clearinghouse for Hazardous Wastes*

expansion of educational programs; and the establishment of permanent headquarters in Bethesda, Maryland. He was instrumental in the development of a statement of principles entitled *Forest Policies* and approved by the SAF membership in 1967.

In 1972, Glascock participated in the founding of the Renewable Natural Resources Foundation and was elected chairman of the board. He has served as forestry advisor to the Food and Agriculture Organization of the United Nations and has written several articles on land-use policies and natural resources.

Gofman, John William (September 21, 1918–   )

Emeritus professor of medical physics at the Donner Laboratory of Medical Physics of the University of California, Berkeley, John William Gofman researched the health effects of exposure to radiation for the Atomic Energy Commission in the mid-1960s while working at the Lawrence Livermore Laboratory. Gofman and colleague Arthur Tamplin found that the standard of radiation exposure accepted at the time would cause 74,000 more deaths than were to be expected normally. The standard exposure deemed safe for the general public was 170 millirems of radiation per year from human sources, double the exposure humans normally received over a 30-year period from natural sources. The two researchers proposed lowering the standard drastically—to 17 millirems per year—but met with skepticism from other scientists and the Atomic Energy Commission. While the debate over acceptable limits and a study by the National Academy of Sciences were under way, the responsibility for setting acceptable standards of radiation exposure was taken away from the Atomic Energy Commission and assigned to the ENVIRONMENTAL PROTECTION AGENCY. Over the following several years, the EPA lowered the standard to 25 millirems per year.

In 1971, Gofman and Tamplin wrote *Poisoned Power: The Case Against Nuclear Power Plants,* alerting the public to the dangers of nuclear power—dangers that the government-controlled nuclear power industry was not willing to divulge. The book was directed at citizen groups who wished to learn more about nuclear power so that they could effectively combat the construction of plants in their communities. In 1981, the SIERRA CLUB published Gofman's *Radiation and Human Health,* which linked the hazards of low-level radiation exposure to cancer and provided risk ratios to project cancer incidence by dose amount and age. Ten years later, Gofman wrote *Radiation-Induced Cancer from Low-Dose Exposure: An Independent Analysis,* for the Committee for Nuclear Responsibility. Gofman argued that currently available data on the ef-

fects of radiation on human epidemiology was inadequate, that no safe level of exposure existed, that exposures over long periods of time offered no less risk of cancer than doses received in a short period of time and that the risk for young people was significantly higher than for older people. In addition, he asserted that approximately 400,000 people in Europe and the Soviet Union could be expected to die over the next several decades from radiation exposure caused by the Chernobyl nuclear accident.

Born in Cleveland, Ohio, Gofman received a Ph.D. in chemistry and an M.D. from the University of California. Before joining the staff of the Donner Laboratory, he was a professor and associate director of the Lawrence Radiation Laboratory and in 1963 was named director of biology and medicine there. He has been chairman of the Committee for Nuclear Responsibility since 1971.

Goldman Environmental Foundation
(Founded: 1989)
One Lombard Street, Suite 303, San Francisco, California 94111; (415) 788-9090

The Goldman Environmental Foundation was established in 1989 by the Richard and Rhoda Goldman Fund. The foundation awards annual monetary prizes of $60,000 each to "environmental heroes—one from each of six continental regions: North America; South/Central America; Europe; Asia; Africa; and Australia/Oceania." The prizes, which recognize sustained and important efforts to preserve or enhance the environment, are awarded primarily to private citizens active in grass-roots initiatives rather than scientists, academic professionals or government officials. Nominations are accepted from a network of environmental organizations, including the CENTER FOR MARINE CONSERVATION, CONSERVATION INTERNATIONAL, Environmental Liaison Centre International, ENVIRONMENTAL DEFENSE FUND, FRIENDS OF THE EARTH, International Rivers Network, INTERNATIONAL UNION FOR THE CONSERVATION OF NATURE AND NATURAL RESOURCES, NATIONAL AUDUBON SOCIETY, NATIONAL GEOGRAPHIC SOCIETY, NATIONAL WILDLIFE FEDERATION, NATURAL RESOURCES DEFENSE COUNCIL, NATURE CONSERVANCY, RAINFOREST ACTION NETWORK, SIERRA CLUB, WILDLIFE CONSERVATION INTERNATIONAL, WORLDWATCH INSTITUTE, WORLD RESOURCES INSTITUTE, WORLDWIDE FUND FOR NATURE and WORLD WILDLIFE FUND. A prize jury, which includes members of the foundation as well individuals active in environmental causes, evaluates and acts on the nominations.

Richard N. Goldman, president of the foundation, is chairman of a major insurance brokerage firm in

San Francisco and active with many environmental organizations. Rhoda H. Goldman, secretary-treasurer of the foundation, is a member of the board of directors of Levi Strauss Inc. and is active in numerous philanthropic and cultural organizations.

Gordon, John C. (June 10, 1939–   )

Born in Nampa, Idaho, John Gordon worked as a forestry instructor at Iowa State University from 1965 to 1966 before joining the staff of the U.S. FOREST SERVICE as a plant physiologist, a position he held until 1970. He then returned to teaching at Iowa State and, later, Oregon State University, where he headed the department of forestry. In 1983, he moved to Yale University to serve as dean of forestry and environmental studies.

From 1988 to 1989, Gordon chaired the Commission on Research and Resource Management in National Parks, a project that recommended an end to what Gordon called a "short-term 'brush-fire' approach to research funding and design." Since 1989, he has served as chairman of forestry research for the National Academy of Sciences. Gordon's research has focused on photosynthesis and translocation in trees, enzymes in woody plants and nitrogen fixation.

Gordon, Seth Edwin (April 2, 1890–June 22, 1983)

As one of the drafters of the Model Game Law of 1934, which established the standards of modern wildlife management, Seth Edwin Gordon was a crucial figure in the campaign to gain public acceptance of the need for game management. A native of Richfield, Pennsylvania, he joined the staff of the Pennsylvania Game Commission as a game protector in 1913. In 1915, he was named assistant secretary of the commission, and four years later was named secretary and chief game protector. In 1926, he moved to the IZAAK WALTON LEAGUE OF AMERICA, where he served as conservation director. Ten years later, he returned to state government, accepting the job of executive director of the Pennsylvania Game Commission in 1936.

As a private consultant from 1948 to 1951, Gordon worked for various state commissions, including the California Department of Fish and Game, which offered him a permanent position in 1951 as director.

Gordon served several conservation organizations as an officer or board member, including the American Game Association (president, 1931–34), the American Wildlife Institute (secretary, 1935), the North American Wildlife Foundation (trustee and vice-president, 1947–75) and the International Association of Fish and Wildlife Agencies (general counsel, 1963–83). He served on the Forest Research Advisory Committee to the U.S. Secretary of Agriculture (1952–62) and as a member of the President's Water Pollution Control Advisory Board to the Surgeon General of the United States (1958–61).

Gore, Albert, Jr. (March 31, 1948–   )

Elected a U.S. representative from 1976 to 1984 and Tennessee senator from 1984 until his 1992 election as vice-president of the United States, Albert Gore Jr. devoted much of his congressional career to environmental issues. In the House, Gore, a native of Washington, D.C., was instrumental in drafting the "Superfund" bill to clean up chemical spills and hazardous waste dumps, and he was a sponsor of the resolution creating Earth Day 1990. In addition, he worked to create the Interparliamentary Conference on the Global Environment and served as chairman of the conference. Gore also conducted congressional hearings on the greenhouse effect.

Among the environmental legislation Albert Gore Jr. has drafted are the World Environment Policy Act, which called for a five-year phase-out of chlorofluorocarbons, a ban on nonrecyclable packaging and reductions in greenhouse gas emissions and deforestation; a bill to encourage recycling and increase markets for recycled products; and a resolution to protect Antarctica from mining and minerals development and to preserve the continent as a global ecological commons. He also introduced a proposal to create a Nobel Prize for environmental protection. Gore recently secured passage of amendments to the Clean Air Act to ban hydrochlorofluorocarbons, to include carbon dioxide among the chemicals measured by the ENVIRONMENTAL PROTECTION AGENCY and to prohibit industries from purchasing land to use as "dead zones" around sources of pollution.

During his 1988 bid for the Democratic Party's presidential nomination, Gore raised America's consciousness of environmental issues. Seen by many as a Paul Revere of impending environmental catastrophe, Gore has argued that the environment is "becoming a matter of national security" and strongly criticized former President George Bush for inattention to environmental issues.

Further reading: Gore, *Earth in the Balance: Ecology and the Human Spirit* (Boston: Houghton, Mifflin, 1992).

Gorsuch, Anne McGill See BURFORD, ANNE MCGILL (GORSUCH).

Grassland Heritage Foundation (Founded [as the Tallgrass Prairie Foundation]: 1976)

P.O. Box 344, Shawnee Mission, Kansas 66201-0394; (913) 377-3326

This 1,500-member organization has set as its mission the fostering of appreciation for America's native grassland prairie. It works to increase understanding of the prairie and to purchase, lease or acquire tall-grass prairie for the public benefit, including recreation and scientific research. The foundation seeks to protect the tallgrass prairie from forces alien to the natural prairie environment or a grazing economy.

The foundation currently manages several prairie properties, including 395 acres at Malvern Reservoir, Kansas; the Prairie Center, a site for environmental study, near Kansas City; and 160 acres near Topeka. It is affiliated with the Tallgrass Prairie Alliance.

Grassland Heritage Foundation maintains a speakers' bureau and publishes a quarterly newsletter, *The Prairie Dog's Companion*. Philip S. Brown is the organization's president.

Graves, Henry Solon (May 3, 1871–March 7, 1951)

Graves, a native of Marietta, Ohio, met Gifford PIN-CHOT when both were students at Yale; Pinchot, a senior, advised freshman Graves to go to Germany to study forestry, and the two men subsequently formed a partnership as private consulting foresters and coauthored *The White Pine* (1896). Appointed chief of the U.S. Division of Forestry (later called the U.S. FOREST SERVICE) in 1898, Pinchot made Graves his assistant. Two years later, Graves became director of the new Yale School of Forestry and wrote *Forest Mensuration* (1906) and *Principles of Handling Woodlands* (1911). Graves succeeded Pinchot as chief of the Forest Service in 1910, serving until 1920 and introducing a number of programs, including the investigation of private land claims within national forests, improved recreational use of forests and cooperative fire-protection programs with state and local agencies.

Graves served as dean of the Yale School of Forestry from 1922 to 1939 and collaborated with Cedric H. Guise on a major textbook, *Forest Education* (1932). Following World War II, Graves was chairman of a joint committee of the National Research Council and the SOCIETY OF AMERICAN FORESTERS, which published its findings as *Problems and Progress of Forestry in the United States* (1947). Graves also worked to include forestry in programs of the United Nations Food and Agriculture Organization.

Further reading: William B. Greeley, "Henry Graves: The Great Conserver," *American Forests* 61 (April. 1955): 20–21, 40, 42, 44, 46–48; Harold K. Steen, *The U.S. Forest Service: A History* (Seattle: University of Washington Press, 1976).

Gray, Asa (November 18, 1810–January 30, 1888)

Born in Sauquoit, New York, Asa Gray was the leading botanical taxonomist in the United States

Asa Gray. *Courtesy of the Library of Congress, Brady-Handy Collection*

during the 19th century. A firm believer in Charles DARWIN's theory of evolution, Gray pioneered plant geography in America and was a prominent professor of natural history.

After studying medicine at Fairfield Medical School in Connecticut and teaching high school in New York, Gray took a job as an assistant to John Torrey, a chemistry professor at the College of Physicians and Surgeons in New York. Gray had developed an early interest in botany, and he was able to turn his avocation into a livelihood in 1835 when he was named curator and librarian of the New York Lyceum of Natural History. In 1838, he traveled to Europe to study and to acquire books for the Lyceum library. Shortly after his return to the United States, he was offered a professorship of natural history at Harvard University and taught there from 1842 to 1873. Upon his retirement, he donated his extensive collection of plants and books to the university.

Extraordinarily prolific, Gray wrote more than 360 books, monographs and papers. His best-known book is *Manual of Botany of the Northern United States, from New England to Wisconsin and South to Ohio and Pennsylvania Inclusive* (1848)—usually abbreviated to *Gray's Manual*. A standard in the field, the book has been

Sequoia/Kings Canyon National Park. *U.S. Department of the Interior, National Park Service photo by Richard Frear*

issued in many editions. He also wrote *Flora of North America* (with John Torrey), which was expanded in 1878 and republished as the first volume of *Synoptical Flora of North America.*

Gray was vitally interested in plant geography and spent much time conducting comparative studies of plants found in Japan, Europe and North America. While Darwin was working on his theory of evolution and natural selection, he asked Gray to critique his writings on plant distribution.

Further reading: A. Hunter Dupresa, *Asa Gray* (New York: Atheneum, 1968).

Greeley, William Buckhout (September 6, 1879–November 30, 1955)

The third chief of the U.S. FOREST SERVICE, William Greeley engineered a policy of cooperation among the federal government, state agencies and private industry in the management of the nation's forests.

In 1890, Greeley's family moved from Oswego, New York, to California, where the young man grew to love the woods. He graduated from the University of California in 1901, having majored in history and English. After a brief stint as a public school teacher, Greeley enrolled in the Yale School of Forestry, re-

ceiving an M.F. degree in 1904. In that same year, he began working for the Bureau of Forestry, becoming supervisor of Sequoia National Forest in 1906. In 1908, he was named first district forester in the northern Rockies. After fires ravaged his district in 1910, he worked to create a pioneering cooperative fire-protection program among private timber owners.

Greeley became chief of the Branch of Forest Management in 1911 and moved to Washington, D.C. During this period, he formulated his ideas on cooperation among federal, state and private interests in forest resource management, which he published in *Some Public and Economic Aspects of the Lumber Industry* (1917). His cooperative approach brought him into direct conflict with pioneering forester Gifford PINCHOT, who advocated strong federal regulation of forests. Following two years of service overseas in World War I, Greeley resumed his duties as chief of the Branch of Forest Management and, in 1920, succeeded his Yale forestry professor, Henry GRAVES, as the third head of the Forest Service. For the next four years, against the opposition of Pinchot, Greeley attempted to implement a cooperative federal-state program of reforestation and fire protection. He prevailed in 1924 with the passage of the Clarke-McNary Act. Four years later, he was instrumental in the passage of the McSweeney-McNary Act, which established the research program of the U.S. Forest Service.

Greeley left the Forest Service in 1928 to become secretary-manager of the West Coast Lumbermen's Association in Seattle, a position he held until his retirement in 1946. Active in the SOCIETY OF AMERICAN FORESTERS as president (1915) and a member of its governing council (1944-49), Greeley contributed generously to his alma mater, the Yale School of Forestry, which named its William B. Greeley Memorial Laboratory in his honor. The university awarded him the Yale Medal in 1955, the University of California made him an honorary doctor of letters in 1927; and the Society of American Foresters presented him with the Sir William Schlich Memorial Medal in 1946.

Further reading: Greeley, *Forests and Men* (Garden City, N.Y. Doubleday,: 1951); George T. Morgan Jr., *William B. Greeley: A Practical Forester* (St. Paul, Minn.: Forest History Society, 1961).

Green Party (Die Grünen) (Founded: 1979)

Postfach 1422, W-5300 Bonn, 1, Germany; (228) 692021

A German political party that represents members of the Green movement, the Green Party developed from a band of antinuclear and ecological activists. In 1979, the party received 3.2% of the vote, making it eligible to receive public funds amounting to 4.8 million marks. By 1983, the party had received more than 5% of the vote, making it eligible for state and federal parliamentary representation.

The German Green Party is the strongest of several "green parties" in Europe. These include AGALEV and ECOLO of Belgium; the Greens of France; Alternative Ecologists, the Greek Democratic Ecological Movement, and Ecological Movement-Political Renaissance of Greece; the Green Party of Ireland; the Green List and the Rainbow Greens of Italy; the Green List-Ecological Alternative, the Green Alternative and the Green Alternative Alliance of Luxembourg; the Rainbow Party of the Netherlands; the United Democratic Coalition and the Portuguese Democratic Movement of Portugal; and the Green List, the Ecological Greens, V.E.R.D.E. and the Green Alternative of Spain. Germany has two ecological parties in addition to the Green Party: the Ecological Democratic Party and the Ecological Union. There is also a Green Party of the United Kingdom. Similar "green parties" have also appeared in other countries, including Sweden and Tasmania.

The Green Party in Germany advocates nothing less than a transformation of society away from goals of economic growth at the expense of the environment. The Greens also support full equality of the sexes and state-guaranteed medical care, social services and full employment. In addition, the party advocates worldwide demilitarization, the disbanding of military alliances and the withdrawal of troops from foreign territories. Of late, the German Greens have suffered considerable factionalism in their diversified ranks and a diminished presence in German politics. In 1990, the party polled less than the 5% necessary for parliamentary representation.

Further reading: Wolfgang Rudig, "Green Party Politics Around the World, *Environment* 33, no. 8 (October 1991): 7–31.

Greenpeace International (Founded: 1971)
Keizersgracht 176, NL-1016 DW Amsterdam, Netherlands; (20) 5236555

Originally a loosely organized band of Canadian ecologists, pacifists and Quakers, Greenpeace International today boasts 4 million members worldwide and a staff of 750. Under the leadership of Stephen Sawyer, executive director, and David MCTAGGART, chairman of the board, the organization manages an annual budget of $40 million, much of which comes in the form of $5 and $10 individual contributions.

Greenpeace staffers and members engage in "direct nonviolent action" against individuals, corporations and governments that use the environment or

Greenpeace activist Grace O'Sullivan climbs the anchor chain of a Soviet nuclear warship in the Mediterranean 10 miles off the Greek island of Nissos Kithera on September 29, 1989. The gesture is a vintage example of Greenpeace "direct action." © *Greenpeace/Midgley*

wildlife in an irresponsible or negligent manner. The most dramatic incident of such nonviolent action occurred in 1985 when the organization's ship, the *Rainbow Warrior,* sailed to the South Pacific to protest the French government's nuclear tests there. The ship, anchored in the harbor of Auckland, New Zealand, was sunk by French secret service agents, and a Greenpeace photographer was killed. In November 1992, the organization staged a dramatic protest against a plutonium shipment France made to Japan. On November 7, French marines seized the Greenpeace vessel *Moby Dick* and roughed up members of the crew. On November 8, a Japanese military vessel escorting the plutonium shipment rammed another Greenpeace ship, the *Solo.*

Greenpeace has been active in reducing the slaughter of harp seal pups, in banning commercial whaling, in stopping toxic waste dumping and in restricting the exploration of oil in Antarctica. Greenpeace International is affiliated with GREENPEACE U.S.A.

Greenpeace U.S.A. (Founded: 1979)
1436 U Street NW, Washington, D.C. 20009; (202) 462–1177

Affiliated with GREENPEACE INTERNATIONAL, Greenpeace U.S.A. carries out nonviolent, active protests to protect the environment. Of particular concern to the organization's more than 1.5 million national members are freeing the earth of nuclear and other pollution, ending the commercial slaughter of marine mammals and stopping the production and testing of nuclear weapons. Through grass-roots lobbying efforts, the organization brings pressure to bear on local and national governments. Funded mainly through many small donations, Greenpeace sponsors scientific research and monitors the greenhouse effect and radioactive and toxic waste dumping. The organization publishes the bimonthly *Greenpeace* magazine and frequent campaign fact sheets. The national organization is divided into five regional groups, with Peter BAHOUTH as overall executive director.

Gregg, Frank (December 15, 1925–   )
A native of Denver, Frank Gregg was editor of *Colorado Outdoors* and the publications of the Colorado Department of Game and Fish from 1951 to 1957, when he was named executive director of the IZAAK WALTON LEAGUE OF AMERICA. In that position he garnered support for strong federal restrictions on water pollution. In 1961, he was named staff assistant in the office of the secretary of the interior, a position he held until 1963 and in which he developed legislation for the Land and Water Conservation Fund. Between 1963 and 1965, Gregg directed the Citizens Committee for the Outdoor Recreation Resources Review Commission, and in 1965, he became vicepresident of the CONSERVATION FOUNDATION. Gregg was chairman of the New England River Basins Commission from 1967 to 1978 and director of the U.S. Bureau of LAND MANAGEMENT from 1978 to 1981.

Gregg has served as a visiting instructor in the School of Renewable Natural Resources at the University of Arizona and has written widely on natural resources policy, planning, management and administration. His articles have appeared in numerous scholarly journals, and he has contributed chapters to *Redesigning National Water Policy: New Roles and Directions* (1988), *Government and Environment: Essays on Historical Development Since World War II* (1990) and other books on resource management.

George Bird Grinnell. *Courtesy of the National Park Service, Glacier National Park*

Grinnell, George Bird (September 20, 1849– April 11, 1938)
In an obituary, the *New York Times* called George Bird Grinnell the "father of American conservation." He was actually better known in his own day for his writings on the Plains Indians, but his most lasting contribution to American history was, indeed, his pioneering work in wilderness preservation and environmentalism.

A native of Brooklyn, New York, Grinnell was born into a family of means, and he grew up enjoying hunting and the study of nature. Young Grinnell was educated at Yale University, from which he took a B.A. in 1870 and a Ph.D. in paleontology 10 years later. In 1921, the university also conferred upon him an honorary doctor of letters degree. He served as naturalist on several expeditions into the West, including one led by paleontologist Othniel C. Marsh in 1870 and another, in 1874, with Lieutenant Colonel George Armstrong Custer, into the Black Hills. In 1875, he accompanied William Ludlow, an engineer, into the newly established Yellowstone National Park.

In 1875, Grinnell became natural history editor of *Field and Stream,* taking over the magazine as its

Glacier National Park. *U.S. Department of the Interior, National Park Service photo by Richard Frear*

owner and publisher in 1880. From this time until he retired from the journal in 1911, Grinnell used the pages of *Field and Stream* to conduct a series of pioneering conservation campaigns, including one begun in 1882, aimed at securing full and proper protection for Yellowstone National Park and to establish for all time the concept that a national park should be an inviolate sanctuary for wilderness and wildlife.

In 1894, in large part due to Grinnell's sustained editorial efforts, Congress passed An Act to Protect the Birds and Animals in Yellowstone National Park. Later, in 1901, Grinnell—this time in an editorial written for *Century Magazine*—began a campaign to promote the creation of Glacier National Park in Montana, one of the areas he had earlier explored. Again, Grinnell's promotional persistence paid off. On May 11, 1910, President William Howard Taft signed the bill creating Glacier National Park.

Grinnell, an early admirer of the professional forestry techniques long practiced in Europe, began an effort in 1882 to persuade American foresters to adopt European standards of training and professionalism. Through a carefully orchestrated program of persuasion, Grinnell prepared the way for the establishment of a New York State Forest Preserve in the Adirondacks in 1885 and was responsible for initiating federal legislation to grant the president the right to set aside federal forest reserves.

In 1886, Grinnell founded the first Audubon Society, dedicated to the study and preservation of non-

game bird species. He joined Theodore ROOSEVELT and other well-heeled naturalists, sportsmen and nature enthusiasts in founding the BOONE AND CROCKETT CLUB (1887–88). With Roosevelt, Grinnell edited the club's series of books on hunting, natural history and conservation. Historians of American environmentalism credit Grinnell as a formative influence on the future president's positive ideas concerning conservation.

Grisebach, August (April 17, 1814–May 9, 1879)

August Grisebach, professor of botany at Göttingen, Germany, and later director of the botanical garden there, was the first scientist to classify plants according to the climate in which they are found. In *Die Vegetation der Erde* (1872), he described more than 50 different "formations," assemblages of plants within a given climatic region. He argued that plants found in the tropical rainforests of Africa, South America and the Indian Archipelago were part of a single plant formation, regardless of their different geographical locations.

Plant geographers who followed Grisebach incorporated three of his basic principles: Plants are classified according to their adaptive forms rather than according to taxonomy alone; plants are viewed as members of integrated societies; and climate is the factor that determines the constitution of plant communities.

A native of Hanover, Grisebach died in Göttingen.

H

Haeckel, Ernst Heinrich (February 16, 1834–
August 8, 1919)
The German zoologist Ernst Heinrich Haeckel (born
in Potsdam, Prussia) is best known for coining the
term *ecology* and for creating genealogical trees of
organisms, a valuable illustrative device he developed after adopting Charles DARWIN's theory of evolution. After studying medicine at the University of
Wurzburg and the University of Berlin, Haeckel traveled in Italy and then returned to Prussia to practice.
In 1861, after a year of private practice, he was
appointed lecturer at the University of Jena, and in
1862, he became Extraordinary Professor of Comparative Anatomy at the Zoological Institute in that city.
In 1865 Haeckel was appointed full professor at the
University of Jena.

In addition to his genealogical trees, Haeckel also
developed a theory of recapitulation, proposed in his
Generelle Morpholgie der Organismen (1866). As Haeckel
saw it, ontogeny (the development of a fertilized egg
into an adult organism) recapitulates phylogeny (the
developmental history of a species); that is, as a
fertilized egg of a species develops, it resembles in
its various stages the adult versions of less evolved
species. Haeckel also theorized that the origin of life
is determined by chemical and physical factors, such
as sunlight, oxygen, water and methane.

Finally, it was Haeckel who coined the term *ecology*,
which has been used since the 19th century to mean
the study of living organisms in relation to each other
and to their environment. The word is derived from
oikos, the Greek word meaning "economy." Haeckel
saw *oecologie* (to use his spelling) as encompassing
the study of groups of organisms that live together,
forming a unit similar to a family living in the same
dwelling. The concept of ecology, as Haeckel developed it, turned the life sciences away from studying
particular organisms in isolation and toward analyzing organisms holistically, in the context of other
organisms and natural elements.

Further reading: Wilhelm Bolsche, *Haeckel: His Life and Work*
(Philadelphia: Jacobs, 1906).

Hair, Jay Dee (November 30, 1945–   )
Miami native Jay Dee Hair holds a B.S. in biology
and an M.S. in zoology from Clemson University,
South Carolina, and a Ph.D. in zoology from the
University of Alberta, Canada. In 1973, he returned
to Clemson, after serving in the U.S. Army, to become an assistant professor of wildlife biology. In
1977 he moved to North Carolina State University,
where he was named associate professor of zoology
and forestry and administrator of Fisheries and Wildlife Sciences.

In 1978, Hair was employed by the U.S. Department of the INTERIOR as director of the U.S. FISH AND
WILDLIFE SERVICE, where he worked to formulate a
national policy on fish and wildlife conservation. In
1981 he was named executive vice-president and in
1982 president of the NATIONAL WILDLIFE FEDERA-
TION.

Hair has belonged to many environmental and
conservation organizations, including the Acid Rain
Clearinghouse Professional Advisory Council, the
American Fisheries Society and the Association for
the Advancement of Science. He has served on the
board of directors of the American League of Anglers,
the Boy Scouts of America National Conservation
Committee, ECOLOGICAL SOCIETY OF AMERICA, International Commission on Ecology, National Coordinating Committee on Fish and Wildlife in Federal
Water Resources Projects, the SOCIETY OF AMERICAN
FORESTERS and the WILDLIFE SOCIETY.

He was named South Carolina Governor's Wildlife
Conservationist of the Year in 1977 and North Carolina Governor's Conservationist of the Year in 1980.

He has written several articles on the management of ecological resources and has served as editor of *Ecological Perspectives of Wildlife Management* in 1977.

As president of the National Wildlife Federation since 1982, Hair draws on a budget of $75 million and a membership of 5.8 million to lobby Congress on environmental issues. One of his goals is to make the director of the ENVIRONMENTAL PROTECTION AGENCY a member of the president's cabinet.

Hall, Ansel Franklin (May 6, 1894–March 28, 1962)

Born in Oakland, California, Ansel Franklin Hall was educated at the University of California, taking his B.S. degree in 1917. After graduating, he became a ranger with the NATIONAL PARK SERVICE. World War I interrupted his park service career between 1917 and 1918, when he served as a second lieutenant with the U.S. Engineering Corps, Allied Expeditionary Force, in France. Hall briefly taught forestry at the A.E.F. University in Beaune, France.

Returning to the United States in 1918, Hall resumed his work as a ranger until 1923, when he became chief naturalist for the park service. In 1930, he was named senior naturalist and chief forester; in 1932, chief of the Division of Education and Forestry; and in 1933, chief of the Field Division of Education, a position he held until 1937, when he left the National Park Service to head his own firm, the Mesa Verde Company (later called Mesa Verde Enterprises Inc.).

Both under the auspices of the park service and with his own company, Hall organized naturalist and educational expeditions, including the Rainbow Bridge-Monument Valley Expedition (1933–38) and the Alaska-Yukon Expedition (1936). From 1939 until his death, Hall served as research director of the Navajo Trail Association.

Hall was active in various environmentally related organizations, conferences and commissions, including the Anasazi Association Inc.; the American Association of Museums; the Grand Canyon Committee (1929–32) and the Crater Lake Committee (1924–37) of the National Academy of Sciences; and the First Pan Pacific Conference on Education, Rehabilitation, Reclamation and Recreation (serving as secretary of the recreation section in 1927). Hall was a member of the SOCIETY OF AMERICAN FORESTERS, the American Association of Museums, the California Academy of Science, the Explorers' Club, the American Alpine Club and the SIERRA CLUB. He wrote two important guidebooks, to Mesa Verde National Park (1937) and to the entire Mesa Verde region (1952). Hall served

as editor of *Yosemite Nature Notes* from 1919 to 1925. He died at his home in Mesa Verde.

Hansen, James (March 24, 1941–   )

For the past 16 years James Hansen has used computer models to study the greenhouse effect and has publicized the dangers to the atmosphere posed by carbon dioxide, methane and chlorofluorocarbons. Director of NASA's Goddard Institute for Space Sciences, he testified before Congress in 1988 and announced that "the greenhouse effect has been detected and is changing our climate now." Under fire from some other scientists for his dire predictions, Hansen nevertheless has continued his campaign and in 1990 told a group of climatologists meeting at the Goddard Institute in New York that within the following three years, the world would break century-old high-temperature records. Indeed, for much of the world, the summer of 1991 was warmer than usual and the winter exceptionally mild.

Hardin, Garrett (James) (April 21, 1915–   )

Dallas-born Garrett Hardin, biologist and human ecologist, is best known for his controversial and uncompromising theories of human overpopulation, its consequences and, most of all, policies for coping with it.

At the core of Hardin's beliefs are two metaphors: "the tragedy of the commons" and "living in a lifeboat." The first he coined in a 1968 essay for *Science* (December 13):

> The tragedy of the commons develops in this way. Picture a pasture open to all. It is to be expected that each herdsman will try to keep as many cattle as possible on the commons. Such an arrangement may work reasonably satisfactorily for centuries because tribal wars, poaching, and disease keep the numbers of both man and beast well below the carrying capacity of the land. Finally, however, comes the day of reckoning, that is, the day when the long-desired goal of social stability becomes a reality. At this point, the inherent logic of the commons remorselessly generates tragedy.

Five years later, Hardin developed the lifeboat analogy as a dramatic illustration of his answer to the "tragedy of the commons." What to do about overpopulation and consequent starvation among the poor nations?

Let millions die.

At some point, the population of each poor nation will decline to the carrying capacity of the country. During this harsh process, the governments of the poor nations, realizing that they cannot look to outside sources for aid, will be compelled to develop policies to control overpopulation in the future. "Metaphorically," Hardin wrote,

> each rich nation amounts to a lifeboat full of comparatively rich people. The poor of the world are in other, much more crowded lifeboats. Continuously . . . the poor fall out of their lifeboats and swim for a while in the water outside, hoping to be admitted to a rich lifeboat. . . . What should the passengers on a rich lifeboat do? This is the central problem of "the ethics of a lifeboat."

Hardin's solution to the "problem" was an injunction to the rich passengers to let the others drown.

Hardin's twin metaphors were severely criticized by humanitarian thinkers as "obscene" and as examples of "eco-imperialism." It must be observed, however, that Hardin saw the policy embodied in his metaphors as a method of implementing the kind of "mutual coercion mutually agreed upon" that is necessary to enforce regulation of population and prevent universal—that is, "common"—tragedy. The price, as the metaphors demonstrate, is high and even morally repugnant, but with a characteristic lack of sentimentality (some would say absence of sensitivity or even decency), Hardin observed in 1980: "Cherishing individual lives in the short run diminishes the number of lives in the long run. It also diminishes the quality of life and increases the pain of living it."

Garrett Hardin was educated at the University of Chicago (Sc. B., 1936) and Stanford University (Ph.D., biology, 1941). He taught at Stanford (1936–37; 1938–42) and at Chicago City Junior College (1938), served on the staff of the Division of Plant Biology of the Carnegie Institute (1942–46) and taught at the University of California, Santa Barbara, where he is currently professor emeritus of Human Ecology. He has also served on the visiting faculty of other institutions, including Stanford; California Institute of Technology; University of California, Los Angeles; University of California, Berkeley; and the University of Chicago. In addition to his career as an educator, Hardin has been active with the ENVIRONMENTAL DEFENSE FUND, which he served as president from 1980 to 1988; the American Association for the Advancement of Science; the ECOLOGICAL SOCIETY OF AMERICA; the American Philosophical Society; the American Academy of Arts and Sciences; and the International Society of Ecological Economics.

In addition to numerous contributions to scientific and learned journals, Hardin has published *Biology: Its Principles and Implications* (1949), *Nature and Man's Fate* (1959), *Population, Evolution, and Birth Control*

(1964), *Exploring New Ethics for Survival* (1972), *Stalking the Wild Taboo* (1973) and *Mandatory Motherhood* (1974). In 1980, he received the Margaret Sanger Award.

Hartzog, George Benjamin, Jr. (March 17, 1920–   )

Born in rural Colleton County, South Carolina, Hartzog graduated from American University and studied law under J. M. Moore from 1939 to 1942. After being admitted to the bar, he was named attorney for and administrator of the Bureau of LAND MANAGEMENT and the NATIONAL PARK SERVICE in 1946. He served as assistant superintendent of Rocky Mountain National Park from 1955 to 1957, of the Great Smoky Mountains National Park from 1957 to 1959 and as superintendent of Jefferson National Expansion Memorial in St. Louis from 1959 to 1962. From 1962 to 1963, he directed Downtown Saint Louis, before taking a position as associate director of the National Park Service in 1963. The following year he was promoted to director of the park service, a position he held until 1972.

Hartzog's 1988 book *Battling for the National Parks* chronicles the development of the National Park Service during the 1960s, its years of greatest expansion.

Harvey, Hal (July 18, 1960–   )

Hal Harvey is the first executive director of the ENERGY FOUNDATION, which seeks to assist the nation in making a transition to a sustainable energy future.

Harvey was born in Aspen, Colorado, and was educated at Stanford University, earning B.S. (1982) and M.S. (1984) degrees in engineering, specializing in energy planning. He is the author of energy policy articles in numerous journals and magazines and has lectured widely. From 1986 to 1989, Harvey was director of the Security Program at the Rocky Mountain Institute and led a research team investigating the links between resources—especially energy—and international security. From 1989 to 1990, he served as executive vice-president of the International Foundation, directing their energy project and the GlasNet computer network project.

In addition to his post at the Energy Foundation, Harvey is on the board of directors of the Joyce Mertz-Gilmore Foundation and the Ploughshares Fund. He is vice-president of the board of directors of the New-Land Foundation and chairs the board of directors of the Institute for Global Communications. Hal Harvey was a member of the Energy Task Force of President Bush's Commission on Environmental Quality.

Hayes, Dennis Allen (August 29, 1944–)

A native of Wisconsin Rapids, Wisconsin, Denis Allen Hayes was executive director of the 1970 and 1990 Earth Day celebrations and is currently an attorney with the San Francisco law firm of Cooley, Godward, Castro, Huddleston & Tatum. He served as a visiting scholar at the Smithsonian Institution from 1971 to 1972 and directed the Illinois State Energy Office from 1974 to 1975. Hayes joined the staff of WORLDWATCH INSTITUTE in Washington, D.C., in 1975 as a senior researcher, and from 1979 to 1981, he was director of the Solar Energy Research Institute in Golden, California.

Writing about Earth Day 1970 in *The Progressive*, Hayes called for a holistic approach to ecological problems. "It is absolute folly to continue to pursue piecemeal solutions—when we know full well that the pesticides, the detergents, and the dams are all fouling the same river," he explained. He criticized the "neo-Keynesian mentality" that "has yet to grapple with the elementary fact that infinite expansion is impossible on a finite planet." Twenty years later, writing about Earth Day 1990 in *Natural History*, Hayes asserted that no real improvement had been made on the environmental front. "How could we have fought so hard, and won so many battles, only to find ourselves now on the verge of losing the war?" he asked. One answer, he suggested, was that new problems have appeared in the environment at every turn. Chlorofluorocarbons, for example, were viewed at the time of the first Earth Day as a "triumph of modern chemistry." Four years later, scientists at the University of California, Irvine, found that they damaged the earth's ozone layer. Hayes called for the environmental movement to face such new issues as the draining of government coffers to fund the defense budget at the expense of programs to research and solve problems such as global warming and ozone destruction. "The world cannot build a sustainable future," he wrote, "so long as it spends $1 trillion annually . . . on military ends." Another issue he claimed environmentalists ignore is population. Writing that "current population levels are undermining the biological basis for the future," he called on environmentalists to confront the issue of overpopulation and advocate family planning, even at the risk of alienating some individuals from the environmental cause. He also called for environmental organizations to spend less on lobbying and more on solving problems directly.

Hayes has won awards from the American Institute for Public Service, the SIERRA CLUB and the American Solar Energy Society.

Hays, Samuel Pfrimmer (April 5, 1921–)

Whereas most writers on environmental topics devote themselves to environmental *policy*, Samuel P. Hays is a historian of environmental *politics* and, specifically, the political origins of the conservation movement. His special areas of concentration have been the analysis of changes in popular beliefs and environmental practices in the United States following World War II and, more broadly, understanding how post-Civil War industrialism shaped the liberal movement that gave rise to an active concern for the environment and the organization of public interest lobbies to bring about policy change.

Born in Corydon, Indiana, Hays was educated at Swarthmore College (B.A., 1948) and Harvard University (M.A., 1949; Ph.D., 1953). He served on the faculties of the University of Illinois (1952–53) and the University of Iowa (1953–60) before coming to the University of Pittsburgh as head of the history department in 1960. Hays has been Distinguished Service Professor of history at Pittsburgh since 1973.

Hays is a prolific author. In addition to numerous contributions to learned journals, he has written *Response to Industrialization, 1885–1914* (1957), *Conservation and the Gospel of Efficiency: The Progressive Conservation Movement, 1890–1920* (1959), *American Political History as Social Analysis: Essays by Samuel P. Hays* (1980) and *Beauty, Health, and Permanence: Environmental Politics in the United States, 1955–1985* (1987).

Hazelwood, Joseph (September 24, 1946–)

On March 24, 1989, the 987-foot supertanker Exxon *Valdez* ran aground 25 miles south of Valdez, Alaska, spewing 240,000 barrels of oil into Prince William Sound. Exxon quickly dismissed the vessel's captain, Joseph Hazelwood of Huntington, New York, who was subsequently charged with criminal mischief, reckless endangerment, operating a vessel while intoxicated and negligent discharge of oil. In March 1990, he was found guilty of negligent discharge of oil and was sentenced to perform 1,000 hours of community service, specifically assisting in the cleanup of beaches polluted by the oil. In addition, he was ordered to pay $58,500 in restitution to the state of Alaska. However, on July 10, 1992, the Alaska State Court of Appeals threw out the conviction, based on a Federal statute granting immunity to those who report oil spills to the authorities. Hazelwood had radioed a report to the Coast Guard.

The Valdez oil slick covered more than 2,600 square miles, killed thousands of birds and marine animals and polluted hundreds of miles of beaches. Exxon spent more than $2 billion cleaning up the spill, which is considered to be the worst environmental disaster in American history. On May 7, 1992, the Maritime College of the State University of New York hired Hazelwood as a "watch officer" for a two-month training cruise.

Further reading: John D. Keeble, *Out of the Channel: The* Exxon Valdez *Oil Spill in Prince William Sound* (New York: HarperCollins, 1991).

Heald, Weldon F. (May 1, 1901–July 28, 1967)

Trained as an architect at the Massachusetts Institute of Technology, Weldon F. Heald (born in Milford, New Hampshire) abandoned a career in the building arts to become a full-time writer on conservation subjects. Over his prolific career, he produced more than 750 articles on history, ecology, deserts, mountains, state and national parks, national forests and other topics. Among the magazines and journals in which his work appeared were *National Wildlife News, Sierra Club Bulletin, National Parks Magazine, Western Outdoor Quarterly* and *Westways*. Between 1945 and 1946 and again from 1947 to 1949, he was director of the SIERRA CLUB. From 1961 until his death in 1967, he was an advisor to the secretary of the interior on national parks and monuments and conducted field inspections for the NATIONAL PARK SERVICE and the U.S. FOREST SERVICE.

Herbst, Robert LeRoy (October 5, 1935–   )

Before being named national executive director of Trout Unlimited in 1981, Minneapolis-born Robert LeRoy Herbst worked for the U.S. FOREST SERVICE and the University of Minnesota. From 1957 to 1963, he was forester for the Minnesota Conservation Department and was responsible for preparing more than 2,000 wildlife management plans. Between 1963 and 1966, he served as executive director of Keep Minnesota Green, and over the next three years, he was deputy commissioner and acting commissioner of the Minnesota Conservation Department. As executive director of the IZAAK WALTON LEAGUE OF AMERICA, he was successful in halting mining activities in the Boundary Waters Canoe Area, and he coordinated the National Citizens Crusade for Clean Water. He returned to work for state government as Minnesota's first commissioner of natural resources.

From 1977 to 1981, Herbst participated in the national conservation arena as assistant secretary of the interior for fish and wildlife and parks.

Hodel, Donald Paul (May 23, 1935–   )

A former Portland, Oregon, attorney and Georgia-Pacific Company executive, Donald Hodel began his government career as deputy (1969–72) and chief administrator (1972–79) of the Bonneville Power Administration, the federal agency that markets the hydroelectric energy produced by the Northwest's New Deal-era dams. Warning that "homes will be cold and dark or factories will close," Hodel vastly overestimated the region's future energy needs and pursued an aggressive plan of expansion that included the construction of five new nuclear power plants under the Washington Public Power Supply System. With enormous cost overruns, WPPSS earned the nickname WHOOPS for its record-setting ($2.25 billion) default of municipal bonds, and four of the nuclear stations, proven wildly superfluous, were ultimately cancelled.

After a stint as president of the National Electricity Reliability Council and as a private energy consultant, in 1981 Hodel was appointed deputy to Secretary of the Interior James WATT. An administration loyalist who had campaigned for Reagan's presidency as early as 1968, Hodel helped formulate and implement Watt's devil-may-care programs to exploit the natural resources of wilderness areas, ocean-floor acreage and other federally owned lands.

A year later, Hodel's BPA background and reputation for low-profile efficiency won his appointment as secretary of the U.S. Department of ENERGY, which the president wished to cut back significantly and eventually dismantle. Although Hodel managed to strengthen the department and protect some funding for solar power and energy conservation programs, environmentalists found his consistently pro-nuclear, pro-industry record unimpressive and protested his 1985 return to the U.S. Department of INTERIOR as successor to William P. Clark.

During his tenure as interior secretary (1985–89), Hodel quietly maintained and extended such policies as cut-rate oil and gas leasing of the outer continental shelf, largely unsupervised mining of parks and wilderness areas, subsidization of irrigation water for otherwise unsustainable western agribusiness, nonenforcement of environmental regulations and noncollection of offender fines.

Although Hodel's rhetoric was generally less inflammatory than that of his former boss, he did attract widespread ridicule in June of 1987. Urging the administration to reconsider its initiative for international limits on chlorofluorocarbon emissions, Hodel suggested that the populace might best be protected against ozone-layer damage by a government advisory to wear hats, sunscreen lotions and dark glasses.

Holdgate, Martin W. (January 14, 1931–)

A former polar expeditionist and high-ranking government scientist, British environmentalist and author Martin Holdgate is director general of the INTERNATIONAL UNION FOR CONSERVATION OF NATURE AND NATURAL RESOURCES, a global organization with headquarters in Switzerland.

Born in Horsham, England, Holdgate earned his degrees at Queens College, Cambridge University (B.A., 1952; M.A., 1956; Ph.D., 1955). In 1955, he traveled as senior scientist with the Gough Island Scientific Survey; the following year, he lectured in zoology at Manchester University and published his first book, *A History of Appleby, County Town of Westmoreland* (reprinted 1970). Holdgate's chronicle of the Gough Island expedition, *Mountains in the Sea*, was released in 1958. Teaching next at the Durham Colleges (1957–60), he led the 1958 Royal Society expedition to southern Chile. In 1960 he was named assistant director of research at the Scott Polar Research Institute in Cambridge, and in 1963, he began work as senior biologist for the British Antarctic Survey. With R. Carrick and J. Prevost, he edited *Antarctic Biology* (1964). In 1966, he moved on to London's Nature Conservancy, where he was deputy director of research for the next four years. Also during this period, Holdgate served as secretary of the Working Group on Biology for the Scientific Committee on Antarctic Resources (1964–68) and edited another volume, *Antarctic Ecology* (1970).

In 1970 Holdgate joined Britain's Department of the Environment as director of its Central Unit of Environmental Pollution, and he held this London post until 1974, when he left to head the Institute of Terrestrial Ecology for the Natural Environment Research Council. Two years later, Holdgate returned to government policy-making and the Department of the Environment with his appointment as director general of resources (1976–79). A fellow of the Institute of Biology, the Royal Geographic Society, the Zoological Society and the British School Exploring Society (chairman, 1967–78), he was created Companion of the Bath in 1979, the same year he became chief scientist and deputy secretary of the Departments of the Environment and Transport and his book *A Perspective of Environmental Pollution* was published. Throughout his career, Holdgate's articles on

Antarctic ecology and other environmental topics have appeared in biological and conservation journals.

Since becoming director general of IUCN in 1988, Holdgate has helped the scientific federation and its more than 600 member entities lead the way in creating international conservation agreements and establishing innovative, locally managed projects for sustainable development of natural resources.

Further reading: Holdgate (ed., with M. Kassas and G. F. White), *The World Environment 1972–1982* (Dublin, Ireland: Tycooly Institute, 1982); *Environmental Issues* (joint editor; New York: Norton, 1977).

Holdren, John Paul (March 1, 1944–)

As a professor of energy and resources at the University of California, Berkeley, and senior investigator at the Rocky Mountain Biological Laboratory, John Paul Holdren is highly critical of the federal government's lack of commitment to energy. A political realist, Holdren believes that the government is unlikely to devote adequate funds to researching new sources of energy while energy remains cheap. But, he argues, the apparent low price of energy is false. Americans need to make the connection between the price of energy and the price of cleaning up air pollution or of military deployment in the Persian Gulf (necessary, Holdren argues, because of the nation's dependence on Middle Eastern oil) before they can appreciate the full cost of energy consumption. Holdren has called for gasoline taxes that would more nearly cover the real cost of the country's reliance on petroleum fuel. He also calls for carbon taxes that would be imposed on energy sources in proportion to the amount of carbon dioxide they release into the atmosphere.

A native of Sewickley, Pennsylvania, Holdren has a Ph.D. from Stanford University in aeronautical, astronautical and electrical engineering. Before joining the faculty of the University of California, Berkeley, he was a physicist with the Lawrence Livermore National Laboratory. He has served on the International Environmental Program Committee for the National Academy of Sciences and National Academy of Engineering and as a member of the committee on nuclear and alternative energy systems. From 1978 to 1979, he was a member of the Energy Resources Advisory Board of the U.S. Department of ENERGY. His research activities have centered on the environmental aspects of coal, fusion, fission, the international problems of nuclear weapons and arms control as they relate to the environment and energy and on population and arms control.

Hornaday, William Temple (December 1, 1854–May 7, 1937)

In his chapter on William T. Hornaday in *Man's Dominion: The Story of Conservation in America* (1971), author Frank Graham quotes this Hornaday pronouncement as typical of the uncompromising stance of this prickly, militant, unyielding, controversial and highly effective pioneer of conservation: "Fully ten per cent of the human race consists of people who will lie, steal, throw rubbish in parks, and destroy wildlife whenever and wherever they can do so without being stopped by a policeman and a club." Graham suggests that, as Hornaday grew older, he would have retained this methodology but revised his percentage estimate upward.

Hornaday was born in Plainfield, Indiana, and moved with his family to Iowa, where he was educated at Iowa State College. In 1873, he traveled to Rochester, New York, to study zoology and "scientific taxidermy" at Ward's Natural Science Establishment. In 1874, he set off on his first specimen-collecting expedition to the Bahamas, Cuba and Florida. In 1876, he collected in the West Indies and South America and, later in the year, set out on a three-year collecting tour around the world, including India, Ceylon, the Malay Peninsula and Borneo.

From 1882 to 1890, Hornaday served as chief taxidermist of the U.S. National Museum and in 1896 became director of the New York Zoological Park (Bronx Zoo), serving in that capacity until 1926. Hornaday provoked controversy and outrage in 1905 when he displayed Ota Benga, a young pygmy brought to America from the Belgian Congo the year before, in a Bronx Zoo cage with a parrot and an orangutan. Hornaday, yielding to pressure from clergy white and black, removed Ota Benga from display.

William T. Hornaday was one of the early activists who fought to stave off the extinction of the American bison. He was instrumental in establishing Montana and Wichita national bison ranges and the Elk River game reserve in Montana. He campaigned on behalf of the Audubon Plumage Bill to prohibit the importation of plumage from wild birds for millinery purposes (enacted 1911) and the Bayne Law to prohibit the sale of native American game (enacted 1913). Hornaday was successful in urging passage of the Federal Tariff Act, which closed loopholes in the prohibition against plumage importation (enacted 1913), and the Federal Migratory Bird Act, which protected migratory birds from the depredations of "sportsmen" (enacted 1913).

Hornaday wrote many pamphlets and circulars urging the cause of conservation. He was also a prolific author of book-length works, including *The Extermination of the American Bison* (1887), *Camp Fires*

William Temple Hornaday. *Courtesy of the New York Zoological Society*

in the Canadian Rockies (1906), *Camp Fires on Desert and Lava* (1908), *Wild Life Conservation in Theory and Practice* (1914), *Minds and Manners of Wild Animals* (1922), *Tales from Nature's Wonderlands* (1924), *A Wild-Animal Roundup* (1925), *Wild Animal Interviews* (1928) and *Thirty Years' War for Wild Life* (1931).

Further reading: Frank Graham, *Man's Dominion: The Story of Conservation in America* (New York: M. Evans, 1971).

Hough, Emerson (June 28, 1857–April 30, 1923)

Born near Newton, Iowa, Emerson Hough was educated at the State University of Iowa, earning a Ph.D. degree in 1880. At his father's insistence, Hough studied law and was admitted to the Iowa bar in 1881, but left that state to practice in the western frontier town of Whiteoaks, New Mexico. Here Hough indulged his passion for the wilderness, for hunting and fishing. He began selling brief sketches and essays on hunting and fishing to magazines and soon decided to become a professional writer. After working briefly on newspapers in Des Moines, Iowa, and Sandusky, Ohio, he became head of the Chicago office of *Forest and Stream* magazine in 1889.

In the winter of 1894, Hough toured Yellowstone Park on skis in order to study big game conditions there. He discovered that the park's buffalo herd had been nearly exterminated by poachers, and he made an eloquent report to the government concerning this situation. Hough's report is credited with moving Congress to enact legislation on May 7, 1894, extending federal protection to the park's herd. Years later, from 1916 to 1918, he campaigned for similar protection of the park's elk, which were threatened by the encroachment of grazing sheep.

Hough published his first book, *The Singing Mouse Stories*, studies and meditations on the outdoor life, in 1895. After this, he launched a highly successful career as a writer of popular western novels, including, most famously, *The Covered Wagon* (1922). But he never stopped campaigning on behalf of the wilderness and its preservation, writing hundreds of newspaper and magazine articles on the national parks and other conservation subjects.

Hough, Franklin Benjamin (July 22, 1822–June 11, 1885)

Gifford PINCHOT called Hough "perhaps the chief pioneer in forestry in the United States." By profession a country doctor in upstate New York, Hough directed the state censuses in 1854 and 1865. Distressed by the forest depletion the census data indicated, Hough became increasingly interested in forestry and, in 1873, urged the American Association for the Advancement of Science to petition Congress to create a commission to investigate national forest conditions. The commission was created in 1876, with Hough as its head. He produced a four-volume *Report upon Forestry* (1878–84) and was named chief of the Division of Forestry when it was created in 1881. His *Elements of Forestry* (1881) was the first American book on the subject, and he also edited the *American Journal of Forestry.*

As Division of Forestry chief, Hough worked to establish strong federal regulation of timber harvesting on public lands, to create federal forest experiment stations and planting programs as well as programs of public outreach and education.

Further reading: Edna L. Jacobsen, "Franklin B. Hough, A Pioneer in Scientific Forestry in America," *New York History* 15 (July 1934): 317–21; Harold K. Steen, *The U.S. Forest Service: A History* (Seattle: University of Washington Press, 1976).

Hughes, J(ohnson) Donald (June 5, 1932–)

J. Donald Hughes is an environmental historian and editor of *Environmental Review* magazine. His areas of special interest are the role of ecology in the ancient world and in American Indian culture. Hughes's writings include *The Story of Man in the Grand Canyon* (1967), *Ecology in Ancient Civilization* (1975), *American Indians in Colorado* (1976), *Ecological Consciousness* (1981) and *American Indian Ecology* (1983).

Hughes was educated at Oregon State University (1950–52) and the University of California, Los Angeles, from which he received an A.B. in 1954. He received his Ph.D. from Boston University in 1960 and also attended Cambridge University (1958–59) and the American School of Classical Studies in Athens (1966–67). Hughes was assistant professor of history at California Western University from 1961 to 1966 and professor of history at Pierce College, Athens, Greece, from 1966 to 1967. At the University of Denver, he served as assistant professor (1967–72) and associate professor (1972–77) and has been professor of history since 1977. During the summers of 1952, 1957 and 1958, Hughes worked as a park ranger at Yosemite National Park and as a ranger-naturalist at Grand Canyon National Park during the summers from 1960 to 1968. He is a member of the American Historical Association, the Association of Ancient Historians, the American Society for Environmental History, the American Indian Historical Society, the NATIONAL PARKS AND CONSERVATION ASSOCIATION, the SIERRA CLUB, the Colorado Mountain Club and Phi Beta Kappa.

Humboldt, Baron Alexander von (September 14, 1769–May 6, 1859)

The German naturalist and explorer Baron Alexander von Humboldt began his extensive fieldwork in geology, mineralogy and botany as a student at the universities of Göttingen, Frankfurt-on-Oder and Freiburg. Next, he traveled to Mexico, Cuba and South America on an expedition spanning 1799 to 1804. Over the next 20 years, he organized and published his research in a monumental 30-volume work entitled *Voyage de Humboldt et Bonpland* (1807–1817) (translated into English as *Personal Narrative*).

The *Voyage* earned him worldwide acclaim, and he was invited by Czar Nicholas I to explore the Urals and Asiatic Russia. Humboldt described these regions in the three-volume *Asia Central* (1843).

Humboldt is credited with devising a system of classifying plants according to the environmental conditions in which they are found. Not only did he provide clear and accurate descriptions of flora and fauna, he also incorporated romantic accounts of the exotic landscapes he visited. Throughout his writings, Humboldt attempted to portray nature as a complex unity. "In short," he wrote, "I must find out about the harmony of nature." Accordingly,

Humboldt adopted a holistic approach, which later influenced Charles DARWIN and other scientists.

One of the volumes of his *Personal Narrative, Essay on the Geography of Plants,* written in collaboration with Aimé Bonpland, who accompanied Humboldt to South America and Central America, argues not only for taxonomic analysis of plants, but also for geographical or environmental analysis. Humboldt and Bonpland divided plants into 15 *"divisions physiognomiques"* named for the single plant whose presence in a given locale most determined the appearance of the region's flora. The authors also explored the origins of the plant groups they identified and decided that climate was the most powerful determinant.

To some, Humboldt represents a turning away from the romantic vision of nature to a scientific one. Others, however, have seen in his work a merging of these two views. In *Cosmos,* his last major work, which appeared in 15 volumes between 1845 and 1862, Humboldt repeatedly refers to "one great whole animated by the breath of life," and he adopts as his central theme the growing, creative and unfinished quality of nature.

Humboldt was born and died in Berlin.

Further reading: Thomas M. Zottmann, *Alexander von Humboldt: Scientist, Explorer, Adventurer* (New York: Pantheon, 1960).

Hussein, Saddam (April 23, 1937–   )

Saddam Hussein, president of Iraq, conducted a form of ecological warfare during the Persian Gulf War in 1991. In late January, Hussein ordered the valves opened at Sea Island Terminal in Kuwait, the nation he had invaded. Thousands of barrels of oil spewed into the Persian Gulf. At al Ahmadi, he ordered plugs pulled on five Kuwaiti tankers loaded with 3 million gallons of petroleum. Three days after the oil began flowing into the gulf waters, the oil slick caught fire. In addition to these deliberate discharges, Hussein set ablaze oil fields at Wafra, Khafji and elsewhere in Kuwait.

The oil spill contaminated sea-grass regions that provided food for marsh birds, ruined mangrove stands and severely damaged the area's fishing industry. The spill also threatened the operation of desalinization plants, on which the populations of the region depend for drinking water. The oil-field fires, which burned out of control for months, created massive air pollution. Only time will tell the full extent of damage caused by these unprecedented acts of ecological terrorism.

Further reading: Efraim Karsh and Inari Rautsi, *Saddam Hussein: A Political Biography* (New York: Free Press, 1991); Elaine Sciolino, *The Outlaw State: Saddam Hussein's Quest for Power and the War in the Gulf* (New York: Wiley, 1991).

Hutchinson, George Evelyn (January 30, 1903– May 17, 1991)

Professor of biology from 1928 to 1965 and Sterling professor of zoology from 1965 to 1972 at Yale University, George Evelyn Hutchinson was one of the founders of the modern science of ecology. Early in his career, he claimed that the burning of forests had direct impact on global warming, and as early as 1943 he wrote that the most important goal of science was to teach human beings how to avoid destroying their environment. Much of his work was devoted to limnology, the study of life in lakes and ponds, and his four-volume *A Treatise on Limnology* (1957) is considered a standard reference.

Born in Cambridge, England, Hutchinson began his teaching career in 1926 at the University of Witwatersrand in South Africa. Three years later, he moved to Yale University, where he remained until his retirement in 1972. Among his other published works are *The Clear Mirror* (1936), *The Itinerant Ivory Tower* (1958), *The Enchanted Voyage* (1962), *The Ecological Theater and the Evolutionary Play* (1965) and *An Introduction to Population Ecology* (1978).

Hutchinson received numerous awards for his scientific work, including the Eminent Ecologist Award of the ECOLOGICAL SOCIETY OF AMERICA in 1962, the Daniel Giraud Elliot Medal of the National Academy of Sciences in 1984 and the Kyoto Prize in Basic Science from Japan in 1986.

Hutchinson died in London.

I

Ickes, Harold LeClair (March 15, 1874–
February 3, 1952)

As secretary of the interior during Franklin D. ROO-
SEVELT's administration, Ickes brought a vigorous
spirit of reform to his department, developing a strong
national parks system, ending racial segregation
throughout the department (including the parks) and
enforcing the department's stewardship of and authority over the nation's forests and public lands,
preserving them from unregulated exploitation by
real estate investors and lumber, mining and power
companies.

Born on a farm in Frankstown Township, Pennsylvania, Ickes moved to Chicago at 16 following the
death of his mother. He received a B.A. from the
University of Chicago in 1897, worked briefly as a
newspaper reporter and took a law degree in 1907.
From the beginning, Ickes was a reformer, endorsing
Theodore ROOSEVELT's Bull Moose candidacy for
president in 1912 and working for civic improvement,
civil rights for African-Americans and conservation
causes. He made little headway in these pursuits
until 1932, when he swung the liberal midwestern
Republican vote to Franklin D. Roosevelt and was
subsequently appointed to the post of secretary of
the U.S. Department of the INTERIOR.

In addition to his reforms within the department
and the extension of its authority, Ickes, as head of
the Depression-era Public Works Administration, initiated massive reclamation projects, including the
construction of the Grand Coulee, Bonneville and
Boulder (Hoover) dams. In addition to his cabinet
post and direction of the PWA, Ickes was oil administrator under the National Recovery Administration
(NRA). He was a strong proponent of federal regulation of natural resources and of preservation of the
wilderness. During World War II, when demand for
natural resources was especially great, he managed

to stave off private attempts to exploit mineral and
timber resources within the national parks.

An extraordinarily able administrator, Ickes was
contentious and could even be petty and suspicious.
After Roosevelt's death in April 1945, President Truman retained Ickes as Interior secretary. However,
in 1946, the president nominated a California oil man
as undersecretary of the Navy, a move Ickes saw as

Secretary of the Interior Harold L. Ickes at the dedication
of the new Department of the Interior Building, Washington, D.C., April 1936. *Courtesy of the National Park Service*

inviting a conflict of interest scandal similar to the Teapot Dome debacle that had marred the Harding administration. In protest, Ickes resigned from the cabinet.

A widower since the death of his wife in a 1935 auto accident, Ickes, 64, married 25-year-old Jane Dahlman in 1938. After leaving Truman's cabinet, he retired to his Olney, Maryland, farm with his young wife and their two children.

Further reading: Ickes, *The Secret Diary of Harold L. Ickes* (New York: Simon and Schuster, 1953–54); *The Autobiography of a Curmudgeon* (New York: Simon and Schuster, 1948); Elmo Richardson, *Dams, Parks, and Politics* (Lexington: University Press of Kentucky, 1973).

Institute for Energy and Environmental Research (Founded: 1985)
6935 Laurel Avenue, Takoma Park, Maryland 20912; (301) 270-5500

IEER was formed to provide citizens and policy makers alike with scientific and technical studies on a wide range of policy issues of importance to public health and safety and the protection and restoration of the environment. The institute has as its primary goal the democratization of science and the promotion of a safer and healthier environment by bringing to bear upon public policy issues the latest in scientific thought.

IEER works with a variety of citizens' groups, environmental organizations, law firms and governments to analyze environmental problems and issues in such areas as health risks to personnel working in nuclear fuel cycle facilities, energy conservation, electric utility investment planning, municipal solid waste management, long-term military and civilian radioactive waste management, stratospheric ozone depletion, global climate change and Third World energy policy.

IEER has worked with the Congressional Office of Technology Assessment, International Physicians for the Prevention of Nuclear War, the State of Nevada Nuclear Waste Project Office, Hanford Education Action League, ENVIRONMENTAL POLICY INSTITUTE, Three Mile Island Public Health Fund, Edison Electric Institute and GREENPEACE, Germany. IEER's work is supported in part by foundation grants, concerned individuals and consulting contracts. Two special programs, Project on the Protection of the Global Atmosphere and Project on the Nuclear Weapons Complex, are supported by foundation grants. IEER has a collaborative relationship with a sister institute, Institut für Energie und Umweltforschung, in Heidelberg, Germany.

IEER's president is Arjun MAKHIJANI, and its executive director is Bernd Franke.

Institution of Environmental Sciences
(Founded: 1971)
14 Princes Gate, Hyde Park, London 8W7 1PU, England

With 700 members representing professional and educational institutions, industry, environmental agencies and universities in 50 countries, the Institution of Environmental Sciences works to increase public awareness of and involvement in environmental issues. The organization encourages interdisciplinary studies of the environment and advises schools, agencies, libraries and the public on current issues. In addition, the organization engages British school-age children in environmental issues through an annual essay competition. Directed by Alistair Baillie, the organization publishes *The Environmentalist*, a quarterly, the IES Monograph Series, the *IES Newsheet*, the *IES Proceedings* and a *Membership Directory*. The organization supports six regional and 10 national groups and holds quarterly conferences and monthly meetings.

Interior, U.S. Department of the (Founded: 1849)
Washington, D.C. 20240; (202) 208-6416

The Department of the Interior was created by Congress to manage myriad responsibilities, including the administration of public lands; mineral, timber and water resources; Indian affairs; war-related pensions; the Patent Office; and the Census Bureau. Three major divisions of the department were formed soon after its creation: Lands and Railroads, Indians, and Patents and Miscellaneous.

In the late 19th century, public concern over the disposal of land and the management of natural resources led to a new direction for the department. Conservationists such as John Wesley POWELL and William E. Smythe and, later, Gifford PINCHOT and Theodore ROOSEVELT, pushed the department toward adopting policies of sustained-yield management of timber, stricter grazing restrictions and reclamation. In addition, other conservationists, such as George Perkins MARSH, John MUIR and Aldo LEOPOLD, urged the department to promote policies aimed at preserving a portion of the nation's land resources in their natural state.

In 1891, the General Revision Act authorized the creation of forest reserves, and seven years later, the department began selling timber from the reserves and leasing grazing rights, under the provisions of the Forest Management Act.

Throughout the 20th century, the department's policies have focused not on the disposal of land but on its management, as evidenced by the creation of the Bureau of RECLAMATION in 1903, the Bureau of MINES in 1920, the NATIONAL PARK SERVICE in 1916, the United States FISH AND WILDLIFE SERVICE in 1939 and the Bureau of LAND MANAGEMENT in 1946. Legislation during this century, including the Antiquities Act of 1906, the Wilderness Act of 1964 and the Federal Land Policy and Management Act of 1976, has further strengthened the department's position that the disposal of land is no longer a viable solution to land management problems. These acts and others have increasingly drawn the department into the role of environmental defender, and today the department's own brochure proclaims its preeminence as the "nation's principal conservation agency."

Manuel LUJAN Jr., former congressman from New Mexico, was appointed secretary of the interior by George Bush in 1989 and was replaced by Mike Espy in the Cabinet of President Bill Clinton.

Under the assistant secretary for fish and wildlife and parks are the National Park Service and the U.S. Fish and Wildlife Service. The National Park Service administers 350 areas, including national parks, monuments, historic sites, battlefields, seashores and recreation areas. The service also administers the Land and Water Conservation Fund for the states and manages the Urban Park and Recreation Recovery Program, in addition to carrying out educational programs and maintaining the National Register of Historic Places. The U.S. Fish and Wildlife Service oversees the management of migratory birds, endangered species, freshwater and anadromous fisheries and marine mammals. With seven regional offices and several field units, the service manages 450 national wildlife refuges and determines regulations for the hunting of migratory birds.

Under the assistant secretary of Indian affairs is the Bureau of Indian Affairs. In addition to its work with the governments of recognized Native American tribes, the bureau manages 53 million acres of land held by the United States government in trust for the tribes.

Under the assistant secretary of lands and minerals management are the Bureau of Land Management; the Office of Surface Mining, Reclamation and Enforcement; and the Minerals Management Service. The Bureau of Land Management manages the 270 million acres of public land owned by the United States government—a land mass that constitutes one-eighth of the total land area of the country. Under the Federal Land Policy and Management Act of 1976, the bureau carries out a program of multiple use and sustained yield. The Office of Surface Mining

regulates coal mining practices and oversees the reclamation of mined areas. The Minerals Management Service oversees drilling leases on the Federal Outer Continental Shelf and manages the funds collected from those leases.

Under the assistant secretary of water and science are the U.S. GEOLOGICAL SURVEY, the Bureau of Mines and the Bureau of Reclamation. The Geological Survey conducts research on global environmental conditions and the nation's surface and ground water resources, assesses energy and mineral resources and produces geographic and cartographic materials. The Bureau of Mines, originally created to oversee mining operations and secure safe working conditions for miners, today manages the nation's mineral resources and conducts research on their availability and use. The Bureau of Reclamation was chartered in 1902 to reclaim the arid lands of the West through a major dam and power plant building program.

In addition, a fifth assistant secretary directs the department's territorial and international affairs.

International Council for Bird Preservation
(Founded: 1922)
32 Cambridge Road, Girton, Cambridge CB3 OPJ, England; (223) 277318

The International Council for Bird Preservation is a federation of organizations devoted to the preservation of bird species. The council gathers and disseminates information on bird conservation and sponsors research and conservation-related activities. In July 1988, the council reported that of the 9,000 species of birds in the world, 1,029 were facing extinction and cited forest cutting in tropical regions and illegal trade in exotic species as primary causes of the increase in the number of threatened species.

The organization holds an international conference every four years and publishes the annual *Bulletin*, a quarterly *Newsletter*, various reports, monographs and the *Bird Red Data Book*. Christoph Imboden is director of the International Council for Bird Preservation.

International Crane Foundation (Founded: 1973)
E-11376 Shady Lane Road, Baraboo, Wisconsin 53913–9778; (608) 356-9462

With 4,000 members worldwide, the International Crane Foundation works to preserve the natural habitats of cranes and to increase crane populations. The organization, under the direction of George W. Archibald and with an annual budget of $500,000, conducts research projects in cooperation with universities, provides tours, operates a speakers' bureau and sponsors a seminar series. Members receive the *ICF*

Bugle, a quarterly publication. Other publications include *Crane Research Around the World* and *Proceedings of the International Crane Workshops.* Members convene for an annual meeting each September.

International Ecology Society (Founded: 1975)

1471 Barclay Street, St. Paul, Minnesota 55106-1405; (612) 774-4971

The International Ecology Society acts on a broad agenda of legislative advocacy, litigation, public programs and education in order to protect wildlife, domestic animals and the environment. Focusing on the protection of wetlands, the control of acid rain and hazardous and toxic wastes, the promotion of national wildlife refuges, the protection of endangered species and the humane treatment of all animals, the organization compiles statistics and publishes a periodic newsletter, the *Eco-Humane Letter,* and a monthly newspaper, *Sunrise.* R. J. Kramer is president of the organization, which has an annual budget of $50,000 and 6,000 members.

International Mountain Society (Founded: 1980)

P. O. Box 1978, Davis, California 95617-1978; (916) 758-7618

The 1,100-member International Mountain Society works to protect mountain lands and people. Through its research programs on mountain regions, the organization publishes issue papers, including *Mountain Ecosystems: Stability and Instability, The Himalaya-Ganges Problem, African Mountains and Highlands* and *Frost and Drought in the Highlands of Papua New Guinea.* The organization sponsors seminars and workshops on mountain-related problems and, as of 1992, had plans to develop an information center and register of professionals with skills related to mountain environments. Jack D. Ives is president of the organization, which has an annual budget of $70,000. Members receive the quarterly publication *Mountain Research and Development.*

International Professional Association for Environmental Affairs (Founded: 1976)

31, rue Montoyer, Boîte Postale 1, B-1040 Brussels, Belgium; (2) 5136083

The International Professional Association for Environmental Affairs is a professional membership organization made up of 200 individuals working in governments, industries, universities and public interest groups on environmental affairs. The association sponsors seminars and workshops on environmental problems and provides a forum for the discussion of these issues through its semiannual conventions. The association is headed by Mark Dubrulle, executive vice president.

International Society for Ecological Modelling (Founded: 1978)

Lanngkaer Vaenge 9, DK-3500 Vaerloese, Denmark; (45) 42480600

Working to promote the exchange of ideas, research results and knowledge in ecological and environmental modeling, the International Society for Ecological Modelling provides its members with information on computer programs, data sources, model construction and equations used in models. In addition, the organization provides computer software useful in ecological modeling. The group, headed by S. E. Joergensen, executive officer, has 457 members in 47 countries. Members receive a semiannual *Ecomod Newsletter.* Other society publications include *Comparison of Forest Water and Energy Exchange Models, Handbook of Environmental Data and Ecological Parameters* and *Principles of Environmental Science and Technology.*

International Society for the Planting and Protection of Trees See MEN OF THE TREES.

International Solar Energy Society (Founded: 1954)

P.O. Box 124, Caulfield East, VIC 3145, Australia; (3) 5717557

This pioneering solar energy advocacy group consists of 4,100 members, most of them solar energy researchers, scientists, engineers and organizations— as well as interested members of the lay public.

The society is affiliated with the American Solar Energy Society and publishes *International Congress Proceedings, ISES News, Solar Energy Journal* and *Sunworld,* a quarterly popular magazine. W. R. Read is secretary treasurer of ISES.

International Union for Conservation of Nature and Natural Resources (Founded: 1948)

Avenue du Mont-Blanc, CH-1196 Gland, Switzerland; (22) 649114

The largest international conservation organization, the International Union for Conservation of Nature and Natural Resources (IUCN) counts among its members 116 of the 160 national governments of the world, 126 government agencies and 342 nongovernmental agencies. The union has been active in work carried out by the United Nations, including the

World Heritage program and the Convention on International Trade in Endangered Species.

With 2,000 researchers around the world, the union studies tropical forests, wetlands, deserts, marine zones and population. In 1980, the IUCN launched the World Conservation Strategy, focusing on the preservation of genetic diversity, the maintenance of essential ecological systems and the "discriminative" use of species and ecosystems through programs that will keep those species and ecosystems at sustainable levels.

In addition to researching conservation issues, the union finances and directs conservation projects around the world. In seven Central African countries, the IUCN provides training in forest management; in the Karakoram Mountains of Pakistan, it provides villagers with learning packages that instruct them in establishing nurseries and selecting trees for timber, firewood, fruit and shade; in Costa Rica, it trains local people in the raising of iguanas for food and for limited trade.

IUCN research around the world has furnished data used to persuade governments to establish parks and preserves and to pass legislation to protect wildlife. In addition, the union has drafted international treaties to regulate trafficking in endangered species and to enforce the conservation of species and ecosystems. The IUCN maintains special committees on ecology, education and training, environmental policy, law and administration, national parks and protected areas, species survival and sustainable development. It publishes a quarterly *IUCN Bulletin*, periodic *Protected Areas Systems Reviews* and other reports and monographs. Martin W. HOLDGATE is currently the director general.

International Union of Radioecologists
(Founded: 1978)
5, rue Cardinal Cardijn, B-4480 Oupeye, Belgium; (41) 642564

With 250 members who work as radioecologists in 35 countries, the International Union of Radioecologists promotes study of the effects of radioactivity on the environment. Through workshops, seminars and fellowships for students, the union fosters the exchange of ideas among members, who participate in working groups devoted to specific topics: Environmental Assessment Modeling, Future Objectives in Radioecology, Marine Radioecology: Plant-Animal Transfer Factors, Radioecology of Major Rivers, Soil-to-Plant Transfer Factors, Specific Needs of Developing Countries in the Field of Radioecology and Waste Storage. Publications of the union include a periodic *Information Bulletin* and *Proceedings of Workshops* and a booklet entitled *Actual and Future Objectives in Radioecology.*

International Whaling Commission (Founded: 1976)
The Red House, 135 Station Road, Histon, Cambridge CB4 4NP, England; (223) 233971

Composed of representatives from 36 countries, the International Whaling Commission regulates the whaling industry in an effort to conserve whale populations. The group commissions research reports on whales and whaling, gathers data on current whale populations and disseminates information on whale stocks.

In July 1990, representatives to the commission from Japan and Norway asked the organization to lift its ban on the commercial hunting of minke whales, which was imposed in 1986 as part of the commission's ban on all commercial whaling. The commission voted to uphold the ban, without exception, by more than a two-thirds majority, despite Japan's threat to pull out of the commission.

The commission publishes an *Annual Report*, which includes papers and reports of its scientific committee. It holds a convention in June or July of each year. R. Cambell serves as secretary.

International Wildlife Coalition (Founded: 1982)
634 North Falmouth Highway, P. O. Box 388, North Falmouth, Massachusetts 02556; (508) 564-9980

The International Wildlife Coalition works to preserve wildlife and wildlife habitats. The organization sponsors a research program and publishes Information Packets and a quarterly entitled *Whalewatch*. David J. Morast is president of the organization, which has 130,000 supporters. The group was formerly known as I-KARE (Killing Animals for Recreational Enjoyment).

Ives, John (Jack) David (October 15, 1931–   )
A native of Grimsby, England, Jack Ives is a physical geographer whose research centers on glaciers, deglaciation and the effects of erosion by glacier melt water and the history of the recession of the last major ice sheets. In addition to studying glaciers and deglaciation, Ives researches the geoecology of mountain regions, including renewable resources in the mountains of Nepal, China, Thailand, South America and the former Soviet Union.

Ives, a Canadian citizen, was educated at the University of Nottingham (B.A., 1953) and McGill University, from which he received a Ph.D. in geography (1956). Beginning in 1955, Ives worked as a geographer at the Sub-Arctic Research Laboratory of McGill University, becoming director of geography at the laboratory and assistant professor at the university in 1957. He left these positions in 1960 to become director of the division of physical geography of the Geography Branch, Canadian Department of Mines and Technical Survey. From 1964 to 1967, he served as director of the branch.

Ives left the Department of Mines and Technical Survey to become director of the Institute of Arctic and Alpine Research of the University of Colorado at Boulder, a post he held until 1979. From 1967 to 1989, Ives was also professor of geography at the university. He moved to the University of California at Davis in 1989 as chairperson of the department of geography.

Ives has been active in many geographical and ecological organizations and research bodies, including the subcommittee on glaciers of Canada's National Resource Council (1960–67) and the Canadian committee of the International Geographical Union (1961–67). Since 1974, Ives has served as chairman of the U.S. Directorate Project on Human Impacts on Mountain Ecosystems. Also in 1974, he became chairman of the International Geographical Union Commission on Mountain Geoecology and the United Nations University Project on Highland-Lowland Interactive Systems. He held this latter post until 1990, when he became chairman of the United Nations University Project on Ecology and Sustainable Development. Ives is a member of the Glaciological Society, Asian-American Geographers, the International Mountain Society (serving as president since 1980) and the Arctic Institute of North America.

Ives was a Guggenheim fellow (1976–77) and visiting professor at Bern University, Switzerland.

In 1969, Ives founded the *Journal of Arctic and Alpine Research*, serving as its editor until 1981, when he founded the *Journal of Mountain Research and Development*.

Izaak Walton League of America (Founded: 1922)

1401 Wilson Boulevard, Level B, Arlington, Virginia 22209; (703) 528-1818

Named for the celebrated 17th-century English author of *The Compleat Angler*, the Izaak Walton League of America was founded in Chicago, Illinois, by fishermen who were dismayed over the deteriorating condition of America's streams, rivers and lakes. First concentrating on legislation to control water pollution, wetland drainage and logging along waterways, the IWLA then expanded its scope to include soil conservation and air pollution.

In 1927, at the request of President Calvin Coolidge, the IWLA undertook a survey of water pollution. Following this, and after years of IWLA campaigning, Congress finally passed the Water Pollution Control Law of 1948. Since then, the league has campaigned against the building of dams in national parks and in Superior National Forest and against the use of national forests and public lands for private livestock grazing.

The league had 50,000 members in 400 local groups in 1991.

J

Jackson, Wes (June 15, 1936–　　　　)

With his wife, Dana, Topeka-born Wes Jackson is codirector of the LAND INSTITUTE in Salina, Kansas, which is working to change the face of agriculture. At the organization's headquarters, the Jacksons work with a handful of staff members and students to explore the feasibility of changing the crops grown on American farms, replacing nutrient-depleting, soil-eroding annuals with soil-increasing, self-sustaining perennials.

Jackson holds a B.A. from Kansas Wesleyan University, an M.A. from the University of Kansas and a Ph.D. in genetics from North Carolina State University. He has written widely on the subjects of agriculture and ecology. His book-length works include *Man and the Environment* (1971), *New Roots for Agriculture* (1980), *Meeting the Expectations of the Land* (with Wendell Berry and Bruce Colman, 1985) and *Altars of Unhewn Stone* (1987). Throughout his research, Jackson has maintained a single goal: to find through the study of the natural environment a sustainable agriculture and to discover the system's underlying principles. From that discovery, Jackson hopes to devise a workable crop plan that does not require the introduction of harmful chemicals into the environment, that reduces the use of fossil fuel by farmers and that minimizes erosion of topsoil.

Organized in 1976, the Land Institute is a combination research center and school. The institute has investigated alternative energy technologies, including wind turbines and solar collectors, but its primary focus is on finding ways to prevent soil erosion. What led Jackson to this focus was his discovery that soil losses during the Dust Bowl years were no greater than those of today. The major culprit is agribusiness, which every year cultivates huge expanses of single crops and then plows them under, leaving the soil susceptible to erosion.

Jackson, his staff and students are examining perennials native to the prairie. Although he carefully tends crops of Maximillian sunflower, eastern gama grass, Illinois bundleflower, bee balm, light poppy mallow and others, he admits that using them for food is not feasible at this point. Still, he hopes that over the next 50 to 100 years, variations of these plants will be cultivated that can indeed replace corn and wheat and other soil-depleting crops in human diets. The ideal he is working toward is a farm field that closely resembles a virgin prairie, where the roots of perennials firmly bind the soil and provide new growth year after year. In addition, many of the plants grown in this ideal farm field would provide natural protection from pests, and because the fields would not be plowed under each year, less fossil fuel would be required to sustain the crops.

Jackson's institute has an annual budget of around $500,000. Funds are obtained from foundations, individual donations, tuition and proceeds from the sale of organically grown crops from the institute's garden. Students enroll for a 43-week term. Their courses range from ecology to philosophy, and they sign up for specific research projects and for farming duties. The institute also publishes a magazine, *The Land Report*, which Dana Jackson has edited since 1976.

Jahn, Laurence Roy (June 26, 1926–　　　　)

This noted biologist, a native of Jefferson, Wisconsin, joined the staff of the WILDLIFE MANAGEMENT INSTITUTE in 1959 as the north central field representative. In 1970, he moved to the institute's headquarters in Washington, D.C., as director of conservation. Seventeen years later, he was named president of the organization.

Jahn has held leadership positions with the North American Wildlife Foundation and the WILDLIFE SO-

120

CIETY (he was president 1979 to 1980). He has also served on various national committees and commissions, including an advisory committee on marine fisheries of the U.S. Department of Commerce, an advisory committee on wildlife of the Department of State and an advisory committee on fish, wildlife and parks of the U.S. Department of the INTERIOR. He was named a fellow of the American Association for the Advancement of Science in 1971.

Jahn holds a B.S. in zoology, an M.S. in wildlife management and a Ph.D. in wildlife ecology and zoology, all from the University of Wisconsin, Madison. He has conducted extensive research on wildlife populations and ways to minimize the impact of development on natural habitats.

Jamison, (Delos) Cy (April 12, 1949–   )

Appointed director of the Bureau of LAND MANAGEMENT by President George Bush in 1989, Cy Jamison was born in Billings, Montana, and educated at Eastern Montana College, earning a B.S. in secondary education in 1971.

Jamison began his career in government in 1973 as a public affairs specialist in the Denver, Colorado, field office of the secretary of the U.S. Department of the INTERIOR. He left this post in 1974 to become a public affairs specialist with the Bureau of Land Management's Montana state office in Billings. In 1976, he served as employee development specialist for the office, moving on to youth program manager in 1978. From 1980 to 1981, Jamison was legislative affairs specialist in the Billings office. He moved to Washington, D.C., in 1981 to become Republican consultant on the Oversight and Investigations Subcommittee of the House Committee on Interior and Insular Affairs, and in 1983, he became House liaison for the secretary of the interior. He returned to Billings in 1984 as district field director for Montana Congressman Marlenee.

Jamison became legislative advisor on the National Parks and Public Lands Subcommittee of the House Committee on Interior and Insular Affairs in 1985, serving until his appointment to the directorship of the BLM in 1989. He left the BLM upon the inauguration of Bill Clinton, who nominated Jim Baca as the new director.

Johnson, Lady Bird (Claudia Alta) (December 22, 1912–   )

The wife of President Lyndon B. JOHNSON, Lady Bird Johnson used her position as the nation's First Lady to further the cause of what was termed in the early 1960s "beautification." She began her campaign in February 1965, when she and Secretary of the Interior

Mrs. Lyndon B. Johnson is named an "honorary ranger" in the National Park Service, 1974. At right are Ron Walker and Nathaniel P. Reed. *Photo by James Aycock, courtesy of the National Park Service*

Stewart UDALL gathered a group of philanthropists, designers, publishers, officials and civic leaders to form the Committee for a More Beautiful Capital. The committee organized clean-up and fix-up projects in Washington's neighborhoods, planted flowers and generally refurbished the city and its surrounding suburbs. The committee landscaped parks, planted some 2 million bulbs, 83,000 spring-flowering plants, 50,000 shrubs, 25,000 trees and 137,000 annuals.

From this beginning, Lady Bird Johnson was instrumental in securing public support for a host of environmental and "beautification" legislative acts during her husband's administration. Mrs. Johnson believed that "beautification," despite the superficial and cosmetic connotation of the term, encouraged a deep respect for the land and the environment, including a desire to protect such resources as clean air and clean water.

Lady Bird Johnson's best-remembered "beautification" campaign from the White House years is her effort to abate litter and advertising "pollution" along the nation's highways. It was largely her efforts, which heightened public awareness of the visual blight along many American roadways, that made possible the passage of the Highway Beautification Act of 1965, a measure that regulated billboard advertising along interstate and primary highways.

Lady Bird Johnson's concern for the environment did not end when she and her husband left the White House in 1969. Returning to Texas, she began to work with the Highway Department of that state to encourage the cultivation of wildflowers along the roads. Mrs. Johnson became increasingly interested in the subject of wildflowers and, in 1982, donated funds and 60 acres of land on the Colorado River just outside of Austin, Texas, for the establishment of the National Wildflower Research Center. Directed by Dr. David Northington, the center has as its goals (in Mrs. Johnson's words) "to learn as much as we can about wildflower propagation and growth and to be a clearinghouse to spread knowledge to developers, park managers, and private citizens everywhere."

Johnson, Lyndon Baines (August 27, 1908–January 22, 1973)

Lyndon Baines Johnson, elected vice-president in 1960, became the 36th president of the United States following the assassination of John F. Kennedy on November 22, 1963. He was reelected in 1964.

Johnson's presidency was marked, on the one hand, by the escalating war in Vietnam and, on the other, by a liberal agenda for national social change that included epochal advances in the areas of civil rights, education and the environment. Programs in these areas were grouped under the umbrella of what Johnson termed the "Great Society"—his version of what FRANKLIN DELANO ROOSEVELT had called the New Deal and John F. Kennedy, the New Frontier.

President Johnson appointed an Environmental Pollution Panel and, in the course of his administration, signed into law such important measures as the 1964 amendments to the Federal Insecticide, Fungicide and Rodenticide Act, more effectively regulating the use of biocides. Congress expanded the scope of the 1956 Water Pollution Control Act Amendments through the Water Quality Act of 1965, enjoining the states to establish and enforce water-quality standards. The legislation involved the federal government more deeply than ever before in water quality issues. President Johnson also commissioned from the President's Science Advisory Committee (PSAC) a 317-page report called *Restoring the Quality of Our Environment*, which appeared in 1965 and which stressed the importance of setting threshold limits (tolerance levels) for pollutants affecting human health. The year 1965 also saw passage of the Solid Waste Disposal Act, which called for research and aid to the states in dealing with the nation's ever-mounting pile of garbage.

The Johnson administration's concern with the environment extended beyond controlling pollution. In large part encouraged and aided—perhaps even prodded—by his wife LADY BIRD JOHNSON, Lyndon Johnson directed the national attention to issues relating to the "beautification" of the environment. The Public Land Law Review Commission, established in

President Lyndon B. Johnson signing the North Cascades National Park Act. *U.S. Department of the Interior, National Park Service photo by Cecil Stoughton*

1964, studied public land policy and land law, issuing a report entitled *One-third of the Nation's Land*. While critics called it bland, "weighted heavily on the side of mining, timber, and other commercial users," it did succeed in heading off proposals to sell much of the public domain to private interests. The Wilderness Act of 1964 gave legislative protection to some 9.1 million acres, forming the core of a federally protected wilderness that would be greatly expanded over succeeding years. In 1965, the Highway Beautification Act instituted controls on billboard advertising along interstate and federally funded highways. The Redwood National Park Act of 1968 set aside 58,000 forest acres in northern California, site of the nation's oldest and, many would say, grandest trees. Also in 1968, President Johnson sent a special message to Congress. Entitled "To Renew a Nation," it was broadcast on radio and television, and called on "all Americans . . . to join us in this urgent task of conserving America the beautiful." One additional act, not directly related to the environment, nevertheless proved invaluable to generations of environmental activists. The Freedom of Information Act of 1966, which mandated the public availability of all "matters of official record," gave environmentalists a powerful tool for creating political and administrative change.

Lyndon Baines Johnson was born near Stonewall, Texas, the son of a state legislator, schoolteacher and rancher. He was educated at Southwest Texas State College, graduating in 1930 with a B.S. degree. He had taught grade school from 1928 to 1929 in Cotulla, Texas, and public speaking and debate at Sam Houston High School, Houston, from 1930 to 1931. Johnson served as secretary to Representative Richard Kleberg, a Texas Democrat, from 1932 to 1935; was state director for Texas of the National Youth Administration from 1935 to 1937; and won a special election to fill a U.S. House of Representatives seat left vacant by the death of James Paul Buchanan. Johnson was reelected to the seat five times, serving until 1948. In December 1941, he obtained consent from the House for a leave of absence to enter service in the U.S. Naval Reserve, thereby becoming the first member of Congress during World War II to enter active duty. Johnson was awarded the silver star for gallantry under fire.

In 1948, Johnson was elected to the Senate and was reelected in 1954 and 1960. A 1955 heart attack threatened to cut short his political career, but he recovered and, in 1960, was nominated for the presidency of the United States. Defeated by John F. Kennedy, he served as Kennedy's running mate. Johnson was elected vice-president even as he was reelected senator from Texas. He was sworn in as senator on January 3, 1961, resigned three minutes later, and was sworn in as vice-president on January 20.

On March 31, 1968, President Johnson, convinced that his role in the Vietnam War made him unelectable, announced in a televised speech that he would not seek another term. Lyndon Baines Johnson succumbed to a heart attack four years and two days after he left office.

Jorling, Thomas C. (June 25, 1940–   )
From 1977 to 1979, during the administration of President Jimmy Carter, Thomas C. Jorling served as assistant administrator of the ENVIRONMENTAL PROTECTION AGENCY for water and hazardous materials. In this capacity, he was responsible for developing and enforcing some of the nation's most ambitious and most costly antipollution regulations, including those pursuant to the Clean Water Act, the Ocean Dumping Act, the Safe Drinking Water Act and the Resource Conservation and Recovery Act.

Jorling received his B.S. degree from the University of Notre Dame in 1962 and went on to earn an M.S. in ecology from Washington State University in 1969. Jorling combined his scientific education with legal training, earning a law degree from Boston College in 1966 and gaining admission to the Massachusetts and District of Columbia bars.

Jorling served as assistant counsel to the Smithsonian Institution and attorney-advisor in the Solicitor's Office of the U.S. Department of the INTERIOR before becoming minority counsel to the U.S. Senate Committee on Public Works from 1969 to 1972. In this capacity, he advised on the creation of the environmental legislation he was later responsible for implementing and enforcing at the EPA.

Jorling left Washington in 1972 to become professor of environmental studies and director of the Center for Environmental Studies at Williams College in Williamstown, Massachusetts. He returned to Washington in 1977 to take up the EPA post. Jorling resigned as assistant EPA administrator in 1979 to return to Williams College. In 1980, he served on the President's Commission on an Agenda for the Eighties, and from 1982 to 1983, he was visiting professor at the University of California, Santa Cruz. In 1987, New York governor Mario M. Cuomo appointed Jorling commissioner of environmental conservation, Department of Environmental Conservation.

Jorling is a member of the American Association for the Advancement of Science and the ECOLOGICAL SOCIETY OF AMERICA.

K

Kahn, Herman (February 15, 1922–July 7, 1983)

Born in Bayonne, New Jersey, Herman Kahn was educated at the University of California, Los Angeles (B.A., 1945) and the California Institute of Technology (M.A., 1948). From 1948 to 1960, he was a member of the Rand Corporation's "think tank" of technological and political consultants, and from 1961 until his death, he was associated with the Hudson Institute in Croton-on-Hudson, New York. A center he helped to found, the Hudson Institute researched defense work for the United States government and also delved into research on the future of American policy.

Kahn became widely known to the scientific and political communities, as well as to the public at large, during the 1960s for his efforts to think about "the unthinkable": the consequences of thermonuclear war. His *On Thermonuclear War* appeared in 1962, and *Thinking about the Unthinkable* was published the same year.

In addition to his works on thermonuclear war, Kahn was one of the earliest and most important "futurists." His speculations about the future include *The Year 2000* (1967), *The Emerging Japanese Superstate* (1970), *The Future of the Corporation,* (1974) and *The Next 200 Years: A Scenario for America and the World* (1976).

Kahn's thought, particularly in the 1960s and 1970s, was highly influential in government circles, including those responsible for establishing environmental policy. A member of the Council on Foreign Relations, the Center for Inter-American Relations, the American Political Science Association, Phi Beta Kappa and Phi Mu Epsilon, Kahn was awarded two honorary Ph.D.s, from the University of Puget Sound and from the Worcester Polytechnic Institute, both in 1976.

Keep America Beautiful Inc. (Founded: 1953)
9 West Broad Street, Stamford, Connecticut 06902; (203) 323-8987

Originally founded to mount a nationwide campaign against litter, Keep America Beautiful Inc. has branched out from its original mission to encompass the promotion of sound waste-handling principles in the United States. Today, the organization disseminates information to the public on waste reduction at its source, recycling, waste-to-energy programs, sanitary landfills and composting. Roger E. Powers is president of the organization.

Through its KAB System, the group's principal program, 450 communities across the country work to promote responsible attitudes and approaches to waste handling. Launched in 1976, the system engages community residents in a results-oriented program. Keep America Beautiful Inc. trains community leaders in carrying out the program, which includes a community-specific analysis of litter and solid wastes, the development of goals and the setting of priorities for the community. Fees to cover the training of community leaders are based on the community's size.

Recently, the KAB System has been expanded to include states that wish to participate. So far, 18 states have been certified through the program. The organization has documented the savings created by the KAB System in various communities and has found that, within three years of implementation, communities enjoyed a 55% reduction in litter and realized a cost-benefit of $9 for every $1 invested.

In addition to the KAB System, Keep America Beautiful Inc. has also developed curriculum programs: Waste in Place, for elementary schools; and Waste: A Hidden Resource, for secondary schools. The organization worked with the TENNESSEE VAL-

Aluminum cans collected at a recycling center run by the Warner-Robins Clean Community Commission, Georgia, are loaded for delivery to a processing plant. The commission is a local affiliate of Keep America Beautiful, Inc. *Keep America Beautiful, Inc.*

LEY AUTHORITY to produce and test the latter program.

KAB has carried out extensive public service campaigns, including the familiar "weeping Indian" ad of the 1980s, in which a Native American guides a canoe along a polluted and littered stream and is shown at the end of the advertisement with a single tear running down his face. In 1990, KAB adopted as its new slogan, "Let's not waste the 90s."

Keep America Beautiful Inc. publishes a six-page quarterly newsletter, *KAB Vision,* featuring news about the national organization and its community programs and articles on litter prevention, voluntary recycling and community improvement programs. *Keep America Beautiful—Annual Review* includes a list of all communities certified through the KAB System and those working toward certification.

Kelly, Petra Karin (November 29, 1947–October 1992)

Kelly was a political leader and environmental activist. A member of the Green Party, she served in the West German Bundestag from 1983 to 1987. She was a founding member of the Green Party in 1979. Born in Gunzberg, West Germany, Kelly moved to the United States with her mother and stepfather, a U.S. Army officer, in 1960. She graduated from American University's School of International Service in Washington, D.C., in 1970. While a student there, she campaigned actively for Robert F. Kennedy during his bid for the 1968 Democratic nomination and founded Students for Kennedy in Washington. After Kennedy's assassination, she worked for Hubert H. Humphrey's campaign.

After graduating from American University, Kelly enrolled at the University of Amsterdam to study political science and worked as a research assistant at the Europa Institute until October 1971. Later that year, she joined the staff of the European Community in Brussels as an assistant in its general secretariat. In October 1973, she was named administrative counselor in the secretariat, a post she held until 1982.

As a founder of the Green Party, Kelly helped transform the loosely knit band of environmentalists, feminists and pacifists into a strong political force. In the March 1983 elections in West Germany, the Greens received 5.6% of the vote and were therefore entitled to send 17 representatives, including Kelly, to the 498-member Bundestag. Although the Greens were aware that their bloc of votes was small, their parliamentary representatives, including Kelly, vowed to engage in acts of civil disobedience in order to effect change. They pledged to disclose secret military and political documents they believed to be of interest to the public; to boycott the national census; to participate in peace marches in Moscow, Washington and Geneva; and to investigate financial irregularities.

In 1987, the Greens received 8.3% of the vote, but in a crushing defeat in 1990, they received only 3.9% a total that was 1.1% below the level required for parliamentary representation. Some party representatives cited the group's opposition to the reunification of Germany as a major cause of its defeat. Kelly, a pacifist, died a violent death when she was shot by her companion, 69-year-old Gert Bastian, who then killed himself. The bodies were discovered on October 19, 1992, but the exact date of death is unknown.

Kinney, Abbot (November 16, 1850–November 14, 1920)

Best known as a southern California real estate developer, Kinney was a social reformer (his special concern was the California Mission Indians) and an advocate of forest and watershed protection throughout semi-arid southern California. His *Eucalyptus* (1895) promoted the spread of this Australian hardwood in

California, and *Forest and Water* (1900) convincingly made the case for watershed protection in the state.

Kinney served as chairman of the California State Board of Forestry from 1886 to 1889, which carried out the state's first forest resource survey. Kinney was also an effective Yosemite Valley commissioner (1897–1901) and an early supporter of professional forestry education.

Kinney, Jay P. (September 18, 1875–December 2, 1975)

Recipient of the first master of forestry degree granted by Cornell University (1913), Kinney joined the U.S. Indian Service in 1910, charged with establishing its first branch of forestry. He served as head of this branch until 1933, when he became general production supervisor for CIVILIAN CONSERVATION CORPS (CCC) projects on Indian reservations. In 1942, he became associate director of soil conservation in the Office of Land Utilization of the Department of the INTERIOR. Three years later, despite a policy of mandatory retirement at 70, Kinney was appointed adviser in forestry for the U.S. Department of Justice. Among Kinney's distinguished publications are *The Essentials of American Timber Law* (1917), *The Development of Forest Law in America* (1917), *A Continent Lost— A Civilization Won: Indian Land Tenure in America* (1937) and *Indian Forest and Range* (1950).

Born in Snowden, New York, Jay P. Kinney died in Hartwick, New York.

Further reading: George S. Kephart, "Kinney, Jay P." *The Encyclopedia of American Forestry and Conservation* 1.

Kroegel, Paul (January 4, 1864–March 8, 1948)

Born in Chemnitz, Germany, Paul Kroegel immigrated as a young child to the United States with his father. He first lived in New York and Chicago, then moved to Florida at 17, settling in Sebastian, near a small mangrove-covered island at the mouth of the Indian River. Here Kroegel developed an avid interest in the welfare of the pelicans that came to nest year after year. Despite a state law that banned the killing of almost all birds in the region, the pelicans were primary targets of vacationer-hunters in the state. After unsuccessfully trying to buy the island, the American Ornithologists' Union hired Kroegel to protect the pelicans. This meant, on many occasions, positioning himself between the pelicans and the gun-toting vacationers passing by the island on yachts.

Conservationists, including Kroegel, grew more determined to save the pelicans and lobbied President THEODORE ROOSEVELT to set Pelican Island aside as a national bird refuge. On March 14, 1903, the president signed the necessary order and named

Fred Krupp, executive director of the Environmental Defense Fund. © *T. Charles Erickson, courtesy of the Environmental Defense Fund*

Kroegel commissioner of the refuge. He remained in that post until 1919, when the federal government cut the funds used to pay the warden's salary.

In November 1963, the Pelican Island refuge, the first wildlife refuge in the United States, was designated a national historical monument.

Krupp, Fred (March 21, 1954–   )

Executive director of the ENVIRONMENTAL DEFENSE FUND since 1984, Fred Krupp, a native of Mineola, New York, worked in private law firms after his graduation in 1978 from the University of Michigan Law School. He was general counsel for the Connecticut Fund for the Environment in New Haven from 1978 to 1984 and currently serves on the organization's board of directors. In addition, he is a member of the board of RESOURCES FOR THE FUTURE. Krupp is a member of the President's Commission on Environmental Quality, the National Recycling Advisory Council and New York Governor Mario Cuomo's Environmental Advisory Board.

Krupp was instrumental in securing congressional passage of the 1990 Clean Air Act, which includes a plan designed by the Environmental Defense Fund for reducing acid rain. He worked with EDF's task force with the McDonald's fast food chain to devise a solid waste-reduction plan, including the phaseout of styrofoam packaging and the use of recycled and reusable materials.

Since Krupp joined EDF in 1984, its annual budget increased from $3 million to more than $18 million, and full-time staff has more than doubled from 50 to 130. Membership rose from 40,000 to 200,000.

Krutch, Joseph Wood (November 25, 1893–May 22, 1970)

Joseph Wood Krutch originally planned a career teaching high school mathematics, but during his undergraduate study in his native Knoxville, at the University of Tennessee, he became interested in literature. He enrolled in Columbia University's graduate school in 1915 and completed his master's degree in English the following year. After service during World War I in the Army Psychological Corps, Krutch returned to Columbia and received a Ph.D., writing his dissertation on English Restoration comedy.

After traveling in Europe on a fellowship, Krutch became professor of English at Brooklyn Polytechnic Institute until 1924, when he left to become associate editor of the *Nation* from 1924 to 1937. In 1937, he was appointed professor of English at Columbia University.

In 1948, Krutch published a still-standard biography of Henry David Thoreau. Drawing inspiration from the subject of his work, Krutch himself began writing more about natural history and, in 1949, published a collection of essays, *The Twelve Seasons*, in which he reflected on the human significance of various natural phenomena. During a 1950–51 sabbatical, Krutch lived in Tucson, Arizona, a location that provided the inspiration for *The Desert Year*, published in 1952. That year, he resigned his teaching post at Columbia and relocated permanently in Tucson. He published numerous essays in the *Saturday Review* and the *American Scholar*, many of which were collected in *Human Nature and the Human Condition* (1959), *If You Don't Mind My Saying So* (1964) and *And Even If You Do* (1967).

Early in his writing career, Krutch had maintained—in *The Modern Temper* (1929)—that it was necessary for humankind to separate from nature in order to attain its full development. With the publication of *The Twelve Seasons*, however, he reversed his position. He attributed humanity's sense of alienation to a divorce from other living things. "We must be a part not only of the human community, but of the whole community," he wrote. "It is not a sentimental but a grimly literal fact that unless we share this terrestrial globe with creatures other than ourselves, we shall not be able to live on it for long." Because of his advocacy of organicism, Krutch is viewed as a leading proponent of the new ecology and ecological ethic.

Further reading: John D. Margolis, *Joseph Wood Krutch: A Writer's Life* (Knoxville: University of Tennessee Press, 1980).

Kuroda, Yoichi (January 24, 1954–   )

For many years, the island nation of Japan had imported ivory and tropical woods and had engaged in ecologically damaging fishing practices. Yoichi Kuroda, an environmental activist, exposed these practices through his Japan Tropical Action Network, which he founded in 1987. As a result of his publicity campaign, many of the harmful practices have been discontinued or modified. Kuroda may be credited with having insisted that Japan play its part in preserving the global environment. In 1991, he was awarded a Goldman Environmental Prize of $60,000 for his work to curb hardwood imports to Japan.

L

Lacy, John Fletcher (May 30, 1841–September 30, 1913)

Called the "Father of Game Legislation," Lacey was elected to the Iowa House of Representatives in 1869 —his family had moved to Iowa from his native New Martinsville, Virginia (now West Virginia), in 1855— and the U.S. Congress in 1888. During his 16 years in Congress (1889–91; 1893–1907), Lacey was the driving force behind legislation to protect wildlife in Yellowstone National Park, and he sponsored the Lacey Act of 1900, which prohibited interstate shipment of wildlife killed in violation of state law, and the Antiquities Act of 1906, which enabled the establishment of national monuments. Lacey was a close associate of Gifford PINCHOT and Theodore ROOSEVELT, advocating the "wise use" of natural resources through strong federal regulation.

Land Institute (Founded: 1976)

2440 East Water Well Road, Salina, Kansas 76401; (913) 832-5376

Under the direction of Dana and Wes JACKSON, the Land Institute researches sustainable agriculture, promoting responsible stewardship of the earth through programs of research and study of relevant environmental and agricultural issues that use the prairies of the western United States as a model. Of primary interest to the organization are perennial grain crops for American grasslands that require no pesticides or fertilizers, that can be adapted for use as food and that, as perennials, are not plowed under after harvesting. Among the crops under study are Illinois bundleflower, Maximillian sunflower, leymus and eastern gama grass. The organization's land holdings include a 98-acre tract that has never been turned by plow.

With a membership of 2,100 and an annual budget of $700,000, the organization publishes *The Land Re-port* three times a year and an annual *Land Institute Research Report*. It also offers postgraduate internships to students who wish to research sustainable agriculture. Support for the institute comes from private contributions, foundations and subscriptions to *The Land Report*.

Land Management, Bureau of (Established: 1946)

Department of the Interior, Washington, D.C. 20240; (202) 208-5717

The Bureau of Land Management represents a consolidation of the General Land Office (created in 1812) and the Grazing Service (created in 1934) and is a bureau within the U.S. Department of the INTERIOR. The Federal Land Policy and Management Act of 1976 defined the BLM's present mission, which is to oversee and manage the development of energy and mineral leases and ensure compliance with applicable regulations governing extraction of these resources. The bureau is responsible for the survey of federal lands and establishes and maintains public land records and records of mining claims. Other resources the bureau manages include timber, wildlife habitat, endangered plant and animal species, rangeland vegetation, recreation and cultural values, wild and scenic rivers, designated conservation and wilderness areas and open space. BLM programs provide for the protection (including fire suppression), orderly development and use of public lands and resources under principles of multiple use and sustained yield. In all, the BLM is responsible for administering some 270 million acres, located primarily in the West and Alaska, as well as administering subsurface resource management of an additional 300 million acres of land where mineral rights are owned by the federal government.

Hot Springs, Yellowstone National Park. *U.S. Department of the Interior, National Park Service photo by C. H. Hanson*

The extent and complexity of the BLM's mission and authority have often involved the bureau in environmental controversy, most recently during the administration of President Ronald REAGAN, who appointed ROBERT BURFORD, a prominent rancher and pro-business conservative, to head the bureau. Many criticized the appointment for introducing potential conflicts of interest into the administration of the BLM. Environmentalists protested Burford's maintenance of grazing subsidies, his scaling back of environmental programs and his drive to increase industry access to wilderness areas.

In addition to its headquarters in Washington, D.C., the BLM maintains state offices in Alaska, Arizona, California, Idaho, Montana, Nevada, New Mexico, Oregon, Utah and Wyoming, as well as a regional office in Alexandria, Virginia, for the eastern states, the Boise Interagency Fire Center in Idaho and the Denver Service Center.

Langford, Nathaniel Pitt (August 9, 1832– October 18, 1911)

In 1870, Nathaniel P. Langford helped organize and participated in an expedition into the region that is now Yellowstone National Park. He was so affected by the grandeur and beauty of the country that he undertook a campaign of articles, lectures and lobbying successfully aimed at persuading Congress to make Yellowstone the nation's first national park in 1872. Langford served—without compensation—as the park's first superintendent until 1877. Langford's extensive journal notes of the expedition were published in 1905 as *Diary of the Washburn Expedition of the Yellowstone and Fire Hole Rivers in the Year 1870.*

Nathaniel P. Langford, a native of Westmoreland, New York, moved to St. Paul, Minnesota, in 1854, becoming a bank cashier. In 1862, when news reached him of a gold discovery in Montana, Langford joined Captain James L. Fiske's Northern Overland Expedition. At Bannock, Montana, a frontier town in the heart of Montana gold country, Langford gained prominence as the organizer of a vigilante committee to enforce law and order in this most reckless and violent place. His narrative of his early Montana experiences, published in 1890 as *Vigilante Days and Ways*, is still considered the best available firsthand account of frontier law enforcement.

Langford held various public offices in Montana and was appointed by President Andrew Johnson to the post of collector of Internal Revenue in 1868 (the Senate failed to confirm the appointment, however).

After leaving his unpaid post as Yellowstone superintendent, Langford returned to St. Paul but was active in Montana politics for some 10 years. He spent his later years in the quiet study of the history and natural history of the region he loved.

Lavelle, Rita Marie (September 8, 1947–   )
Rita Lavelle served in the ENVIRONMENTAL PROTECTION AGENCY as assistant administrator for solid waste and emergency response, with direct responsibility for overseeing the Superfund for toxic-waste site clean-up. Lavelle was one of the most controversial environmental appointees of Ronald REAGAN's administration. Immediately before her appointment in 1982, she had been director of communications for Arrowjet Liquid Rocket Company, a subsidiary of Arrowjet-General Corporation of California. According to the EPA itself, Arrowjet-General had, at the time of Lavelle's appointment to EPA, the third worst pollution record in the state and was charged with improperly dumping some 20,000 gallons per day of

Mammoth Hot Springs, Yellowstone National Park. *U.S. Department of the Interior, National Park Service photo by M. Woodbridge Williams*

carcinogens and other toxic wastes. To many, including the House Energy and Commerce Committee Subcommittee on Oversight and Investigations, appointing Lavelle to a sensitive and vital EPA post seemed a manifest conflict of interest.

Lavelle's tenure was stormy. Congress, in 1983, began a series of hearings into the conduct of the EPA, particularly investigating charges of manipulations of the Superfund program; conflicts of interest and perjury involving EPA administrator Anne Gorsuch BURFORD, Lavelle and others; the existence of political "hit lists" and the practice of surveillance of agency employees; and the showing of favoritism toward certain toxic dumpers. In the course of its investigation, Congress subpoenaed EPA documents. Invoking "executive privilege," however, Burford refused to surrender subpoenaed documents and was summarily cited for contempt of Congress.

At the heart of the congressional charges was the matter of Rita Lavelle's administration of the Superfund, which was most directly criticized for foot-dragging and political favoritism in cleaning up waste sites. During the investigation, Burford ordered Lavelle to resign, reportedly over a memo Lavelle had sent to White House counsel Robert J. Perry, accusing him of "alienating" President Reagan's "primary constituents"—that is, business interests. The memo was embarrassing to the EPA, already under such heavy fire for siding with business and industry rather than enforcing toxic waste regulations. The EPA issued a letter of resignation on behalf of Lavelle, which Lavelle subsequently disclaimed. President Reagan thereupon removed her from office.

In the thick of this controversy, it was discovered that certain of Lavelle's official records, which were under subpoena, had apparently disappeared—most notably appointment calendars, which might have provided evidence of contacts with industry and business interests. After the Reagan administration reached a compromise with Congress and backed down from supporting Burford's invocation of executive privilege, Lavelle agreed to produce and surrender the appointment calendars. However, she also filed a suit questioning the validity of a subpoena calling on her to testify before the House Energy and Commerce Committee's Subcommittee on Oversight and Investigations concerning favoritism alledgedly shown to her former employer, Arrowjet-General. In May 1983, because of her refusal to testify, Lavelle was indicted by a federal grand jury for contempt of Congress. She pleaded not guilty and was tried, a federal jury finding her guilty of perjury and of impeding congressional investigations of hazardous waste programs. The guilty verdicts involved charges of her having lied about her knowledge that her previous employer, Arrowjet-General, was among the illegal dumpers of hazardous waste in the Stringfellow Acid Pits in California. She was found not guilty of perjury in her assertions that she had not injected political considerations into her decisions concerning hazardous waste issues.

Lavelle was sentenced to six months' imprisonment, a fine of $10,000, community service and five years' probation. She was released after serving four and a half months of the sentence.

A native of Portsmouth, Virginia, Lavelle was educated at the College of Holy Names (B.A., 1969) and at Pepperdine University (M.B.A., 1980). From 1969 to 1971, she was publicity assistant to the governor of California; from 1971 to 1976, information officer and director of consumer education in the California Department of Consumer Affairs; from 1976 to 1978, director of marketing for Intercontinental and Continental Chemicals; from 1978 to 1979, communications director for Cordova Chemicals; and from 1979 to 1982, director of communications for Arrowjet.

League of Conservation Voters (Founded: 1970)
1150 Connecticut Avenue NW, Suite 201, Washington, D.C. 20002; (202) 785-8683

The League of Conservation Voters was founded by the FRIENDS OF THE EARTH to raise funds to support the political candidates whose conservation policies are consonant with those of the founding organization. The steering committee, made up of officials of the SIERRA CLUB, the IZAAK WALTON LEAGUE OF AMERICA, the WILDERNESS SOCIETY and other conservation groups, annually supports 15 to 20 candidates nationwide in local, state and congressional election campaigns. The league publishes an annual *How Congress Voted on Energy and the Environment* and other analyses of politicians' records on environmental issues. It has a membership of 10,000, and Jim Maddy serves as executive director.

League of Women Voters of the United States (Founded: 1920)
1730 M Street NW, Washington, D.C. 20036; (202) 429-1965.

The League of Women Voters of the United States is a national nonpartisan organization that promotes participation of all citizens in government and politics. The organization conducts research, maintains an information clearinghouse, holds public education programs and undertakes political action. Of particular concern to the league are international relations, the environment and social policy. Through its research programs, the league compiles information on candidates for political office and distributes that information to the public in order to generate interest in the issues and promote more widespread participation in elections. In addition, the league takes stands on legislative issues, such as its attack on the proposed rollback of emission standards for truck and car manufacturers in 1984.

In the mid-1980s, state and local chapters of the League of Women Voters spearheaded a campaign for improved labeling of hazardous household chemicals and management of hazardous wastes. In Massachusetts, the league promoted a household hazardous waste collection day in which 55 communities participated. On the heels of that success, the state league developed a video program on household chemicals and established a nationwide public education campaign. The video program, "Beginning at Home: Tackling Household Hazardous Wastes," encourages community leaders to institute collection plans in order to prevent flammable, toxic and corrosive materials—such as creosote, insect spray, and photo processing chemicals—from being dumped in landfills.

The league publishes an annual report and two bimonthly publications: *National Voter* and *Report From the Hill*. Gracia Hillman is executive director of the organization, which has 110,000 members nationwide and a staff of 50.

Leahy, Patrick J. (March 31, 1940–)

Liberal Democratic senator from Vermont, Patrick J. Leahy has chaired the Senate Agriculture Committee since 1987. His pesticide law of 1988 was a major compromise between agricultural interests, who favored deregulation and subsidy, and environmentalists, who wanted strict controls on pesticide use.

In securing passage of the 1990 farm bill, Leahy shaped legislation that was as much environmental as it was agricultural. He attempted to include a "circle of poison" provision in the law, barring export of pesticides banned in this country, lest they be reimported as residues in food and fiber. Although this was ultimately excluded from the farm bill, he reintroduced the measure separately in 1991. Leahy was successful in making funding for research on less toxic pesticides part of the 1990 legislation, and he preserved strong wetlands protection provisions as part of the bill. Leahy is active in environmental causes in his own state as well, and he has worked to secure for Lake Champlain a designation as a Great Lake, in order to bring it under the umbrella of federal environmental protection.

Understandably, Leahy gets consistently high marks from the LEAGUE OF CONSERVATION VOTERS (a perfect 100 score in 1989 and a 92 in 1990).

Born in Montpelier, Vermont, Leahy was educated at St. Michael's College, earning his B.A. in 1961, and at Georgetown University, from which he received his law degree in 1964. From 1964 to 1974, he was a practicing attorney, and from 1966 to 1974, he was state's attorney for Chittenden County. He was first elected to the Senate in 1974.

Leland, Mickey (George Thomas) (November 27, 1944–August 14, 1989)

A former civil rights activist, instructor in clinical pharmacy at Texas Southern University and member of the Texas state legislature, Mickey Leland was elected to the U.S. Congress in 1978. He served as the first chairman of the House Select Committee on World Hunger and as a member of the Energy and Commerce Subcommittee on Telecommunications. Before he was killed in an airplane crash in Ethiopia, he was actively sponsoring a bill that would strengthen restrictions on airborne toxics. Leland was born in Lubbock, Texas.

Leonard, Richard Manning (October 22, 1908–)

Born in Elyria, Ohio, Leonard went west to practice law and was a San Francisco attorney in the 1930s, when he first climbed in the Sierra Nevada Mountains. An avid climber, he perfected the rope-and-piton method and used mathematical planning techniques previously unheard of in the sport. He later outlined his methods in *Belaying the Leader*, published in 1946.

Leonard served as a board member of the SIERRA CLUB from 1938 to 1973, as the club's secretary from 1947 to 1953 and as its president from 1953 to 1955. Since 1976, he has been honorary president. During his presidency, the Sierra Club undertook a major campaign to save Dinosaur National Monument.

Other organizations Leonard has served include the SAVE-THE-REDWOODS LEAGUE (board member since 1954 and president from 1975 to 1980) and the WILDERNESS SOCIETY (board member from 1948 to 1982). Continuing his interest in both conservation and law, he formed the Conservation Law Society of America in 1963.

Leopold, Aldo (January 11, 1886–April 21, 1948)

Although he died in 1948, Aldo Leopold is considered by many environmentalists to be the father of the new conservation movement that developed during the 1960s and 1970s, and of the wildlife management profession. His attitude toward conservation, traced through the nearly 350 articles he wrote, evolved over his long career from a belief in humankind's ability to control the environment for its own benefit to a conviction that wildlife species should be left to thrive in their own self-regulating ecosystem without human interference or intervention.

One of the first graduates of the Yale Forest School, Leopold went to work for the U.S. FOREST SERVICE's Southwestern District in 1909 and was promoted to supervisor of the Carson National Forest in New Mexico in 1912. Illness forced him to leave the post temporarily in 1913, and he spent the next year and a half recuperating. When he was able to return to work, he organized management programs for game and fish for the Forest Service and created game protective associations in New Mexico.

As assistant district forester for the Forest Service, he created new forest-control procedures, better personnel practices and worked on methods of forest inspection. It was his work on watershed protection in the Southwest that led him to the conviction that humankind was responsible for preserving the health of the environment. In addition, he began the preliminary work of setting aside 500,000 acres of the Gila National Forest as a wilderness area, a move that predated the passage of the Wilderness Act of 1964 by 40 years.

Leopold worked as associate director of the Forest Products Laboratory in Madison, Wisconsin, and in the research branch of the Forest Service from 1924 to 1928. He then left the Forest Service and began work on creating a new profession of wildlife management based on the already established forestry profession. After conducting surveys and writing reports, he wrote *Game Management* in 1933, still considered a classic in the wildlife protection field. That year, he became the first professor of wildlife management in the country when he was awarded a newly created chair of game management at the University of Wisconsin. In this position, he taught the next generation of wildlife preservationists and instilled in them his own brand of conservation.

As an officer, director and chairman of scores of professional environmental associations, including the SOCIETY OF AMERICAN FORESTERS, the WILDLIFE SOCIETY, the WILDERNESS SOCIETY and the ECOLOGICAL SOCIETY OF AMERICA, Leopold slowly persuaded conservation professionals across the country to adopt a new ethic of ecological responsibility. He broadcast his message of conservation to the general public through such popular writings as *A Sand County Almanac*, published the year after his death. Selling

more than 1 million copies, it chronicled in a series of vignettes the work Leopold had conducted at a Wisconsin farm, which he was restoring to its ecologically pristine condition, and included his most famous essay, "The Land Ethic." Writing in the style of a farmer's monthly almanac, Leopold catalogued the horrors modern farmers had inflicted upon their lands and blamed much of the resulting devastation on farming methods taught by state agricultural colleges. To cure the ills caused by modern farmers, Leopold argued, would be to cure the ills of the environment as a whole. This, however, could be achieved only if farmers adopted a new attitude of living in "mutual toleration" with the creatures and plants of the land.

Leopold was adamant in his belief that past environmentalists had made a fatal mistake in their isolation of species from their total environment in misguided attempts to preserve them. Yellowstone National Park, for example, where officials had weeded out the natural predators of elk and Kaibab deer in order to preserve them, taught Leopold that it was not ecologically sound to select some species for survival while rejecting others. The ultimately diminished numbers of elk and Kaibab deer, whose unchecked proliferation resulted in a shortage of food, demonstrated that the survival of any species actually depends on the survival of its predators.

Equally to blame for the worsening environment, according to Leopold, were the conservationists who espoused saving portions of the environment as wilderness areas for the public to use as retreats from daily life. Conservation practices that set aside some land for preservation in pristine condition while ignoring the land that humans inhabited on a daily basis were doomed to tragic failure.

Further reading: Susan L. Flader, *Thinking Like a Mountain: Aldo Leopold and the Evolution of an Ecological Attitude Toward Deer, Wolves, and Forests* (Columbia: University of Missouri Press, 1974).

Leopold, A(ldo) Starker (October 22, 1913–August 23, 1983)

A son of the pioneering wilderness ecologist Aldo LEOPOLD, A. Starker Leopold also earned distinction as a naturalist, educator and author.

Born in Burlington, Iowa, Leopold received his bachelor's degree in agriculture from the University of Wisconsin in 1936, then studied for a year at the Yale University School of Forestry. He worked as a biologist with the USDA Soil Erosion Service and the Missouri State Conservation Commission until 1944, when he took his doctorate in zoology at the University of California, Berkeley. Leopold taught at

Left to right: George L. Collins, Aldo Starker Leopold and Frank Fraser Darling, Umiat, Alaska, 1952. *Photo by Lowell Sumner, courtesy of the National Park Service*

Berkeley from 1946 to 1978, retiring as a professor emeritus of zoology and forestry. He wrote scores of articles and several books on birds and wildlife; from 1959 to 1971, he served as president of the California Academy of Sciences.

A committed conservationist and wildlife proponent, Leopold gained a position of key influence in 1962, when he was appointed head of a federal advisory commission on the National Park system. The panel's report, advocating the maximum restoration and preservation of natural conditions throughout America's parklands, resulted in crucial changes to existing INTERIOR Department policies.

Further reading: Leopold, *The California Quail* (Berkeley: University of California Press, 1977); *Game Birds and Mammals of California* (Berkeley: University of California Press, 1951); Leopold (with editors of *Life*), *The Desert* (New York: Time-Life, 1961).

Leopold, Luna Bergere (October 8, 1915–   )

An internationally honored expert on hydrology and geomorphology, Luna Leopold is a professor of geology at the University of California at Berkeley.

A son of the early forest preservationist Aldo LEOPOLD, Luna Leopold was born in Albuquerque, New Mexico. After graduating from the University of Wisconsin (B.S., 1936), Leopold returned to his birth state as a junior and then associate engineer with the SOIL CONSERVATION SERVICE. He worked for a time at the U.S. Engineer's office in Los Angeles (1941–42), and during World War II, he joined the U.S. Air Force, where he was made a captain in the air weather service. He earned his M.A. at the University of California at Los Angeles in 1945 and worked with the U.S. Interior Department's Bureau of RECLAMATION until his appointment, in 1947, as head meteorologist at the Pineapple Research Institute of Hawaii in Honolulu. He remained in this position until 1949, gained his doctorate in geology from Harvard University the following year, and began work as a hydraulic engineer with the U.S. GEOLOGICAL SURVEY. In 1957, he was promoted to chief hydrologist, and from 1966 to 1972, he held the title of senior research hydrologist. Since leaving his agency post in 1972, Leopold has taught at Berkeley.

Leopold's intensive study of natural water systems and their interaction with the landscape made him a key contributor to several important texts on hydrology and river morphology, including *The Flood Control Controversy* (with T. Maddock, Jr., 1954), *Water* (with Time-Life editors, 1965; revised edition 1980), *Water: A Primer* (1974) and *Water in Environmental Planning* (with T. Dunne, 1978). He has also written over 100 papers for scientific journals and edited *Round River: From the Journals of Aldo Leopold* (1972).

A lifelong conservationist and vocal advocate for the protection of free-flowing river systems, Leopold has served on the board of directors of the SIERRA CLUB since 1968. He is a member of the American Academy of Arts and Sciences, the American Geophysical Union, the American Meteorological Society, the American Philosophical Society, the American Society of Civil Engineers, the Cosmos Club, the Geological Society of America (president, 1971) and the National Academy of Sciences. The recipient of five honorary degrees and numerous distinguished service awards, Leopold was presented with the National Medal of Science in 1991.

Leydet, François G(uillaume) (August 26, 1927–   )

A native of Neuilly-sur-Seine, François G. Leydet is a popular writer on environmental and wilderness topics. The son of novelist Bruno Leydet (whose pseudonym is Bertrand Defos), he was educated at the University of Paris, from which he received a Bachelier-es-lettres-philosophie in 1945; at Harvard University, which awarded him an A.B. degree in 1947 and where he undertook graduate study from 1950 to 1952; and at Johns Hopkins University, where he was a graduate student from 1952 to 1953. From 1947 to 1948, Leydet served in the Tank Corps of the French army, leaving the service with the rank of first lieutenant.

Leydet was a staff writer for "This World," the *San Francisco Chronicle* Sunday supplement, from 1954 to 1962. He worked for the *San Francisco Examiner* from 1962 to 1963 in the copy editing, layout and make-up departments. Leydet was editor of *Tomorrow's Wilderness*, a 1963 SIERRA CLUB publication and coauthor (with Philip Hyde) of *The Last Redwoods*, published by the Sierra Club the following year. Also in 1964, Leydet's *Time and the River Flowing: Grand Canyon* was published by the Sierra Club in a version edited by David BROWER. An abridged edition of this book was published in 1968 by the Sierra Club and Ballantine Books, which also brought out *The Last Redwoods, and the Parkland of Redwood Creek* in 1969. His *The Coyote: Defiant Songdog of the West* appeared in 1977.

Leydet is active in numerous environmental organizations, including the board of advisors, Research Ranch, Elgin, Arizona, and the American Wilderness Alliance. He is a member of the National Parks Association, the WILDERNESS SOCIETY, the Sierra Club, the NATIONAL AUDUBON SOCIETY, the WORLDWIDE FUND FOR NATURE, the American Museum of Natural History, the Union of Concerned Scientists, the ENVIRONMENTAL DEFENSE FUND, FRIENDS OF THE EARTH, Arizona-Sonora Desert Museums and the Arizona Historical Society.

Lindbergh, Anne (Spencer) Morrow (June 22, 1906–   )

Born in New York City, the daughter of Dwight Whitney Morrow, former U.S. ambassador to Mexico, Anne Morrow was educated at Smith College, graduating with a B.A. in 1928. In 1929, she met and married Charles A. LINDBERGH, the young aviator who, two years earlier, had become the first person to pilot an aircraft solo from New York to Paris. Anne Morrow Lindbergh rapidly gained an enthusiasm for flying and often served as her husband's navigator and copilot, logging more than 40,000 miles in the air doing aerial survey work, which earned the couple the Hubbard Medal from the NATIONAL GEOGRAPHIC SOCIETY in 1934.

Anne Morrow Lindbergh began her writing career in 1935, with *North to the Orient,* and followed this with other highly acclaimed works of autobiography and poetry, including the 1955 *Gift from the Sea,* a collection of essays concerning the healing power of nature. This work was born of her tragic experience 23 years earlier, in 1932, when her infant son was kidnapped from the Lindberghs' rural New Jersey home and murdered. *Gift from the Sea* narrates the role nature played in drawing Lindbergh out of her depression and deep sense of loss. Environmentalists have hailed the book as dramatic testimony to the intimate relationship between humankind and nature and the intrinsic emotional and spiritual value of the natural environment.

Further reading: Lindbergh, *Gift from the Sea* (New York: Pantheon, 1955); *Hour of Gold, Hour of Lead: Diaries and Letters of Anne Morrow Lindbergh, 1929–1932* (New York: Harcourt, 1973).

Lindbergh, Charles A(ugustus, Jr.) (February 4, 1902–August 26, 1974)

Son of a U.S. congressman from Michigan, Charles A. Lindbergh attended the University of Wisconsin from 1920 to 1922, but soon decided that he wanted to learn to fly. After taking lessons at the Nebraska Aircraft Corporation flying school in 1922, he became an itinerant stunt flier, barnstormer and aircraft mechanic in the Midwest. He joined the U.S. Army Air Service in 1924, largely to receive further flight instruction, and then worked as an airmail pilot. In 1927, flying *The Spirit of St. Louis,* he became solo pilot of the first transcontinental flight between New York and Paris—a feat that made him instantly a national and international hero.

Following his triumph, Lindbergh became an aviation researcher and a consultant to Pan American Airways and to the U.S. War Department. America's favorite hero suffered profound personal tragedy in 1932 when his infant son was kidnapped and murdered. He provoked considerable controversy throughout the 1930s for his steadfastly pacifist and isolationist beliefs, which he expressed widely and publicly. Despite this pacifism, however, Lindbergh immediately volunteered his services to the government in the wake of Pearl Harbor at the close of 1941. When President Franklin Delano ROOSEVELT declined his offer, Lindbergh resigned his commission in the Army Air Corps reserve, but did serve in the Pacific theater as a civilian technician for United Aircraft Corporation. Although he was a civilian, Lindbergh covertly flew more than 50 missions that resulted in the downing of Japanese aircraft.

After the war Lindbergh served as consultant on several advanced aviation projects, including the design of the giant Boeing 747. In later years, however, he became an ardent conservationist, declaring he had "felt the godlike power man derives from his machines. . . . But I have seen the science I worshiped and the aircraft I loved destroying the civilization I expected them to serve." In 1964, while he was lying under an acacia tree in Africa "with the sounds of dawn" around him, he "realized more clearly the fact that man should never overlook: that the construction of an airplane, for instance, is simple when compared to the evolutionary achievement of a bird; that airplanes depend on an advanced civilization, and that where civilization is most advanced few birds exist. I realized that if I had to choose, I would rather have birds than planes."

Lindbergh worked to save the humpbacked and blue whales from extinction, and he studied monkey-eating eagles and primitive tribes in the Philippines. He also campaigned against the supersonic transport (SST) project as environmentally destructive.

Lindbergh died of cancer at his home on Maui, Hawaii. He was married to author ANNE MORROW LINDBERGH.

Further reading: Lindbergh, *Autobiography of Values* (New York: Harcourt, 1978); *Banana River* (New York: Harcourt, 1976); *We* (New York: Putnam, 1927).

Ling, Joseph Tso-ti (June 10, 1919–   )

Environmental engineer Joseph Tso-ti Ling has been instrumental in changing American industry's approach to pollution from a perspective of control to one of prevention. Born in Beijing, China, he immigrated to the United States in 1948 and became a citizen in 1963. He holds a B.S. degree from Hangchow Christian College in Shanghai, and an M.S. and Ph.D. in sanitary engineering and public health from the University of Minnesota. From 1948 to 1952, he was a research assistant sanitation engineer at the university. From 1953 to 1955, Ling was senior staff engineer for General Mills Inc., returning in 1956 to China as director of environmental science at the Natural Resources Institute. Ling was professor of civil engineering at Hong Kong's Baptist University from 1958 to 1959, and in 1960 joined the staff of the 3M Company as manager of water and sanitation engineering. He was subsequently appointed manager of sanitation and civil engineering and director of environmental engineering and pollution control for the corporation. From 1974 to 1984, Ling served 3M as vice-president for environmental engineering and pollution control, and since 1984, he has been an executive consultant with Community Service Executive Program.

At the 3M Company, Ling was instrumental in changing the company's manufacturing processes. He argued that "pollution prevention pays" and set up an internal process whereby employees could suggest changes to production processes. In his foreword to Michael G. Royston's 1979 book entitled *Pollution Prevention Pays,* Ling wrote that American industry should devise new methods that use "a minimum of resources while causing a minimum of pollution," and he criticized federal laws and agencies that devote effort to cleaning up pollution rather than to preventing it. He argued that controlling pollution does not solve the problem, but merely alters it, and he cited, as examples, the creation of sludge from waste-water purification and the emission of fumes and particulates from chemical waste burning. In addition, Ling claimed that pollution controls themselves use valuable resources.

In addition to his work at the 3M Company, Ling has served as an adviser to the Ohio River Water Sanitation Commission, as a member of the Environmental Pollution Panel of the U.S. Chamber of Commerce, as the technical contact for the National Industrial Pollution Control Council and as a member of the scientific advisory board of the ENVIRONMENTAL PROTECTION AGENCY.

Linnaeus, Carolus (May 23, 1707–January 10, 1778)

Carolus Linnaeus (Latinized form of the Swedish Carl von Linné) was the premier botanist of the 18th century. Born in Råshult, Sweden, Linnaeus took his M.D. degree at Harderwijk in 1735. That year, his *Systema naturae* was also published. In it, he proposed a standard binomial nomenclature for plants, which included genus and species. His system of neatly categorized species gained immediate popularity and was taught to university students throughout Europe. Even casual gardeners came to a fuller understanding of nature through an introduction to the Linnaean system.

From 1735 to 1738, Linnaeus studied in Holland, where he published more than a dozen works. Returning to Sweden, he was awarded a chair in medicine at Uppsala in 1741.

In 1749, Linnaeus published an essay entitled "The Oeconomy of Nature." He wrote that every living creature had its "allotted place" in nature, but that its "place" was more than just its location; it encompassed the role or function of the organism in the "economy" of nature. Linnaeus noted the existence of a food chain that links all organisms and that was created by God to maintain a peaceful coexistence among the creatures of earth. He advocated for humankind a role of dominion over nature and believed that humanity could and should increase the bounty of nature to its own benefit.

Although Linnaeus himself believed in the fixity of species, his system of classification was, in fact, a first step toward the development of theories of evolution.

Linnaeus died in Uppsala, Sweden.

Further reading: Wilfred Blunt, *The Compleat Naturalist: A Life of Linnaeus* (New York: Viking,1971); James L. Larson, *Reason and Experience: The Representation of Natural Order in the Work of Carl von Linné* (Berkeley: University of California Press, 1971).

London, Jack (January 12, 1876–November 22, 1916)

The celebrated American novelist, short-story writer and journalist Jack London based some of his most famous works on his travels to the Yukon during the Klondike gold rush of 1897. His first collection of short stories, *The Son of the Wolf* (1900), explores the violent world of men and animals trying to survive in the wilderness of the Yukon. *The Call of the Wild* (1903) and *White Fang* (1906) portray the struggle between civilization and savagery in the wilds of Alaska. Greatly influenced by the writings of the German philosopher Friedrich Nietzsche, London

Jack London

developed ruggedly individual characters, who considered themselves above social regulation, law and convention, especially in *The Call of the Wild* and *The Sea-Wolf* (1904).

Further reading: Joan London: *Jack London: An Unconventional Biography* (Seattle: University of Washington Press, 1968); Irving Stone, *Sailor on Horseback: The Biography of Jack London* (Boston: Houghton Mifflin, 1938).

Long, George Smith (December 3, 1853–August 22, 1930)

For 30 years, from 1900 to 1930, George S. Long was operating manager of the Weyerhaeuser Timber Company. He earned a reputation as one of the most influential and most highly respected lumbermen in the Pacific Northwest. Responsible for the expansion of Weyerhaeuser's tremendous holdings, Long was an ardent proponent of timber conservation, securing the first effective fire-protection measures from Washington and Oregon lawmakers. He worked with Gifford PINCHOT to introduce fire prevention and tax reforms to encourage the practice of professional, responsible forestry. Long did break with Pinchot, however, over the issue of federal regulation of timber cutting on private lands.

Lopez, Barry Holstun (January 6, 1945–   )
A photographer and writer, Lopez brings to his subject—the natural world around him—the transcendental sensibility of a latter-day Henry David THOREAU. His feeling for the environment is epitomized in *Of Wolves and Men* (1978). In this book, as in all of his writing, Lopez combines meticulous observation with a romantic, metaphysical vision that attempts to rejuvenate man's relation to nature. By increasing to a profound degree man's understanding of the wolf—a creature traditionally persecuted or, at least, shunned—Lopez hoped to teach a more sensitive approach to natural surroundings generally. As an environmentalist writer, Lopez is a poet and Transcendentalist—but he is also always a realist.

Born in Port Chester, New York, Lopez spent his early years in the rural San Fernando Valley of California. There, during trips to the Santa Monica Mountains, Malibu Beach, the Mojave Desert and the Grand Canyon, he came to an early knowledge and love of the Southwest. At 11, he moved with his family to Manhattan and was educated at a Jesuit high school there and at the University of Notre Dame (South Bend, Indiana), where he majored in history and English. After graduating cum laude, he worked briefly as a publisher's sales representative, returned to Notre Dame for his M.A. in education, then studied journalism and folklore at the University of Oregon. He left graduate school in 1970 to settle with his wife in remote Finn Rock, a logging village in Oregon's Cascade Range. He has lived there ever since.

The fiction and nonfiction of Barry Lopez address wildlife, the landscape of the southwestern desert and of the great Northwest, the Arctic, Native American culture and mythology and issues of micro- and macro-ecology. ''I write now in a country and at a time when man's own brutal nature is cause for concern,'' Lopez observed of his work, ''and when the wolf, whom man has historically accused of craven savagery, has begun to emerge as a benign creature.'' His beautiful prose and passionate stance toward the environment have made Lopez a popular and critical success who has appeared on television talk shows and who is much in demand as a lecturer on college campuses. He received the John Burroughs Medal in 1979 for *Of Wolves and Men*, and his *Arctic Dreams* won a 1986 National Book Award.

Further reading: Lopez, *Desert Notes: Reflections in the Eye of a Raven* (Kansas City, Mo.: Sheed, Andrews & McNeel, 1976), *Giving Birth to Thunder, Sleeping with His Daughter:*

Everglades National Park. *U.S. Department of the Interior, National Park Service photo*

Coyote Builds North America (Kansas City, Mo.: Sheed, Andrew & McNeel, 1977), *Of Wolves and Men* (New York: Scribner's, 1978), *Winter Count* (New York: Scribner's, 1981); Peter Wild, *Barry Lopez*, Boise State University Western Writers Series No. 64 (Boise: Boise State University Press, 1984).

Lorenz, Jack (March 14, 1939–   )
St. Louis-born Jack Lorenz has served as executive director of the IZAAK WALTON LEAGUE OF AMERICA since 1974. Previously he worked as editor of *Outdoor America*, the league's magazine (1973–74), and as the director of environmental affairs for Falstaff Brewing Corporation (1969–72). He has also served as chairman of the board of the American League of Anglers since 1981 and as a member of the advisory boards of the Everglades Protection Association, the National Arbor Foundation and the Hunter Education Council. The author of many articles on topics ranging from the impact of sport fishing on the economy to the environmental impact of dredging in the salt marshes along the Atlantic Coast, Lorenz is a member of the Outdoor Writers Association of America. He also serves as a member of the board of advisory governors of the National Freshwater Fishing Hall of

Fame, the steering committee for National Hunting and Fishing Day and the board of directors of the Global Tomorrow Coalition.

Lovejoy, Arthur Oncken (October 10, 1873– December 30, 1962)

A preeminent American philosopher of the early 20th century, Berlin-born Arthur Oncken Lovejoy turned to philosophy in his youth, hoping to escape the oppressive influence of his father's evangelical religion. Late 19th-century idealism held no appeal for him, however, and he was drawn instead to realism and dualism. Lovejoy explored critical realism in *The Revolt Against Dualism* (1930). Most influential in the field of environmental studies, however, was his brilliant analysis of the chain of being and the theory of emergence in *The Great Chain of Being: A Study of the History of an Idea* (1936).

Lovejoy received a B.A. from the University of California, Berkeley, and an M.A. from Harvard University. He taught at Stanford University, Washington University in St. Louis, Columbia University, the University of Missouri and Johns Hopkins University. He was a founder of the American Association of University Professors and created the *Journal of the History of Ideas* in 1940.

Lovejoy, Thomas Eugene (August 22, 1941–   )

A widely known researcher in the field of tropical forests, Thomas Eugene Lovejoy is the assistant secretary for external affairs at the Smithsonian Institution. Previously he worked as vice-president for science at the WORLD WILDLIFE FUND, where he devised the Minimum Critical Size project, an ambitious long-term experiment aimed at determining just what conditions are needed to sustain the ecological diversity of a given parcel of land; the ongoing project is now administered by the Smithsonian Institution.

Born in New York City, Lovejoy holds a Ph.D. in biology from Yale University and has conducted extensive field work, including studies of rainforest bird populations, the epidemiology of arboviruses in Brazil and the decrease in population of ospreys at the mouth of the Connecticut River. He was named research associate in ornithology at the Academy of Natural Sciences of Philadelphia in 1971 and served as executive assistant to the science director at the academy from 1972 to 1973. In 1974, he was named chairman of the Wildlife Preservation Trust International and has served as treasurer of the International Council for Bird Preservation, Pan-American Section. In 1974, he became the coordinator of the J. Paul Getty Wildlife Conservation Prize and, in 1975, a member of the Species Survival Commission of the

INTERNATIONAL UNION FOR THE CONSERVATION OF NATURE AND NATURAL RESOURCES.

In 1985, Lovejoy played a critical role in developing the "debt-for-nature swap" program, in which Third World countries agree to protect their environment in exchange for American banks forgiving portions of their debts. In addition, he was the founder of the widely viewed and critically acclaimed "Nature" series on public television.

Further reading: Marjorie Sun, "How Do You Measure the Lovejoy Effect," *Science* 247 (March 9, 1990): 1174–1176.

Lovelock, James E. (July 26, 1919–   )

Born in Letchworth, Hertfordshire, England, James E. Lovelock was educated at Birbeck College, London (1938–39), Manchester University (B.Sc., 1941) and the University of London (Ph.D., 1949; D.Sc., 1959). In 1941, he embarked on a full, varied and successful career in science, as staff scientist with the National Institute for Medical Research, London (1941–61) and as professor of chemistry at the Baylor University College of Medicine in Houston, Texas (1961–64). He was a Rockefeller fellow at Harvard (1954–55) and at Yale (1958–59). However, since 1964—except for a visiting professorship in engineering and cybernetics at the University of Reading—he has been a self-described "independent scientist" and "inventor," living with his wife and grown son on 30 acres in England's West Country and manifesting, if not contempt for, at least impatience with institutionally affiliated science and scientists.

Lovelock's estrangement from traditional science roughly coincided with his stint as consultant to NASA's Jet Propulsion Laboratory. JPL sought Lovelock's help in the quest to discover whether there is life on Mars, and in 1965, Lovelock proposed a series of tests, including a "top-down view" of the whole planet rather than a local search at the site of a space probe's landing. His idea was to analyze the chemistry of the planet's atmosphere. If the planet were lifeless, it would have an atmosphere determined exclusively by chemistry and physics and would therefore be close to the chemical equilibrium state. If the planet supported life, however, the atmosphere would depart from equilibrium due to the effect of organisms consuming raw materials and depositing wastes. Using evidence from the infrared astronomy of Mars, Lovelock determined that the planet's atmosphere was, in fact, in close equilibrium and dominated by carbon dioxide. In sharp contrast, the atmosphere of the earth is in a state of chemical disequilibrium. On earth carbon dioxide is only a trace gas, and the coexistence of abundant oxygen and such reactive gases as methane would be impossible on a lifeless planet. Even the presence of abundant nitrogen and water, Lovelock realized, is difficult to explain on the basis of geochemistry alone. He concluded that Mars is lifeless, but more important, he also concluded that the constancy of the earth's atmosphere, in defiance of geochemistry alone, requires the existence of an active control system.

What constitutes this control system?

Lovelock theorized that it is life itself. "Conditions on Earth," Lovelock declared, "are made congenial for life by the presence of life." Lovelock discussed his idea with his neighbor, the novelist William Golding (*Lord of the Flies*), who suggested a name for the hypothesis: Gaia, after the Greek earth goddess. In 1979, Lovelock developed his theory in a book, *Gaia: A New Look at Life on Earth.* "The Earth's atmosphere was so far from any conceivable chemical equilibrium state," he explained, "that not only must life be present but also that it interacts so closely with the atmosphere that the atmosphere itself might be considered as an extension of life. . . . [The] Earth can be regarded as a single living system which includes the biosphere, the atmosphere, the oceans and the soil." In effect, the earth is the living embodiment of that Greek goddess; it is a single vast organism.

The notion of the earth as an organism—of such phenomena as the level of carbon dioxide and other gases, the temperature of the earth's surface, the formation of clouds, the rate of rainfall, the saltiness of the oceans and many others being controlled by biological process—provoked great controversy among scientists, but it also proved appealing to many ecologists, who saw a new urgency added to their field. Here was a theory that posited not only a delicate and complex balance among living things, as in traditional ecology, but also a creative feedback relationship between the organic and the inorganic realms.

The Gaia hypothesis was further elaborated in Lovelock's 1988 book, *The Ages of Gaia: A Biography of Our Living Earth,* and Lovelock continues to develop and debate the hypothesis while he also directs his attention to such ongoing environmental problems as the greenhouse effect and acid rain. A member of the American Chemical Society, the Marine Biology Association and Sigma Xi, Havelock is a fellow of the Royal Society and has received awards from the CIBA Foundation (1955); certificates of recognition from NASA (1972); TSWETT Medals from chromatography societies in the United States and the former Soviet Union; an award from the American Chemical Society (1980); and an honorary D. Sc. from the University of East Anglia (1982).

Further reading: Lovelock, *Gaia: A New Look at Life on Earth* (New York: Oxford University Press, 1979); *The Ages of Gaia: A Biography of Our Living Earth* (New York: Norton, 1988).

Lovins, Amory Bloch (November 13, 1947–   )

Cofounder of the Rocky Mountain Institute in Old Snowmass, Colorado, Amory Bloch Lovins is the nation's leading advocate of energy efficiency. A native of Washington, D.C., he became interested in ecology and environmental studies while a graduate student in England. Hiking through the Snowdonia region of North Wales, he noted that the mountain park land was threatened by neighboring nuclear power plants, an aluminum smelter and other industrial complexes. In addition, he learned that Rio Tinto Zinc was proposing a copper mine in the region. To draw attention to these environmental threats, Lovins wrote *Eryri: The Mountains of Longing* (1971), which was adapted to a documentary format by the BBC and created a public outcry against the offending industries.

Lovins returned to the United States in 1971 to take a position with FRIENDS OF THE EARTH. At first, he was a proponent of nuclear energy as a cleaner alternative to fossil fuels, but by the early 1970s, he turned toward what he termed the "soft path" and wrote *Soft Energy Paths: Toward a Durable Peace* (1977), which argues that instead of increasing energy resources, a better solution to the energy crisis is to conserve energy and to use it more efficiently. Lovins argued that hydropower, biomass and solar technologies are more suitable sources of energy than fossil fuels and nuclear power.

Lovins attended Harvard University from 1964 to 1965 and Magdalen College of Oxford University from 1967 to 1969. He received an M.A. from Merton College, Oxford University, in 1971. In addition to his work for Friends of the Earth from 1971 to 1984, he has been a lecturer at the University of California at Berkeley and at Riverside.

The Rocky Mountain Institute, founded in 1982 by Lovins and his wife, Hunter, is a research and educational center devoted to energy efficiency. Among the energy-saving features of the institute's own headquarters are a greenhouse that supplies heat, a toilet of Swedish design that uses only a gallon of water per flush, a shower that incorporates efficiency designs used in submarines and a refrigerator that is six times more efficient than common commercial models. Lovins and his staff earn half the center's million-dollar annual budget by consulting with energy companies, utilities and government agencies in more than 20 countries.

Lovins and his institute have suggested many practical means of energy conservation, from the use of compact fluorescent lamps to decrease consumption of electricity to innovative programs to encourage consumers to buy energy-efficient cars. Lovins's approach is characteristically practical, economic and political rather than romantic and idealistic. For example, he criticizes automobile manufacturers for their delays in releasing cars that get 67 to 138 miles per gallon, pointing out in a 1991 article for *Mother Jones* that a savings of three miles per gallon in the design of family cars would "displace our imports from Iraq and Kuwait" and that an 11-miles-per-gallon savings would end America's dependence on all imports from the Persian Gulf. In *Brittle Power: Energy Strategy for National Security* (1982), coauthored with his wife, Lovins argues that the United States' dependence on foreign oil makes national security a practical impossibility.

In addition to energy sources and use, the Rocky Mountain Institute also studies the conservation of natural resources. In 1989, the institute issued a report that showed how, by adopting water efficiency measures, Denver residents could save twice as much water as the proposed Two Forks Dam—a threat to the natural environment—would provide. After the report was released, the ENVIRONMENTAL PROTECTION AGENCY scuttled plans for the dam, and the Denver Water Board instituted many of Lovins's water-conservation suggestions.

In addition to the books mentioned above, Lovins has written *The Stockholm Conference: Only One Earth* (1972), *Openpit Mining* (1973) and *World Energy Strategies: Facts, Issues and Options* (1975). In 1975, he coauthored *Non-Nuclear Futures: The Case for an Ethical Energy Strategy* with J. Price and, in 1980, wrote *Energy/War: Breaking the Nuclear Link* with Hunter Lovins.

Lovins, Hunter See LOVINS, AMORY BLOCH.

Lujan, Manuel, Jr. (May 12, 1928–   )
Named secretary of the interior in February 1989, Manuel Lujan Jr. first entered politics as vice-chairman of the Republican Party in New Mexico. A native of San Ildefonso, New Mexico, he defeated a five-term incumbent and became the state's first Hispanic congressman in 1968. Reelected throughout the 1970s and 1980s, Lujan served on the House Interior and Insular Affairs Committee and was the ranking Republican on the committee during President Ronald REAGAN's first administration.

His conservative positions have led environmentalists to criticize Lujan's congressional record. He

Secretary of the Interior Manuel Lujan standing before the Fallen Monarch in the Mariposa Grove of giant Sequoias, California. *Photo by Brian Grogan, courtesy of the National Park Service*

cosponsored a bill that would allow oil and gas companies to tap into the resources of the Arctic National Wildlife Refuge, approved cuts to federal subsidies for water and energy programs and remained firmly behind nuclear power projects.

Although Lujan announced his retirement in January 1988, to take effect at the end of his 10th term in Congress, President George Bush named him secretary of the interior on December 22 of that year. Many saw the appointment as an attempt to balance conservative outcries against Bush's appointment of William K. REILLY, former head of the CONSERVATION FOUNDATION, as head of the ENVIRONMENTAL PROTECTION AGENCY.

After the Senate confirmed his appointment on February 2, 1989, Lujan was almost immediately faced with a controversy over classifying the spotted owl from Oregon's timber country as an endangered species. In April 1989, he clashed with the Environmental Protection Agency by approving a water project that had been scheduled for review by the COUNCIL ON ENVIRONMENTAL QUALITY, the federal agency created to mediate disputes between federal agencies over environmental issues. In 1993, Lujan was succeeded as secretary of the interior by President Bill Clinton's nominee, Bruce Babbitt.

Lutzenberger, José A. (December 17, 1926–   )

The Brazilian agronomist and environmental activist José Lutzenberger has staunchly fought to preserve the beleaguered Amazon rainforest, a position that angered former Brazilian President José Sarney. Despite his controversial activism on behalf of the rainforest, Lutzenberger was named secretary of the environment in March 1990 by Sarney's successor, Fernando Collor de Mello. Lutzenberger made it the main priority of his office to halt Amazon deforestation, while also promising to protect the country's forests along the Atlantic and the region's savannahs.

Lutzenberger's tenure as secretary of the environment was brief and turbulent. President Mello dismissed him, together with Eduardo Martins, president of Brazil's environmental agency, in March 1992, just four mouth's before the start of the U.N. Conference on Environment and Development, which was held in Rio de Janeiro.

Before entering government service, Lutzenberger worked for the German chemical company BASF to promote the use of pesticides and fertilizers. In the 1980s, however, he became convinced that these chemicals were not only harming the environment directly but were also causing additional indirect damage by forcing impoverished peasants off their lands and into the employ of the land speculators clearing the Amazon forests. Lutzenberger left BASF to start a consulting service aimed at teaching farmers in southern Brazil how to use organic methods of pest control and fertilization as alternatives to chemicals.

Lyell, Charles (November 14, 1797–February 22, 1875)

Known as the scientist who popularized the theory that the earth was created by gradual, long-term natural forces rather than in the six days of Genesis, Charles Lyell was a proponent of the geological theory of uniformitarianism.

Born in Kinnordy, Forfarshire, Scotland and educated at Oxford University, Lyell began his geologic observations during family trips through Britain and on the European continent. Although he became a practicing attorney, Lyell pursued his interest in geology and natural history and was named secretary of the Geological Society in 1823. In 1831, he was named professor of geology at King's College in London.

His widely read *Principles of Geology*, published in three volumes (1830–33), examined the earth's geologic structure and the forces that have historically worked to mold it and those that continue to do so. Although he was aware of theories that the earth's development had been shaped primarily by momentous catastrophes—theories especially popular in Europe—Lyell emphasized instead the gradual effects of wind and weather, and contrary to the Linnaean model, which postulated a fixed place in the natural order for each species, Lyell argued that species continually alter their relationships with each other and their environment, as they compete for nourishment or migrate to new areas. He also recognized a new disturbance to the natural order: man. Everywhere humankind settled, the number and diversity of species dwindled. Nevertheless, Lyell believed that natural geological forces were far more powerful than man as agents of change.

Significantly, Lyell did not extend his theories of change to species. Although relations among species were subject to continual alteration and adjustment, species themselves were, for Lyell, a fixed part of nature. Although some had become extinct, as evidenced in the fossils he studied in geological formations, no new species are created.

Charles DARWIN found much in the work of Charles Lyell to amplify his theories of evolution and natural selection. He incorporated into his system Lyell's emphasis on violence and competition as a natural law. As for Lyell, after Darwin's *On the Origin of Species* was published, he radically altered his own thinking to accept the theory of the evolution of species and went on to attempt to trace the evolution of man through archaeological evidence. The result of this study was *The Geological Evidence of the Antiquity of Man with Remarks on Theories of the Origin of Species by Variation* (1863).

Further reading: Leonard Wilson, *Charles Lyell: The Years to 1841* (New Haven, Conn.: Yale University Press, 1972); *Sir Charles Lyell's Scientific Journals on the Species Question* (New Haven, Conn.: Yale University Press, 1970).

Lysenko, Trofim Denisovich (September 29, 1898–November 20, 1976)

Born in Karlovka, Ukraine, Lysenko graduated from the Uman School of Horticulture and the Kiev Agricultural Institute. He was stationed at the Gandzha Experimental Station from 1925 to 1929 and named senior specialist in the Department of Physiology at the Ukrainian All-Union Institute of Selection and Genetics in Odessa. He was promoted to scientific director and then director, a post he held until 1938.

In 1940, due in part to his close ties to Joseph Stalin, he was named director of the Institute of Genetics of the USSR Academy of Sciences, but he was stripped of this position in 1965 after Nikita Khrushchev fell from power.

Lysenko first became well known for his work with vernalization, a process in which seeds are moistened just enough to force germination and are then cooled to slightly above freezing. Seeds treated in this manner develop quickly when planted, thereby increasing crop yields, a result greatly beneficial to Soviet farmers, who are hampered by a short growing season.

Lysenko later turned his attention to genetics. He believed that traits acquired by an organism in response to new environmental conditions could be passed on to its descendants, a version of the supposedly discredited Lamarckian doctrine of the inheritance of acquired characteristics. Instead of scientifically refuting Gregor Mendel's widely accepted theory of chromosome heredity, Lysenko and his followers simply denounced the accepted view as "reactionary" and forced adherence to their own theories within the Soviet Union.

As the leader of the Soviet scientific community, Lysenko promulgated other theories—some well-grounded, others unverified—including the doctrine of noncellular life forms and the theory that viruses could transform themselves into bacteria.

M

Maathai, Wangari (April 1, 1940–   )
Organizer of the Green Belt Movement in Kenya, Africa, Wangari Maathai works to check her country's advancing desert. The movement has put 50,000 women to work establishing nurseries and persuading farmers to plant seedlings. The women earn 2 cents for each native tree they plant; and the farmers who promise to raise the seedlings are provided them free of charge. In all, more than 10 million trees were planted in Kenya between 1977 and 1990.

Maathai was honored for her work in 1991 with a $60,000 award from the GOLDMAN ENVIRONMENTAL FOUNDATION of San Francisco and in 1989 by the UNITED NATIONS ENVIRONMENT PROGRAMME. But in 1990, she was denounced by her own government. When Kenyan officials announced plans to allow commercial development in Uhuru Park, the last significant park in Nairobi, Maathai sued the developers. The Kenyan Parliament berated Maathai and her Green Belt Movement, and the courts refused to hear the lawsuit. But public opinion mounted against the development project to such a degree that the World Bank warned the Kenyan government that foreign financial aid might be jeopardized if the government persisted in supporting such a harmful investment. Maathai was arrested by Kenyan police in 1992, an action that sparked public demonstrations on her behalf. After her release, she went into hiding, but presented herself to a Kenyan court in March 1993, where she was told that no charges had been leveled against her.

MacEwen, Ann Maitland (August 15, 1918–   )
Ann M. MacEwen is an ecologically minded British urban planner, who was educated at the Architectural Association School of Architecture, and at the Association for Planning and Regional Reconstruc-

tion School of Planning. After World War II, she was active in many of Great Britain's rebuilding and planning projects, as a specialist in transportation and traffic issues.

Ann MacEwen was a senior lecturer at the Bristol University School of Advanced Urban Studies from 1974 to 1977 and has served as a member of the Noise Advisory Council.

With her husband, MALCOLM MACEWEN, she has written important studies of conservation and Britain's national parks, including *National Parks: Conservation or Cosmetics?* (1982) and *Greenprints for the Countryside? The Story of Britain's National Parks* (1987). With Joan Davidson, she is the author of *The Livable City* (1983), an important study of modern urban planning.

MacEwen, Malcolm (December 24, 1911–   )
Born in Inverness, Scotland, Malcolm MacEwen was educated at Aberdeen University and at Edinburgh University, receiving an M.A. in 1931 and an LL.B in 1936. A motorbike accident when he was 21 resulted in the amputation of one of his legs and a long convalescence, during which MacEwen became an avid reader and a confirmed Marxist. He practiced law in Inverness on the eve of World War II, became a local politician and a correspondent for the communist *Daily Worker*. By 1956, MacEwen, like many others, had become disillusioned with communism. He left the *Daily Worker*, finding a position on *The Architects' Journal*. His growing interest in architecture led to his writing *Crisis in Architecture* in 1974 and editing *Future Landscapes* (1976). The first book is a report on the failure of modern architecture and development to meet man's social and aesthetic needs and the requirements of sound environmentalism. The second book is a collection of 12 essays on such issues as transportation in the countryside, agricul-

ture in a time of inflation, planning and the prospects for wildlife. MacEwen also writes on conflicts between agriculture and conservation.

MacEwen is a member of Great Britain's National Park Committee. Expected to rubber-stamp decisions of the landowners who generally controlled the committee, MacEwen characteristically rebelled. He and his wife, ANN MACEWEN, made themselves authorities on conservation in the national parks, writing together *National Parks: Conservation or Cosmetics?* (1982) and *New Life for the Hills* (1983). The first book addresses the problems of conservation and the political economy of rural England. The second is a study of the agricultural and forestry policies for hill and mountain areas in England and Wales. It is critical of British and European Community policies, which MacEwen sees as major factors promoting rural depopulation and deterioration of the landscape. It recommends alternatives intended to support a rural population and wildlife by encouraging farmers to manage their livestock enterprises in ways compatible with conservation. He and his wife have also written *Greenprints for the Countryside? The Story of Britain's National Parks* (1987).

MacKaye, Benton (March 6, 1879–December 11, 1975)

A U.S. FOREST SERVICE researcher specializing in timber and water resources, MacKaye was also interested in the recreational uses of wild places and in urban forestry. His 1921 article in the *Journal of the American Institute of Architects*, "An Appalachian Trail: A Project in Regional Planning," ultimately resulted in the 2,000-mile-long hiking path from Georgia to Maine. On behalf of the Forest Service, the U.S. Department of Labor and, later, as a private consultant, MacKaye traveled widely, making regional surveys, investigating timber and water resources and making land colonization studies. He was a founding member of the WILDERNESS SOCIETY and served as its president from 1945 to 1950 (and as honorary president from 1950 until his death). MacKaye was born in Stamford, Connecticut.

Further reading: Lewis Mumford et al, "Benton MacKaye: A Tribute," *Living Wilderness* 39 (January/March 1976): 6–34.

Makhijani, Arjun (January 1, 1945–)

President of the INSTITUTE FOR ENERGY AND ENVIRONMENTAL RESEARCH (IEER) in Takoma Park, Maryland, and senior fellow of the Systems Research Institute in Pune, India, Arjun Makhijani received his Bachelor of Engineering (Electrical) degree from the University of Bombay in 1965, his M.S. in electrical engineering

from Washington State University in 1967 and his Ph.D. in engineering, specializing in controlled nuclear fusion, from the University of California, Berkeley, in 1972.

Makhijani has worked with scientific institutions, government agencies and private industry as a consultant on a wide variety of issues relating to the technical and economic analysis of alternative energy sources, electric utility rates and investment planning, energy conservation, energy use in agriculture, energy policy for the United States and energy policy for the Third World. He has participated in evaluative studies of portions of the nuclear fuel cycle.

Makhijani was assistant electrical engineer with Kaiser Engineers, Oakland, California, from 1969 to 1970, and, from 1972 to 1974, was a project specialist with the Ford Foundation Energy Policy Project, researching and writing on the technical and economic aspects of energy conservation and supply in the United States and on rural energy issues in the Third World. He was visiting professor at the National Institute of Bank Management, Bombay, India, from 1977 to 1979, with principal responsibility for evaluating the institute's extensive pilot rural development program. From 1983 to 1988, he was assistant, then associate, professor at Capitol College, Laurel, Maryland.

Makhijani is the author of numerous professional reports and publications, including contributions to *A Time to Choose: America's Energy Future* (Ford Foundation Energy Policy Project, 1974), *Evading the Deadly Issues: Corporate Management of America's Nuclear Weapons Production* (with Robert Alvarez and Brent Blackwelder, 1987), *Saving Our Skins: Technical Potential and Policies for the Elimination of Ozone-Depleting Chlorine Compounds* (with Annie Makhijani and Amanda Bickel, 1988), *Reducing the Risks: Policies for the Management of Highly Radioactive Nuclear Waste* (1989), *Radioactive Heaven and Earth: The Health and Environmental Effects of Nuclear Weapons Testing In, On, and Above the Earth* (1991) and many other works.

Affiliated with the American Association for the Advancement of Science, the Institute of Electrical and Electronics Engineers, the American Geophysical Union, the American Institute of Physics and the American Chemical Society, Makhijani is the recipient of the John Bartlow Martin Award for Public Interest Magazine Journalism, presented by Northwestern University's Medill School of Journalism in 1989.

Malin, James Claude (February 8, 1893– January 26, 1979)

Historian and author James Claude Malin turned his attention to ecology in 1947 with *The Grassland of*

North America. In this collection of essays, the first attempt by a historian to incorporate ecology into the study of a region, Malin refuted Frederic CLEMENTS's climax theory of nature and defended the farmers of the grassland region, who had come under attack for "causing" the Dust Bowl disaster of the 1930s. "No more brazen falsehood was ever perpetrated upon a gullible public." he wrote, "than the allegation that the dust storms of the 1930s were caused by the 'plow that broke the Plains.'" Malin argued that nature did not consist of an "equilibrium," which man had disturbed. Instead, nature was always in flux, and civilization could indeed impose productive order on it through agriculture.

Malin was a member of the faculty of the University of Kansas from 1921 until his death in 1979. In addition to *Grassland of North America,* he also wrote *An Interpretation of Recent American History* (1926), *Winter Wheat in the Golden Belt of Kansas* (1944), *Grassland Historical Studies: Natural Resources Utilization in a Background of Science and Technology,* vol. 1 (1950) and many other titles. Born in Edgely, North Dakota, Malin died in Lawrence, Kansas.

Malthus, Thomas Robert (February 14, 1766– December 23, 1834)

The first serious student of human population trends, Thomas Robert Malthus, born in Dorking, Surrey, was educated at Cambridge University and ordained an Anglican minister in 1788. In 1796, he was appointed curate in Albury, Surrey, and nine years later he accepted a position as professor of history and political economy at Haileybury College.

Published anonymously in 1798, Malthus's *An Essay on the Principle of Population* created much concern over the future of human society. Malthus reasoned that human population, increasing geometrically, would soon outgrow available resources, which increase arithmetically. Only disease, famine or war could stop the deadly progression. Malthus's dismal view was mitigated somewhat by his belief that man was indeed advancing toward civilization, but it was an advance negatively motivated by the ever-present threat of hunger. Malthus's strict adherence to set rates of fertility brought the most criticism. In the first edition of his work, Malthus presented fixed fertility rates for species and offered no occasion for variation. In a later revision, he conceded that human beings could exercise control over their fertility rates, thus slowing the rate of population growth and stemming the impending disaster.

Malthus's theories profoundly influenced Charles DARWIN, who read the *Essay* in 1838 and later wrote that reading Malthus prompted the kernel of his own theory of natural selection, which holds that, during the struggle for existence, "favourable [adaptive] variations would tend to be preserved and unfavourable ones to be destroyed. The result of this would be the formation of new species."

In addition to *An Essay on the Principle of Population,* Malthus also wrote *An Inquiry into the Nature and Progress of Rent* (1815) and *Principles of Political Economy* (1820). He was named a fellow of the Royal Society in 1819.

Malthus died in Bath, England.

Further reading: David Glass, *Introduction to Malthus* (New York: Wiley, 1953); George McCleary, *The Malthusian Population Theory* (London: Faber & Faber, 1953); William Petersen, *Malthus* (Cambridge: Harvard University Press, 1979).

Manes, Christopher (May 24, 1957–)

Associated with the radical environmental organization EARTH FIRST!, Christopher Manes is a writer and documentary film maker. He made a 1988 video documentary called *Earth First! The Politics of Radical Environmentalism* and served as associate editor of the *Earth First! Journal* from 1984 to 1987. *Green Rage: Radical Environmentalism and the Unmaking of Civilization* was published by Little, Brown in 1990, and Manes is a frequent contributor to such journals as *English Language Notes* and *Environmental Ethics.*

Manes was born in Chicago and educated at the University of California, Los Angeles, graduating summa cum laude in 1979. He received his M.A. from the University of Wisconsin, Madison, and engaged in doctoral study at the University of Oregon from 1981 to 1991. He attended the University of Iceland from 1985 to 1986 and the University of California, Berkeley, in 1991.

Marsh, George Perkins (March 15, 1801–July 23, 1882)

The noted author of *Man and Nature; or, Physical Geography as Modified by Human Action* (1864), George Perkins Marsh learned as a child about the negative effect man can have on his environment. Growing up at the base of a mountain along the Quechee River in Woodstock, Vermont, he came to recognize the dangers posed by lumbering and sheep grazing, practices that denuded the mountainside, causing rainwater to run off into the river, which flooded each spring.

Marsh studied law, was elected to the Vermont legislature and later was named ambassador to Turkey. While traveling in the Mediterranean region and France, he witnessed more evidence of the damage man could do to the environment. When he returned to America, he was appointed fish commissioner by the governor of Vermont. In this role, he published

George Perkins Marsh, in an engraving by Henry B. Hall, Jr.

Report on the Artificial Propagation of Fish (1857), which pointed to the bad effects of logging, sheep grazing, farming and industry on streams and rivers.

In 1861, Marsh took on another diplomatic job, as ambassador to Italy. While living in France and Italy, he completed work on *Man and Nature*, which included chapters on wildlife, waters, sands and forests and examined the impact of industry and engineering projects on the environment. Translated into Italian in 1869, the book influenced environmental policy not only in America but in Europe as well.

Further reading: David Lowenthal, *George Perkins Marsh: Versatile Vermonter* (Burlington: University of Vermont Press, 1958); Marsh; *Man and Nature* (New York: Scribner's, 1864).

Marshall, George (February 11, 1904–   )

A founder of the WILDERNESS SOCIETY, George Marshall has served on the group's board of directors since 1936. Born in New York City, he established a career in publishing during the 1920s as assistant editor of the *Encyclopedia of the Social Sciences*. Marshall worked as managing editor of *Living Wilderness* between 1957 and 1961 and, in 1956, edited his brother

Robert's book *Arctic Wilderness*. In 1959, Marshall was elected to the board of directors of the SIERRA CLUB, and between 1966 and 1967, he served as the club's president.

Marshall, Robert (January 2, 1901–November 11, 1939)

Son of Louis Marshall, a constitutional lawyer, social reformer and supporter of an Adirondack preserve, Robert Marshall grew up with a zeal for reform and a reverence for nature. In his brief life—cut short by a heart attack at 38—Marshall combined a brilliant career as a forester and forest administrator with that of a fine writer on wilderness subjects.

He published his first book, *High Peaks of the Adirondacks,* in 1922, which was based on his early experiences on and about his family's Lower Saranac Lake estate. He received a B.S. degree from the New York State College of Forestry in 1924 and an M.F. from the Harvard Forestry School the next year. Between 1925 and 1928, Marshall worked for the U.S. FOREST SERVICE's Northern Rocky Mountain Forest Experimental Station, Missoula, Montana. He left to enter the Ph.D. program at the Johns Hopkins University Laboratory of Plant Physiology, receiving his degree in 1930.

During the summers of 1929, 1930 and 1931, Marshall traveled in the Alaskan frontier, where he studied tree growth at the Arctic timberline and mapped the Brooks Range. His *Arctic Village* (1933), based on his observations of Eskimo and "sourdough" (Alaskan settler) life in the wilderness hamlet of Wiseman, was a popular and critical success. He would return to the Brooks Range in 1938 and 1939, gathering material for *Arctic Wilderness,* a book published posthumously in 1956.

In 1932 and 1933, Marshall worked for the Forest Service, contributing a highly detailed program for forest recreation to the *National Plan for American Forestry.* He was named director of forestry for the Office of Indian Affairs in 1933 and advocated the greater participation of Indians in the management of forests on their reservations. Marshall returned to the Forest Service in 1937 as chief of the Division of Recreation and Lands, where he developed a program for greater protection of primitive areas in the national forests. He also pioneered the development of recreational areas intended to serve lower-income groups. Marshall advocated strong federal management of public forest lands and was a signer of Gifford PINCHOT's and George P. AHERN's "Letter to Foresters" (1930), an indictment of the mismanagement of private forest lands. In 1930, Marshall wrote his own pamphlet on the subject of forest management, *The Social Management of American Forests*, and

Robert Marshall, chief, Division of Recreation and Lands, National Forest Administration, U.S. Forest Service (May 1937–November 1939) and a founder of the Wilderness Society. *Photo by U.S. Forest Service, courtesy of the Wilderness Society*

in 1933 devoted a book to the subject, *The People's Forests.*

Marshall was neither a dogmatic advocate of the preservation of forest lands in their primeval state, nor of their exploitation either for recreation or timber. In place of dogma, he developed a detailed program of management apportioned into distinct categories of use, ranging from primeval to "superlative" wilderness recreation areas, to roadside areas, to residential areas. While he advocated livestock grazing and logging in certain recreational areas, he believed both should be subject to careful regulation.

A bachelor of means, Marshall was a founder and major benefactor of the WILDERNESS SOCIETY in 1935. He left a large portion of his estate to the advancement of socialist utopian projects and civil liberties, and to the Wilderness Society. In 1940, the U.S. Forest Service combined three Montana primitive areas as the Bob Marshall Wilderness Area.

Further reading: George Marshall, "Robert Marshall as a Writer," *Living Wilderness* 16 (Autumn 1951): 14–20; Robert Marshall, *The People's Forest* (New York: Harrison Smith and Robert Haas, 1933); Marshall, *Arctic Village* (New York: Harrison Smith and Robert Haas, 1933); Roderick Nash, "The Strenuous Life of Bob Marshall," *Forest History* 10 (October 1966): 18–25.

Mason, David Townsend (March 11, 1883– September 3, 1973)

David Mason served with the U.S. FOREST SERVICE, was a professor of forestry at the University of California, head of the timber section of the Bureau of Internal Revenue and a highly respected private consultant who championed the theory of sustained yield—in his words, "the policy of managing . . . lands for permanent timber production." As the leading private forester in the Pacific Northwest, a project planner for many lumber companies, manager of the Western Pine Association (1931–35) and member of Herbert Hoover's Timber Conservation Board (1931), Mason was in an ideal position to persuade lumbermen to adopt sustained yield practices. In 1933, he helped write the National Recovery Administration lumber code, which *required* the adoption of such conservation measures. In 1937 and 1944, he helped draft additional federal sustained-yield legislation.

Further reading: Rodney C. Loehr (ed.), *Forests for the Future: The Story of Sustained Yield as Told in the Diaries and Papers of David T. Mason, 1907–1950* (St. Paul: Minnesota Historical Society, 1952).

Mather, Stephen Tyng (July 4, 1867–January 22, 1930)

A native of San Francisco, Stephen Tyng Mather, the first director of the NATIONAL PARK SERVICE, began his professional life as a reporter for the *New York Sun* in 1887. Five years later he joined the staff of the Pacific Coast Borax Company and subsequently became a partner in the creation of the Thorkildsen-Mather Borax Company of Chicago, from which Mather made a modest fortune.

He first became involved in the environmental field as a member of the SIERRA CLUB in 1905. After hiking and camping in the High Sierra Mountains in 1914, Mather wrote to Franklin K. Lane, secretary of the interior, to complain about the condition of the national parks in the West. Lane had been looking for someone to take over the management of the parks system, and he replied to Mather's complaint with a job offer.

After accepting appointment as assistant to the secretary of the interior in January 1915, Mather set out to develop a means by which the national parks would be managed well financially. On August 25, 1916, Congress approved legislation to form the National Park Service, and by early the next year, Mather was named director of the agency, and Horace M. ALBRIGHT was appointed assistant director.

One of Mather's first tasks was to win public support for the national parks. Mather wanted to provide improved tourist facilities in the parks in order to attract more visitors. This required far larger appropriations for the National Park Service than had ever been attained for the parks before. Mather also wanted to expand the holdings of the park service to include deserts of the Southwest and mountains of the Southeast.

Mather was successful in achieving both of these formidable goals. In addition, he succeeded in a campaign against the transformation of Yellowstone Lake into an irrigation reservoir. He enlisted railroad companies in promoting tourism in the national parks by asking them to offer excursion fares to tourists traveling on any line to any of the major parks. And to forestall any possible intrusion into the parks—such as that represented by the Hetch Hetchy dam in Yosemite—Mather promoted the economic value of the park system.

In January 1917, he convened a meeting of congressmen, park officials, railroad representatives and others in Washington, D.C., to discuss the potential of the park service. There many of the speakers adopted the "See America First" campaign in an attempt to keep Americans in their own country for vacations rather than going to Europe; Congressman Scott Ferris of Oklahoma estimated that $500 million was spent annually by American tourists abroad. Mather also instigated a rethinking of the aesthetic values that were considered for each new park added to the system. The fact that Yellowstone National Park included more than 3,000 acres of wilderness went largely unappreciated by the public, who thought the significance of the park lay in its geysers alone. Distributing 275,000 copies of the *National Parks Portfolio* (1917) to leaders of American business and culture, Mather's infant agency attempted to broaden the definition of land suitable for parks to include wilderness areas and wildlife sanctuaries. As Joseph Grinnell and Tracy Storer wrote in the *Portfolio*, the parks should "furnish examples of the earth as it was before the advent of the white man."

New parks added during Mather's directorship were the Grand Canyon, Zion, Bryce Canyon, Acadia, Shenandoah and the Great Smoky Mountains. Mather and his employees saw the parks as "outdoor classrooms," rather than simply as playgrounds for vacationers. In the 1920s, the park service instituted

Stephen T. Mather (right) with Secretary of the Interior Albert B. Fall at Yosemite, 1921. *Photo by F. P. Farquhar*

an educational branch with park museums and interpretive programs.

Realizing that not all scenic lands could be added to the national system, Mather spurred the growth of the state park system by sponsoring a National Conference on State Parks, an ongoing series of annual meetings first held in Des Moines, Iowa, in 1921.

Mather retired from the National Park Service in 1929 and died a few months later at his home in Brookline, Massachusetts. His able assistant, Horace M. Albright, succeeded him as director of the National Park Service.

Further reading: Robert Shankland, *Steve Mather of the National Parks* (New York: Tudor, 1951).

Matthiessen, Peter (May 22, 1927–   )

Considered one of the most important wilderness writers of the 20th century, Peter Matthiessen creates works of fiction and nonfiction that explore endangered species—both animal and human. His works characteristically chronicle the inexorable encroachment of technological civilization on isolated nature and isolated peoples.

Matthiessen was born in New York City and raised in rural New York State and Connecticut. His surroundings, no less than the fact that his architect father was a trustee of the NATIONAL AUDUBON SOCIETY, stimulated an enduring fascination with nature. Educated at the Sorbonne in Paris (1948–49) and Yale University (B.A., 1950), Matthiessen went to live in Paris, where he was co-founder of the *Paris Review*, which quickly became one of the most influential vehicles of contemporary literature. Matthiessen still serves as one of the journal's editors.

In Paris, Matthiessen completed his first novel, *Race Rock* (1954), then returned to the United States, where he continued to write while supporting himself as a commercial fisherman on Long Island. This experience resulted years later in his *Men's Lives: The Surfmen and Baymen of the South Fork* (1986). In 1956, Matthiessen set out on a three-year journey to visit *every* wildlife refuge in the United States. His *Wildlife in America*, published in 1959, was a critical and commercial success, and it was clear that Matthiessen had found his true vocation as a writer: one who travels to the wild places of the world, records his impressions and shapes them into books.

In 1961, he wrote *The Cloud Forest: A Chronicle of the South American Wilderness*. This was followed the next year by *Under the Mountain Wall: A Chronicle of Two Seasons in the Stone Age*. In 1967, he published *Oomingmuk: The Expedition to the Musk Ox Island in the Bering Sea*, and that year was also coauthor of *The Shorebirds of North America*. *Blue Meridian: The Search for the Great White Shark* appeared in 1971, as did a SIERRA CLUB volume titled *Everglades: With Selections from the Writings of Peter Matthiessen*. With photographer Eliot Porter he produced *The Tree Where Man Was Born/The African Experience* in 1972, and with artist Robert Gilmore, he wrote *The Wind Birds*, which appeared the same year. *The Snow Leopard* (1978) is one of Matthiessen's richest works, an autobiographical and spiritual account of a journey undertaken with biologist George Schaller into the most remote reaches of Nepal. The book received the National Book Award and the American Book Award.

Matthiessen's *In the Spirit of Crazy Horse* (1983) and *Indian Country* (1984) chronicle the struggle of modern American Indians to preserve their way of life on the nation's last open land.

McArdle, Richard Edwin (February 25, 1899– October 4, 1983)

Born in Lexington, Kentucky, Richard McArdle was a forester of national and international reputation.

He entered the U.S. FOREST SERVICE in 1924 as a silviculturalist after receiving his B.S. (1923) and M.S. degrees (1924) in forestry from the University of Michigan. Taking a three-year leave of absence from the Forest Service (1927–30), McArdle earned his Ph.D. and returned to become an important Forest Service fire researcher in the Northwest. In 1934, he served as dean of the School of Forestry, University of Idaho, then became the first director of the Rocky Mountain Forest and Range Experiment Station, Fort Collins, Colorado. Three years later, he became director of the Southeastern Station (then called the Appalachian Station) at Asheville, North Carolina. He was called to the Forest Service headquarters, Washington, D.C., in 1944, where he served as assistant chief for state and private forestry cooperative programs. He became chief of the U.S. Forest Service in 1952, a post he held for the next decade.

As chief, McArdle improved and expanded Forest Service recreation development, timber management, reforestation and the regulation of mining and grazing. He also turned his attention to upgrading Forest Service personnel. By abandoning attempts to enforce federal regulation of timber harvesting on private forest lands in favor of cooperative relations between the Forest Service and private owners, McArdle improved relations between the federal government and forest industries.

McArdle extended his influence beyond national boundaries when he helped found the North American Forestry Commission of the United Nations Food and Agriculture Organization. In 1960, he was an organizer of the Fifth World Forestry Congress. Director of the American Forestry Association (now AMERICAN FORESTS) from 1958 to 1981, his lifetime awards and honors are legion and include honorary degrees from the universities of Michigan and Maine as well as Syracuse University; the U.S. Department of Agriculture Distinguished Service Award; Rockefeller Public Service Award; the President's Gold Medal for Distinguished Federal Civil Service; the Sir William Schlich Memorial Medal of the Society of American Foresters; the John Aston Warder Medal of the American Forestry Association; the Knight Commander Order of Merit (Germany); and Order of Merit for Forestry (Mexico).

McCloskey, John Michael (April 26, 1934–)

Chairman of the board of the SIERRA CLUB since 1985, John Michael McCloskey went to work for the organization in 1961 as its Northwest representative. In 1965, he became assistant to the president, in 1966 was named the club's first conservation director, and from 1969 to 1985, he was executive director.

A native of Eugene, Oregon, McCloskey holds a B.A. in American government from Harvard College and a J.D. from the University of Oregon. At the Sierra Club, McCloskey has been instrumental in various environmental and conservation campaigns. He advocated the establishment of Redwood National Park in 1968 and fostered the idea of executive orders to protect roadless areas in the national forests. He was the principal author of the United Nation's Charter for Nature and has written articles on environmental subjects published in professional and legal journals.

From 1978 to 1988, McCloskey was a member of the Commission on Environmental Law and Policy of the INTERNATIONAL UNION FOR CONSERVATION OF NATURE. He served on President Jimmy Carter's Commission on an Agenda for the 1980s. Since 1988, he has served on the board of directors of the NATURAL RESOURCES COUNCIL OF AMERICA and, since 1989, as chairman of the Advocacy Forum. From 1983 to 1987, he was cochairman of the OSHA-Environmental Conference in Washington, D.C.

When McCloskey first became associated with the Sierra Club, the primary reason most members joined was to take advantage of its outings or to purchase its exhibit-format books. During the 1960s, however, the organization shifted its focus from the enjoyment of nature to the preservation of the environment, and in 1970, McCloskey called for nothing less than an environmental revolution: "That other revolution, the industrial one that is turning sour, needs to be replaced by a revolution of new attitudes toward growth, goods, space, and living things." Under McCloskey's leadership, the Sierra Club has broadened its work to an international scope since, as McCloskey has observed, "a catastrophic environmental policy in one country can affect environmental quality in a neighboring country."

During McCloskey's tenure as chairman of the board, the Sierra Club has focused its activities on toxic waste disposal, acid rain and the whaling industry of Japan. McCloskey has called on industrial leaders to change their environmentally unsound practices, commending such companies as StarKist, for changing its tuna-fishing practices to methods that are safe for dolphins, and Conoco, for using double-hulled tankers to transport oil. However, he has stated that few American corporations are "good environmental citizens" and urges that industry voluntarily alter its environmentally dangerous practices before governmental regulations force them to do so.

McFarland, J(ohn) Horace (September 24, 1859–October 2, 1948)

McFarland, a newspaper publisher, philanthropist and civic activist, was an early and important crusader on behalf of urban beautification and scenic preservation. Born in McAlisterville, Pennsylvania, he became editor of the influential "Beautiful America" column of the *Ladies' Home Journal* in 1904, the year in which he was elected president of the new American Civic Association. McFarland fought to preserve Niagara Falls from disfigurement by power company interests and supported the struggle (1908–13) of the SIERRA CLUB against the building of the Hetch Hetchy Valley Dam, which threatened Yosemite National Park. His experience doing battle with commercial exploiters of natural resources moved McFarland to lobby for the creation of a NATIONAL PARK SERVICE, an effort that spanned 1911 to 1916.

Further reading: Alfred Runte, *National Parks: The American Experience* (Lincoln: University of Nebraska Press, 1979).

McGovern, George (July 19, 1922–   )

George McGovern was a longtime advocate of many liberal social and environmental programs, both as a three-term senator from South Dakota and an unsuccessful candidate for president in 1972. He was especially active in the fight to end hunger, both domestically and abroad.

In 1961, John F. Kennedy appointed McGovern director of Food for Peace, a program which, by the end of 1961, was feeding 64 million people overseas with free U.S. farm surpluses. McGovern was elected to the Senate in 1962. As head of the Select Committee on Nutrition and Human Needs, McGovern won passage of a $1.75 billion food stamp program and of an expanded school lunch program in 1970. McGovern was a strong supporter of mass transit and affordable housing, and he fought against the supersonic transport (SST). McGovern's longshot candidacy in 1972 was spearheaded by a promise to end American involvement in the Vietnam War. He also promised to expand domestic social welfare programs, funding them in part with a major cut in the defense budget. After a campaign beset by difficulties, he lost to Richard M. NIXON by a wide margin.

McGovern was born in Avon, South Dakota. He earned a B.A. from Dakota Wesleyan University in 1946, and a Ph.D. degree from Northwestern in 1953. From 1953 to 1956, McGovern worked for the Democratic party. He served in the U.S. House of Representatives from 1957 to 1961. It was soon after an unsuccessful run for the Senate in 1960 that Mc-

Govern was picked to run the Food for Peace Program.

McHarg, Ian Lennox (November 20, 1920–)

Ian Lennox McHarg moved to the United States from his native Scotland (he was born in Clydebank) in 1946 and attended Harvard University. After receiving a master's in landscape architecture in 1950 and in city planning in 1951, he returned to Scotland to work as a planner in the Department of Health. In 1954, McHarg came to the United States again and joined the faculty of the University of Pennsylvania as assistant professor, achieving promotion to professor, and, finally, chairman of the Department of Landscape Architecture and Regional Planning. In 1962, he left the university to become a partner in the architectural and planning firm of Wallace-McHarg, Roberts & Todd in Philadelphia.

McHarg is noted for his acute sensitivity to nature in his urban landscape designs. His book *Design with Nature* (1969) called on developers to assess fully the local ecosystem before any building or alterations are scheduled. In his own projects, McHarg identifies flood plains, erosion-prone areas, frigid sites, soil drainage capacity, water table polluting areas, unstable bedrock, animal and flora patterns and other factors to determine building or development sites that have the least impact on ecosystems.

McKibben, William Ernest (December 8, 1960–)

A former *New Yorker* staff writer and editor, Palo Alto-born William Ernest McKibben became a prophet of ecological doom with the publication of *The End of Nature* (1989). Using research on the greenhouse effect, McKibben warned of the certainty of ecological disaster unless industry and government modify practices that contribute to global warming. Such practices, McKibben declared, "will lead us, if not straight to hell, then straight to a place with a similar temperature." McKibben proposed a new global society that consumes fewer resources.

In addition to criticizing the consumer society, McKibben takes to task governmental agencies and environmental groups that base their arguments for saving natural landscapes on economics. Environmentalists, he contends, have been forced to couch their arguments in terms of nature's economic benefits rather than on the intrinsic beauty and uniqueness of the regions they want to save.

While forceful and persuasive, McKibben's work has been criticized by the press and some scientists, and McKibben himself has been called an "apocalypse abuser."

McNary, Charles Linza (June 12, 1874– February 25, 1944)

As U.S. senator from Oregon (he was born near Salem) from 1917 to 1944, Charles L. McNary sponsored some of the most important pieces of forestry legislation in the history of the nation. A lawyer, prosecutor and dean of the Willamette University law school, McNary was first appointed to fill a Senate vacancy in 1917 and was subsequently elected and reelected for the rest of his life.

The Clarke-McNary Act of 1924 provided funding for forest fire prevention and for a study on the impact of tax laws on private reforestation efforts. The McSweeney-McNary Act of 1928 established a federal forestry research program and mandated a survey of forest conditions nationwide. The Sustained-Yield Forest Management Act, passed one day after McNary's death, empowered the U.S. FOREST SERVICE and the U.S. Department of the INTERIOR to work with private timber owners in creating cooperative sustained-yield units to help stabilize the industry and ensure the welfare of small towns wholly dependent on logging and milling.

Charles L. McNary was essentially a conservative on forestry issues, advocating federal cooperation with private industry, but not "interference" with private enterprise in the name of the public good. In opposition to Gifford PINCHOT, McNary fought such federal regulatory measures as attempts to control timber cutting on private lands.

In addition to forestry legislation, McNary also sponsored measures to provide federal aid to state parks and to encourage preservation of timber along scenic highways. A farmer, McNary introduced the filbert into the United States from Spain.

McPhee, John (March 8, 1931–)

A native of Princeton, New Jersey, John McPhee was educated at Princeton University, from which he took an A.B. in 1953, and at Cambridge University, where he did graduate work from 1953 to 1954. Almost certainly the most prolific and widely read of contemporary popular environmental writers, having published nearly a book a year since 1965, McPhee began his writing career in 1955 as a screenwriter for television's "Robert Montgomery Presents." He left this position in 1957 to become associate editor of *Time* magazine, serving in that capacity until 1964, when he became a staff writer for the *New Yorker*. Most of his subsequent books have appeared first as series of articles in that magazine.

McPhee's writing is characterized by an ability to penetrate a subject and explore it lucidly and thoroughly with a great narrative immediacy of style. His environmentally oriented works are wide ranging.

The 1967 *Oranges* is a historical, geographical, botanical and anecdotal study of the fruit; *The Pine Barrens* (1968) is a fascinating exploration of a surprisingly remote and wild portion of the nation's most densely populated state, New Jersey; *A Roomful of Hovings and Other Profiles* (1969) is a collection of biographical sketches of contemporary environmentalists; *Encounters with the Archdruid* (1972) is a portrait of the SIERRA CLUB's controversial David BROWER and others; *The Deltoid Pumpkin Seed* (1973) deals with an experimental aircraft; *The Curve of Binding Energy* (1974) is a profile of Theodore Taylor and the world's nuclear materials safeguards problems. Other works relevant to nature and the environment include *The Survival of the Bark Canoe* (1975), *Giving Good Weight* (1979), *In Suspect Terrain* (1983), *Rising from the Plains* (1986), *The Control of Nature* (1989) and *Looking for a Ship* (1990).

A fellow of the Geological Society of America and the American Academy of Arts and Letters, McPhee has been Ferris Professor of Journalism at Princeton since 1975.

McTaggart, David, (June 24, 1932–   )

Controversial chairman of the board of GREENPEACE INTERNATIONAL from 1979 to 1991, David McTaggart began his career of protest against environmental offenders in 1973. McTaggart had dropped out of a successful construction company to sail a 38-foot ketch, the *Vega*, around the South Pacific. There he learned that members of Greenpeace, a loosely organized band of Canadian ecologists, pacifists and Quakers, were demonstrating against the testing of nuclear weapons in the South Pacific. He decided to join the protest. When he sailed into the test site, a French minesweeper rammed his boat and removed it from the area. The next year, McTaggart returned to the test site, and this time French security personnel boarded his boat and beat him, permanently damaging one eye. He returned home to Canada (McTaggart is a native of Vancouver, British Columbia) and successfully sued the French government. Opposition against nuclear testing in international waters was mounting, and McTaggart began organizing supporters into Greenpeace International, which now has chapters worldwide and commands a budget in excess of $14 million.

Until he stepped down on September 2, 1991, McTaggart oversaw the organization's "nonviolent direct actions," which call attention to environmental problems. Greenpeace members have painted the coats of harp seals green to make their hides commercially undesirable; they have parachuted from industrial smokestacks to protest acid rain; and they

Former chairman—now honorary chairman—of Greenpeace International, David McTaggart. © 1985 *Greenpeace*

have stopped the flow of toxics into lakes and streams by plugging factory drainpipes.

McTaggert is now honorary chairman of Greenpeace International, which is currently headed by Matti WUORI.

Men of the Trees (Founded: 1922)

Sandy Lane, Crawley Down, West Sussex RH10 4HS, England; (342) 742536

An international organization, Men of the Trees encourages the planting and preservation of trees; supports the reclamation of arid regions; plants trees; advises businesses, governments and the public on tree planting; and publishes information on tree preservation and forestry. The organization, also known as the International Society for the Planting and Protection of Trees, publishes *Trees* and *Trees Are News*. Mrs. E. Sandwell is executive secretary of the organization.

Merriam, C(linton) Hart (December 15, 1855–March 19, 1942)

A New York-born graduate of Yale University's Sheffield Scientific School and Columbia University College of Physicians and Surgeons, Clinton Hart Merriam practiced medicine from 1879 to 1885, when he was appointed head of the Division of Economic Ornithology and Mammalogy. In 1905, when the division became the U.S. Bureau of BIOLOGICAL SURVEY within the Department of AGRICULTURE, Merriam remained at its helm. In 1910, he retired from the survey to become a research associate at the Smithsonian Institution where, for the next 30 years, he conducted research in botany, zoology and ethnology. His dioramas and exhibits instructed a generation of Smithsonian visitors.

In the late 1880s, Merriam traveled to the San Francisco mountains of northern Arizona to study the fauna there. From his observations of life forms in the low desert, the mountain peaks and the more temperate zone in between, he developed his theories of life zones, postulating that all mountainous regions of the world could be "flattened out" for the purposes of study, so that each mile of altitude equaled 800 miles of latitude. From this he reasoned that the United States and Canada comprised two life areas: a southern austral zone and a northern boreal zone. Within these expanses were six life zones: the lower austral, upper austral, transition, Canadian, Hudsonian and arctic-alpine. Each of these zones was characterized by a specific range of temperatures.

Various scientists argued against the life zone theory, pointing out that geographical succession was sometimes more gradual than Merriam had presented and that, occasionally, as in the American grasslands, progression moved from east to west, according to quantities of rainfall, rather than from south to north, according to temperature. Although Merriam's theories have been criticized as reductive and simplistic, he was a pioneer in nature study who looked not simply at the various species themselves but at their habitats and communities as well.

Merriam was president of the American Ornithologists' Union from 1900 to 1902, president of the Biological Section of the Washington Academy of Sciences from 1891 to 1892, chairman of the U.S. Geographic Board from 1917 to 1925, president of the American Society of Mammalogists from 1919 to 1921 and president of the American Society of Naturalists from 1924 to 1925. In addition, he was an associate editor of *National Geographic Magazine* and zoological editor of *Science*. He wrote 29 books and reports, including *Birds of Connecticut* (1877), *Mammals of the Adirondacks* (1882–84) and *Life Zones and Crop Zones of the United States* (1898).

C. Hart Merriam

Merriam, John Campbell (October 20, 1869–October 20, 1945)

Merriam was a native Iowan who went to the University of Munich to study vertebrate paleontology, receiving his doctorate in 1893. He taught at the University of California, Berkeley, from 1894 to 1920 and was president of the Carnegie Institution of Washington, D.C., from 1920 to 1938. A popularizer of Darwin, he wrote *The Living Past* (1926) and *The Garment of God: The Influence of Nature in Human Experience* (1943) and was very active in the cause of scenic preservation. Merriam was president of the SAVE-THE-REDWOODS LEAGUE from 1920 until his death and a key figure on the advisory board of the NATIONAL PARK SERVICE from 1920 to 1933. He was also active in international preservation organizations, including the Commission du Parc National Albert in Zaire and La Asociacion Conservadoro de los Monumentos Arquelogicos de Yucatán.

Perhaps his most significant contribution to the cause of American wilderness preservation was his conviction that state and national parks should serve as laboratories crucial for the present and future study of nature and as places where everyone might draw inspiration and enlightenment from the earth's geological and biological past. Merriam believed in minimizing the recreational use of wilderness parks in order to preserve them in as pristine a state as possible. It was Merriam who personally supervised the development of the Yavapai Point observation station on the rim of the Grand Canyon.

Metcalf, Robert Lee (November 13, 1916–   )

Robert Lee Metcalf is a leading authority on entomology and on insect pest management, including the ecologically responsible use of chemical pesticides.

He was born in Columbus, Ohio, and educated at the University of Illinois (B.A., 1939 and M.A., 1940) and at Cornell University (Ph.D., 1942). From 1946 to 1948, he taught at the University of California, Riverside, becoming chairman of the Department of Entomology there in 1950 and vice-chancellor of the university in 1963, serving in that capacity until 1966. Since 1968, Metcalf has been a member of the faculty of the University of Illinois and was head of the Department of Zoology from 1969 to 1973.

Metcalf served as a member of the pesticide science advisory committee of the ENVIRONMENTAL PROTECTION AGENCY from 1976 to 1982 and has been a member of the Board of Natural Resources and Conservation of the state of Illinois since 1982. He is the author of *Organic Insecticides* (1957), *Destructive and Useful Insects* (1962) and coeditor (with W. H. Luckmann) of *Introduction to Insect Pest Management* (1974).

Professor Metcalf has received many honors, including the Order Cherubini from the University of Pisa. He is a fellow of the American Association for the Advancement of Science and of the American Academy of Arts and Sciences. The Entomological Society of America (of which Metcalf was president in 1958) presented him with its Founder's Award, the Ciba-Geigy Award, the International Award in Pesticide Chemistry and the Charles F. Spencer Award. The Society of Environmental Toxicological Chemistry presented him with its Founder's Award in 1983. Metcalf is also a member of the American Chemical Society, Phi Beta Kappa, Phi Beta Phi and Sigma Xi.

Mines, U.S. Bureau of (Established: 1910)
Department of the Interior, 2401 E Street NW, Washington, D.C. 20241; (202) 634-1004

Established by the Organic Act of May 16, 1910, the Bureau of Mines is primarily a research and fact-finding agency. Its goals are to help ensure that the nation has adequate supplies of nonfuel minerals for security and other needs. The bureau conducts research to provide technology for the extraction, processing, use and recycling of nonfuel mineral resources at a reasonable cost and without jeopardizing the safety of the workers involved in the industry or harming the environment.

Although the bureau has no regulatory functions or enforcement authority, it collects, compiles, analyzes and publishes statistical and economic information on all phases of nonfuel mineral resource development, much of which bears directly on environmental issues. From time to time, the bureau engages in special studies, such as the effect of potential economic, technological and legal developments on source availability and is responsible for analyzing the effect of policy alternatives—including those mandated by environmental regulations—on mineral supply and demand.

Mitchell, George John (August 20, 1933–   )

Senate majority leader George J. Mitchell is a leading voice of the Democratic Party today and a strong supporter of environmental issues. He is a member of the Committee on Environment and Public Works and played a key role in the passage of the Clean Air Act in 1989. Mitchell is also the author of *World On Fire: Saving an Endangered Earth* (1991), a detailed account of what he calls the "Four Horsemen of the Apocalypse riding over today's world environment": the build-up of carbon dioxide and other greenhouse gases, the destruction of the rainforests, the destruction of the ozone layer and the phenomenon of acid rain. To combat these threats, Mitchell has called for the creation of a world atmosphere fund that would be financed by taxes on fossil fuels and forgiveness of the debts of Third World nations that agree to follow ecologically sound courses of development.

Mitchell was born in Waterville, Maine, the son of a janitor at Colby College; his mother was a Lebanese immigrant. Supporting himself, he attended Bowdoin College (B.A., 1954) and served in army counterintelligence from 1954 to 1956. After leaving the service, he attended Georgetown University, receiving his law degree in 1960, then taking a position with the U.S. Department of Justice. In 1962, he became executive assistant to Maine's Senator Edmund S. Muskie. From 1965 to 1977, Mitchell practiced law and also served—in 1971—as the assistant attorney for Cumberland County, Maine. From 1977 to 1979, Mitchell was United States attorney for Maine, and from 1979 to 1980, he served as U.S. district judge for Maine. When Senator Muskie succeeded Cyrus Vance as secretary of state in 1980, Maine Governor Joseph Brennan appointed Mitchell to serve out his Senate term. Mitchell won election to the seat in 1982 and has served since.

Conservation International president Russell Mittermeier with a bamboo lemur. © *Conservation International*

Mittermeier, Russell A. (November 8, 1949–   )

Bronx-born and Ivy League-educated, Russell Mittermeier is a leading primate expert and the president of CONSERVATION INTERNATIONAL, a worldwide organization dedicated to the preservation of tropical rainforests and other biologically diverse ecosystems and to the sustainable, conservation-based economic development of related communities.

Active also in the INTERNATIONAL UNION FOR CONSERVATION OF NATURE AND NATURAL RESOURCES, a global federation of environmental groups, Mittermeier is vice-chairman for International Programs of the IUCN Species Survival Commission, a member of the commission's steering committee, chairman of the organization's Primate Specialist Group (and editor of *Primate Conservation*, its newsletter and journal) and a consultant to the IUCN/SSC Crocodile Specialist Group.

Mittermeier graduated from Dartmouth College in 1971 and earned his M.A. (1973) and Ph.D. (1977) in biological anthropology at Harvard University. He

joined the New York Zoological Society in 1976, serving first as a conservation associate and then, from 1977 to 1979, as a World Wildlife Fund Conservation Fellow in primate ecology. Also in 1977, Mittermeier began teaching at the State University of New York at Stony Brook, where he is now an adjunct professor in the Department of Anatomical Sciences and an adjunct assistant professor of anthropology. From 1979 to 1989, he directed the primate program of the WORLD WILDLIFE FUND (U.S.), and during his tenure with WWF he also served as director (1985–89) and vice-president (1986–88) of the Species Conservation Program and vice-president for Science (1987–89). In 1988, he became chairman of the World Bank Task Force of Biological Diversity, and in 1989, he accepted the presidency of Conservation International, which is headquartered in Washington, D.C.

With 10 years of field experience and expedition leadership in Central and South America, Africa and Asia, Mittermeier is fluent in several languages: French, German, Portuguese, Spanish and Surinamese creole. He has written five books and over 200 papers for scientific journals, including numerous studies of South American turtle species. He serves on the editorial boards of *Biology and Conservation*, *Journal of Medical Primatology*, *Orion Nature Quarterly*, *Revue de Zoologie Africaine* (Belgium) and *Zoo Biology*. A Scientific Fellow of the New York Zoological Society and a member of the Linnaean Society of London, Mittermeier serves on the advisory boards of the American Society of Primatologists Conservation Committee, FUNATURA (Brazil), the International Primatological Society Conservation Committee, the Peruvian Conservation Foundation and Primarily Primates Inc. He has been the recipient of several awards and fellowships, including the Gold Medal of the San Diego Zoological Society.

Moore, Barrington (September 25, 1883– October 19, 1966)

This forester and ecologist was born in Ossining, New York, and educated at Yale University (A.B., 1906) and the Yale University School of Forestry (M.F., 1908). After taking his master's degree, he became an assistant in the U.S. FOREST SERVICE, which sent him to France, Germany, British India, the Philippines and Japan to study forestry practices. From 1909 to 1911, he worked as forest assistant in New Mexico and then was assigned, from 1911 to 1914, as forest examiner, working out of the Forest Service headquarters in Washington, D.C. During his tenure in Washington, Moore worked on methods of mapping and estimating timber lands. Active in the SOCIETY OF AMERICAN FORESTERS, he was editor of

Proceedings of the Society of American Foresters, subsequently called *Journal of Forestry*.

In 1914, he left the Forest Service to devote himself to forest research, becoming associate curator of woods and forestry at the American Museum of Natural History in New York. After serving in the 10th (Forestry) Engineer regiment during World War I, organizing a force to supply wood for American military operations in Europe, Moore returned to the Museum of Natural History, staying at that institution until 1920. Moore next worked for the ECOLOGICAL SOCIETY OF AMERICA and the National Research Council, and from 1920 to 1931, served as editor of the journal *Ecology*.

Moran, Thomas (January 12, 1837–August 26, 1926)

The greatest of three artist brothers, Thomas Moran was one of the finest of all western landscape painters. His oils and watercolors, prized for their intrinsic beauty, were also instrumental in raising public consciousness of the natural wonders of the West and thereby generating public and political support for the cause of conservation and the formation of the national park system and the NATIONAL PARK SERVICE.

Born in Bolton, England, Moran immigrated to Philadelphia with his parents in 1844. He was apprenticed to a wood engraver in 1853 and studied etching and painting with his older brother, Edward.

Thomas Moran made his first western painting expedition in 1860, to Lake Superior, and the following year returned to England with Edward. While he was abroad, Moran discovered the artist who would prove to be his first great influence, the British landscapist and seascapist J. M. W. Turner. A second European trip (1866–67) resulted in an encounter with the work of the French painter Jean-Baptiste-Camille Corot, Moran's second important artistic influence.

Moran translated the lessons of Turner and Corot into a vision unique to the American western landscape. In 1871, he accompanied geologist Dr. Ferdinand V. Hayden to the relatively unexplored upper Yellowstone River. The next year, he ventured into California's Yosemite Valley, and in 1873, he accompanied John Wesley POWELL in southern Utah and Arizona. In 1874, Moran explored central Colorado in search of the Mountain of the Holy Cross, which he painted later that year. In 1879, in company with his younger brother, Peter, Thomas Moran explored and sketched the Tetons. For the next two decades, the artist continued to travel widely, especially in the West.

Moran turned his studies and sketches into magnificent, emotionally intense and almost always large-scale paintings in his Newark, New Jersey, studio. Two of his canvases, *The Great Canyon of the Yellowstone* and *Chasm of the Colorado*, were purchased by Congress in 1872 for the then lordly sum of $10,000 each to decorate the rotunda of the U.S. Capitol. These and a series of watercolors Moran executed to illustrate Hayden's scientific report of his expedition are credited with having influenced the federal government to create in the Yellowstone region America's first national park.

Thomas Moran's is one of the happier stories of American art. Admired by critics during his own time and since, he had a prolific, long and prosperous career, painting until the very end of his life. It was reported that, on his deathbed at 90, Moran gazed at the ceiling and calmly gestured, envisioning landscapes yet to be painted.

Further reading: Alan Axelrod, *Art of the Golden West* (New York: Abbeville Press, 1990).

More, Henry (October 1614–September 1, 1687)

The 17th-century philosopher Henry More wrote important works on nature and the structure of the natural world, which profoundly influenced generations of later philosophers and scientists. Born in Grantham, Lincolnshire, More was a fellow of Christ's College, Cambridge. His first major work, *An Antidote Against Atheisme* (1652), lists and describes natural phenomena that, for More, could be understood only as manifestations of divine providence. John RAY used this section of More's work in developing his *Wisdom of God Manifested in the Works of Creation* (1691). In the *Immortality of the Soul* (1659), More provides elaborate descriptions of nature and spirits. In *Enchiridion Metaphysicum* (1671), he rejected Robert Boyle's theories on the mechanism of gravity, magnetism and hydrostatics. More generally rejected all mechanistic views of nature, arguing instead that a divine *Anima Mundi*—world soul—infuses nature with an active force. Man cannot reduce this to mere mechanism, and for that reason, humankind's relation to nature is rightly one of wonder and humility. More's work, stressing the divine, mystic and organic order of nature and the cosmos, forms a cornerstone of so-called arcadian ecology.

More died where he had taught, in Cambridge, England.

Further reading: Edwin A. Burtt, *The Metaphysical Foundations of Modern Physical Science: A Historical and Critical Essay* (London: Routledge and Kegan Paul, 1932).

The Teton Range and the Snake River, Grand Teton National Park. *U.S. Department of the Interior, National Park Service photo by George A. Grant*

Mott, William Penn, Jr. (October 19, 1909–September 21, 1992)

As director of the NATIONAL PARK SERVICE during President Ronald REAGAN's second term, William Penn Mott worked to expand the park system despite the president's reluctance to do so. In addition, he tackled problems of park overcrowding, pollution and concessionaires.

Mott began working for the National Park Service in 1933 as a landscape architect in the San Francisco Bay area. From 1940 to 1943, he was planning and housing advisor for the California Housing Authority, Contra Costa County, after which he went into private practice as a landscape architect until 1946. Between 1946 and 1962, Mott served as superintendent of parks for the city of Oakland. Moving to the state level in 1946, he managed the regional parks in northern California and then became director of the California State Parks.

While conservationists were delighted with Mott's appointment as director of the National Park Service, his tenure ended soon after President Reagan left office. Early in 1989, President George Bush and Interior Secretary Manuel LUJAN announced that James RIDENOUR would succeed Mott. Ridenour was director of the Department of Natural Resources in Indiana and had been campaign finance chief for Vice-President Dan Quayle's Senate campaign in 1980.

Mowat, Farley (McGill) (May 12, 1921–   )

Farley Mowat is probably Canada's best known living writer. A prolific author, he has published some 30 volumes, including fiction and nonfiction. His works most characteristically focus on nature, especially the wilderness and ecology. He has a particular affinity for the far Canadian North and is an outspoken and eloquent critic of much in his government's official position on these remote regions.

Mowat was born in Belleville, Ontario, and earned a B.A. at the University of Toronto in 1949. After serving as a captain in the Canadian army during World War II, he took a position as a government biologist in the Barren Lands of northern Canada. He was assigned to study the area's wolves and their diet, since the government suspected that the wolves were responsible for the thinning of the caribou population. What Mowat observed was that, far from being rapacious and predatory, the wolves were intelligent animals that ate only what they needed. They lived primarily on field mice, attacking only weak or sickly caribou—and thereby actually strengthened the herd.

Mowat's findings were not well received in official circles and were, in fact, largely ignored by the bureaucracy. However, he based one of his best-known books, *Never Cry Wolf* (1963; revised edition, 1973) on his observations, and the public did respond. Indeed, singlehandedly, Mowat had rehabilitated the popular reputation of this animal, elevating it into a kind of romantic symbol of the wilderness and of the values of that wilderness.

Never Cry Wolf was not the first of Mowat's books to issue from his experiences in the Barren Lands. *People of the Deer*, first published in 1952, publicized the plight of the Ihalmiut tribe, whose numbers were dwindling in the face of government apathy over their welfare.

Of Mowat's many books, however, perhaps none is more powerful than *Sea of Slaughter*, published in 1984. It is a long, mournful history of the extinction and near-extinction of sea and land animals along the Atlantic seaboard of North America, from Cape Cod to Labrador. "The living world," Mowat observes in this work, "is dying in our time." Astoundingly, United States immigration officials refused to allow Mowat into this country to publicize the book in 1984. The author, who believes that the "gun lobby and anti-environmentalists" were behind his exclusion, wrote a 1985 book, *My Discovery of America*, about his frustrated attempts to determine why he was not allowed entry.

Mowat's 1987 biography of gorilla researcher and environmentalist Dian Fossey, *Woman in the Mists: The Story of Dian Fossey*, was made into a popular motion picture.

Farley Mowat's other environmentally oriented books include *The Polar Passion: The Quest for the North Pole* (editor, 1967; revised edition, 1973), *Canada North* (1967), *The Siberians* (1970), *A Whale for the Killing* (1972), *Top of the World Trilogy* (1976) and *The Great Betrayal: Arctic Canada Now* (1976). Mowat has received many awards and honors for his writing, including honorary degrees from four universities and the Curran Award (1977) "for contributions to the understanding of wolves."

Muir, John (April 21, 1838–December 24, 1914)

A native of Scotland who came to Wisconsin with his family in 1849, John Muir matured into a conser-

vationist of the Transcendentalist mold. He argued passionately for the need to preserve wilderness areas to serve as a respite from daily life for an increasingly urbanized nation peopled by individuals he described as "tired, nerve-shaken, over-civilized." His position was taken up by conservationists of the day and sparked tremendous growth in the environmental field during the late 19th and early 20th centuries.

As a student of literature and science at the University of Wisconsin from 1859 to 1863, Muir was profoundly influenced by the Transcendentalist writings of Ralph Waldo EMERSON and Henry David THOREAU and by the scientific theories of Louis AGASSIZ and Asa GRAY. Like Thoreau, Muir broke with the popular Christian notion that the universe had been created for man's use. All living things, Muir believed, contributed equally to a universal whole.

After his university work, he began his lifelong study of plant life, beginning with a 1,000-mile trek from Indiana to the Gulf of Mexico. In 1868, Muir moved to California's Yosemite Valley, where he lived intermittently over the next several years, climbing the high peaks of the Sierra Nevada while continuing his study of geology and botany. Becoming alarmed by the devastation lumbermen and sheep grazers were creating in the region, he began writing and speaking about the need to preserve the forests—not only because of their scenic beauty but also because of their importance as watersheds for California farmers.

During the early 1880s, Muir became a successful farmer himself, but he did not remain apart from the wilderness preservation movement for long. He promoted the creation of Yosemite National Park, which was established in 1890. Next he worked to establish the SIERRA CLUB and served as the group's first president. Under his leadership, the club campaigned against the building of a dam in the Hetch Hetchy Valley of Yosemite National Park. Although the organization waged the battle mightily for years, the "Hetch Hetchy Steal," as it was called, became fact in 1913, and Muir died the next year.

In the struggle against the Hetch Hetchy dam, proponents of preserving the valley discovered their strongest weapon too late to win the battle. They realized that the proposed dam and reservoir would decrease tourist revenues—but, by the time of that realization, the battle had been lost.

The battle had been lost, but not the lesson. Conservationists had now learned to include the economic rationale in their defense of wilderness. Moreover, the team Muir had assembled to fight the "Hetch Hetchy Steal" was a valuable and enduring one, which included not only conservationists, but railroad officials and tourism promoters as well. This

John Muir at Yosemite National Park. *Courtesy of the National Park Service*

coalition was instrumental in the creation of a government agency to administer the national parks. Three years after Hetch Hetchy, and two years after the death of John Muir, Congress created the NATIONAL PARK SERVICE.

John Muir was a fine writer who contributed to leading magazines, including *Harper's Monthly*, *Scribner's Monthly*, *Atlantic Monthly*, *Century* and *Overland Monthly*. His books—*The Mountains of California* (1894), *Our National Parks* (1901) and *My First Summer in the Sierra* (1911)—are classics of environmental prose.

Further reading: William Frederic Badé, *The Life and Letters of John Muir* (Boston: Houghton Mifflin, 1924); Holway R. Jones, *John Muir and the Sierra Club: The Battle for Yosemite* (San Francisco: Sierra Club, 1965); Herbert F. Smith, *John Muir* (Boston: Twayne, 1965); Linnie Marsh Wolfe, *Son of the Wilderness: The Life of John Muir* (Boston: Houghton Mifflin, 1945).

Murdoch, William W. (January 28, 1939–   )

Population biologist and ecologist William W. Murdoch is a professor of biological science at the University of California, Santa Barbara. Educated at the University of Glasgow (he was born in Glassford, Scotland) and at Oxford University, Murdoch became a research associate and instructor in ecology at the University of Michigan in 1963. In 1965, he moved to the University of California, Santa Barbara, as an assistant professor, where his research has focused on the population and community dynamics of organisms.

In the January 1970 issue of *The Center Magazine*, published by the Center for the Study of Democratic Institutions in Santa Barbara, Murdoch and Joseph CONNELL published an article entitled "All About Ecology." The two authors claim that ecologists have a responsibility to correct the public's blind acceptance of technology as a solution to environmental problems. New technologies, they assert, create new problems. The authors advocate a rethinking of growth and progress. They write, "In short, the ecologist must convince the population that the only solution to the problem of growth is not to grow."

Murie, Olaus Johan (March 1, 1889–October 21, 1963)

A wildlife field biologist and preservation activist, Murie combined the goals of science with an aesthetic and spiritual appreciation of nature. A native of Moorhead, Minnesota, Murie studied biology at Fargo College, North Dakota, and Pacific University, Oregon (A.B., 1912), was mammal curator at the Carnegie Museum in Pittsburgh and, from 1920 to 1927, was a field biologist for the U.S. Bureau of BIOLOGICAL SURVEY, working mainly in the northern extremity of Hudson's Bay and in Alaska. This, combined with a study of North American elk conducted near Jackson Hole, Wyoming, from 1927 on, led Murie to an appreciation of the fragile ecosystem in which wildlife and modern civilization uneasily coexist. He was, in 1935, a founding member of the WILDERNESS SOCIETY and became its director in 1945. His years of lecturing, writing and campaigning aided in the formulation, public acceptance and passage of the Wilderness Act of 1964.

Further reading: Crandall Bay, "Murie, Olaus Johan," *The Encyclopedia of American Forestry and Conservation* 2; Murie, *The Elk of North America* (Harrisburg, Pa.: Stackpole, 1951).

Myers, Norman (August 24, 1934–   )

Norman Myers is a conservationist who has written widely on wildlife and the environment. Commissioned by the National Academy of Sciences to report on the state of the world's rain forests, he produced *The Primary Source: Tropical Forests and Our Future* in 1984 (second edition, 1985). Directed at a popular audience, the book argues that tropical forests are being exploited unnecessarily, that timber products from other, less vulnerable forests can almost always adequately meet demand and that untold numbers of species of plants unique to the rainforest ecosystem—potentially useful as food, fuel or medicine—are being utterly destroyed. Myers also illustrates how the massive deforestation of these tropical lands will affect the global climate, quite possibly with catastrophic results.

Born in Whitwell, Yorkshire, England, Myers was educated at Oxford University (M.A., 1957; Diploma in Overseas Administration, 1958) and the University of California, Berkeley (Ph.D., 1973). He served as a district officer with H. M. Overseas Civil Service in Kenya, Africa, from 1958 to 1961. From 1961 to 1966, he was a high school teacher in Nairobi and, from 1966 to 1969, a writer, photographer, film maker and broadcaster specializing in the conservation of the African wildlands. From 1972 to 1973, he was an ecological consultant in Kenya, and from 1974 to 1975, he was a parks officer for Africa, under the auspices of the UNITED NATIONS FOOD AND AGRICULTURE ORGANIZATION. Since 1981, he has worked as a consultant in environment and development, conducting projects for various organizations and agencies, including the Agency for International Development, Rockefeller Fund, National Academy of Sciences and the WORLD WILDLIFE FUND. He has lectured widely, including at the University of California, Berkeley and Santa Barbara, and has been visiting scholar at the Rockefeller Foundation and visiting fellow at the WORLD RESOURCES INSTITUTE. A senior associate with the INTERNATIONAL UNION FOR CONSERVATION OF NATURE AND NATURAL RESOURCES, Myers is a member of the board of directors of the Center for Conservation Biology at Stanford University.

Myers has been awarded the Gold Medal and Order of the Golden Ark from World Wildlife Fund International, the Gold Medal of the New York Zoological Society and the Achievement Award presented by the Christophers "for significant contribution to the betterment of humankind."

In addition to *The Primary Source,* Myers's writings include *The Long African Day* (1972; third edition, 1976), *Nairobi National Park: An Annotated Bibliography* (1973), *The Cheetah (Acinonys Jubatus) in Africa* (1975), *The Leopard (Panthera Pardus) in Africa* (1975), *The Sinking Ark: A New Look at the Problem of Disappearing Species* (1979), *Conversion of Tropical Moist Forests* (1980), *Multinational Timber Corporations and Tropical Forests* (1980), *A Wealth of Wild Species: Storehouse for Human Welfare* (1983), *GAIA: An Atlas of Planet Management* (with the GAIA Books staff, 1984), *Economics of Ecosystem Management* (editor, with others, 1985), *Causes of Loss of Biological Diversity* (1985) and *A Comparison of Tropical Forest Surveys* (with others, 1986).

N

Nader, Ralph (February 27, 1934–   )
Consumer advocate, lawyer and author Ralph Nader was catapulted to national attention in 1965 with the publication of his *Unsafe at Any Speed: The Designed-in Dangers of the American Automobile.*

Born in Winsted, Connecticut, and a graduate of Princeton University's Woodrow Wilson School of Public and International Affairs and Harvard Law School, Nader set up a small legal practice in Hartford, Connecticut, in 1959. During the early 1960s, he was a free-lance journalist for *Atlantic Monthly* and the *Christian Science Monitor,* work that took him to the Soviet Union, Africa, South America and Scandinavia. In 1964, he went to work for Daniel Patrick Moynihan, then assistant secretary of labor, as a staff consultant on highway safety. Over the next year, he conducted extensive research and produced "A Report on the Context, Condition and Recommended Direction of Federal Activity in Highway Safety." The findings presented in this governmental report became the basis for his ground-breaking first book.

An instant folk-hero after the publication of *Unsafe at Any Speed,* Nader then directed his attention to other consumer issues, working to improve safety standards in the construction of natural gas pipelines and to regulate conditions at slaughterhouses and meat-processing plants. He traveled extensively, lecturing across the country. Recognizing a need for consumer activist organizations, he founded in 1969 the Center for Study of Responsive Law, which is headquartered in Washington, D.C. The center monitors government agencies and regulatory committees to ensure that they are not influenced by the industries they were formed to regulate. In 1970, Nader created the Corporate Accountability Research Group and the Public Interest Research Group. The follow-

ing year, he formed PUBLIC CITIZEN, a consumer lobbying group, which in turn has spawned other organizations designed to lobby Congress or to serve as congressional watchdogs.

Nader was instrumental in the fight to create the ENVIRONMENTAL PROTECTION AGENCY and to pass the Clean Air Act of 1970. Later, he was instrumental in the creation of the Occupational Safety and Health Administration. Nader was unsuccessful in his campaign to gain congressional approval of a Consumer Protection Agency, however, and, during the 1980s, his consumer groups declined in effectiveness. Nader complained that the REAGAN administration gave the American people a "government *of* General Motors, *by* Exxon, *for* Du Pont."

In May 1990, speaking at "Early Warnings," an environmental conference sponsored by *Utne Reader,* Nader commented to journalists and environmentalists on the pervasive influence of corporations in contemporary life. "Corporations," he said, "are more important in raising children than parents. . . . Who's raising the kids? Kindercare is raising them. McDonald's is feeding them. HBO and Disneyland are entertaining them. . . . This is what it means to grow up corporate."

In 1972, Nader published *Working of the System: A Manual for Citizen's Access to Federal Agencies.* He has coauthored several other books, including *What To Do with Your Bad Car* (1971), *Action for a Change* (1972), *You and Your Pension* (1973), *Taming the Giant Corporation* (1976), *Menace of Atomic Energy* (1977) and *The Lemon Book* (1980).

Further reading: Robert F. Buckhorn, *Nader: The People's Lawyer* (Englewood Cliffs, N.J.: Prentice Hall, 1972); Hays Gorey, *Nader and the Power of Everyman* (New York: Grosset and Dunlop, 1975); Charles McCarry, *Citizen Nader* (New York: Saturday Review Press, 1972).

Nash, Roderick Frazier (January 7, 1939–)

Roderick Nash turned his interest in fishing and wilderness travel into a vocation after graduating from Harvard University with an A.B. in 1960 and earning a master's degree and a Ph.D. from the University of Wisconsin in 1961 and 1964 respectively. During his student days, he worked as a professional fishing guide, and after he became a professor at the University of California, Santa Barbara, in 1966, he began writing about his outdoor experiences. The New York-born Nash currently serves as professor of history and environmental studies and chairman of environmental studies at the university.

His environmental writings include *Wilderness and the American Mind* (1967), *The American Environment: Readings in the History of Conservation* (1968), *Grand Canyon of the Living Colorado* (1970), *Environment and Americans: The Problem of Priorities* (1972), *The Big Drops: Ten Legendary Rapids* (1978) and *The Rights of Nature: A History of Environmental Ethics* (1989). In addition, he has contributed articles to *Living Wilderness*, *Forest History* and various historical publications.

National Association of Environmental Professionals (Founded: 1975)
P.O. Box 15210, Alexandria, Virginia 22309-0210; (703) 660-2364

The 2,400 members of the National Association of Environmental Professionals are all persons whose occupations are either directly or indirectly related to environmental management and assessment. The organization sets as its goal the improvement of interdisciplinary communications and the advancement of the state of the art in the environmental planning process. The association has formulated a Code of Ethical Practices for environmental professionals, and it conducts a professional certification program. *Environmental Professional* is its quarterly publication, and a *Newsletter* is issued bimonthly. Joan A. Schroeder is executive secretary of the association.

National Audubon Society (Founded: 1886)
950 Third Avenue, New York, New York 10022; (212) 832-3200

Named for John James Audubon, naturalist, ornithologist and wildlife artist, the National Audubon Society first directed its attention toward protecting wild birds from hunters, egg collectors and the insatiable demand for feathers created by the millinery business during the late 19th century. Led by George Bird GRINNELL, editor of *Forest and Stream* magazine

and BOONE AND CROCKETT CLUB publications, the society quickly grew to 39,000 members but was disbanded before the end of the decade. In 1905, however, the various state chapters of the old society incorporated themselves as the National Association of Audubon Societies.

Early society conservation efforts included patrolling colonies of wild birds, promoting legislation to protect birds and their natural habitats and instituting educational programs. In the 1920s, the society began purchasing land to serve as wildlife preserves. Today, the society owns about 250,000 acres in 76 separate preserves and has become the largest private owner of preserves.

The organization's magazines, *Audubon* and *American Birds*; its newsletter, *Audubon Activist*; and its publications for children reach more than 500,000 members. Since the 1960s, the society has branched out beyond the preservation and study of wild birds to include the preservation of all types of wildlife and the promotion of sound ecological practices.

Further reading: Carl W. Buchheister and Frank Graham Jr., "From the Swamps and Back: A Concise and Candid History of the Audubon Movement," *Audubon* 75 (January 1973): 4–45.

National Clean Air Coalition (Founded: 1973)
1400 16th Street NW, Washington, D.C. 20036; (703) 256-4021

The National Clean Air Coalition is a lobbying organization that works to strengthen the nation's clean air policies and implementation programs. The organization, including representatives of state and local organizations and individuals concerned about the environment, health, labor, parks and other resources, sponsors workshops for the public on air pollution and its control and prevention. Richard AYRES is chairman of the coalition.

National Coalition for Marine Conservation (Founded: 1973)
P.O. Box 23298, Savannah, Georgia 31403; (912) 234-8062

The National Coalition for Marine Conservation works to ensure the protection of marine resources and ocean environments through legislative advocacy and publications. The organization is the only national body representing both recreational and commercial fishermen who want to protect the marine environments and ensure the long-term productivity of the oceans.

The coalition worked to pass the Magnuson Fishery Conservation and Management Act in 1975 and later helped strengthen the law by calling for the regulation of longlines used in tuna fishing, which kill thousands of marlin, sharks and other fish. Long-lines were not the only fishing gear attacked by the coalition; it also raised public awareness about the adverse effects associated with drift nets, shrimp trawls and fish traps. In addition, the coalition worked to reduce development near fisheries and to increase government funding of scientific research and enforcement of regulations.

Other action aimed at legislation has included helping to enact a conservation plan covering billfish in the Atlantic Ocean, a federal ban on dumping sludge and plastic waste into the oceans, regulations to protect reefs from damage caused by trawlers and a plan to protect bluefish along the East Coast.

Under the direction of Ken Hinman, the coalition publishes a bimonthly newsletter, *Currents*, the monthly *Marine Bulletin* and *Ocean Views*, a periodical that includes position papers on marine-environment issues, including licensing, fisheries and fishing equipment. The organization holds an annual Marine Recreational Fisheries Symposium for its 5,000 members and publishes the proceedings from that event.

National Council for Environmental Balance
(Founded: 1972)
4169 Westport Road, P.O. Box 7732, Louisville, Kentucky 40207; (502) 896-8731

Made up of some 1,320 science professionals, students, educators and others concerned about what the organization calls "the facts" of the environmental movement, the council "is dedicated to a balanced approach to solving environmental and energy problems without destroying the economy and people's right to a responsible life." The council coordinates the efforts of members of the scientific and academic communities who are willing to study, research and speak on topics related to energy, the environment and economics.

The National Council for Environmental Balance publishes *Energy and Environment Alert: Brief Notes About NCED and NCEB Associates*, a bimonthly newsletter. It also issues such pamphlets as *Worried About Pesticides in Your Water? Here Are the Facts, Danger in Environmentalism, Organic Farming* and *Environmental Guidelines. U.S. Energy Today* is the organization's annual.

I. W. Tucker is president of the council.

National Environmental Satellite, Data, and Information Service
(Established: 1965)
2069 Federal Building 4, Washington, D.C. 20233; (301) 763-7190

The National Environmental Satellite, Data, and Information Service (NESDIS) collects and disseminates environmental data and research on the atmosphere, oceans, earth and space. Information collected and stored in the archives of the service is used by government agencies, researchers around the world, industry and the public. Among its collections are studies of environmental fluctuations that affect the national economy, world food supplies, natural resources and human health. The service also maintains all data acquired by NATIONAL OCEANIC AND ATMOSPHERIC ADMINISTRATION (NOAA) satellites. In addition to maintaining the database, the service also operates the National Climatic Data Center in Asheville, North Carolina; the National Oceanographic Data Center and Assessment and Information Services Center in Washington, D.C.; and the National Geophysical Data Center in Boulder, Colorado. Publications of the service include *Climatic Data for the World* (monthly), *Local Climatological Data* (monthly), *Mariners Weather Log* (bimonthly), *Solar Geophysical Data* (monthly) and *Storm Data* (monthly).

National Geographic Society (Founded: 1888)
17th and M Streets NW, Washington, D.C. 20036; (202) 857-7000

Staffed by 2,400 employees and numbering 10 million members, the National Geographic Society is dedicated to the "increase and diffusion of geographic knowledge." Most people are familiar with the society through its enormously popular monthly *National Geographic Magazine*, which is renowned for its globe-spanning full-color stories on the human and natural world. The society also promotes research and exploration in geography and allied sciences and has sponsored, often in cooperation with other institutions, expeditions to the polar regions, to the farthest reaches of the earth, under the sea and even into outer space.

The National Geographic Society maintains a library of 78,000 volumes, 100,000 maps and 1,500,000 pieces of related material at its Washington headquarters. It produces a wide variety of books on subjects in geography, natural history, astronomy, archaeology, anthropology and ethnology, and has created an array of films, filmstrips and popular television programing. The society also conducts a Geography Education Program designed for use at the kindergarten through high school levels.

The society's Hubbard Medal and Special Gold Medals are awarded to explorers and scientists for outstanding achievements in geography. Gilbert M. Grosvenor is chairman of the board and president of the society, and William Graves is editor of *National Geographic Magazine*.

National Oceanic and Atmospheric Administration (Established: 1970)
U.S. Department of Commerce, Washington, D.C. 20230; (202) 377-2985

The mission of the administration is to explore, chart and map the global ocean and its living resources. The administration is charged with managing and conserving these resources, and with describing, monitoring and predicting conditions in the atmosphere, oceans, space and sun in order to issue warnings against impending destructive natural events, such as hurricanes, tornadoes, floods and so on. The National Weather Service, a branch of NOAA, is directly responsible for issuing such warnings.

The National Oceanic and Atmospheric Administration is also responsible for enforcing the Coastal Zone Management Act, the Marine Mammals Protection Act and the Marine Protection, Research, and Estuaries Act—all important environmental legislation.

NOAA regulates ocean fisheries, minerals exploration and mining. It researches alternatives to ocean dumping of hazardous waste. The administration maintains artificial satellites for environmental data gathering and provides the nation's precise geodetic surveys.

NOAA is divided into four branches: the National Ocean Survey; the National Marine Fisheries Service; the National Weather Service; and the National Environmental Satellite, Data, and Information Service.

National Park Foundation (Established: 1967)
1101 17th Street NW, Suite 1008, Washington, D.C. 20036; (202) 785-4500

The National Park Foundation was chartered by the U.S. Congress for the purposes of generating and maintaining private sector support for the National Park Service and its activities. Contributors to the foundation include individuals, corporations, unions and other foundations. The foundation offers grants for projects that support the National Park Service and publishes the biennial *Complete Guide to America's National Parks*, a directory of 370 parks with information on visitor facilities and other features.

National Park Service (Established: 1916)
Room 3104, Department of the Interior Building, Washington, D.C. 20240; (202) 208-6843

Established by Congress on August 25, 1916, the National Park Service today manages 80 million acres of land in 357 parks and monument areas in 49 states, the District of Columbia, American Samoa, Guam,

Puerto Rico, Saipan and the Virgin Islands. The roots of the system can be traced back to 1864, when Yosemite Park was established in California. Although the federal government turned over the land to the state of California to manage, it was done with the understanding that the land would be held "inalienable" for future generations to enjoy. The first truly *national* park was Yellowstone, created on March 1, 1872, when President Ulysses S. Grant approved the Yellowstone Park Act, which preserved some 3,300 square miles of land. Not until 1877, however, did Congress appropriate money for the park's management, and not until 1883 was the U.S. Cavalry authorized to patrol the park to prevent vandals and poachers from destroying its resources.

In 1890, Congress again added park lands to the nation's holdings by creating Yosemite, Sequoia and General Grant parks in California's High Sierra. Over the next several years, Congress added Mount Rainier in Washington (1899), Crater Lake in Oregon (1902), Mesa Verde in Colorado (1906), Glacier in Montana (1910), Rocky Mountain in Colorado (1915) and Mount Lassen in California (1916). During this period of expansion, Congress passed the Antiquities Act of 1906, giving the president the power to create national monuments from land deemed historically or scientifically important.

The period of expansion was marked by the belief among legislators that land set aside for parks or monuments should be "worthless" for other commercial purposes—in effect the leftovers of the public domain. The notion of worthlessness brought about two reversals in the national park system. In 1905, Yosemite National Park was reduced by 542 square miles because some of the land was deemed valuable for lumbering, mining and grazing, and in 1913, San Francisco city managers won approval for their plan to lease the Hetch Hetchy Valley of Yosemite for building a dam and water reservoir.

Following these two reversals, momentum for the idea of a park service increased. Stephen T. MATHER became assistant to the secretary of the interior in January 1915, and preservationists looked to him to direct efforts toward the creation of a separate agency to manage the 4.75 million acres of park land. Railroad companies joined the movement with a "See America First" campaign, promoting tourism, and, on August 25, 1916, Congress created the National Park Service with Mather as its first director and Horace M. ALBRIGHT his assistant. Their accomplishments included the creation of national parks in the East—the Acadia, Shenandoah, Great Smoky Mountains and Everglades national parks—and the addition of more western parks—Zion, Bryce and Grand Teton.

The Grand Canyon. *U.S. Department of the Interior, National Park Service photo by George A. Grant*

During its 75-year history, the National Park Service has enjoyed stretches of autonomy and has endured periods of congressional pressure and undue influence from political appointees in the U.S. Department of the INTERIOR. Issues of management have frequently raised controversy. Some park supporters consistently argue for improved facilities to promote tourism, while others complain that tourists themselves have destroyed much of the parks' natural resources. Some argue for the primacy of the parks' mission of recreation over the preservation of wildlife in a pristine setting, while others blast park policies for ignoring the needs of wildlife. Some criticize the park service for imposing restrictions on use by visitors, while others see the service's allocation of more than 80% of its budget to visitor needs as disproportionate.

In 1980, the land managed by the National Park Service was more than doubled by the addition of 40 million acres in Alaska. Visitation to the parks has grown from a half-million in 1916 to 300 million in 1989.

National Parks and Conservation Association
(Founded: 1919)
1015 31st Street NW, Washington, D.C. 20007; (202) 944-8530

The National Parks and Conservation Association boasts a membership of more than 100,000. With a staff of 30 and an annual budget of $3.4 million, the organization promotes the preservation and improvement of national parks. It publishes *National Parks*, a bimonthly magazine, periodic *NPCAlerts* and books on environmental issues.

Originally called the National Parks Association, the organization was founded by Stephen T. MATHER, the first director of the National Park Service, and Robert Sterling YARD, information officer for the park service, who served as the group's first executive secretary. Under Yard's leadership, the organization successfully blocked efforts to use Yellowstone Lake as an irrigation reservoir. However, several other association campaigns mired the group in controversy, as Yard, uncompromising in his purism, resisted all alternative uses for national park resources and blasted officials for accepting into the park system the Everglades, the Grand Teton and the Shenandoah national parks, because he felt they were not worthy of inclusion. (Yard called the Everglades a "promoters' proposition," and Jackson Hole, he said, "borrowed its grandeur" from the Tetons.)

The 1940s brought the issue of hydroelectric power generation to the forefront of the association's concerns. Campaigns were successfully undertaken to block proposed dams in Glacier National Park, Mammoth Cave, the Grand Canyon and Kings Canyon. During the 1960s and 1970s, the organization defeated another Grand Canyon dam project as well as the Everglades jetport and successfully campaigned for the creation of Redwood National Park and the preservation of wilderness lands in Alaska. Reflecting a new commitment to conservation beyond the holdings of the National Park Service, the organization has campaigned in recent years for increased public transportation facilities, pollution abatement and control of human population growth.

National Wildlife Federation (Founded: 1936)
1400 16th Street NW, Washington, D.C. 20036-2266; (202) 797-6800

With over 5.8 million members, 51 affiliates, 6,500 local groups and a permanent staff of 800 employees, the National Wildlife Federation is the largest private, nonprofit conservation education organization in the United States. Its primary mission is to promote the wise use of natural resources through programs of education, publication, research and interaction with legislators and other government and private groups.

Founded as the General Wildlife Federation by Jay "Ding" DARLING at the First North American Wildlife Conference in 1936, and launched with the blessings of President Franklin D. ROOSEVELT, the organization quickly exerted influence as a major proponent of early conservation legislation. In 1938, the group changed its name to the National Wildlife Federation and sponsored its first National Wildlife Week, an annual public awareness initiative. Supported with the proceeds from colorful wildlife stamps by artists such as Roger Tory PETERSON, and promoted by celebrity Wildlife Week chairpersons such as Shirley Temple, Hopalong Cassidy and Walt Disney, the group's yearly theme-oriented campaigns have brought environmental issues before the public for over five decades.

Currently, the National Wildlife Federation administrates an enormous variety of public education programs: conservation summits and guided nature tours, teen adventure programs, NWF Wildlife Camps, Ranger Rick's Nature Club, NatureQuest (a certified training program for outdoor educators) and the Urban and Backyard Wildlife Habitat Program. The group sponsors the National Conservation Achievement Awards, student publication awards and graduate fellowships in environmental research, and operates a Conservation Hall of Fame and Wildlife Gallery of Art. The NWF's Institute for Wildlife Research is a clearinghouse for wildlife information, and the Laurel Ridge Conservation Education Center in Vienna, Virginia, includes the wheelchair-accessible Mountain Laurel Nature Trail.

In addition to the four-color bimonthly magazines *National Wildlife* and *International Wildlife*, the federation publishes the monthly *Ranger Rick's Nature Magazine* and (for preschool children) *Your Big Backyard*, as well as a host of materials for use in schools from elementary to college level: NatureScope (science and nature activity series curriculum supplements), CLASS (Conservation Learning Activities for Science and Social Studies) and other books, fact sheets, teacher's guides and audiovisual materials on wildlife and conservation topics. The organization produces a syndicated biweekly newspaper column titled "The Backyard Naturalist," the daily radio program *Nature NewsBreak* and has copresented the PBS television series "Conserving America." The federation publishes a twice-yearly newsletter on raptor (bird of prey) research titled *EYAS*, the quarterly *Conservation Exchange*, the legislative reports *Enviro-Action* and *Action Alerts*, the *Leader* (a monthly newpaper for state and local affiliates) and several annuals: *The Conservation Directory, Environmental Quality Index, Media Guide to Environmental Resources* and a *Survey of Compensation in the Fields of Fish and Wildlife Management*.

The National Wildlife Federation also prepares wildlife and natural resource policy studies and sponsors research by outside institutions and agencies. The federation's Resources Conservation Department

Jay D. Hair, president of the National Wildlife Federation. *National Wildlife Federation photo by Robert Rathe*

conducts investigations, litigation and legislative campaigns, and operates a "Legislative Hotline"— (202) 797-6655—to provide twice-weekly summaries of environmental developments in the nation's capital. Recently, the federation has created a Corporate Conservation Council to encourage environmental discussions with private industry and established a National Biotechnology Policy Center to address the environmental implications of biotechnology. Since its founding in 1936, the National Wildlife Federation's stated purpose has been to "bring together all interested organizations, agencies and individuals on behalf of restoration of land, water, forests, and wildlife resources."

Natural Resources Council of America
(Founded: 1946)
801 Pennsylvania Avenue NW, No. 410, Washington, D.C. 20003; (202) 547-7553

More than 70 national and regional organizations working in the conservation field are represented on the Natural Resources Council of America. The council offers a broad range of programs to encourage member organizations to cooperate in the conservation efforts. The Conservation Round Table is a monthly forum held at the National Press Club in Washington, D.C., where representatives discuss the efforts of the conservation movement, industry and government. The Conservation Community Banquet and Award Program annually presents awards to individuals in the private sector and in government who have made significant contributions to natural resources conservation.

Membership in the Natural Resources Council of America is by invitation only. Organizations included in the council's membership include conservation associations, scientific societies and resource conservation committees of national organizations.

In recent years, the council has published a study of public opinion on energy needs and conservation and a report on ways to increase minority participation in conservation activity. In addition, the council was instrumental in shaping the Wilderness Act of 1964 and the Farm Bill of 1985 and helped member organizations in 1986 understand the effects of the the federal government's deficit-reduction plan on natural resource agency budgets.

Andrea J. Yank serves as executive director of the council, which operates with an annual budget of $150,000.

Among the organization's publications are *NRCA News*, a bimonthly newsletter, and such books as *National Leaders of American Conservation, Careers in Conservation, Hard-Rock Mining—Modern Industry Under an Ancient Law, What's Ahead for Our Public Lands? Origins of American Conservation* and *America's Natural Resources.*

Natural Resources Defense Council (Founded: 1970)

40 West 20th Street, New York, New York 10011;
(212) 727-4412, Fax (212) 727-1773

With a large and expert staff of attorneys, research scientists and policy specialists, and a current annual operating budget of over $17 million, the Natural Resources Defense Council is widely considered the single most influential organization in the history and ongoing practice of public interest environmental law. Founded in 1970, the council pioneered the use of litigation to establish broadly applicable legal precedents safeguarding natural resources and public health, and the organization has also mounted lawsuits to halt, prohibit or strategically delay specific instances of hazardous development or habitat destruction. Many of the NRDC's legal actions have

won landmark decisions directly affecting U.S. law and public policy on such critical ecological and public health issues as air and water pollution, nuclear power safety, wilderness preservation, energy conservation, toxic waste disposal and pesticide regulation. The group also monitors federal departments and regulatory agencies to help ensure enforcement of environmental and public interest legislation. In conjunction with other organizations in the U.S. and abroad, the NRDC works to establish international agreements for global resource protection and nuclear disarmament.

The Council produces books, research reports, pamphlets and other publications, including the bimonthly newsletter *NRDC Newsline* and the quarterlies *Amicus Journal* and *Truly Loving Care: For Our Kids and for Our Planet*. In 1991, the organization won awards from the American Institute of Architects and *Interiors* magazine for the renovation of its New York City headquarters, which uses one-half the energy of a conventional office design.

The Nature Conservancy (Founded: 1951)

1815 North Lynn Street, Arlington, Virginia 22209;
(703) 841-5300

The Nature Conservancy identifies natural areas to be saved, acquires the land and manages it as nature reserves or turns it over to other conservation groups for management. In recent years, the organization helped community leaders in Boulder, Colorado, purchase the White Rocks Natural Area, noted for its diversity of ferns and for its mining bee population, an insect that drills holes in rocks for nests. The organization bought a swamp area in southern Illinois containing the nation's largest locust tree and several endangered species of plants. Other preserves include Lower Tubbs Island, a 330-acre bird sanctuary in San Francisco Bay; Redbud Valley, an 85-acre tract in Oklahoma; and Clausland Mountain, a 500-acre tract of woods north of Manhattan. In all, the Nature Conservancy has preserved 5 million acres of land in the United States, the Virgin Islands, Canada, the Caribbean and Latin America, and operates more than 1,000 sanctuaries.

An unusual land deal occurred in the wake of the nationwide savings and loan debacle of the late 1980s and early 1990s. In September 1991, the Nature Conservancy announced that it would receive 10,000 acres of land formerly under the control of a failed savings and loan corporation in Texas. The Nature Conservancy planned to sell or transfer some of the land to the city of Austin, Texas, for use as a nature preserve.

A 1985 article in *Industry Week* dubbed the Nature Conservancy a "friendly foe" and "industry's favorite environmental group." Its nonconfrontational approach, according to the article, had attracted some $35 million annually over the preceding five years.

The organizaton, under the direction of Richard S. Weinstein, chairman, and John C. SAWHILL, president, publishes a bimonthly magazine, *Nature Conservancy*, for its 600,000 members. The publication includes articles on wildlife and information on the organization's local projects. The organization maintains the National Natural Heritage Inventory, a database of flora and fauna throughout the United States and in other countries. In addition, the group holds an annual meeting and conducts an awards program.

The Nature Conservancy was reorganized in 1951 from the Ecologists Union and the former Committee on Preservation of Natural Conditions of the ECOLOGICAL SOCIETY OF AMERICA.

Nearing, Scott (August 6, 1883– August 23, 1983)

A blacklisted radical pacifist and early forerunner of the back-to-nature movement, author and social scientist Scott Nearing dedicated most of his 100 years of life to a passionate and uncompromising advocacy of global peace, economic justice and direct, harmonious coexistence with nature.

Born in Morris Run, Pennsylvania, to merchant Louis Nearing and Minnie (Zabriskie) Nearing, Scott Nearing and his five siblings shared a prosperous and conservative upbringing. Nearing graduated from a Philadelphia high school in 1901, briefly studied law and, in 1905, earned a degree in oratory from Temple College and a bachelor of science in economics from the University of Pennsylvania.

Soon after, Nearing began his extraordinarily prolific writing career, collaborating with Frank D. Watson on the textbook *Economics,* which was published in 1908. Also in that year, Nearing married his first wife, Nellie Seeds, with whom he later cowrote *Women and Social Progress* (1912).

In 1909, he completed his doctorate in economics at the University of Pennsylvania, and he served as instructor there and at Swarthmore College for the next five years. Nearing published two more books, *Wages in the United States* (1911) and *Solution of the Child Labor Problem* (1911), and in 1914 he was promoted to assistant professor at the Wharton School of Finance. But the following year, his outspoken opposition to Pennsylvania's child labor policies resulted in his nationally reported academic dismissal. (Ironically, the Wharton School was to honor Nearing as professor emeritus in 1973.)

Nearing lectured for a semester at the socialist Rand School in New York City, and in 1915, he moved to Ohio as professor of social science and dean of the College of Arts and Sciences at the University of Toledo. But Nearing's iconoclastic views again cost him his livelihood when, in 1917, the Rand School published *The Great Madness: A Victory for the American Plutocracy,* his 32-page tract denouncing U.S. involvement in World War I. Indicted by a federal grand jury for inciting resistance to military recruitment, Nearing was fired from his university post. Although his 1919 trial ended in acquittal, the author was blacklisted by academic institutions and the mainstream press for many years thereafter.

Nearing continued to write, however, and his independent commentary on domestic and international affairs found publication in dozens of books, pamphlets and syndicated articles. His major works of the 1920s and 1930s included *Dollar Diplomacy* (with Joseph Freeman, 1925), *Education in Soviet Russia* (1926), *Whither China?* (1927), *Black America* (1929), *The Twilight of Empire* (1930), *War* (1931) and *Fascism* (1933). Although his political philosophy was fundamentally socialist, Nearing remained a quintessential freethinker, and in 1929, the Communist Party expelled him for his nonconformism.

In 1932, Nearing and his eventual second wife, violinist Helen Knothe (they married in 1947), renounced New York City life and moved to a wooded mountainside in Pike Valley, Vermont. Using hand tools only, the maverick homesteaders built their own fieldstone house and established a self-sufficient, strictly organic sugarbush "forest farm." Vegetarians, the Nearings enthusiastically embraced the physical rigors and spiritual rewards of their subsistence lifestyle. During this period Nearing wrote *United World* (1944) and *Tragedy of Empire* (1945); the couple's jointly authored *Maple Sugar Book: Together with Remarks on Pioneering as a Way of Living in the Twentieth Century* was published in 1950.

Two years later, local ski resort development prompted the Nearings to seek more isolated surroundings, and they purchased 100 acres of coastal timberland in Harborside, Maine. Growing vegetables and blueberries, the Nearings intensified their commitment to a daily regimen of organic farming, intellectual activity and social activism. They founded their own Social Science Institute and, in 1954, cowrote and self-published another book describing their experiences and philosophy. Reprinted in 1971, their *Living the Good Life: How to Live Simply and Sanely in a Troubled World* was hailed by critics as a visionary document in the growing environmental movement.

Indeed, during the 1960s and 1970s, the Nearings gained a large and admiring following in America's youthful counterculture and in the ecologically minded community, and the couple began to lecture widely and frequently. The Nearings also journeyed to China, the Soviet Union and other countries around the world, reporting their observations on international social and political conditions in numerous books and articles.

When Scott Nearing was in his nineties, he and Helen Nearing handbuilt another stone farmhouse. The self-described "tough U.S.A. radical" died there 18 days after his 100th birthday.

Further reading: Nearing, *The Making of a Radical: A Political Autobiography* (New York: Harper and Row, 1972); Nearing and Nearing, *Continuing the Good Life: Half a Century of Homesteading* (New York: Schocken, 1979).

Nelson, Gaylord Anton (June 4, 1916–)

More than just the inventor of Earth Day, Senator Gaylord Nelson of Wisconsin was one of the driving forces behind the environmental movement of the 1960s, a man whose political leadership helped put environmental issues on the national agenda.

In 1963, Senator Nelson wrote President Kennedy, "Though the public is dimly aware that all around them, here and there, outdoor assets are disappearing, they really don't see the awful dimension of the catastrophe. The real failure has been in political leadership. . . . But strangely, politicians don't talk about it." Nelson got Congress to embrace the issue, working for curbs against industrial pollution of the Great Lakes, and introducing legislation to ban the pesticide DDT and to force industry to restore strip-mined land. In a speech to the Senate in 1970, he charged that the environmental crisis was threatening constitutional rights to life, liberty and the pursuit of happiness. He suggested observation of an "Earth Day," which would heighten public awareness of environmental issues. When Earth Day happened on April 22, 1970, it was estimated that some 20 million people participated. In 1972, DDT was finally banned.

Born in Clear Lake, Wisconsin, Nelson graduated from San Diego State College and Wisconsin Law School. He rose through Wisconsin state politics to become governor in 1959. His environmental activism dates at least as far back as his governorship, when he imposed a tax on cigarettes that was used to buy wetlands and park lands for the state. He served as senator from 1963 until his defeat at the hands of national conservative organizations in 1980. He lives in the Washington, D.C., area, where, as counselor for the WILDERNESS SOCIETY, he continues to work for environmental causes.

New Alchemy Institute (Founded: 1969)

237 Hatchville Road, East Falmouth, Massachusetts 02536; (508) 564-6301

The New Alchemy Institute is a research and educational organization that studies such topics as housing and landscaping that use natural resources efficiently, organic gardening, solar greenhouses, pest control and the use of toxins in homes and gardens. The group sponsors internships and seminars for teachers and community leaders and has developed a Green Classroom Project curriculum for schools.

On its 12-acre Cape Cod site, the New Alchemy Institute raises a market garden that employs compost, green manures and animal manures to create highly fertile soil for growing crops that are resistant to disease and pests. In addition, the organization operates three greenhouses: the Cape Cod Arc, heated by solar energy and containing a year-round garden of food crops; the Composting Greenhouse, which uses the heat emitted by decomposing weeds, leaves, food scraps, grass clippings and manure; and the Pillar Dome, a goedesic structure that uses solar heat to grow vegetables year round. In addition, the Cape Cod site features an auditorium, which incorporates superinsulation, air-vapor barriers, air-to-air heat exchange, low-flow toilets and a tankless hot water heater. It features a visitor's center with an exhibit area and store.

In recent years, the institute has administered a program engaging 20 New England farmers in integrated pest management and cover cropping programs. The group has found that pests can be controlled without chemicals by using strictly biological solutions. The cover crop program has developed effective ways to control weeds, reduce erosion and sustain fertility without using chemical fertilizers or herbicides.

The 10,000 members of the institute receive the periodic *New Alchemy Institute Catalogue: Books and Products for Ecological Living* and the *New Alchemy Quarterly*, which publishes research on sustainable technologies, book reviews and calendars of events. Virginia Rasmussen is the executive director of the organization.

Newell, Frederick Haynes (March 5, 1862–July 5, 1932)

Newell was a pioneering water conservationist with the U.S. GEOLOGICAL SURVEY. As chief of the USGS Hydrographic Branch, he developed programs of coordinated water use, encompassing navigation, irrigation, power and flood control. Newell worked with Nevada Congressman (later Senator) Francis G. Newlands and George H. Maxwell of the National

Reclamation Association to formulate Newlands's Reclamation Act of 1902.

Appointed head of the Reclamation Service (later called the Bureau of RECLAMATION) created by the act, Newell built dams, water tunnels and canals that served 20,000 farms. While all of these were successful from an engineering point of view, many failed economically, and Newell was removed as director of the Reclamation Service in 1914. He served as chairman of the Civil Engineering Department of the University of Illinois from 1915 to 1919 and as an engineering consultant thereafter. Dedicated to engineering and conservation, he was the first secretary of the NATIONAL GEOGRAPHIC SOCIETY and the first corresponding secretary of the American Forestry Association (now AMERICAN FORESTS). Newell was born in Bradford, Pennsylvania.

Further reading: Michael C. Robinson, "Frederick Haynes Newell," *APWA Reporter* 47 (March 1980): 6-7.

Nixon, Richard Milhous (January 9, 1913–   )

Richard M. Nixon became the 37th president of the United States in 1969 and played an important role in launching what many have called the "environmental decade" of the 1970s. Although most historians point out that the environmental legislation of this period was the product of congressional initiative and pressure from environmental and consumer groups, it is true that President Nixon, like Lyndon Johnson before him, largely endorsed the environmental movement. He also established (through Congress) a Commission on Population Growth and the American Future, acceded to environmentalists' demands to block construction of an Everglades jetport and to halt construction on the Cross-Florida Barge Canal project, signed into law the sweeping National Environmental Policy Act (NEPA), established the COUNCIL ON ENVIRONMENTAL QUALITY (CEQ) and the ENVIRONMENTAL PROTECTION AGENCY (EPA). Together, these measures constitute the single most important body of conservation law ever enacted.

President Nixon signed the NEPA legislation in January 1970. It declared "a national policy which will encourage productive and enjoyable harmony between man and his environment [and] enrich the understanding of the ecological systems and natural resources important to the Nation." The law required each federal agency to prepare an estimate of environmental impact (environmental impact statement) before taking any action that might harm the environment, and it established the Council on Environmental Quality, an executive agency that was to set long-term policy, advise the president and monitor

the environmental impact statement process. Six months after NEPA was signed into law, President Nixon established the Environmental Protection Agency, which started with a staff of 6,673 and an annual budget of $1.28 billion, growing to $5.6 billion by 1980. Nixon also established an advisory council representing industry to convey business concerns over emerging environmental regulation, and through the OFFICE OF MANAGEMENT AND BUDGET (OMB), he set up a system of "quality of life" reviews of environmental regulation.

Despite the epoch-making environmental legislation enacted during his administration, President Nixon was by no means an unconditional and ardent environmentalist. As early as the summer of 1971, in the wake of the legislation he had endorsed, President Nixon had serious afterthoughts concerning the economic impact of wholesale environmental regulation. In August, the president responded to a memo concerning the "negative economic impact of . . . the environmental movement": "I completely agree," he wrote. "We have gone overboard on the environment—& are going to reap the whirlwind for our excesses." He even requested White House counsel John Ehrlichman to "get me a plan for cooling off the excesses." Nixon also came to blows with the EPA over its move to ban the use of the pesticide DDT, and in 1972, he vetoed the Federal Water Pollution Control Act Amendments because of their nearly $25 billion price tag. Congress overrode the veto, and the legislation became popularly known as the Clean Water Act—according to the NATURAL RESOURCES DEFENSE COUNCIL, "one of the strongest environmental laws ever written."

In addition to attacking such afterthoughts and backsliding on environment issues, some Nixon critics have suggested that the president's endorsement of environmental legislation was, to begin with, largely motivated by a desire to reduce national unrest by distracting attention from the seemingly endless nightmare of the Vietnam War. Whether this was the case or not, Vietnam was the scene of the Nixon administration's single greatest offense against the environment. All war, of course, is destructive to life, but Vietnam saw the use of a new defoliant called Agent Orange, a dioxin compound designed to deprive the enemy of concealing camouflage by denuding vast tracts of jungle. Not only did this intended effect of Agent Orange damage the environment, but unanticipated side effects continue to threaten long-term animal and human consequences, including nervous disorders and cancer among some Vietnam veterans.

Richard Milhous Nixon was born in Yorba Linda, California, the son of an oil field worker, who later became a street car motorman and then a service station owner. Nixon was educated at Whittier College, earning a B.A. in 1934. He graduated from Duke University Law School in 1937 and, despite his Quaker religion, served with the United States Navy from 1942 to 1945. After World War II, he practiced law in Whittier, California, briefly and was elected to the U.S. House of Representatives in 1946 and again in 1948. Nixon, who earned a reputation as an ardent anti-Communist on the House Un-American Activities Committee (HUAC) during the height of the Cold War, was elected to the U.S. Senate in 1950 and was nominated as Dwight Eisenhower's running mate in 1952. He served two terms as Eisenhower's vice president and was nominated as the Republican presidential candidate in 1960, suffering a narrow defeat by John F. Kennedy. In 1962, he was defeated in his bid for the governorship of California, but in 1968, the Republicans again made him their nominee for president, and he defeated the Democratic candidate, Hubert H. Humphrey. Nixon was elected to a second term in 1972, defeating George S. McGovern.

President Nixon is often praised for his foreign policy, which included ending America's involvement in the Vietnam War and opening a dialogue with Communist China. However, during his second presidential bid, on June 17, 1972, five employees of the Campaign to Re-elect the President (better known by its remarkable acronym, CREEP) were arrested as they broke into the Democratic National Committee's headquarters, located in a Washington, D.C., apartment complex called the Watergate. The resulting scandal mushroomed during Nixon's second term as, one by one, the "president's men"—high-ranking administration officials—were implicated in a widespread conspiracy to sabotage the Democratic Party's campaign and to impede the investigation of the scandal itself. From July 27 to July 30, 1974, the House Judiciary Committee voted to recommend Nixon's impeachment on grounds of obstruction of justice, abuse of power and contempt of Congress. On August 8, 1974, Richard M. Nixon became the first U.S. president in history to resign his office. He was succeeded by vice president Gerald R. Ford, who granted Nixon a pardon for all federal offenses he "committed or may have committed."

North American Radon Association (Founded: 1989)
8445 River Birch, Roswell, Georgia 30075; (404) 993-5033

The North American Radon Association engages scientists, educators and other professionals in research on the elimination of health problems caused by radon, a radioactive gas that occurs naturally in soils and whose byproducts can accumulate in buildings, posing radiation-related health risks. The organization works to establish exposure standards and to improve methods of radon detection and abatement. The 800 members of the organization receive the bimonthly *NARA Newsletter*. Stewart M. Huey is the administrative director of the organization, which was founded with the merger of the American Radon Association and the National Radon Association.

North American Wildlife Foundation (Founded: 1911)
102 Wilmot Road, Suite 410, Deerfield, Illinois 60015; (708) 940-7776

The North American Wildlife Foundation, with an annual budget of $1.7 million, supports research on the practical management of wildlife and other natural resources. Funds for research are awarded annually to other organizations and agencies. The organization administers the Delta Waterfowl Research Station in Manitoba, Canada, and maintains a library of natural science and wildlife management publications. It was known formerly as the American Game Protective Association, the American Wildlife Institute and the American Wildlife Foundation.

Nuclear Regulatory Commission (Established: 1974)
Washington, D.C. 20555; (301) 492-7000

Created as an independent federal regulatory agency pursuant to provisions of the Energy Reorganization Act of 1974, the Nuclear Regulatory Commission assumed all licensing and regulatory functions formerly assigned to the Atomic Energy Commission (AEC), which was established by the Atomic Energy Act of 1946. The NRC consists principally of the Office of Nuclear Reactor Regulation, the Office of Nuclear Material Safety and Safeguards and the Office of Nuclear Regulatory Research. The commission licenses and regulates civilian use of nuclear energy to protect public health and safety and the environment. In order to do this, the NRC is charged with the responsibility of licensing all persons and companies that build and operate reactors and other facilities that own or use nuclear materials. The commission sets the standards for the various types of licenses granted and ensures that all safety and environmental requirements are met. Most of the NRC's efforts are directed toward regulating the nuclear power industry.

The NRC investigates all nuclear-related "incidents," no matter how minor, that occur in connection with reactor operation. The commission is also responsible for coordinating efforts with other federal agencies and state and local authorities to formulate disaster and evacuation plans in the event of a nuclear emergency. After the 1979 accident at the Three Mile Island reactor near Harrisburg, Pennsylvania, the commission opened a special Program Office to deal with the aftermath of the incident.

Nuttall, Thomas (January 5, 1786–September 10, 1859)

Thomas Nuttall came to America from his native England in 1808. Although he had been apprenticed to a printer as a young man, his real passion was for natural history, and in Benjamin Smith Barton of Philadelphia, Nuttall found a patron who supported his interest in nature and employed him as a plant collector. Barton financed an expedition into the American West in 1810, which led to Nuttall's joining elements of John Jacob Astor's Pacific Fur Company as they traveled up the Missouri River and into the Far West. Nuttall returned to England in 1811 to write up the work he had done in the course of his American travels. *The Genera of North American Plants and a Catalogue of the Species through 1817* was published in 1818—the first American flora to be published in the United States and in the English language.

Nuttall returned to America in 1815 and spent the next five years collecting specimens along the Arkansas River in Indian territory. He served as curator of the botanic garden in Cambridge, Massachusetts, from 1823 to 1833 and was a lecturer in natural history at Harvard University. He published *An Introduction to Systematic and Physiological Botany* (1827 and 1830) and *A Manual of the Ornithology of the U.S. and Canada* (1832 and 1834).

In 1834, Nuttall again ventured west, this time with Nathaniel Jarvis Wyeth, the pioneering settler of Oregon country. Nuttall collected along the Pacific Northwest and then in Hawaii, returning to Boston in 1836. His far western and Hawaiian work was incorporated into Torrey and Gray's *Flora of North America* and into a three-volume appendix Nuttall wrote to accompany André Michaux's *North American Sylva* (1842–49).

Nuttall returned to England in 1842, visiting America one last time (1847–48).

Oberholtzer, Ernest Carl (February 6, 1884–June 6, 1977)

A student of the great landscape architect FREDERICK LAW OLMSTED, JR., Oberholtzer was a dedicated conservationist who worked for international protection of the Rainy Lake and Pigeon River watersheds along the Minnesota-Ontario border. He began his campaign in 1925, when the Minnesota and Ontario Paper Company proposed to build power dams along the border and harvest the forest for pulpwood. For the next nine years, Oberholtzer lobbied for the creation of an international wilderness, which resulted in the Shipstead-Nolan Act of 1930. A native of Davenport, Iowa, Oberholtzer was a founding member of the WILDERNESS SOCIETY.

Further reading: R. Newell Searle, *Saving Quetico-Superior: A Land Set Apart* (St. Paul: Minnesota Historical Society, 1977).

Occupational Safety and Health Administration (OSHA) (Established: 1970)

U.S. Department of Labor, 200 Constitution Avenue NW, Washington, D.C. 20210; (202) 523-8017

OSHA is responsible for occupational safety and health activities and is charged with promoting safe and healthful conditions in the workplace. Its chief environmental function is to regulate toxic and carcinogenic or otherwise harmful materials in the workplace. In addition to its Washington, D.C., headquarters, OSHA maintains the Toxicology Information Response Center (TIRC) in Oak Ridge, Tennessee, which responds to inquiries concerning the toxicity of materials and their regulation.

Odum, Eugene Pleasants (September 17, 1913–   )

Eugene Pleasants Odum is a leader in the field of the "new" ecology, which focuses on energy flow in ecosystems. Born in Lake Sunapee, New Hampshire Odum received his A.B. degree at the University of North Carolina and began his career at the university as an assistant zoologist. Between 1936 and 1937, he was an instructor in biology and ornithology at Western Reserve University in Cleveland. He then enrolled in the doctoral program at the University of Illinois, completing his degree in ecology and ornithology in 1939 and, that year, was appointed research biologist at the Edmund Niles Huyck Preserve in New York. In 1940, he moved to the University of Georgia, where he taught for the next four decades, progressing from zoology instructor to emeritus professor and director of the university's Institute of Ecology.

Odum was chosen as a delegate to the first Atoms-for-Peace Conference in Geneva in 1955. A pioneer in radiation ecology, he received a senior postdoctoral fellowship from the National Science Foundation in 1957. He also served as chief scientist of the Special Training Division, Oak Ridge Associated Universities, and as an instructor in the Marine Biology Laboratory at Woods Hole, Massachusetts (1957–61).

He has advised numerous environmental organizations and governmental agencies, including the National Science Foundation, Oak Ridge National Health Laboratory, U.S. FISH AND WILDLIFE SERVICE and the National Academy of Sciences, and he has served on the governing boards and as a trustee of the American Institute of Biological Sciences, the NATURE CONSERVANCY and the CONSERVATION FOUNDATION.

Odum's publications include *Fundamentals of Ecology* (1953) and *Ecology* (1962), both of which have been reissued in revised editions, and *Ecology and Our Endangered Life-Support System* (1989). In this most recent work, he compared the earth to the Apollo 13 spacecraft, which was perilously close to destruction when an explosion crippled its life-support system.

Odum has received awards from the ECOLOGICAL SOCIETY OF AMERICA, L'Institut de la vie, the American Institute of Biological Sciences and the Association of Southeastern Biologists. He is a fellow of the American Academy of Arts and Sciences and has been elected to the National Academy of Sciences.

Office of Management and Budget (OMB)
(Established: 1970)
Executive Office Building, Washington, D.C. 20503; (202) 395-3080

Created by President Richard M. NIXON as an office within the Executive Office of the President, the Office of Management and Budget functions *officially* to assist the president in his program to develop and maintain effective government by reviewing the organizational structure and management of the executive branch; to assist in developing efficient government activities and to expand interagency cooperation; to supervise and control the administration of the budget; to assist the president by clearing and coordinating departmental advice on proposed legislation; to assist in the development of regulatory reform and programs for paperwork reduction; to assist in the preparation of proposed executive orders and proclamations; to develop information systems to provide the president with program performance data; to assist the president in evaluating program efficiency; and to assist the president in preparing budget recommendations to Congress.

Unofficially, the OMB is a particularly powerful body in that it can block or hinder the implementation of any agency's programs, policies or regulations if it feels that these conflict with overall federal policy or with the policies or regulations of other agencies. During the administration of Ronald REAGAN, OMB Director David STOCKMAN became notorious among environmentalists for using the OMB to defeat the implementation of various environmental programs.

Olmsted, Frederick Erskine (November 8, 1872–February 19, 1925)
The cousin of FREDERICK LAW OLMSTED JR., Frederick Erskine Olmsted worked for more than two decades in forestry conservation. Born in Hartford, Connecticut, he studied at the Sheffield Scientific School of Yale University, the Biltmore Forest School and the University of Munich before joining the Bureau of Forestry under Gifford PINCHOT. When the U.S. FOREST SERVICE was established, Olmsted was named chief inspector in the field service. He resigned in 1911 to work as a consulting forester with Fisher and

Bryant, a private firm in Boston. In 1914, he returned to California to direct the Tamalpais Fire Protection Association and the Diamond Match Company, where he designed new plans for conservative forest cutting. Five years later, he was elected president of the SOCIETY OF AMERICAN FORESTERS.

Throughout his career, Olmsted made major contributions to forestry conservation, both in the public and private sectors.

Further reading: Coert duBois, "Frederick Erskine Olmsted," *American Forest and Forest Life* 30 (1925): 234.

Olmsted, Frederick Law, Jr. (July 24, 1870–December 25, 1957)
In 1903, when FREDERICK LAW OLMSTED SR. died, his sons, Frederick Law Olmsted Jr. and John Olmsted, assumed the leadership of the country's largest and most prestigious landscape architecture firm. Among Frederick Jr.'s early assignments, in 1901, was a position on the Senate Park Commission, which was charged with restoring and developing L'Enfant's original plan for the nation's capital. This project included work on the grounds of the White House, Lafayette Park, the Jefferson Memorial, the National Arboretum and Rock Creek Park. Between 1926 and 1932, Olmsted worked on the National Capital Park and Planning Commission. Both commission seats allowed Olmsted to continue the important work in Washington begun by his father.

In scenic preservation, the younger Olmsted was engaged to assess the impact of a planned diversion of water from the Niagara River in 1906. Other work included surveying potential park sites in California in 1928 and investigating the possibility of preserving the Everglades in southern Florida as a national park in 1932.

Olmsted was instrumental in drafting the legislation that created the NATIONAL PARK SERVICE in 1916. Supporters of the National Park Service Act relied on him to compose the language describing the purpose of the national parks, and his words were later written into the law: "to conserve the scenery and the natural and historic objects and the wild life therein and to provide for the enjoyment of the same in such manner and by such means as will leave them unimpaired for the enjoyment of future generations."

In addition to legislative support and work on projects across the country, Olmsted also developed the nation's first academic program in landscape architecture, begun in 1900 as part of Harvard University's curriculum. Olmsted served on the Harvard faculty until 1914.

In 1950, after a lifetime of landscape design, preservation work and teaching, Olmsted retired and moved to California, where he was active in campaigns to save the redwood forests along the coast and to improve the management of Yosemite Valley.

Further reading: Laura Wood Roper, *FLO: A Biography of Frederick Law Olmsted* (Baltimore: John Hopkins University Press, 1973).

Olmsted, Frederick Law, Sr. (April 26, 1822–August 28, 1903)

The landscape architecture careers of Frederick Law Olmsted Sr. and his son FREDERICK LAW OLMSTED JR. span a century, from 1850, when the father began writing about public parks in England, to 1950, when the son retired from his active professional life.

Born in Hartford, Connecticut, Frederick Law Olmsted Sr. studied at Yale University, but his education was interrupted by an eye ailment caused by contact with poison sumac. In 1850, he traveled to Europe, a trip that inspired his first book, *Walks and Talks of an American Farmer in England* (1852).

Greatly impressed with the English public park system, Olmsted spread his message among American politicians, and in 1857, he was appointed superintendent of the embryonic Central Park in New York City. After he and his partner, the architect Calvert Vaux, won the design competition for the new park, Olmsted took on the role of architect-in-chief of Central Park.

Olmsted's work on the park was interrupted by the Civil War, when Olmsted became general secretary of the United States Sanitary Commission, which was charged with the daunting task of providing decent medical care to wounded soldiers. Olmsted next moved to California to head the Mariposa Mining Estate in the Sierra Nevada Mountains. As the head of the Yosemite Park Commission, Olmsted presented in 1865 a report detailing his vision of future conservation problems the park would face. (The report subsequently disappeared and was lost for some 87 years. By the time it resurfaced, it was apparent that many of the problems Olmsted predicted had come true.)

It was also in 1865 that Olmsted resumed his partnership with Vaux and his work as landscape architect for Central Park. While Manhattan's great park emerged as Olmsted and Vaux's masterpiece, the company also created other great urban parks and landscape projects incorporating Olmsted's controlling principle of balancing wild with more domesticated and formal elements. Prospect Park in Brooklyn, the city parks in Boston, important parks in Chicago as well as the suburban community of Riverside near that city and the grounds of the U. S. Capitol Building are among Olmsted's works.

Frederick Law Olmsted Sr.

In 1879, Olmsted returned to the field of natural preservation with his efforts to restore Niagara Falls, threatened by water erosion and uncontrolled tourism. This work culminated in the establishment of the Niagara Falls State Reservation in 1888.

Olmsted died in Waverly, Massachusetts.

Further reading: Laura Wood Roper, *FLO: A Biography of Frederick Law Olmsted* (Baltimore: John Hopkins University Press, 1973).

Olson, Sigurd Ferdinand (April 4, 1899–January 13, 1982)

A lyrical writer of several books and essays on environmental topics, Chicago-born Sigurd Ferdinand Olson was also a conservationist and teacher. Believing that people needed a direct relationship with nature in order to retain their humanity, Olson first put his philosophy into practice as a teacher of biology and agriculture in Nashawk, Minnesota. In 1922, he moved to Ely, Minnesota, where he began teaching at a junior college and established a canoeing and camping outfitter company, which he operated until 1947.

Beginning in 1932, Olson wrote a series of philosophical essays, but even more important was his study of the ecology of timber wolves, prepared as part of his work toward a master's degree in ecology (University of Illinois, 1931). His first book was *Singing Wilderness* (1956), a collection of essays organized along seasonal themes. His next book, *Listening Point* (1958), focused on the Quetico-Superior country, a region in which he had a lifelong interest. His other book-length works include *Lonely Land* (1961), *Runes of the North* (1963), *Hidden Forest* (1969), *Open Horizons* (1969), *Wilderness Days* (1972) and *Reflections from the North Country* (1978).

Olson was president of the NATIONAL PARKS AND CONSERVATION ASSOCIATION from 1954 to 1959 and of the WILDERNESS SOCIETY from 1968 to 1972. He also served as a wilderness ecologist for the IZAAK WALTON LEAGUE OF AMERICA, as a wilderness consultant on the President's Quetico-Superior Committee and as a consultant to the director of the NATIONAL PARKS SERVICE and to the U. S. Department of the INTERIOR's Committee on Wilderness Preservation, Wildlife Refuges, National Parks and Archaeological and Historic Sites.

Further reading: R. Newell Searle, *Saving Quetico-Superior: A Land Set Apart* (St. Paul: Minnesota Historical Society, 1977).

Onthank, Karl William (August 7, 1890– October 27, 1967)

A conservation-minded educator, Onthank was most active in Oregon, where he worked as a public school administrator. He participated in debate over proposed hydroelectric facilities at Beaver Marsh on the upper McKenzie River; over a proposal for an Oregon Dunes National Seashore; over the proposed exclusion of prime commercial timberland from the Three Sisters Wilderness Area in the Cascades; and over development in the vicinity of Waldo Lake, also in the Cascades. He was instrumental in initiating a long-term program to clean up the Willamette River and to create a belt of parks and wild lands along its course. Onthank served as president of the FEDERATION OF WESTERN OUTDOOR CLUBS (1955–57) and of the Oregon County Parks Association. He served as chairman of the Oregon Water Resources Board, was a founder of the Friends of the Three Sisters Wilderness and the Save the McKenzie River Association. Onthank was also active in other conservation organizations, including the Columbia Basin Inter-Agency Committee and the SIERRA CLUB.

Open Space Institute (Founded: 1974)

145 Main Street, Ossining, New York 10562; (914) 762-4630

Operating with a staff of four and a budget of $2 million, the Open Space Institute assists qualified groups in protecting open space and promoting positive environmental values. The institute offers help with educational programs, litigation and land conservation, and provides technical and administrative aid to citizen environmental projects.

O'Riordan, Timothy (February 21, 1942–   )

An environmental science educator and researcher, Timothy O'Riordan, a native of Edinburgh, Scotland, teaches at the School of Environmental Sciences of the University of East Anglia in Norwich, England. O'Riordan also serves as executive editor of *Environment* magazine, published by the Helen Dwight Reid Educational Foundation.

O'Riordan is the author of *Perspectives on Resource Management* (1957) and *Environmentalism* (1976). In addition, he coauthored *Sizewell B: An Anatomy of the Inquiry* (1988), a report on the three-year-long public inquiry that preceded the construction of the Sizewell B pressurized water reactor (PWR) in East Suffolk, England. The *Sizewell* book is an extensive analysis of the scientific and political procedures that constitute—or should constitute—the process of licensing and managing nuclear projects.

O'Riordan also served as editor of the four-volume *Progress in Resource Management and Environmental Planning* (1979–83), and he serves with important English environmental organizations, including the Advisory Committee on Engineering of the Nature Conservancy Council and the Social Science Research Council for the Environmental and Planning Committee, of which he is vice-chairman. He is also a member of the Iven Commission on Environmental Planning in Switzerland.

Osborn, Fairfield (January 15, 1887–September 16, 1969)

The founder of the CONSERVATION FOUNDATION in 1948, Fairfield Osborn served as the organization's first president until 1962, when he became chairman of the board. He also served as honorary vice-president of the Fauna Preservation Society in London and of the AMERICAN FORESTRY ASSOCIATION. He was a member of the secretary of the interior's Advisory Committee on Conservation in 1952.

Osborn's publications include *Our Plundered Planet* (1948) and *Limits of the Earth* (1953). In addition, he was the editor of *The Pacific World* (1944) and *Our Crowded Planet* (1962).

A native of Princeton, New Jersey, he received numerous awards, including the Medal of Honor of the City of New York, the Louis Bromfield Memorial Medal from the Friends of the Land, the Gold Medal of the New York Zoological Society, the First Conservation Medal of the San Diego Zoological Society and the Medal of Honor of the Theodore Roosevelt Memorial Association.

Osborn was a member of various conservation organizations, including the council of the SAVE-THE-REDWOODS LEAGUE and the International Committee for Bird Preservation.

Outdoor Recreation and Heritage Conservation and Recreation Service, Bureau of (Established: 1962; Abolished: 1981)

Created by Secretary of the Interior STEWART UDALL, the BOR was expected to promote coordination of the nation's outdoor recreation programs and to prepare a National Plan for Outdoor Recreation. While the BOR did administer various recreational and environmental programs, it was never able to create the plan that was its central mandate. Indeed, the BOR found itself in a state of continual friction with other agencies, most notably the NATIONAL PARK SERVICE, usually over conflicting perceptions of responsibility and jurisdiction.

After years of low morale and progressive dismantling, the BOR was finally abolished by Ronald REAGAN's Secretary of the Interior James WATT in 1981.

Owings, Margaret Wentworth (March 29, 1913–   )

Born in Berkeley, California, conservationist and artist Margaret Wentworth Owings first entered the conservation movement as a commissioner of the California State Parks Commission from 1963 to 1969. During her tenure on the commission, she led the fight against the proposed construction of a freeway through Pacific Creek Redwoods State Park. In 1969, she became the first woman to be elected to the board of the American Wildlife Leadership Foundation. That year she also became associated with DEFENDERS OF WILDLIFE, an organization she served as a board member until 1974. In addition, she has worked for the ENVIRONMENTAL DEFENSE FUND as a trustee since 1972.

Owings founded the Friends of the Sea Otter in 1969 and currently serves as president of the organization. In addition, she chaired the California Mountain Lion Preservation Foundation in 1987. Her contributions to conservation magazines and journals include "They're Still Shooting the Tule Elk" (*Audubon*, September 1965), "Perils of the Southern Sea Otter (*Humane Society News,* Spring 1981) and "The Southern Sea Otter" (*Monterey Life,* November 1980).

Her work in conservation has been honored by the U.S. Department of the INTERIOR, the California Academy of Scientists, the Humane Society of the United States and the NATIONAL AUDUBON SOCIETY.

P

Pack, Charles Lathrop (May 7, 1857–June 14, 1937)

A businessman and forester born in Lexington, Michigan, Charles Pack served as a forestry advisor at the 1908 White House Conference of Governors and as a member of the National Conservation Commission. Director of the American Forestry Association (now AMERICAN FORESTS) from 1911 to 1916, he was elected president of the National Conservation Congress in 1913 and served as AFA president from 1916 to 1922. During World War I, Pack organized the National War Garden Commission, forerunner of the World War II-era Victory Garden movement. After the war, he developed and financed gifts of tree seeds to Belgium, France and Italy to reforest devastated woodlands. Great Britain and France also received seeds to replant forests that had been heavily harvested for war-related lumber.

With his son, Arthur Newton Pack, Charles Pack founded the AMERICAN TREE ASSOCIATION and the AMERICAN NATURE ASSOCIATION, both intended to heighten public awareness of conservation. *Forestry News Digest,* a journal he founded in 1923 and circulated free to foresters, also advocated conservation programs. Pack endowed forestry school scholarships, subsidized demonstration forests in New York State and Washington State, endowed a chair of forest soils and two fellowships at Cornell University and funded other conservation and forestry programs. In 1930, he created the Charles Lathrop Pack Forestry Foundation.

Further reading: Pack and Thomas Harvey Gill, *Forests and Mankind* (New York: Macmillan, 1929).

Paley, William (July 1743–May 25, 1805)

A principal proponent of theological utilitarianism, Bishop William Paley outlined his belief in the precision of the economy of nature in *Natural Theology* and other works. His philosophy rested on the belief that God had designed the universe to operate according to integrated natural laws, and Paley frequently compared the workings of the universe to a well-made machine. In the opening pages of *Natural Theology,* Paley argued for the existence of God as "designer" of the universe. He introduced the persuasive analogy of the abandoned watch found on a heath; even in the apparent absence of the maker, the very existence of the watch irrefutably implies the existence of its maker. Paley's mechanistic cosmology, a primitive adumbration of modern ecology, was tremendously popular and influential in the 18th and early 19th centuries.

Born in Peterborough, England, Paley was educated at Christ's College, Cambridge. He was appointed rector of Musgrave in Westmorland in 1776 and archdeacon of Carlisle in 1782. He died in Lincoln.

Parenteau, Patrick Aloysius (May 7, 1947–   )

An attorney with the Oregon firm of Perkins Coie, Patrick Aloysius Parenteau served as commissioner of environmental protection in Vermont and as vice-president of the NATIONAL WILDLIFE FEDERATION, where he drafted testimony and legislation, prepared petitions and comments and analyzed policy. Born in Omaha, Nebraska, he was a teaching fellow in the Natural Resources Law Institute of Northwestern School of Law at Lewis and Clark College from 1975 to 1976. He has conducted seminars in wildlife law at the Vermont Law School and at Northwestern School of Law. In 1979, Parenteau was named director of the Resources Defense Division of the National Wildlife Federation, and in 1981, he was named vice-president for resources conservation.

Patterson, Clair Cameron (June 22, 1922–)

Specializing in geochemical and environmental chemical research, Clair Cameron Patterson has been a geochemist at the California Institute of Technology since 1952. From 1942 to 1944, he was an emission and mass spectroscopist with the Manhattan Project, which developed the atomic bomb that ended World War II. Patterson then moved to the University of Chicago, where he was research associate in geochemistry and geochronology and a teaching fellow.

His research has focused on the esotopic evolution of lead and the age of the earth, biogeochemistry of lead in marine and terrestrial ecosystems, lead pollution in mammals and the atmosphere, the archaeology of South American metallurgy and the history of ancient metal production. His work on lead pollution, in which he documented that human beings in industrial societies have far higher concentrations of lead in their systems than those in preindustrial societies, brought about increased public awareness of the dangers of lead contamination and governmental controls on lead in gasoline.

Penfold, Joseph Weller (November 18, 1907– May 25, 1973)

As western representative (1949–57) and conservation director (1957–73) of the IZAAK WALTON LEAGUE OF AMERICA, Joseph Weller Penfold worked in cooperation with the federal government to develop important conservation legislation.

Born in Marinette, Wisconsin, Penfold began his career in conservation during the Depression with the National Youth Administration and, after service in World War II, worked with the United Nations Relief and Rehabilitation Administration. His early years with the Izaak Walton League saw him do battle with certain livestock interests, which were challenging U.S. FOREST SERVICE regulation of public rangelands, and with the Bureau of RECLAMATION, which was planning two high dams in Dinosaur National Monument. In 1952, Penfold personally took Congressman Wayne N. Aspinall (member and, later, chairman of the House Interior and Insular Affairs Committee) and Congressman John P. Saylor (ranking minority member of the committee) on a camping tour of the endangered area. Both men subsequently acted to stop the dam projects, and a strong precedent for safeguarding national park lands was established.

Penfold served as a conservation lobbyist for many years and wrote the act that established the Outdoor Recreation and Resources Review Commission in 1958, to which President Eisenhower subsequently appointed him. The commission's report, completed in 1962, resulted in the creation of the Bureau of OUTDOOR RECREATION, the Land and Water Conservation Fund and the establishment of many national recreation areas. The Bureau of Outdoor Recreation also worked cooperatively with all states to create outdoor recreation plans for them. Penfold was an important force behind the environmental legislation of the 1960s, including the Multiple Use-Sustained Yield Act (1960), the Wilderness Act (1964) and the Wild and Scenic Rivers Act (1968).

In addition to his work with the Izaak Walton League, Penfold served as secretary (1957–65), vice-chairman (1966) and chairman (1967–69) of the NATURAL RESOURCES COUNCIL OF AMERICA. The U.S. Department of the INTERIOR presented him with its Conservation Service Award in 1962, and the American Forestry Association (now AMERICAN FORESTS) created an award especially for him in 1969.

Perring, Franklyn Hugh (August 1, 1927–)

British writer, broadcaster and environmental consultant F. H. Perring is the author or editor of many standard works on the distribution of flora in the British Isles. His *Atlas of the British Flora*, which he edited with S. M. Walters, is currently in its third edition and is recognized as a keystone of much important ecological work. Perring is also the author, editor, coauthor or coeditor of *A Flora of Cambridgeshire* (1964), *The Flora of a Changing Britain* (1970), *The British Oak* (1974), *English Names of Wild Flowers* (1974, 1986), *British Red Data Book of Vascular Plants* (1977, 1983), *Ecological Effects of Pesticides* (1977), *RSNC Guide to British Wild Flowers* (1984), *Ecological Flora of the Shropshire Region* (1985), *Changing Attitudes to Nature Conservation* (1988), *The Macmillan Guide to British Wildflowers* (1989), *The Nature of Northamptonshire* (1989), *Tomorrow Is Too Late* (1990), *Britain's Conservation Heritage* (1991) and various scientific papers.

Perring was educated at Queens College, Cambridge, from which he took his M.A. and Ph.D. Long associated with the Biological Records Centre of the Monks Woods Experimental Station, he served as botanical secretary of the Linnaean Society of London from 1973 to 1978 and was general secretary of the Royal Society of Nature Conservation from 1979 to 1987.

Peterson, Ralph Max (July 25, 1917–)

A long-time employee of the U.S. FOREST SERVICE, Ralph Max Peterson is a native of Doniphan, Missouri, who held positions as an engineer in the Plumas, Cleveland and San Bernardino national forests in California and the Northern Regional Office in

Montana before his transfer to the Washington, D.C., headquarters in 1961.

Returning to California in 1966 as regional engineer for the service, he designed new methods of building roads, bridges and recreation areas in the national forests. Promoted to deputy regional forester for the Southern Region in 1971 and regional forester for the Southern Region in 1972, he was next named deputy chief of the U.S. Forest Service for Programs and Legislation, where he worked to secure passage of the National Forest Management Act of 1976. Three years later, he became the first engineer to be named chief of the federal agency, and in that role he worked to improve coordination among the United States, Mexico and Canada in fire control and insect and disease control. He retired from the Forest Service in February 1987.

In addition to his service with the federal government, Peterson is a member of the American Forestry Association (now AMERICAN FORESTS), the SOCIETY OF AMERICAN FORESTERS, the Society of Tropical Foresters, the WILDLIFE SOCIETY and other conservation organizations.

Peterson, Roger Tory (August 28, 1908–)

The author of the popular *Field Guide to Birds,* Roger Tory Peterson a native of Jamestown, New York, worked in the 1930s as an education specialist and art editor of *Audubon* magazine. After military service during World War II, he returned to the NATIONAL AUDUBON SOCIETY, serving as a lecturer, artist, writer and director. In 1946, he was named editor of the Houghton Mifflin Field Guide Series, which had produced the first edition of *A Field Guide to Birds* in 1934, four subsequent editions, *A Field Guide to Western Birds* and other Peterson titles. He has served on the board of the WORLD WILDLIFE FUND and was president from 1948 to 1949 of the American Nature Study Society. Among his many awards are the William Brewster Medal from the American Ornithologists' Union, the John Burroughs medal, the Gold Medal of the World Wildlife Fund and the Medal of Freedom.

Peterson, Russell Wilbur (October 3, 1916–)

Research director and development division director for E. I. Du Pont de Nemours and Company from 1942 until 1969, Russell Wilbur Peterson was elected governor of Delaware and served from 1969 to 1973. During his administration, the state passed the Delaware Coastal Zone Act, a pioneering law that banned industry from a two-mile strip along the state's coast. When his term as governor ended, he continued his efforts in environmental protection, first as chairman of the President's COUNCIL ON ENVIRONMENTAL QUALITY from 1973 to 1976, then as a founder and first president, from 1976 to 1977, of New Directors, a lobbying group devoted to global issues. In 1979, he was elected president of the NATIONAL AUDUBON SOCIETY, a post he held until his retirement in 1985. In addition, in 1979 he served on the commission appointed by President Jimmy Carter to investigate the Three Mile Island nuclear accident. That year he also became involved with the Solar Energy Research Institute by serving on its advisory board.

Other ecological organizations in which Peterson has been active include the Bio-Energy Council (1976–78), WORLD WILDLIFE FUND (1976–82), Population Crisis Committee (since 1973), Global Tomorrow Coalition (since 1981), International Council for Bird Preservation (since 1982) and EARTH ISLAND INSTITUTE (1988).

In 1983, as president of the National Audubon Society, Peterson began working with representatives of other environmental groups to develop a national protection agenda. The product of two years of study, *An Environmental Agenda for the Future* (1985) addresses such issues as nuclear power, human population growth, energy strategies, water resources, toxic waste and pollution control, wildlife, private lands and agriculture, protected land systems, public lands, and the role of national organizations in dealing with urban and international environmental problems.

Among the many awards given to Peterson for conservation work are the Gold Medal of the World Wildlife Fund (1971), the Audubon Award of the National Audubon Society (1977), the Frances K. Hutchinson Medal of the Garden Club of America (1980), Conservationist of the Year Award of the NATIONAL WILDLIFE FEDERATION (1972) and the Robert Marshall Award of the WILDERNESS SOCIETY (1984).

Peterson is a native of Portage, Wisconsin.

Pinchot, Gifford (August 11, 1865–October 4, 1946)

Gifford Pinchot introduced the first systematic forest management in America in February 1892 at Biltmore, the North Carolina estate of George W. Vanderbilt. He went on, in December 1893, to open an office in New York City, where he offered his services as a consulting forester. From 1893 to 1898—when he was appointed chief of the U.S. Department of AGRICULTURE's Division of Forestry (later called the FOREST SERVICE)—Pinchot developed management plans for privately owned forest lands in the Adirondacks, Pennsylvania and New Jersey; he also established the guidelines of academic forestry instruction.

Gifford Pinchot with President Franklin Delano Roosevelt and an unidentified woman. *Courtesy of the National Park Service*

Oldest son of James W. Pinchot, a prominent New York and Pennsylvania manufacturer, and Mary Eno Pinchot, Gifford Pinchot was educated in Paris and New York City, attended Phillips Exeter Academy (New Hampshire) and graduated from Yale University in 1889. He determined to become a forester, but since the profession of forestry was virtually unknown in the United States at the time, Pinchot traveled to France, where he studied at the French Forest School in Nancy and then toured model forests in France, Switzerland and Germany before returning to the United States at the end of 1890.

In 1896, Pinchot was appointed a member of the National Forestry Commission, which was charged with formulating a national forest policy. This led to his appointment as a special agent for the U.S. Department of the INTERIOR the following year and then to his service with the Division of Forestry. With the close cooperation and enthusiastic support of President THEODORE ROOSEVELT, Pinchot began a cooperative forest management program to aid private forest owners, established the National Forest System and generally promulgated the cause of forest regulation and conservation. Pinchot's conservation crusade culminated in his 1908 White House conference on the issue, which led to the establishment of a National Conservation Commission, which he chaired. The commission prepared the nation's first comprehensive inventory of its natural resources.

Pinchot served on many conservation commissions including the Public Lands Commission, Inland Waterways Commission and the Commission on Country Life. A strong-willed man, Pinchot clashed with Secretary of the Interior Richard A. BALLINGER over conservation policy and was removed as Forest Service chief by President William H. Taft in 1910.

Even after he left government service, Pinchot continued his leadership role in the conservation movement. He had founded the SOCIETY OF AMERICAN FORESTERS in 1900 and redoubled his activity in that organization. He also turned increasingly to his duties as professor of forestry (1903–1936) at the Yale University School of Forestry, which he had been instrumental in establishing in 1900. In 1909 he organized the National Conservation Association, an important political pressure group. Pinchot was an unsuccessful candidate for U.S. senator from Pennsylvania in 1920 and 1926 and was Pennsylvania governor for two terms (1923–27 and 1931–35).

Gifford Pinchot was a prolific author. His works include *Biltmore Forest* (1893), *The Adirondack Spruce* (1898), *A Primer of Forestry* (Part 1, 1899; Part 2, 1905), *The Fight for Conservation* (1909), *The Training of a Forester* (1914, 1937) and his polemical autobiography, *Breaking New Ground* (posthumously published, 1947).

Pinchot was born in Simsbury, Connecticut, and died in Milford, Pennsylvania.

Further reading: M. Nelson McGeary, *Gifford Pinchot: Forester-Politician* (Princeton, N.J.: Princeton University Press, 1960); Harold T. Pinkett, *Gifford Pinchot: Private and Public Forester* (Champaign-Urbana: University of Illinois Press, 1970).

Pomerance, Rafe (July 19, 1945–)

Senior associate for policy affairs at the WORLD RESOURCES INSTITUTE, Rafe Pomerance serves as a congressional liaison working to inform policy makers about the greenhouse effect. Before joining the staff of the World Resources Institute, he was an officer and president of FRIENDS OF THE EARTH, founding coordinator of the NATIONAL CLEAN AIR COALITION and chairman of the board of AMERICAN RIVERS. He is credited with having been a moving force behind the 1986 Senate hearings, chaired by Senator John H. Chafee, that brought increased national awareness of the environmental hazards of the greenhouse effect.

Poole, Daniel Arnold (April 11, 1922–)

President of the WILDLIFE MANAGEMENT INSTITUTE from 1970 to 1987 and chairman of the board from 1987 to 1991, Daniel Arnold Poole holds B.S. and M.S. degrees in wildlife management from the University of Montana. Before joining the staff of the institute in 1952, Poole, who was born in New York City, was employed as a field assistant with the Montana Department of Fish and Game and as a biological aide with the U.S. FISH AND WILDLIFE SER-

Yellowstone Canyon and Lower Falls, Yellowstone National Park. *U.S. Department of the Interior, National Park Service photo by George A. Grant*

VICE offices in California and Utah. At the Wildlife Institute, Poole edited the *Outdoor News Bulletin* from 1952 to 1969 and was elected secretary of the institute in 1963.

In addition to his work with the Wildlife Management Institute, Poole was secretary of the NATURAL RESOURCES COUNCIL OF AMERICA from 1966 to 1970 and edited the council's *Executive News Service* from 1960 to 1965. From 1971 to 1972, he was the council's vice-chairman, and from 1973 to 1974, he served as chairman.

Poole consulted with the U.S. Department of AGRICULTURE as a member of a special advisory committee from 1966 to 1967. The committee studied the feasibility of a multiple-use plan for the Magruder Corridor of the Bitterroot National Forest. He also consulted with the NATIONAL PARK SERVICE as a member of the Master Plan Team studying Yellowstone and Grand Teton national parks.

Poole has served as a trustee of the NORTH AMERICAN WILDLIFE FOUNDATION, which issues grants to graduate students in the United States and Canada and owns the Delta Waterfowl Research Station in Manitoba. Since 1974, Poole has been a trustee of Stronghold Inc., which administers Sugarloaf Mountain, a 3,000-acre property in central Maryland near Washington, D.C., that is managed as a natural area open for public use and for scientific and educational purposes.

In 1978, Poole was selected as chairman of the Boy Scouts of America's National Conservation Committee, a group that is reviewing the BSA's conservation efforts at national facilities and is developing new conservation programs.

Poole's articles on wildlife have appeared in numerous newspapers and periodicals, and from 1960 to 1970, he edited a monthly column on wildlife for *American Rifleman*. In 1969, he was honored with the Jade of Chiefs Award of the Outdoor Writers Association of America.

Population Council (Founded: 1952)
One Dag Hammarskjold Plaza, New York, NY 10017; (212) 644-1300

This organization provides support and technical expertise for research in world population control and assists in establishing government policies to stabilize population. Administering an annual budget of $20 million, the council underwrites graduate programs, research seminars and workshops on family planning. The council operates regional offices in the United States, Mexico, Thailand, Egypt and Japan.

Population Institute (Founded: 1969)
110 Maryland Avenue SE, Suite 207, Washington, D.C. 20002; (202) 544-3300

A large organization with a membership of 32,000, the Population Institute collects and collates information on global overpopulation in order to lobby Congress for legislation relating to population policy. The institute runs an internship program for population research and sponsors professional-area interest groups, including Bankers Who Care, Religious Leaders Who Care, and others.

John Karefa-Smart, M.D., is chairperson of the board of directors of the Population Institute, and Werner Fornos is the group's president.

Post, Diana (March 28, 1939–   )
Diana Post, a Washington, D.C.-area veterinarian, is executive director of the RACHEL CARSON COUNCIL. She was educated at Swarthmore College and Temple University and received her veterinary medical doctor degree in 1974 from the University of Pennsylvania. She was in private practice from 1974 to 1977, when she joined the federal FOOD AND DRUG ADMINISTRATION as a veterinary medical officer. Her work at the FDA included analyzing adverse reactions to veterinary drugs and reviewing safety and efficacy data intended to support new animal drug approval.

During her 14 years with the FDA, Dr. Post became interested in the similarity of some veterinary drugs to pesticides, both in their active ingredients and in their reasons for use. This led to her research in pesticide effects on pets and brought her into association with the Rachel Carson Council as a member of the board of directors. In July 1992, she was appointed executive director.

Dr. Post brings to her position an interest in researching pesticide effects on people, pets, wildlife and the environment generally, with emphasis on long-term, chronic and subtle effects.

Potter, Albert Franklin (November 14, 1859– January 1, 1944)

Born in Lone, California, Albert Franklin Potter became a major Arizona sheep rancher. Later, it was Potter who persuaded Gifford PINCHOT, head of the U.S. Division of Forestry, that properly regulated livestock grazing on federal reserves would not damage the land. In 1901, Potter worked with Pinchot to implement federal grazing policies and was instrumental in enlarging forest reserves during President THEODORE ROOSEVELT's administration. Potter was named chief of grazing in 1905 when the forest reserves were transferred to the U.S. Department of AGRICULTURE. In 1910, he became associate forester, and during World War I, he served as acting forester, while Henry GRAVES was in military service in France. Potter resigned from the service in 1920.

Pound, Roscoe (October 17, 1870–July 1, 1964)

Although best known as a lawyer and law professor, Roscoe Pound became interested in botany at an early age and received a B.A., M.A. and Ph.D. in botany from the University of Nebraska in his native Lincoln. His graduate research focused on plant geography, ecology and parasitic fungi. As director of the state's Botanical Survey, he oversaw the production of the *Reports of the Botanical Survey of Nebraska* and *Flora of Nebraska*.

Pound enrolled in the Harvard School of Law in 1889. Straitened finances prevented his completing the program at Harvard, but he was admitted to the Nebraska bar in 1890 nevertheless and started a private practice in Lincoln. He later taught at the University of Nebraska, Northwestern University and the University of Chicago. Between 1916 and 1936, he served as dean of the law school at Harvard University.

As a botany student at the University of Nebraska, Pound studied under Charles BESSEY and worked with Frederic CLEMENTS on *The Phytogeography of Nebraska* (1898), covering not only plant distribution but also ecology, which they defined as "the interrelations of organic elements of this floral covering."

John Wesley Powell

Powell, John Wesley (March 24, 1834– September 23, 1902)

Before John Wesley Powell undertook his famous geographic explorations of the West, this native of Mount Morris, New York, served in the Union Army during the Civil War, attaining the rank of major. He lost his right arm at the Battle of Shiloh and, after the war, took up the quiet profession of teaching, securing a professorship in geology at Illinois Wesleyan College and serving as museum curator at Illinois Normal University.

But he did not let the loss of his right arm keep him sedentary for long. In 1867, Powell turned his attention to the American West. After gaining support from the Smithsonian Institution and securing an appropriation from Congress, he led a 900-mile boat expedition along the Colorado River and the Grand Canyon between May and August of 1869. Powell continued his explorations of the West in 1871 and 1874. In 1875, he became director of the second division of the United States Geological and Geographical Survey of the Territories, which was renamed in 1877 the Survey of the Rocky Mountain Region. In 1880, Powell became director of the United States Geological Survey, a consolidation of all federal survey projects. He held this post until 1894, when Congress forced him to resign because of his unpopular support of irrigation projects and forest preservation in the West.

Powell's reports on his early geological studies were published in 1875 in a 300-page volume entitled *Explorations of the Colorado River of the West and its Tributaries,* which was revised, enlarged and republished in 1885 as *Canyons of the Colorado.* He also wrote *Report on the Lands of the Arid Region of the United States* (1878). From these works emerged not only an understanding of vast tracts of western lands, but much of the terminology used by geologists to this day.

Under Powell's leadership, the Geological Survey grew into a well-organized, well-funded, powerful federal agency. Powell instituted several publications programs, including the Bulletin series (begun in 1883), the Monograph series (begun in 1890) and the folio atlas series (begun in 1894).

Powell's interests were not limited to geography and geology, however. He became an avid student of Native tribes in the West and served as director of the Bureau of Ethnology of the Smithsonian Institution from 1879 until his death in Haven, Maine.

Further reading: John Upton Terreli, *The Man Who Rediscovered America: A Biography of John Wesley Powell* (New York: Weybright and Talley, 1969).

Powers, Roger W. (October 12, 1932–)

A native of Peoria, Illinois, Roger W. Powers was educated at Bradley University, where he earned his B.S. in business administration, and at Rutgers University, where he did postgraduate work in the social sciences. An authority on waste management, Powers is currently president and chief executive officer of KEEP AMERICA BEAUTIFUL INC., a private, nonprofit organization that developed the KAB System of waste management, which is now used by 485 cities and counties in 40 states as well as in several foreign countries.

Before joining KAB in 1970, Powers worked in the business world as a marketing, sales and public affairs specialist. A director of the National Institute for Urban Wildlife and America's Clean Water Foundation, he also serves on the Take Pride in America advisory board, a 21-member board appointed by the U.S. secretary of the interior. Powers is also active in other national conservation and educational organizations.

During his tenure at Keep America Beautiful, Powers has expanded the organization's traditional environmental education programs and has restructured the organization to provide direct services to its large membership, which includes more than 300 companies, unions and trade associations.

Price, Overton Westfeldt (January 27, 1873–July 11, 1914)

An émigré from Liverpool, England, Overton Westfeldt Price attended the Biltmore Forest School in North Carolina from 1895 to 1896. He then enrolled at the University of Munich, where he studied forestry and gained a year of experience working in European forests. In 1899, he was hired as an agent by the Division of Forestry of the U.S. Department of AGRICULTURE, working as an associate forester in the Bureau of Forestry and the U.S. FOREST SERVICE from 1901 to 1910.

Although Price was credited with the establishment of a sound and enduring national forestry policy, he was fired by President William Howard Taft in 1910 for his role in the Richard BALLINGER-Gifford PINCHOT controversy over Alaskan land claims.

Price was one of seven charter members of the SOCIETY OF AMERICAN FORESTERS in 1900, an organization he served as chairman of the executive committee, vice-president and member of the editorial board. After losing his job with the U.S. Forest Service, he became treasurer and vice-president of the National Conservation Association and later consulted with the province of British Columbia on establishing its Forest Branch. He also worked as a forester for the Letchwork Park Arboretum and as an advisor to the George W. Vanderbilt estate.

Pritchard, Paul Clement (August 27, 1944–)

Paul Clement Pritchard, executive director of the NATIONAL PARKS AND CONSERVATION ASSOCIATION since 1980, began working in the field of ecology in 1972 as chief of planning in the Georgia Department of Natural Resources. After serving in that position for two years, he was named Pacific Region coordinator for coastal zone management for the National Oceanic and Atmospheric Administration (1974–75) and then directed the APPALACHIAN TRAIL CONFERENCE (1975–77). In President Jimmy Carter's administration, Pritchard worked as deputy director of the Bureau of OUTDOOR RECREATION OF THE HERITAGE CONSERVATION AND RECREATION SERVICE from 1977 to 1980.

Among his many achievements are his leadership of the Presidential National Heritage Trust Task Force, his work to create the federal Coastal Zone Management Act and the State Heritage Inventory, his implementation of the Washington State coastal zone management program (the first such program in the

United States) and his work to create the South Slough Estuary Sanctuary in Oregon.

Pritchard, who holds an M.S.P. in natural resource and economics planning from the University of Tennessee (1976) and a certificate in business management from Harvard University (1973), is the recipient of numerous awards. In 1973, he was named special fellow by the U.S. Department of Housing and Urban Development and was honored with the Outstanding Service Award of the National Oceanic and Atmospheric Administration in 1975. In addition, the U.S. Department of the INTERIOR conferred its Meritorious Service Award on Pritchard in 1980, and in 1982, he received the Gulf Oil Conservation Award.

Public Citizen (Founded: 1971)
P.O. Box 19404, Washington, D.C. 20036; (202) 833-3000

Founded by consumer advocate Ralph NADER, Public Citizen is a powerful advocacy, information and lobbying organization, numbering some 100,000 supporters and operating on a $7 million annual budget.

In addition to protecting consumer rights and promoting the production of safe products, Public Citizen works to achieve and preserve a healthful environment and workplace, to encourage the development of clean and safe energy sources and ensure that government as well as private industry is responsive to public welfare and public needs.

Public Citizen engages in lobbying, litigation, monitoring of government agencies, research, public education and media campaigning. The organization operates the Public Citizen Foundation, which supports Public Citizen's educational activities, and includes the following subdivisions: Congress Watch, a legislative monitoring group; the Critical Mass Energy Project; the Health Research Group; Buyers Up; and the Litigation Group.

Public Citizen publishes a monthly *Health Letter*; *Public Citizen*, a bimonthly magazine covering consumer and environmental issues; *Buyers Up News*; and a variety of monographs, policy papers, books and reports. Joan Claybrook is president of Public Citizen.

Public Health Service, U.S. (Established: 1798)
200 Independence Avenue SW, Washington, D.C. 20201; (202) 690-6867

A branch of the Department of Health and Human Services, the Public Health Service is the principal health agency of the federal government. In this capacity, the agency has been directly engaged in the drafting of environmental legislation. The Water Pollution Control Acts of 1948 and 1956 and the Clean Air Act of 1963 benefited from research by Public Health Service staff members. In general, the Public Health Service is mandated to protect and improve the health of American citizens. It carries out this mission through a broad range of programs designed to promote greater knowledge of health issues among health professionals and the public, to improve access to health services in communities, to control and eradicate disease, to ensure the safety of food sources and drugs and to collect statistics on the state of the nation's health.

The service is divided into six major agencies: the National Institutes of Health; the FOOD AND DRUG ADMINISTRATION; the Centers for Disease Control; the Alcohol, Drug Abuse, and Mental Health Administration; the Health Resources Administration; and the Health Services Administration.

The Public Health Service was created in 1798 with the passage of a law designed to provide medical services to the merchant marine. Under the provisions of the law, each mariner paid 20 cents a month to a fund administered by the president for providing medical care to seamen and for building hospitals specifically for them. It was the first prepaid medical plan in the country.

Further reading: Ralph Chester Williams, *The United States Public Health Service, 1798–1950* (Washington, D.C.: U.S. Government Printing Office, 1951).

Purcell, Arthur Henry (August 11, 1944–)
An authority on energy and resource waste and waste management, Arthur Henry Purcell was born in Evanston, Illinois. He was educated at the Institute for European Studies, Vienna, Austria (1965), and earned his B.S. from Cornell University in 1966. From Northwestern University, he took his M.S. in 1971 and his Ph.D. the following year.

Purcell worked as a civilian environmentalist for the U.S. Army Environment Office in 1971 and was associate director of the congressional scientific fellow program of the American Association for the Advancement of Science from 1973 to 1974. He was cofounder of the Technical Information Project Inc. in Washington, D.C., in 1975 and has served as its director since its founding. Purcell is also an adjunct professor at George Washington University and American University.

Purcell is the author of *Citizens and Waste*, published by the Technical Information Project in 1976 (volume 1) and 1978 (volume 2), *Tin Cans and Trash Recovery* (Technical Information Project, 1980) and *The*

Waste Watchers (1980). He has contributed to many scientific and technical journals and has served on the President's Scientific Policy Task Force (1976), the President's Commission on Scholars (1978) and the President's Commission on the Accident at Three Mile Island (1979), for which he was a staff principal.

A member of the American Institute of Mining, Metallurgy, and Petroleum Engineers, the American Association for the Advancement of Science, the Federation of Materials Societies and Sigma Xi, Purcell was the recipient of a grant from the German Marshall Fund in 1980.

Q

Quarles, John (April 26, 1935–   )
John Quarles is a partner in the Washington, D.C., law firm of Morgan, Lewis & Bockius. He serves as chairman of the firm's Environmental Practice Group. Quarles is one of the nation's leading attorneys working in litigation over hazardous waste facilities, environmental enforcement prosecutions, permit proceedings, environmental audits and other matters.

Quarles became the first assistant administrator for enforcement and general counsel of the ENVIRONMENTAL PROTECTION AGENCY when it was created in 1971. In April 1973, he became deputy administrator of the EPA, resigning in 1977. Responsible for the general management of EPA programs, he was a principal figure in the formulation of national policy on many environmental issues.

Before taking his position with the EPA, Quarles practiced corporate law in Boston from 1962 to 1969. A native of Boston, he was educated at Yale University, graduating in 1957. He took his law degree, magna cum laude, from Harvard University Law School in 1961. From 1969 to 1970, he was chief staff assistant to the secretary of the interior.

Quarles's articles on environmental regulation have appeared in newspapers and magazines, and he is the author of *Cleaning Up America* (1976), *Federal Regulation of New Industrial Plants* (1979), *Federal Regulation of Hazardous Wastes: A Guide to RCRA* (1982) and *Groundwater Contamination in the United States* (1983; revised edition, 1987).

R

Rachel Carson Council (Founded: 1965)
8940 Jones Mill Road, Chevy Chase, Maryland
20815; (301) 652-1877

Formerly the Rachel Carson Trust for the Living
Environment Inc., the Rachel Carson Council is an
independent, nonprofit scientific organization dedicated to preserving the integrity of the environment
through programs of research and education. The
council employs a board of consulting experts, including environmental scientists and advisers in
medical, legal, social and communications areas, to
find and evaluate the latest data on dangers to the
environment and to bring relevant issues effectively
to the attention of the public.

The Rachel Carson Council is active not only in
the United States, but throughout the world, through
participation in international meetings and programs,
including the UNITED NATIONS ENVIRONMENT PRO-
GRAMME as well as such organizations as the Pesticide
Action Network.

Named after the author of *Silent Spring*, which
brought to worldwide attention the environmental
dangers of pesticides (see CARSON, Rachel), the council concentrates its education and publishing efforts
on pesticides in the environment and on finding
organic alternatives to pesticide use. The organization's major publication is the *Basic Guide to Pesticides*
(1992), a comprehensive work that was 25 years in
the making. In addition, the council has published
such books and pamphlets as *Pesticides and Lawns*
(1991), *Healthy Lawns without Toxic Chemicals* (1971)
and *Pesticides and the Naturalist* (1963). It has issued a
pamphlet on the dangers of pesticides in citrus fruits,
*Beware the Zest of the Lemon-Lime, Orange, Kumquat,
Grapefruit* (1990), and pamphlets on integrated pest
management, including *Gardening with Nature: Your
Role for a Quality Environment* (1991) and *How to Control Garden Pests without Killing Almost Everything Else*
(1977).

Rainforest Action Network (Founded: 1985)
301 Broadway, Suite A, San Francisco, California
94133; (415) 398-4404

The 33,000-member Rainforest Action Network (RAN)
works to protect tropical rainforests around the world.
Focusing on timber imports, logging, cattle ranching,
development banks and the rights of indigenous
people, the organization carries out a broad program
of grass-roots organizing and international public
pressure. Recent accomplishments include preserving a 28,000-acre rainforest in Puerto Rico, pressuring
Burger King to stop purchasing beef raised in rainforest regions, stopping Coca Cola Foods and Minute
Maid Orange Juice from carrying out a plan to cut a
rainforest in Belize in order to plant orange groves
and pressuring Scott Paper Company to stop operations in a 2-million-acre rainforest in Indonesia. In
addition, the organization has lobbied the World
Bank to stop using United States money in loans to
projects that will harm or destroy rainforests. In most
of its campaigns, Rainforest Action Network engages
activists from indigenous rainforest peoples in its
work to pressure governments and corporations.

As of 1992, the group was engaged in a campaign
to halt plans for a power plant on the island of
Hawaii. The proposed project would destroy a large
portion of the lowland tropical rainforest on the island.

Members of the Rainforest Action Network receive
the six-page quarterly *World Rainforest Report*, which
includes news on rainforest issues, and the monthly
single-page *Rainforest Action Network Alert*, which
covers current preservation campaigns and projects.
Other RAN publications include the *Wood User's Guide*,
which helps readers identify woods used in construc-

Hawaiians protest geothermal plant proposed for Wao Kele O Puna, the last rainforest in the United States. *Rainforest Action Network*

tion and suggests alternatives to tropical woods, and the *Rainforest Action Guide,* an information brochure on resources, products and ways to become involved in the campaign to save tropical forests. Working with a full-time staff of 15, Randall Hayes is executive director of RAN.

Rasmussen, Boyd Lester (April 19, 1913–)

Born in Glenns Ferry, Idaho, Rasmussen enrolled at Oregon State University, graduating with a B.S. in forestry in 1935. He joined the staff of the Pacific Northwest Forest and Range Experiment Station of the U.S. FOREST SERVICE and over the next three decades worked as a forest ranger, timber staff officer, supervisor, assistant regional forester and assistant to the deputy chief in charge of national resource management. In 1961, he was named regional forester of the Northern Region, headquartered in Missoula, Montana, and three years later he became deputy chief in charge of cooperative forestry programs and insect and disease control. In 1966, Ras-

mussen was appointed director of the Bureau of LAND MANAGEMENT. In addition, he was a permanent member of the Forestry Panel of United States-Japan and worked on the Arctic Environmental Council.

Ray, John (November 29, 1627–January 17, 1705)

The most important naturalist of the 17th century, John Ray taught at Trinity College, Cambridge, from 1646 to 1659. During his tenure there he became seriously ill, and while convalescing, he wandered through the countryside—an activity that stimulated his interest in natural history, which became his primary academic pursuit.

At Cambridge, Ray befriended a young man named Francis Willughby, who was interested in natural history as well. When Ray was forced to leave the university because of his refusal to conform to the Church of England, Willughby and other friends supported him financially. Willughby and Ray toured Europe from 1663 to 1666, studying the flora and fauna.

Randall Hayes, founder and director of Rainforest Action Network, is arrested at a demonstration protesting World Bank rainforest policy. 1987. *Rainforest Action Network*

Ray published *Catalogue of Plants around Cambridge* (1660), which included descriptions of 558 species compiled from research conducted during his walks through the Cambridge countryside. In 1668, he contributed a table of plants to John Wilkins's *Essay toward a Real Character*; it was Ray's first extensive attempt at comprehensive plant classification. Before Willughby died in 1672, he and Ray published *Catalogue of English Plants* (1670) and made plans for a definitive catalog of plants and animals. Ray continued this work after Willughby's death and published two volumes on zoology under his late friend's name. In addition, Ray wrote *Methodus Plantarum Nova* (1682), in which he devised a systematic taxonomy based on physiology, morphology and anatomy. He categorized plants into cryptogams, monocotyledons and dicotyledons, a system that is still used today. In addition, he established the species as the basic unit of taxonomy.

Between 1686 and 1704, Ray published a three-volume work entitled *Historia Generalis Plantarum*, listing 18,600 species and including information on morphology, distribution, habitats and uses of plants. In addition, he wrote *The Wisdom of God Manifested in the Creation* (1691), in which he rejected the Newtonian model of nature as a machine and suggested that choice, error and randomness play central roles in the natural world.

Ray's zoological titles include *Synopsis of Quadrupeds* (1693), *History of Insects* (1710) and *Synopsis of Birds and Fish* (1713). It was Ray's taxonomic system, however, that earned him an important place in the field of natural history. His work remained the standard until superseded by the system of Carolus LINNAEUS in 1735.

Reagan, Ronald Wilson (February 6, 1911–   )

Ronald Reagan rode the crest of a conservative wave that swept the United States in the 1980s to victory in two presidential elections. Serving from 1981 to 1988, Reagan was hailed by many as the "great communicator," who inspired patriotism, pride and renewed national confidence particularly among big business, investors and industry. He was also widely condemned as having sacrificed the long-term economic and social good to achieve short-term gains. Despite many controversies, Ronald Reagan was a tremendously popular president—except among environmentalists.

Candidate Reagan campaigned on a promise to reduce "big government" and federal "interference" in the private sector. He saw federal environmental regulation as hobbling economic growth and criticized the Carter administration for having loaded the environmental regulatory agencies with "extremists." While campaigning, Reagan declared his intention to invite steel and oil industry representatives to rewrite the ENVIRONMENTAL PROTECTION AGENCY's regulations and even made the quite incredible claim that 80% of America's air pollution problems were caused by gases released by trees.

To the consternation and despair of environmentalists, the Reagan landslide of 1980 also pushed out of office some of the nation's leading champions of the environment, including Iowa's Senator John CULVER, one of the moving forces behind the clean-up of toxic waste dumps; Senator Gaylord NELSON of Wisconsin, one of the founders of Earth Day; Senator George MCGOVERN of South Dakota, a strong voice for the environment on the Senate Agriculture Committee; Senator John Durkin of New Hampshire, proponent of energy conservation; and Idaho's Frank CHURCH, an advocate of wilderness preservation.

During the early years of the Reagan administration, officials discussed the feasibility of selling portions of the National Park System and of reducing or eliminating federal funding for park acquisition. Secretary of Energy James Edwards discontinued and dismantled renewable-energy programs implemented during the Carter administration. Under the guise of reducing government regulation, federal environmental controls were radically reduced or compromised. Mineral leases were let at low prices on public land. The problem of acid rain was pointedly ignored. The Environmental Protection Agency, under ANNE GORSUCH BURFORD, barely administered the Superfund for toxic-waste site clean-up, and the EPA itself went into sharp decline. During Burford's tenure, from 1981 to 1983, no fewer than 20 EPA officials left the agency because of alleged misconduct. Superfund administrator Rita LAVELLE was even jailed. In addition to the EPA, the NATIONAL PARK SERVICE, the U.S. FISH AND WILDLIFE SERVICE and the Bureau of LAND MANAGEMENT endured radical budget cuts and the outright hostility of the administration.

If Anne Gorsuch Burford, placed in a role that demands an advocate for the environment, was among those in the Reagan administration most obviously opposed to environmental regulation, her policies were the rule rather than the exception. Her husband, Robert BURFORD, a Colorado legislator and rancher holding grazing permits for 33,000 acres of federal land, served as director of the Bureau of Land Management. In that capacity, he worked to maintain federal grazing subsidies and to increase industrial access to wilderness lands. John Crowell, assistant secretary of agriculture, was appointed to oversee the U.S. Forest Service. Crowell moved to increase timber sales from national forests, and when members of the SIERRA CLUB protested, he accused them of "socialism and even communism." Donald HODEL, deputy secretary of the interior (1981–82), secretary of energy (1982–85) and secretary of the interior (1985–89), promoted nuclear energy at the expense of renewable energy sources and reduced the budgets of the agencies under his control. David STOCKMAN, director of the OFFICE OF MANAGEMENT AND BUDGET, ruthlessly eliminated or weakened many environmental regulations and radically reduced funding for the EPA.

Most notorious among Reagan's anti-environmental appointees was James WATT, who served as secretary of the interior from 1981 to 1983. Watt attempted to open vast wilderness areas to oil and gas leasing and advocated a halt to the purchase of new federal park lands. He also endorsed a plan to open 1 billion acres of the outer continental shelf to oil exploration, a policy that gave rise to massive legal and congressional disputes. But it was his sheer tactlessness and anti-environmental antagonism that finally proved Watt's undoing. On the verge of a Senate-inspired movement to compel his dismissal from office, Watt resigned.

In 1988, the Sierra Club tallied up the environmental impact of the eight-year Reagan administration: In 1978, 74% of national forest recreation facilities were considered to be adequately maintained; in 1985, that figure had dropped to 29%, yet $6 billion in federal offshore-oil revenue earmarked for park acquisition and development was left unspent by the end of Reagan's second term. Between 1981 and 1984, the EPA budget was cut by 44% and its staff reduced by 29%. During President Reagan's first year in office, the number of violations of environmental laws referred to the Department of Justice declined by 69%. Ninety percent of the Office of Surface Mining's regulations were rewritten under James Watt. By 1985, in the wake of the new surface-mining regulations, 6,000 strip mines operated illegally but with seeming impunity, as the Office of Surface Mining managed to collect only 8% of the fines it assessed. In 1980, the EPA budget accounted for 1% of the total federal budget; in 1987, it accounted for .5%. For fiscal 1989, it was estimated that $100 million was needed to maintain national forest trails, yet the U.S. Forest Service 1989 budget request called for a mere $15.7 million for maintenance and nothing for new trail construction. Federal energy-conservation funding was cut by 70% during the Reagan years, and funding for the development of renewable energy sources was reduced by 85%. High-priority toxic waste dumps numbered 546 at the start of the Reagan years; in 1988, the count had risen to 1,177. During this time, the EPA had cleaned up a paltry total of 16 sites.

If the Reagan years saw an unprecedented and unremitting attack on pro-environment positions, the extremity of the assault ultimately promoted rather than discouraged environmental activism both inside and outside of government. Sierra Club membership may serve as an indicator. In 1980, its members numbered about 180,000. By 1988, membership had risen to 480,000. Public pressure forced Anne Gorsuch Burford and James Watt out of office, and a reinvigorated environmental movement successfully campaigned for the addition of some half-million acres to the National Wilderness Preservation System. During the Reagan years, 200 new plants and animals were added to the endangered species list, and the Clean Water Act, the Clean Air Act, the Resources Conservation and Recovery Act and Superfund legislation were all reauthorized or strengthened.

While Ronald Reagan remained a very popular president, the official environmental policies of his administration proved highly unpopular and were not, in fact, long tolerated. If anything, the national environmental consciousness—in marked opposition to the tenor of the administration—was raised during the Reagan years although, environmentalists warn, it will take decades to assess and repair the damage caused by eight years of abusive or neglectful policies.

Ronald Reagan, a native of Tampico, Illinois, was educated at Eureka College (B.A., 1932). Until he entered California state politics in 1964, becoming governor in 1966, he was best known as a second-tier film actor and television personality. Reagan served as California governor until 1975, when he made an unsuccessful bid for the Republican presidential nomination. He received the nomination in 1980 and won election by a wide margin. In 1984, President Reagan was reelected. Today, he is revered by the Republican party as its elder statesman.

Further reading: Joseph A. Davis, "Reagan Record Makes Environment Hot Topic," *Congressional Quarterly*, September 22, 1984; Samuel P. Hays, *Beauty, Health, and Permanence,*" Chapter 15, "The Reagan Antienvironmental Revolution," (New York: Cambridge University Press, 1989); Michael E. Kraft and Norman J. Vig, "Environmental Policy in the Reagan Presidency," *Political Science Quarterly*, fall 1984; Carl Pope, "The Politics of Plunder," *Sierra*, November/December 1988.

Reclamation, Bureau of (Established: 1907)
Department of the Interior, Washington, D.C. 20240-0001; (202) 208-4662

The Reclamation Act of 1902 authorized the secretary of the interior to administer a reclamation program to provide arid and semiarid lands of the 17 contiguous western states a secure, year-round water supply for irrigation. Pursuant to the act, the Reclamation Service was created within the U.S. GEOLOGICAL SURVEY, and in 1907 was separated from the survey as an independent service. Its name was changed from the Reclamation Service to the Bureau of Reclamation in 1923.

As the West expanded and uses of the land diversified, the mission of the Bureau of Reclamation likewise expanded from its original exclusive focus on irrigation. The bureau now provides water for farms, towns and industries, and is responsible for the generation of hydroelectric power, river regulation and flood control, outdoor recreation opportunities and the enhancement and protection of fish and wildlife habitats. Bureau functions include the development of plans for the conservation and wise use of water resources; design, construction and maintenance of authorized projects; salinity control; groundwater management; hazardous waste management; and water quality and environmental enhancement. Reclamation project facilities currently in operation include 355 storage reservoirs, 254 diversion dams, 15,855 miles of canals, 1,380 miles of pipeline, 276 miles of tunnels, 17,000 miles of project drains and 54 hydroelectric power plants.

Beginning in the late 1950s and with escalating frequency in the 1960s, 1970s and 1980s, the Bureau of Reclamation fell into frequent disputes with environmentalists and the public at large over the advisability and ecological soundness of various dams and other water projects. Most notable, perhaps, was the struggle between longtime bureau Commissioner Floyd E. DOMINY and environmentalists, including the SIERRA CLUB's David BROWER, over the Echo Park Dam to be built in Dinosaur National Monument in the early 1950s.

With the Bureau of LAND MANAGEMENT, the Bureau of Reclamation is the U.S. Department of the INTERIOR agency most deeply—and most controversially—involved in environmental issues and responsible for projects and programs with the greatest environmental impact.

The Bureau of Reclamation was headed by Commissioner Dennis B. Underwood under President George Bush. President Bill Clinton nominated Daniel Beard as Underwood's replacement.

Reed, Nathaniel Pryor (July 22, 1933–   )
Born in New York City and educated at Connecticut's Trinity College, Reed served in the U.S. Air Force before he began managing his family's real estate and hotel business in Hobe Sound, Florida, in 1960. His interest in the environment of Jupiter Island brought him to the attention of three successive Florida governors, each of whom appointed him as an environmental consultant. From 1968 to 1969, he served on the Florida Pollution Control Commission and then was the first chairman of the state's Department of Air and Water Pollution Control. In 1970, he successfully fought to enact the Florida Jetport Pact and to reject the Cross-Florida Barge Canal project, two achievements of national significance in countering environmental deterioration.

In 1971, Reed was named assistant secretary for Fish, Wildlife, and Parks of the U.S. Department of the INTERIOR, a post he held until 1977. After leaving government service, he was elected to the governing boards of several environmental groups, including the NATURAL RESOURCES DEFENSE COUNCIL, the NATIONAL AUDUBON SOCIETY and the NATURE CONSERVANCY.

Reeves, Merilyn Bronson (June 22, 1931–   )
Born in Burley, Idaho, Merilyn Bronson Reeves has worked for more than 20 years in leadership positions for nonprofit organizations. She has conducted statewide drinking-water workshops in Ohio and Washington; recycling conferences in California, New Jersey and Oregon; nuclear education conferences in Georgia and New Mexico; environmental conferences in Maryland; and workshops on surface mining, air pollution, water quality and energy supply and demand in Washington, D.C. In addition to organizing workshops and conferences, between 1980 and 1990 she worked as a member of the National Research

Council's Committee on Irrigation-Induced Water Quality Problems. She is a member of the Council for Agricultural Science and Technology's Committee on Water Quality, a member of the ENVIRONMENTAL PROTECTION AGENCY's Drinking Water Advisory Committee, a member of the Public Advisory Council of the American Water Works Association Research Foundation and a member of the office of Technology Assessment's Committee on Source Reduction.

Among the honors she has received are the 1983 Award of Achievement from the NATURAL RESOURCES COUNCIL OF AMERICA and the 1988 Donald Boyd Award from the American Metropolitan Water Association. In addition, she was named "Admiral of the Chesapeake Bay" by Maryland Governor Harry Hughes in recognition of her work on issues relating to Chesapeake Bay and the environment generally.

Reeves has written several papers and pamphlets on environmental issues. For the League of Women Voters of Maryland, she coproduced pamphlets that include *Energy Conservation: It's Good Business*, *Maryland's Coastal Areas: The Conflict—The Challenge* and *Maryland Land Use*.

Regan, Tom (Thomas Howard) (November 28, 1938–   )

Tom Regan is an ethical philosopher (according to a colleague) "working to expand our moral sensitivities beyond other humans toward a larger respect for the community of life on Earth in its myriad forms." Regan extends the moral reach of the environmental movement by emphasizing the importance of humankind's recognizing the value of all life. He deems life-threatening and life-denying not only such injustices as racism, sexism and other forms of bigotry, but also "speciesism"—the denial of rights to animals. "This arrogant humanistic tradition," he writes, "cannot be rationally defended. More than the human is morally considerable."

In his plea for animal rights, Regan runs counter to the main thrust of traditional Western thought, which has tended to divide humankind from nature. Regan seeks to create a true global, ecological community, that is, a place where a shared sense of community replaces the destructive void of individual alienation and estrangement. Saving the world, Regan argues, is not only a matter of stopping its physical pollution, but also of ending its moral pollution by looking to what he calls a "Thee Generation"—"a generation of service: of giving not taking, of commitment to principles not material possessions, of communal compassion not conspicuous consumption. If the defining question of the present generation is What can I get for me? the central

question of this new generation is What can I do for thee?"

Born in Pittsburgh, Regan was educated at Thiel College (A.B., 1960) and the University of Virginia (M.A., 1962; Ph.D., 1966). He was assistant professor of philosophy at Sweet Briar College from 1965 to 1967 and has taught at North Carolina State University since 1967. He is now University Alumni Distinguished Professor of Philosophy at that institution.

Regan's writings include *Understanding Philosophy* (1974), *Matters of Life and Death* (1980), *The Case for Animal Rights* (1983) and *The Thee Generation: Reflections on the Coming Revolution* (1991). He has contributed widely to philosophy journals. With Australian philosopher Peter SINGER, who is often credited as having "founded" the modern animal rights movement, he served as editor of *Animal Rights and Human Obligations* (1976).

Further reading: Regan, *The Case for Animal Rights* (Berkeley: University of California Press, 1983).

Reich, Charles Alan (May 20, 1928–   )

A prominent attorney and professor of law, Charles A. Reich wrote in 1970 an epoch-making analysis of the so-called youth culture of America, *The Greening of America*.

Reich's thesis in *The Greening of America* is built on three phases of consciousness he sees as constituting the cultural history of the United States: "Consciousness I," the pioneering and entrepreneurial spirit of 19th-century America; "Consciousness II," the subordination of the individual to institutional America; and "Consciousness III," which Reich saw as the informing spirit of the youth generation just coming of age in the late sixties. The new generation, according to Reich, emphasized personal growth rather than institutional conformity, spiritual values rather than materialism and a sense of community rather than alienation, and Consciousness III further entailed a new and all-encompassing respect for the environment.

Indeed, Reich reported in an interview with the editors of *Contemporary Authors* that his own social consciousness was first awakened by the issue of "conservation." Reich recalls that his "family used to go up to the Adirondacks in New York State in the summer. I went there since I was a very small child. . . . even when I was a youngster I was able to recognize the deterioration of the environment. . . . By the time I was 12 or 13, I was already a very ardent environmentalist."

Most environmentalists of the 1970s found *The Greening of America* spiritually and politically encouraging, although many other social thinkers criticized its absolute faith in youth culture as a particularly naive form of messianic longing.

Educated at Oberlin College (B.A., 1949) and Yale University (LL.B., 1952), Reich was admitted to the New York bar in 1952, the bar of the District of Columbia in 1954 and the bar of the U.S. Supreme Court in 1958. He was in private practice until 1960 (from 1955 to 1960, with the prestigious Washington firm of Arnold, Fortas and Porter) and left to teach law at Yale University. He resigned his Yale professorship in 1974 to commence the full-time study of social change.

In addition to *The Greening of America*, Reich is the author of many public affairs articles in popular magazines and law journals and has written an autobiography, *The Sorcerer of Bolinas Reef* (1976).

Further reading: Reich, *The Greening of America* (New York: Random House, 1970).

Reid, Kenneth Alexander (April 14, 1895–May 21, 1956)

Born in Connellsville, Pennsylvania, and educated at Phillips Andover and at Yale University (Ph.B., 1917),

Kenneth Alexander Reid entered the U.S. Army Air Service in World War I and served as a flight instructor. After the war, he became a sales executive, but in the late 1920s he also joined the IZAAK WALTON LEAGUE OF AMERICA, becoming its executive director in 1938 and serving in that capacity until 1949. Under Reid's leadership, the league became a major force in influencing the management of national forests and other federal lands.

The essence of Reid's philosophy was the supremacy of the right of the public and of the federal government in matters relating to public lands. He declared: "No use shall be made . . . that will establish any right superior to that of the public or the Government." Unintimidated by the interests of the timber and mineral industries, livestock raisers and hunters and fishermen, Reid led the league in a 14-year battle that resulted in the passage of the Water Pollution Control Act of 1948.

Reid successfully fought many attempts to co-opt federally protected lands and was notably successful in his efforts to combat a move to abolish Jackson Hole National Monument. In recognition of his con-

The Teton Range, Grand Teton National Park. *U.S. Department of the Interior, National Park Service photo by George A. Grant*

William K. Reilly, former administrator of the U.S. Environmental Protection Agency. *Courtesy of S. C. Delaney/U.S. EPA*

tributions to wilderness preservation, the NATIONAL PARK SERVICE named Mount Reid, in Grand Teton National Park, in his honor.

Reid also was a cofounder of the NATURAL RESOURCES COUNCIL OF AMERICA. Crippled by a stroke in 1948, Reid stepped down the next year as director of the Izaak Walton League, but continued his work in forest preservation by developing policies for the C. V. Whitney lands in the Adirondacks.

Reilly, William Kane (January 26, 1940–   )

President George Bush's appointment of William Kane Reilly as administrator of the ENVIRONMENTAL PROTECTION AGENCY pleased environmentalists across the country. Reilly had a long record of professional work and commitment to environmental issues, and he was the first professional environmentalist appointed to head the EPA since its founding in 1970.

Reilly, a native of Decatur, Illinois, had been named associate director of the Urban Policy Center for Urban Americans in Washington, D.C., in 1969. After working for the National Urban Coalition, he was senior staff member of President Richard Nixon's COUNCIL ON ENVIRONMENTAL QUALITY from 1970 to 1972. He next directed the Rockefeller Brothers Fund Task Force on Land Use and Urban Growth and was

the principal author of *The Use of Land: A Citizens' Guide to Urban Growth*, the group's final report. In 1973, Reilly became president of the CONSERVATION FOUNDATION in Washington, D.C., and engineered a 1985 merger with the WORLD WILDLIFE FUND, serving as its president since then. The WWF, an international organization focusing specifically on the preservation of tropical rainforests, grew under Reilly's leadership to 600,000 members, 200 staff members and an annual budget of $35 million.

In his role as president of the WWF and the Conservation Foundation, Reilly took to task President Ronald REAGAN's lack of concern with environmental issues. He called the first half of the 1980s "a time of retrenchment" on environmental initiatives and blasted the Reagan administration for its lack of commitment to the national parks. He also faulted the administration for decreasing appropriations for the EPA, cutbacks that allowed thousands of toxic substances to go unmonitored and unregulated in the air and water.

In October 1986, speaking at the National Agricultural Forum in Arlington, Virginia, Reilly said that industry and commercial developers were not the only polluters of the environment. To these he added the family farmer. In a report entitled "Agriculture and the Environment in a Changing World Economy," issued by the Conservation Foundation that month, Reilly called the use of land in the United States and Europe "inefficient" and the goal to overproduce "dangerous." Farmers, he said, tended to add too many chemicals to their soil in order to produce crops that governments bought on subsidies.

At the Conservation Foundation and at the World Wildlife Fund, Reilly has drawn on the expertise of other conservation organizations and has involved individuals whose businesses have often been charged with causing environmental problems. In July 1987, for example, the Conservation Foundation gathered a group of environmentalists, developers, industrialists and federal regulators to study over a 16-month period the loss of wetlands in America. The World Wildlife Fund called on Third World government officials and members of the American banking community to develop an innovative "debt-for-nature swap," a plan by which the governments pledge to protect endangered resources in exchange for the banks assuming their debts.

As head of the EPA, Reilly has committed himself and his agency to finding solutions to acid rain pollution, toxic waste disposal, global warming and wetlands protection and has attempted to initiate "vigorous and aggressive enforcement of the environmental law," as he had promised during his confirmation hearings before Congress. In an interview in February 1989, Reilly labeled toxic waste clean-up his top priority. The next month he announced a plan to slow the advance of the greenhouse effect due to carbon dioxide pollution. The plan called for an international agreement among automobile manufacturers to produce new cars that get 40 miles to a gallon of gasoline and employ catalytic converters. It also recommended increased research on alternate forms of energy, a major reforestation project and a ban on all chlorofluorocarbons.

In the field of scenic and wildlife preservation, Reilly turned the EPA against a project to build the Two Forks Dam on the South Platte River in Colorado. Although the project had already been approved by the regional office of the EPA, Reilly overruled that approval to the delight of environmentalists, who claimed that the dam would flood a scenic canyon, alter migration patterns of wildlife and pollute a trout stream.

Reilly's next target was in Alaska, where the worst oil spill in North American history occurred as a result of the 1989 Exxon *Valdez* tanker accident. Reilly and Secretary of Transportation Samuel K. Skinner reported to the president that the response of the federal government and the oil industry was inadequate and that specific plans should be laid for handling future disasters.

Throughout his leadership of the EPA, Reilly claimed greater access to the office of the president than any of his predecessors. He attended cabinet meetings, regularly conferred with the president at Camp David and accompanied him to the July 1989 Paris economic summit.

Reilly stepped down as EPA head after the inauguration of President Bill Clinton, who named Carol Browner to the post. Reilly is now senior fellow at the World Wildlife Fund.

Renew America (Founded: 1986)
1400 16th Street NW, Suite 710, Washington, D.C. 20036; (202) 232-2252

The 6,000 members of Renew America are working toward the goal of achieving a sustainable future and a healthy, safe environment by promoting a variety of environmental programs, including alternative energy source and solar energy research and information gathering.

The group coordinates the Searching for Success environmental awards program, which recognizes positive environmental achievements, and operates the Environmental Success Index, a clearinghouse of more than 1,200 working environmental projects available to civic groups, community organizations, the media, business, policy makers and individuals.

Directed by Tina C. Hobson, executive director, Renew America publishes the quarterly *Renew America Report*, the annual *State of the States* (which analyzes state environmental programs and policies) and such publications as *Environmental Success Index, Reducing the Rate of Global Warming: The States' Role, Communities at Risk: Environmental Dangers in Rural America* and *Sustaining Energy*.

Resources for the Future (Founded: 1952)
1616 P Street NW, Washington, D.C. 20036; (202) 328-5000

Founded under the sponsorship of the Ford Foundation, Resources for the Future is a private, nonprofit organization dedicated to natural resource research and education. Focusing specifically on the relationship of human beings to the natural environment, the organization publishes a triannual journal entitled *Resources*.

Beginning in 1977, Resources for the Future turned its attention to forest policy and fostered cooperation among the SOCIETY OF AMERICAN FORESTERS, the American Forestry Association (now AMERICAN FORESTS), the U.S. FOREST SERVICE and several timber companies. With funding from the Ford Foundation, the U.S. Forest Service and the Weyerhaeuser Company Foundation, the group has published several books and reports and has sponsored conferences on forest economics and policy.

Further reading: Resources for the Future, *The First 25 Years, 1952–1977* (Washington, D.C.: Resources for the Future, 1977).

Ridenour, James M. (January 1, 1942–   )
James M. Ridenour was director of the NATIONAL PARK SERVICE, a bureau of the U.S. Department of the INTERIOR, under President George Bush. Sworn into office in April 1989, Ridenour oversaw the 359 units of the National Park System, which includes national parks, historical parks and sites, recreation areas and many auxiliary parks, trails and other federally protected natural and cultural resource areas throughout the United States. The director heads a park service staff of more than 12,000 permanent employees.

Raised in Wabash, Indiana, Ridenour earned bachelor's (1964) and master's degrees (1965) in parks and recreation from Indiana University, then completed another master's degree in public administration at the University of Colorado (1972). Ridenour served in the U.S. Army from 1966 to 1969, commanding medical companies in Denver, Colorado, and in Viet-

Former National Park Service director James M. Ridenour with Ann Castellana, superintendant of Kenai Fjords National Park, Alaska, after the *Exxon Valdez* oil spill, 1990. *Courtesy of the National Park Service*

nam and directing the Welfare and Recreation Branch of Pennsylvania's Valley Forge General Hospital.

From 1975 to 1978, he was director of state services for the Council of State Governments. He moved to the Great Lakes Chemical Corporation of West Lafayette, Indiana, in 1978, where he was director of administration until 1981. In 1981 he was appointed director of the Indiana Department of Natural Resources and was responsible for managing the state's parks, forests, reservoirs, fish and wildlife areas, museums, memorials and historic sites. One of his initiatives was a Natural Heritage Protection Campaign, a program in which the state matched funds raised by private conservation organizations to preserve 45 parcels of wetlands and other critical wildlife habitats. During his years with the Indiana DNR, Ridenour also worked as research program coordinator with the Purdue University Natural Resources Research Institute in West Lafayette. In 1983, President Reagan appointed Ridenour to the International Great Lakes Fishery Commission, and during his participation, the Indiana administrator became chairman of the commission, serving from 1985 to 1986.

After taking office, Ridenour frequently emphasized the value of gathering data and creating geographical information systems for park service holdings so that management decisions would be "more soundly based on scientific evidence." He stepped down on January 20, 1993, upon the inauguration of President Bill Clinton, and was replaced by Acting Director Herbert Cables. Ridenour now directs the Eppley Institute at Indiana University, Department of Recreation and Park Administration.

Rifkin, Jeremy (January 26, 1945–   )

A vocal opponent of the biotechnical industry's attempts to use recombinant DNA, Denver-born Jeremy Rifkin has organized demonstrations and mounted public support in a campaign against genetic engineering. As head of the Foundation on Economic Trends, he has initiated lawsuits against individuals and corporations that experiment with DNA, claiming that they are threatening life itself.

Rifkin graduated from the University of Pennsylvania with a B.A. in economics and went on to receive a master's degree in international affairs from the Fletcher School of Law and Diplomacy. It was Rifkin who organized the first nationwide protest against the Vietnam War in 1967. He next worked for the Volunteers in Service to America (VISTA) in Harlem and then moved to Washington, D.C., in 1971, where he founded the People's Bicentennial Commission as a response to what he saw as frivolous activities being planned to celebrate the nation's bicentennial. His group protested against large corporations and demanded a redistribution of wealth in America. During his work on the commission, he assembled an anthology entitled *How to Commit Revolution American Style* and wrote *Common Sense II: The Case Against Corporate Tyranny.*

After the bicentennial, Rifkin remained in Washington and started the Foundation on Economic Trends. In his 1977 *Who Should Play God? The Artificial Creation of Life and What It Means for the Future of the Human Race*, he envisioned a time when human beings would control and exploit the genetic composition of life forms through cloning, selective breeding and gene transfers.

Rifkin has published widely on the problems inherent in Western notions of "progress." In *Entropy: A New World View*, written in 1980 with Ted Howard, he argued that the technologies of Western civilization are depleting the planet's energy sources and that humankind must begin to equate progress with the conservation of resources and the protection of the environment rather than with the outdated notion of mastery over the universe. In *Algeny* (1983), written with Nicanor Perlas, he envisioned a time in which parents will be able to design the genetic composition of their children. In his 1987 *Time Wars: The Primary Conflict in Human History*, Rifkin claimed that the increasingly fast pace of modern life contributes to the depletion of resources and adds an enormous burden of stress to daily life. "We have reached a point at which we are producing and consuming at such an accelerated rate that nature can't possibly recycle and replenish at the pace we're demanding," he concluded.

Rifkin has not limited his protests against biotechnology to writing. In the early 1980s, he brought suit against the National Institutes of Health and the University of California, Berkeley. The university had developed a type of bacteria that deterred the formation of frost on potatoes, and Rifkin and his supporters sought to prevent the university from field testing it. In addition, they demanded that university researchers file an environmental impact statement before field testing any new life forms and that the ENVIRONMENTAL PROTECTION AGENCY be empowered to regulate such research.

In 1983, Rifkin tackled the problems he saw in human genetic engineering. He believed that once scientists started destroying or altering the genes that caused sickle cell anemia and cancer, they would expand their work to other "disorders," such as "myopia, color blindness, and left-handedness." Rifkin gathered support for his arguments from religious leaders across the country, and, together, more than 60 leaders submitted to Congress the "Theological Letter Concerning the Moral Arguments Against Genetic Engineering of the Human Germline Cells."

Rifkin next took on the Department of Defense, which in 1986 was planning to build a biological weapons laboratory. He protested against the military's use of genetic engineering to create weapon viruses that, according to Rifkin, might bring about a disaster on the scale of a nuclear holocaust. He established a "Whistleblowers Fund" to provide financial support to scientists or military personnel who disclosed information about the testing of biological weapons.

In 1987, Rifkin created a coalition to oppose the government's decision to issue patents for new animal species created by gene splicing. In addition, he opposed surrogate parenthood and formed the National Coalition Against Surrogacy.

Rockefeller, John Davison, Jr. (January 29, 1874–May 11, 1960)

An heir to one of the nation's most substantial fortunes, Cleveland-born John Davison Rockefeller Jr. drew on his resources to conduct a 23-year campaign to stop the commercialization of Jackson Hole, Wyoming, a battle that equals in importance his project to restore and recreate Colonial Williamsburg in Virginia.

His work at Jackson Hole began in 1926 when he visited the area with Horace M. ALBRIGHT, then superintendent of Yellowstone National Park. Rockefeller started buying privately owned land in the area in order to donate it to the NATIONAL PARK SERVICE,

thus preserving a "frame" around the Grand Teton National Park, founded in 1929, and provide a winter home for the Yellowstone elk population. Over the next 20 years, Rockefeller and conservationists waged a constant battle with farmers, ranchers and various commercial concerns, a contest that culminated in the addition of Jackson Hole to the Grand Teton National Park in 1950.

In addition to his efforts to preserve Jackson Hole, Rockefeller contributed nearly half the money needed to purchase the land forming the Great Smoky Mountain National Park and funds to purchase groves of redwoods along the coast of California. In all, by the time of his death he had donated almost $75 million to historic and scenic preservation causes.

Further reading: Alan Axelrod (ed.), *The Colonial Revival in America* (New York: Norton, 1985); Nancy Newhall (ed.), *A Contribution to the Heritage of Every American: The Conservation Activities of John D. Rockefeller, Jr.* (New York: Knopf, 1957).

Rockefeller, John Davison, IV (Jay) (June 18, 1937–   )

New York-born governor of West Virginia from 1976 to 1984 and senator from that state since 1985, John Davison Rockefeller IV has taken an active role in environmental issues. As governor, he pushed for major clean-up programs in areas ravaged by surface mining. He secured passage of the West Virginia National Interest Rivers Conservation Act, which protects portions of the Gauley, Bluestone and Meadow rivers. He has spearheaded a program in West Virginia to promote safe waste disposal. In the Senate, he successfully fought against programs proposed by President Ronald Reagan that would have threatened New River Gorge and other national parks and forests. Rockefeller has also cosponsored other bills dealing with solid waste, clean water and safe drinking water. In 1990, he received a perfect rating of 100 from the LEAGUE OF CONSERVATION VOTERS.

Rockefeller, Laurance Spelman (May 26, 1910–   )

The third son of John Davison ROCKEFELLER Jr., Laurance Spelman Rockefeller first became active in scenic preservation as trustee and president of the Jackson Hole Preserve Inc., a nonprofit organization created by his father to administer the family's charitable donations to natural preservation causes. Through this organization, the younger Rockefeller purchased land on St. John Island in the Virgin Islands and gave it to the NATIONAL PARK SERVICE, which in 1954 dedicated Virgin Islands National Park.

In 1958, Rockefeller accepted the chairmanship of the Outdoor Recreation Resources Review Commission, an organization created by President Dwight D. Eisenhower to study the country's need for parks and wilderness regions. During President Lyndon B. JOHNSON's administration, Rockefeller served on the White House Conference on Natural Beauty.

In May 1990, President George Bush signed legislation authorizing the creation of a congressional gold medal to honor Rockefeller for his contributions to the nation's parks.

Further reading: Peter Collier and David Horowitz, *The Rockefellers: An American Dynasty* (New York: Henry Holt & Co., 1976).

Rodale, Robert (David) (March 27, 1930–September 20, 1990)

Head of the family-owned Rodale Press, which his father founded in 1942 in Emmaus, Pennsylvania, Robert Rodale began his career at Rodale as a magazine editor and later became the company's chief executive officer and chairman of the board. Under his leadership, Rodale published such environmentally relevant popular magazines as *Organic Gardening and Farming*, *The New Farmer* and *Prevention*. Rodale also published *Compost Science*, a journal begun in 1960, and *Environment Action Bulletin*.

Robert Rodale was a strong advocate of an organic farming method he called "regenerative agriculture." He was the author of *The Challenge of Earthworm Research* (1961), *The Basic Book of Organic Gardening* (1971), *Sane Living in a Mad World* (1972) and *The Best Health Ideas I Know* (1974), and wrote a nationally syndicated newspaper column called "Organic Living."

Rodale served as vice-president of the Lehigh Valley Land Conservancy and was a member of the board of directors of the Trexlertown Playground Association. He was a member of the American Association for the Advancement of Science, the SIERRA CLUB, the NATIONAL AUDUBON SOCIETY and the Pennsylvania Association for the Advancement of Science. A champion skeet shooter, Rodale was a member of the National Rifle Association and the National Skeet Shooting Association. Rodale was killed in an automobile accident in Moscow, while on a business trip to launch a Russian-language edition of *The New Farmer*.

Roosevelt, Franklin Delano (January 30, 1882–April 12, 1945)

As president of the United States from 1933 to 1945, Franklin D. Roosevelt supervised the creation of myriad federal conservation programs. The CIVILIAN CONSERVATION CORPS (CCC) hired more than 3 million young men to work in national forests and parks and financed the purchase of 8 million acres of land for the national forest system. In addition, the CCC and other federal agencies sponsored the shelterbelt project, which resulted in the planting of millions of trees as windbreaks on the Dust Bowl-ravaged Great Plains. During Roosevelt's administration, the NATIONAL PARK SERVICE added Olympic and King Canyon national parks and the Jackson Hole National Monument. The Bureau of RECLAMATION was authorized to build water conservation and hydroelectric power plants, chief among them the Grand Coulee Dam in Washington and the Central Valley Project in California. The TENNESSEE VALLEY AUTHORITY oversaw resources planning for an entire river basin. The SOIL CONSERVATION SERVICE, established in 1935, took dramatic steps to educate the public on the importance of curbing soil erosion, especially in the Dust Bowl region.

Many of Roosevelt's policies on conservation were carried out by Secretary of the Interior Harold ICKES, a strong conservationist and an able administrator.

Further reading: Edgar B. Nixon (ed.), *Franklin D. Roosevelt and Conservation, 1911–1945* (Hyde Park, N.Y.: Franklin D. Roosevelt Library, 1957).

Roosevelt, Theodore (October 27, 1858–January 6, 1919)

Perhaps the greatest achievments of the administration of the 25th president of the United States, Theodore Roosevelt, were innovations and advancements in natural resource conservation.

Born to a wealthy New York City banking family, Roosevelt traveled extensively as a young man and soon developed an avid interest in natural history. In 1880, he graduated from Harvard University and then studied law at Columbia University Law School. Between 1882 and 1898, Roosevelt served as an assemblyman in New York's legislature, ranched in the Dakota Territory, wrote several works of popular history, was a member of the U.S. Civil Service Commission, president of the Board of Police Commissioners of New York City and assistant secretary of the Navy. During the war against Spain, he was in active service as colonel of his celebrated Rough Rider regiment (officially the 1st U.S. Volunteer Cavalry) and returned home a hero.

Roosevelt was elected governor of New York in 1898. President William McKinley selected Roosevelt as his running mate in the president's bid for reelection in 1900, and when McKinley was assassinated the following year, Roosevelt became president. It was during his second term in office that Roosevelt extended the concept of conservation to include coal and mineral lands, oil reserves and power sites. He added nearly 150 million acres of land to national reserves, over the protests of ranchers, mine companies, the timber industry and power companies, all of which had become accustomed to using land in the public domain at will and for their own gain.

National parks benefited from Roosevelt's support as well. During his administrations, Crater Lake National Park and Mesa Verde National Park were added to the system. Roosevelt supported the Antiquities Act of 1906, a law that allowed him to name many scenic areas national monuments. Those so designated included the Grand Canyon in Arizona and the Natural Bridges in Utah. The Reclamation Act of 1902 provided for the irrigation of desert lands and the production of hydroelectric power. About 3 million acres of western desert were included in the irrigation projects, which were transferred to the Reclamation Service of the Department of the Interior in 1907. Roosevelt also promoted the creation of wildlife refuges, the first to be established in the nation.

Further reading: Paul Russell Cutright, *Theodore Roosevelt, the Naturalist* (New York: Harper, 1956); Samuel Hays, *Conservation and the Gospel of Efficiency* (Cambridge: Harvard

Theodore Roosevelt with John Muir at Yosemite. *Courtesy of the National Wildlife Federation.*

President Theodore Roosevelt at Mammoth Cave National Park, Kentucky, April 1903. *U.S. Department of the Interior photo, courtesy of the National Park Service*

convened the American Forest Congress to examine current preservation efforts. The conference culminated in the transfer of federal forest preserves from the U.S. Department of the INTERIOR to the U.S. Department of AGRICULTURE. But forests were not the only resource that Roosevelt wanted to preserve. He

University Press, 1959); George E. Mowry, *The Era of Theodore Roosevelt, 1900–1912* (New York: Harper & Brothers, 1958); Henry F. Pringle, *Theodore Roosevelt* (New York: Harcourt, Brace, 1931); Elmo R. Richardson, *The Politics of Conservation: Crusades and Controversies, 1897–1913* (Berkeley: University of California Press, 1962); Roosevelt, *Autobiography* (New York: Macmillan, 1913).

Rothrock, Joseph Trimble (April 9, 1839–June 2, 1922)

Called the "father of Pennsylvania forestry," Joseph Trimble Rothrock was a student of Asa GRAY at the Lawrence Scientific School of Harvard University. The Civil War interrupted his education (Rothrock was wounded at Fredericksburg), but he received his B.S. in 1864 and went on to earn an M.D. from the University of Pennsylvania in 1867.

Rothrock taught botany from 1867 to 1869 at the Pennsylvania State Agricultural College, then practiced medicine in Wilkes-Barre, Pennsylvania, until 1873, when he served two years as surgeon and botanist for the U.S. GEOLOGICAL SURVEY's expedition west of the 100th meridian. Rothrock wrote the survey's *Catalog of Plants* (1878).

In 1877, Rothrock was named professor of botany on the auxiliary faculty of medicine at the University of Pennsylvania (he served in this capacity until 1904) and Michaux lecturer in forestry under the auspices of the American Philosophical Society in Philadelphia. He traveled to Germany for botanical study in 1880, observing in particular that nation's advanced forestry techniques. Returning to the United States, he wrote a prize-winning essay, "Forestry in Europe and America," and was offered a chair in botany at Harvard. However, Rothrock chose to remain in his native Pennsylvania (he was born in McVeytown), lecturing on professional forestry techniques.

In 1886, Rothrock became the first president of the Pennsylvania Forestry Association, from which position he continued to broadcast the virtues of scientific forestry, using the pages of the association's magazine, *Forest Leaves* (later called *Pennsylvania Forests*). Rothrock was the principal author of the report of a commission on forestry authorized by the Pennsylvania legislature in 1893. The report, issued in 1895, was the first complete information on the state's forest depletion and prompted the state legislature to create a Department of Agriculture that included a Division of Forestry. Rothrock became the state's first commissioner of forestry in 1895, holding this position until 1905. Under his leadership, state forest land was expanded to a total of 443,500 acres, and Rothrock introduced many measures to bring the state's forestry practices up to professional European standards.

Rothrock's *Areas of Desolation in Pennsylvania* (1915) was effective in alerting the public to the urgent need for water and forest conservation. The SOCIETY OF AMERICAN FORESTERS made him an honorary member in 1915.

Royal Society for Nature Conservation, Wildlife Trusts Partnership (Founded: 1912)

The Green, Witham Park, Waterside South, Lincs LN5 7JR, England; (522) 544400

The wildlife trusts of the Royal Society for Nature Conservation boast more than 200,000 members. The organization monitors nature reserves in order to protect threatened wildlife and conducts research on conservation management techniques, advises government departments and produces a national catalog of wildlife sites. Its publications include *Annual Report and Accounts, Annual Review, Natural World* and *Watchword*. T. S. Cordy is chief executive.

Ruckelshaus, William Doyle (July 24, 1932–   )

The first administrator of the ENVIRONMENTAL PROTECTION AGENCY, William Doyle Ruckelshaus is currently chairman and chief executive officer of Browning-Ferris Industries, a Houston-based waste disposal service company which has developed innovative recycling programs.

After serving as EPA's first administrator from 1970 to 1973, Ruckelshaus returned to that agency for a second term, heading it from 1983 to 1985, after ANNE BURFORD had been forced to resign over allegations of conflict of interest and misuse of the toxic waste clean-up "Superfund." Ruckelshaus pledged to return the agency to its proper mission, and during his second term of office, the EPA devoted its resources primarily to cleaning up toxic waste dumps, protecting groundwater from chemical spills and banning the pesticide ethylene dibromide (EDB). Despite these efforts, Ruckelshaus noted in a 1984 article for *Maclean's* magazine his disappointment over the EPA's failure to curb acid rain significantly.

A native of Indianapolis, Ruckelshaus holds a B.A. from Princeton University and an LL.B. from Harvard. In addition to heading the Environmental Protection Agency, he was assistant attorney general in charge of the civil division of the Department of Justice from 1969 to 1970, acting director of the FBI in 1973 and deputy attorney general for one month in 1973. President Nixon removed him from that position for refusing to fire Watergate special prosecutor Archibald Cox.

Runte, Alfred (April 16, 1947–   )

Born in Binghamton, New York, Alfred Runte is an environmental historian. Since 1980, he has taught history at the University of Washington, Seattle. His books include *National Parks: The American Experience* (1987), which documents the growth of the national park system in the United States and the shift in the thought of park advocates from saving land for its beauty to saving it for ecological purposes. In addition, he has written *Trains of Discovery: Western Railroads and the National Parks* (1984) and *Yosemite: The Embattled Wilderness* (1990). In 1978, he was awarded the Frederick K. Weyerhaeuser Award by the *Journal of Forest History* for his article "The National Park Idea: Origins and Paradox of the American Experience." He has contributed articles to *American West*, *Conservationist* and *Pacific Northwest Quarterly* in addition to the *Journal of Forest History*.

S

Sale, (J.) Kirkpatrick (June 27, 1937–   )
This radical environmentalist is best known for his 1980 book *Human Scale,* an analysis of the effects of large-scale technology and urbanization on human beings and the environment. As a result of urbanization, overcrowding and massive technology, Sale argues, people have lost touch with their instincts and are therefore out of harmony with themselves and with the natural environment. To solve this problem of civilization, he proposes the radical step of dismantling many of the trappings and artifacts of contemporary life in a return to the smaller and more humanly scaled social systems of the past, systems "rooted" in local circumstances and guided by local conditions.

In his *Dwellers in the Land: The Bioregional Vision* of 1985, Sale takes the notion of human scale even further. Bioregionalism is an ecological philosophy maintaining that people should live on resources obtained exclusively within their geographic regions. That is, for example, only people living in areas that produce citrus fruit would consume orange juice. Sale holds that the earth's ecological crisis began when humankind viewed the natural world as something to be controlled, exploited, transported and used up for human purposes. Returning to bioregionalism would be a return to roots and, therefore, a radical step toward repairing the planet's ecology.

Sale's revisionist account of the European discovery of America, *The Conquest of Paradise: Christopher Columbus and the Columbian Legacy* (1991), is also, at base, a work of ecology. Sale portrays Columbus as a greedy and embittered man, the product of a rapacious age and people, who simply seizes what he wants. In a larger sense, Columbus is a representative man of the modern age itself, thoughtless and

heedless. He attacks and enslaves the Indians, who, in contrast to himself, live in harmony with nature and within their bioregion.

Sale has also written *The Land and People of Ghana* (1963; revised edition, 1972) and *SDS,* a book about the radical student political organization (1972). A native of Ithaca, New York, he attended Swarthmore College from 1954 to 1955 and received his B.A. from Cornell University in 1958. He was associate editor of the *New Leader* from 1959 to 1961, and he served as foreign correspondent for the *San Francisco Chronicle* and the *Chicago Tribune* in 1961–62. Sale was a lecturer in history at the University of Ghana from 1963 to 1965 and a *New York Times Magazine* editor from 1965 to 1968.

Sale has been active in various political and social organizations, including Project Work, School for Living and Association for Workplace Democracy. He is a member of the P.E.N. American Center.

Salyer, John Clark II (August 16, 1902–August 15, 1966)
A native of the small town of Higgensville, Missouri, John Clark Salyer II began working in 1934 at the U.S. Bureau of BIOLOGICAL SURVEY of the U.S. Department of AGRICULTURE (the predecessor of the Bureau of Sport Fisheries and Wildlife of the U.S. Department of the Interior). Later he directed the Division of Wildlife Refuges, and until 1961, when he retired, he supervised the acquisition of 27.5 million acres of wildlife preserves. Frequently referred to as a "father of the National Wildlife Refuge System," Salyer was honored with the American Motors Conservation Award in 1956 and the Distinguished Service award of the U.S. Department of the Interior in 1962.

Sampson, R(obert) Neil (November 29, 1938–)

Executive vice-president of AMERICAN FORESTS (formerly American Forestry Association) since 1985, R. Neil Sampson, born in Spokane, Washington, started his career in ecology as a soil conservationist with the U.S. SOIL CONSERVATION SERVICE in Idaho. In 1974, he moved to the Washington, D.C., office, where he served as acting director of the Environmental Services Division and worked on land use strategies. From 1978 to 1984, he directed research on soil and water conservation as the executive vice-president of the National Association of Conservation Districts.

At American Forests, Sampson directs a nationwide program called "Global ReLeaf." With a declared goal of planting 100 million trees around homes and businesses by 1992, the program has engaged garden clubs, community associations, city councils and Audubon chapters in its work, which currently consists of more than 1,000 local programs. (No one has actually counted the number of trees planted as a result of the program.)

In 1988, Sampson and American Forests convened a conference called "Natural Resources for the 21st Century," which resulted in the publication of a book by the same name, edited by Sampson and Dwight Hair (1990). This anthology of conference papers develops a holistic approach to environmental problems and stresses the close relationship of world economies and natural resources management.

Sampson's other publications include a 24-minute film entitled *Look to the Land* (1973) and two other books, *Farmland or Wasteland: A Time to Choose* (1981), named Best Book of 1982 by the NATURAL RESOURCES COUNCIL OF AMERICA), and *For Love of the Land* (1985).

Sargent, Charles Sprague (April 24, 1841– March 22, 1927)

A Boston-born Harvard graduate and Civil War staff officer, Charles Sprague Sargent began developing his interest in horticulture and agriculture while traveling in Europe after the war. In 1873, Sprague was named director of the Botanic Garden at Harvard University and the Arnold Arboretum in Jamaica Plain, Massachusetts. At the arboretum, which he designed with Frederick Law OLMSTED Sr., Sargent gathered around him a team of botanists and developed the institution into a leading center for the study of trees.

In 1880, Sargent used his firsthand knowledge to prepare the section on forests for the 10th U.S. Census. His study, *Report on the Forests of North America* (1884), included data on more than 400 species and

Cheatham Grove, Grizzly Creek Redwoods State Park. *Photo by David Swanlund, courtesy of the Save-the-Redwoods League*

soon became a standard reference. While working on his census report, he actively lobbied the New York State legislature in an attempt to persuade the government to maintain the forests and watersheds of the Adirondacks. His efforts led to the establishment of the Adirondack Forest Preserve in 1885. During the early 1880s, he also prepared a forest exhibit for the American Museum of Natural History, and from 1887 to 1897, he edited a popular weekly publication entitled *Garden and Forest* devoted to taxonomy, geology, ecology, agriculture and horticulture.

Silva of North America (1891–1902), a 14-volume reference work, and *Manual of the Trees of North America* (1905) further established Sargent's reputation as a leading scholar of trees.

Save-the-Redwoods League (Founded: 1918)
114 Sansome Street, Room 605, San Francisco, California 94104; (415) 362-2352

The 45,000 members of the Save-the-Redwoods League work primarily in California to preserve stands of redwoods along the coast and in the Sierra Nevada Mountains. The league has enjoyed many successes since its founding in 1918. Among its early accomplishments was securing state legislation to create the California State Park Commission in 1927 and the California State Park Bonds program in 1928. Until the 1960s, the league devoted most of its resources to purchasing first-growth redwood lands from private owners and establishing and expanding the Jedediah Smith, Del Norte Coast, Prairie Creek, Humboldt and Big Basin state parks. In addition, it contributed funds for the purchase of cypress groves at Point Lobos, Monterey, and sequoia stands in North Calaveras.

In more recent years, the league has cooperated with the SIERRA CLUB to expand Redwood National Park and has added to the California state parks system thousands of acres of land, including a 3,000-acre expansion of the Sinkyone Wilderness State Park in 1986.

Save the Whales (Founded: 1971)
P. O. Box 3650, Washington, D.C. 20007; (202) 337-2332

With a membership of 8,000, Save the Whales works to preserve great whales from extinction and to promote the regeneration of whale populations. The organization campaigns against commercial whaling through public service announcements and print-media advertising and through the publication of leaflets, brochures, posters and books, including *Whales vs. Whalers*. Christine STEVENS is president of Save the Whales, which is a special project of the ANIMAL WELFARE INSTITUTE.

Sawhill, John Crittenden (June 12, 1936–   )
The president and chief executive officer of the NATURE CONSERVANCY, John C. Sawhill is a former federal energy administrator and a past president of New York University.

Born in Cleveland, Ohio, and raised in Baltimore, Sawhill studied at Princeton University's Woodrow Wilson School of Public and International Affairs, graduating with a bachelor's degree, cum laude, in 1958. Sawhill worked on Wall Street from 1958 to 1960, then entered New York University's Graduate School of Business Administration, where he earned a Ph.D. in economics, finance and statistics (1963).

Sawhill had held various distinguished positions in the financial community when, in April 1973, the Nixon administration asked him to join the OFFICE OF MANAGEMENT AND BUDGET as one of four associate directors, with particular responsibility for matters of energy, science and natural resources. Within months, the Arab oil embargo made energy policy a front-page issue, and Sawhill was appointed deputy director (under administrator William E. Simon) of the newly established Federal Energy Office. When Simon was made Treasury secretary in 1974, Sawhill succeeded him as head of the FEO, an office further enlarged and empowered, a few months later, in its executive-ordered conversion to the Federal Energy

Nature Conservancy president John C. Sawhill. *Courtesy of the Nature Conservancy*

Administration. In his role as FEA chief, Sawhill was a strong and plain-spoken proponent of a new, nationwide ethic of energy conservation, urging citizens and industry alike to significantly cut fuel consumption or accept compulsory conservation measures. At the same time, he was responsible for creating a blueprint for "Project Independence," a government policy program designed to vastly increase domestic energy production and reduce the nation's dependency on foreign suppliers.

In 1974, Sawhill left government, and in April 1975, he accepted the presidency of New York University.

During the Carter administration, Sawhill was called back to Washington as deputy secretary of the Department of Energy, then in 1980 he joined the United States Synthetic Fuels Corporation as chairman and chief executive officer. In 1981, he returned to McKinsey and Company as its director. He headed the firm's energy-consulting practice, inaugurated its energy research group and directed strategic planning studies for industrial and governmental clients in the U.S., Europe and Latin America, and in 1986, New York Governor Mario Cuomo appointed Sawhill to chair a blue-ribbon task force evaluating options for the financially beleaguered Long Island Lighting Company. In 1990, Sawhill accepted his current position with the Nature Conservancy, an international organization that owns and manages the largest private nature preserve system in the world, comprising over 5 million acres in the Americas and the Caribbean.

With commissions from the Ford Foundation, the Brookings Institution, the Trilateral Commission, Harvard's Center for Energy and Environmental Policy and other organizations, Sawhill has authored numerous books, articles and reports on energy issues and policy, including *Improving the Energy Efficiency of the American Economy* (1979).

Sawhill remains active in the energy field as an advisory board member for Elf Aquitaine, British Petroleum and the Center for Energy and Environmental Policy at Harvard University's Kennedy School of Government, and as a director of Pacific Gas and Electric Company and NACCO Industries. A member of the Council on Foreign Relations and the Trilateral Commission, Sawhill is also chairman of the board of trustees of the Manville Trust, a fund benefiting asbestos disease victims, and of the Whitehead Institute for Biomedical Research at MIT.

Scenic America (Founded: 1981)
216 7th Street SE, Washington, D.C. 20003; (202) 546-1100

Scenic America is a coalition of individuals and organizations dedicated to preserving the nation's scenic beauty by controlling billboards and signage and protecting the landscape. It works with affiliated organizations at the local and state level to secure the regulation of billboard advertising and other elements of scenic aesthetics. SA established the Center for Sign Control in Washington, D.C., to advise communities wishing to develop effective sign control strategies.

Formerly called the National Coalition to Preserve Scenic Beauty (to 1984) and the Coalition for Scenic Beauty (1984–89), Scenic America publishes *Sign Control News* and issues *Ordinance Information Packet* and *Legal Handbook on Sign Control*. Sally Oldham is executive director of Scenic America.

Schenck, Carl Alwin (March 26, 1868–May 15, 1955)
On September 1, 1898, Schenck started the Biltmore Forest School, the first forestry school in the United States, which he ran until 1913. Schenck had been educated in forestry at the Institute of Technology (in his native Darmstadt, Germany), the University of Tübingen and the University of Giessen, which awarded him a doctorate in 1895. That year, Gifford PINCHOT, forest planner for George W. Vanderbilt's 100,000-acre Biltmore estate near Asheville, North Carolina, recommended Schenck for the position of resident forester. He served in this capacity for 14

Claudine Schneider. *Courtesy of Claudine Schneider*

years and opened the Biltmore Forest School on the property.

After service with the German army in World War I, Schenck worked as a forester in Germany. After World War II, the U.S. military government made him chief forester for Greater Hesse.

Schneider, Claudine (March 25, 1947–   )
Claudine Schneider served five terms as Republican congresswoman from Rhode Island's Second District, first elected in 1980. An environmentalist, Schneider first came into the public eye as a leader of the fight against a proposed nuclear power plant to be built near her home. After this, she was active in various environmental causes before an initial—unsuccessful—run for Congress in 1978.

Schneider's environmental agenda has often put her at odds with the prevailing conservative, pro-business, pro-industry tenor of her party, especially during the Reagan years. Although she lost her bid for a seat on the powerful House Energy and Commerce Committee during the 101st Congress, she did become the ranking Republican on the less influential Science, Space and Technology Subcommittee on Natural Resources, Agriculture Research and Environment.

Using her committee position, Schneider successfully argued against approval of the Clinch River nuclear reactor, a project that President Ronald REAGAN, the nuclear industry, the U.S. Chamber of Commerce and a powerful Senate lobby led by Howard H. Baker Jr. vigorously supported.

Schneider was unsuccessful in efforts to introduce a plan to tax hazardous-waste disposal, but she did play a role in legislation, enacted by the 100th Congress, to end ocean dumping of sewage sludge.

A native of Clairton, Pennsylvania, Schneider was educated at Windham College, earning a B.A. in 1969. She did graduate work at the University of Rhode Island in 1975 and worked as a television producer and moderator.

Schneider, Stephen H(enry) (February 11, 1945–   )

Stephen H. Schneider is a research scientist concerned with the effects of climate on society and of society on climate. He quickly came to believe that working as a scientist to investigate, predict and cope with potential climate-related crises was accomplishing only half of the task at hand. The public and government officials alike habitually ignore the warnings of scientists. Therefore, in 1976, Schneider wrote *The Genesis Strategy: Climate and Global Survival* (with Lynne Mesirow), an exploration of climate-related problems and strategies for solving them written for a popular audience.

Schneider was educated at Columbia University, from which he received a B.S. in 1966, an M.S. in 1967 and a Ph.D. in 1971. He was a postdoctoral research associate at the Goddard Institute for Space Studies from 1971 to 1972 and has been associated with the National Center for Atmospheric Research in Boulder, Colorado, since 1972. A member of the American Meteorological Society, the American Geophysical Union, the American Association for the Advancement of Science, the Federation of American Scientists and Sigma Xi, Schneider is also the coauthor (with Lynne Martin) of *The Primordial Bond: Exploring Connections between Man and Nature through the Humanities and Science* (1981), which studies present-day environmental problems from the dual perspectives of science and the humanities.

In 1984, the SIERRA CLUB published Schneider's *The Coevolution of Climate and Life* (written with Randi S. Londer), and Schneider has served as editor of the journal *Climatic Change* since 1975. He is a frequent contributor to professional and popular science journals.

Schurz, Carl (March 2, 1829–May 14, 1906)

The first German-born citizen to hold a seat in a presidential cabinet, Carl Schurz was appointed sec-

Carl Schurz

retary of the interior in 1877. Born in Liblar, Germany, he immigrated to the United States in 1852 after being forced to abandon his studies at the University of Bonn because of his activities in the abortive revolution of 1848. Before being named secretary of the interior, he worked as Washington correspondent of the *New York Tribune* and as editor of the *Detroit Daily Post*, the *Saint Louis Westliche Post* and the *New York Evening Post*. He was elected senator from Missouri in 1869, serving until 1875.

At the U.S. Department of the INTERIOR, Schurz maintained high standards in the enforcement of forest conservation laws and recommended strict policies governing timber sales, forest reserves, the federal Forest Service and the National Forestry Commission.

Further reading: Claude M. Fuess, *Carl Schurz, Reformer* (New York: Dodd, Mead, 1932).

Scott, Douglas Willard (July 16, 1944–   )

Douglas Willard Scott, according to the editor-in-chief of *Sierra* magazine, has achieved through his legislative work and lobbying the preservation of more wilderness acres than any other person working in the environmental fields. Born in Vancouver,

Washington, he entered conservation as a ranger at Carlsbad Caverns National Park during the summers of 1964 and 1965 while he was enrolled in a B.S. program in forestry at the University of Michigan. During the summer of 1967, he worked for the NATIONAL AUDUBON SOCIETY as a Nature Center Planner and the next year as an intern with the WILDERNESS SOCIETY. After working as a staff assistant to Senator Philip Hart—a job in which he helped draft legislation to establish Sleeping Bear Dunes National Lakeshore—Scott returned to the University of Michigan to coordinate "Teach-in on the Environment" during the 1969–70 academic year. Joining the full-time staff of the Wilderness Society in Washington, D.C., he turned his attention to other wilderness legislation, to a campaign for the defeat of the supersonic transport (SST) project and to rally conservationists' support of the Alaska Nature Claims Settlement Act.

In 1973, Scott became the northwest representative for the SIERRA CLUB. In this role he was actively involved in securing the passage of an act to establish the Hells Canyon Natural Recreation Area, the Olympia National Park Expansion Act, the Endangered American Wilderness Act and an act to create the Alpine Lake Wilderness. From 1975 to 1978, he served as coordinator of the Citizens for America's Endangered Wilderness, and from 1978 to 1980, he worked for the enactment of the Alaska National Interest Lands Bill. In 1980, he was appointed federal affairs director for the Sierra Club, and in 1983, he became deputy conservation director. He was working as associate executive director when, in December 1990, he resigned to establish a performing arts center in Washington state.

Sea Shepherd Conservation Society (Founded: 1977)

P. O. Box 7000 S, Redondo Beach, California 90277; (213) 373-6979

The Sea Shepherd Conservation Society seeks to preserve populations of sea mammals, birds and marine life by acting as a policing organization to ensure that protection laws are enforced. Through various programs, including the Reward Program, the Marine Mammal Rescue Progam and the Art and Education Program, the group works to raise public awareness of the threats to marine life and actively engages its members and volunteers in preservation work. The organization's Reward Program offers money to individuals who provide information leading to the conviction of violators of marine protection laws. Volunteers in the Marine Mammal Rescue Program are called upon to disentangle marine mammals from gill nets in the Southern California region. The Art

and Education Program sponsors the creation of life-size murals and other works depicting marine wildlife to educate the public on the need to protect sea mammals.

Since its founding, the society has gained an international reputation for success in preserving sea mammals and birds and has been credited with saving thousands of dolphins, seals and whales. In 1988, the Sea Shepherd Conservation Society joined the EARTH ISLAND INSTITUTE in calling for a nationwide boycott of tuna canned in the United States. The boycott forced the American tuna industry to adopt "dolphin-safe" fishing methods.

In addition to boycotts and public education campaigns, the Sea Shepherd Conservation Society sometimes uses controversial confrontational strategies that have resulted in the sinking of seven whaling vessels. Volunteers of the organization traveled to waters off the coast of the former Soviet Union and gathered evidence of illegal whaling. In the summer of 1990, the volunteer crew of the *Sea Shepherd II*, the organization's ship commanded by Captain Paul Watson, encountered six Japanese fishing boats using 30-mile-long drift nets in the Pacific Ocean. Watson deliberately rammed two of the Japanese ships, damaging their fishing gear and sinking one drift net valued at $1 million.

The Sea Shepherd Conservation Society publishes a four-page quarterly, *The Sea Shepherd Log*, and the monthly *Sea Shepherd News*. Scott Trimingham serves as president of the group, which has 15,000 members and one regional office in Vancouver, British Columbia.

Sears, Paul Bigelow (December 17, 1891–April 30, 1990)

Born in Bucyrus, Ohio, Paul Bigelow Sears began his career as a teacher of botany at Ohio State University in 1915 after graduating from Ohio Wesleyan University (B.S., 1913) and receiving an M.A. from the University of Nebraska (1915). After military service in World War I, Sears taught at Nebraska (1919–28), earning his Ph.D. from the University of Chicago during this period. He also taught at the University of Oklahoma (1928–38) and Ohio's Oberlin College (1938–50). In 1950, he was named professor of conservation and made chairman of the Conservation Program at Yale University, where he developed the nation's first graduate program in the conservation of natural resources.

Sears served on the governing boards of various conservation organizations, including the ECOLOGICAL SOCIETY OF AMERICA (president, 1948) and the American Society of Naturalists (board member, 1958–64). In addition, he served as chairman of the Yale

Sea Shepherd was the first to "paint" seal pups to protect them from fur hunters. *Sea Shepherd Conservation Society*

Nature Preserve and as chairman of the board and honorary president of the NATIONAL AUDUBON SOCIETY.

During his long career as a teacher of botany and conservation, Sears wrote 10 books, including *This Is Our World* (1937), *Life and the Environment* (1939), *The Living Landscape* (1964) and *Lands Beyond the Forest* (1969). In 1980, a fourth edition of his *Deserts on the March*, first published in 1935, was issued by the University of Oklahoma Press. In it, the author updated much of the information in his earlier work and provided a current status report on the balance between man and nature. The original work, which had appeared just as the country was struggling with the Great Depression and the Dust Bowl disaster of the 1930s, examined the causes and effects of the spreading desert in the Midwest and called for strictly supervised land-use programs.

Among Sears's many honors are the Richard Prentiss Etinger Medal from the Rockefeller Institute (1963), Eminent Ecologist Award (1965) from the Ecological

Society of America, the Browning Award (1972) from the Smithsonian Institution and the Distinguished Service Award (1976) from the American Institute of Biological Sciences.

Seton, Ernest Thompson (August 19, 1860–October 23, 1946)

Born in South Shields, England, Seton became a Canadian and U.S. naturalist-artist, whose many sketches, drawings and paintings (some 3,000) and books (40) helped educate both adults and children in the ways of wildlife. His *Studies in the Art Anatomy of Animals* (1896) is a standard work of wildlife art, and his bird identification charts introduced a now-standard method of identifying waterfowl. Although Seton enjoyed popular acclaim for his work, naturalist John Burroughs (and others) criticized the romantic and anthropomorphic tendencies of his illustrations (especially evident in his books for children)—though Seton and Burroughs were eventually reconciled.

In the 1970s, Sharp pushed for expansive energy regulating and conservation legislation. In the 1980s, as economic pressures prompted the dismantling of much of this energy legislation, Sharp's subcommittee sponsored repeal of a 1978 law aimed at encouraging industries to burn coal rather than oil and gas. Sharp also supported the dismantling of the Synthetic Fuels Corporation, which he himself had helped to establish in 1980.

More recently, in the wake of the Persian Gulf War with Iraq, Sharp developed proposed legislation to cut oil consumption and therefore reduce U.S. dependence on oil supplied by nations in the volatile Middle East. These measures include legislation to promote energy efficiency and alternative sources of energy, including solar and wind power. In the 102nd Congress, Sharp launched an extensive series of hearings to review all aspects of energy policy.

Sharp generally takes the environmentalist view in legislation, but this is tempered by his allegiance to an industrial Indiana constituency. He has favored relaxing auto emission standards (though not as much as the auto industry would like) and worked to make clean air legislation more palatable to midwestern

Ernest Thompson Seton. *Courtesy of Mrs. Ernest Thompson Seton*

Paul B. Sears. *Photo by Albertus/Yale News Bureau, courtesy of Yale University*

In 1902, Seton created the Woodcraft Indians (later called the Woodcraft League), on which Lord Baden-Powell may well have modeled the original Boy Scouts. In 1910, Seton chaired a committee that established the Boy Scouts of America.

Further reading: John G. Samson (ed.), *The Worlds of Ernest Thompson Seton* (New York: Knopf, 1976); Seton, *Trail of an Artist Naturalist* (New York: Scribner's, 1940); John Henry Wadland, *Ernest Thompson Seton, Man in Nature and the Progressive Era, 1880–1915* (New York: Arno, 1978).

Sharp, Philip R. (July 15, 1942–   )

Democratic U.S. representative from Indiana's Second Congressional District, Philip R. Sharp has played a key role in energy legislation since he first took office in 1975. He is chairman of the Energy and Power Subcommittee of Energy and Commerce and was chairman of the Fossil Fuels Subcommittee, before it was incorporated into Energy and Power. He also serves on the House Interior and Insular Affairs Committee.

industry. Sharp was instrumental in creating the so-called emission swap system, whereby utilities that exceed federal requirements for reducing sulphur dioxide emissions are given emission tax credits, which they can sell to utilities in other areas that need to expand and would therefore exceed federally allowable emission standards.

Born in Baltimore, Maryland, Sharp holds a B.S. (cum laude, 1964) and a Ph.D. (1974) in government from Georgetown University. He served as legislative aide to Indiana Senator Vance Hartke from 1964 to 1969 and taught political science at Ball State University from 1969 to 1974.

Sharpe, Lois Kremer (November 15, 1906–   )

In 1960, Milwaukee-born Lois Kremer Sharpe joined the staff of the LEAGUE OF WOMEN VOTERS OF THE UNITED STATES as a program specialist in water resources. In 1970, she became the league's coordinator for environmental programs. Kremer has served on various environmental committees and commissions, including the Environmental Advisory Board of the U.S. Army Corps of Engineers and the Environmental Advisory Committee to the Federal Energy Office. She was a consultant to the CONSERVATION FOUNDATION during its planning of a volunteer program in 1972, and she has served on the executive committee of the NATURAL RESOURCES COUNCIL OF AMERICA. From 1979 to 1983, she served as a federal commissioner on the Interstate Commission on the Potomac River Basin, and from 1979 to 1980, she was a member of the Water Data for Public Use Committee of the U.S. Geological Survey. After serving on the Fairfax County, Virginia, Water Authority, she retired in 1986. Kremer is the author of *Know Your River Basin* (1958) and *Who Pays for a Clean Stream?* (1966).

Shelford, Victor Ernest (September 22, 1877– December 27, 1968)

Often called the father of animal ecology, Victor Ernest Shelford was the developer, with Frederic Edward CLEMENTS, of the idea of "bio-ecology," a merging of the studies of plants and animals. His *Animal Communities in Temperate America* (1913) advanced animal ecology further, and 23 years later, he continued that work with Clements in *Bio-Ecology* (1956). In 1963, his last major work, *The Ecology of North America*, described every "biome"—vegetation groups and the animals supported by them—of the continent.

Born in Chemung, New York, Shelford took a B.S. in biology and a Ph.D. in zoology and began his teaching career at the University of West Virginia. After teaching briefly at the University of Chicago, he moved in 1914 to the University of Illinois, where he taught until 1968.

Shelford directed the research laboratories of the Illinois Natural History Survey from 1914 to 1929 and edited *Naturalists' Guide to the Americas* (1926). He served on the editorial board of *Ecology* from 1920 to 1928 and was active in numerous ecology organizations during his long career, including Grasslands Research Foundation, the National Research Council, the Organizing Committee for the ECOLOGICAL SOCIETY OF AMERICA and the Committee on Preservation of Natural Conditions. He was a founder of the Ecologists' Union, later renamed the NATURE CONSERVANCY.

Sierra Club (Founded: 1892)
730 Polk Street, San Francisco, California 94109; (415) 776-2211

The great pioneering naturalist John MUIR merged a citizens' group he had organized to protect the Sierra Nevada from exploitation with the Alpine Club, a small group of mountain-loving University of California, Berkeley, students, to form the Sierra Club. Muir reasoned that those who enjoy the wilderness would also fight to protect it; therefore, the charter of the new club proclaimed a dedication to "exploring, enjoying, and rendering accessible the mountain regions of the Pacific Coast" as well as a commitment to enlist "the support and cooperation of the people and the government in preserving the forests and other features of the Sierra Nevada."

The Sierra Club's first major political action was to arrange the transfer of the Yosemite Valley from state to federal jurisdiction in 1906. Next, the club did legal battle with the city of San Francisco, which proposed to convert Yosemite National Park's Hetch Hetchy Valley to a reservoir. The club lost in 1913, and a year later, Muir died.

After Muir, William E. COLBY became the club's director. During the period between the world wars, the Sierra Club campaigned successfully to enlarge Sequoia National Park, establish Kings Canyon National Park and block logging in Washington's Olympic National Park.

Beginning in 1901, the Sierra Club sponsored annual High Trips in the mountains, which became increasingly popular, so that by 1973, club guides were leading approximately 5,000 persons on almost 500 trips annually. By the 1950s, however, the charter mandate to render the mountains "accessible" began to conflict with the aim of preserving the wilderness. During the 1950s, the Sierra Club was increasingly critical of national policy with regard to outdoor recreation and successfully campaigned for the Out-

Blue Glacier, Olympic National Park. *U.S. Department of the Interior, National Park Service photo by George A. Grant*

door Recreation Resources Review Act of 1958, which compelled public and private agencies to catalog park, wilderness and wildlife resources and their recreational potential with an eye toward curbing overuse. In concert with the WILDERNESS SOCIETY, the Sierra Club campaigned for the National Wilderness Act of 1964, which established a National Wilderness Preservation System.

The 1950s also saw the expansion of the club from an association of independent local chapters to a centrally directed national organization. David R. BROWER, the first executive director of the newly constituted club, led a campaign to preserve Dinosaur National Monument against a Bureau of RECLAMATION dam project in 1952; between 1952 and 1954, Brower established Atlantic and Pacific Northwest club chapters. Beginning with the 1960 publication of naturalist-photographer Ansel ADAMS's *This Is the American Earth*, the club began the highly acclaimed and profitable Exhibit Format book series. The 1960s saw a steady increase in membership and political influence until 1966, when, as a direct result of its

lobbying, the organization lost its tax-exempt status. The later sixties were marked by financial problems and dissension within the organization, a trend that was gradually reversed by the 1970s, when the Sierra Club again assumed a leadership role in battles over Alaskan lands and worldwide environmental issues. Today, the Sierra Club has some 300,000 members in 53 chapters throughout the United States and Canada.

Further reading: Stephen Fox, *John Muir and His Legacy: The American Conservation Movement* (Boston: Little, Brown, 1981); Holway Jones, *John Muir and the Sierra Club: The Battle for Yosemite* (San Francisco: Sierra Club, 1965); Roderick Nash, *Wilderness and the American Mind* (New Haven, Conn.: Yale University Press, 1967).

Silcox, Ferdinand Augustus (December 25, 1882–December 2, 1939)

A native of Columbus, Georgia, Ferdinand A. Silcox was raised in Charleston, South Carolina, and was educated at the College of Charleston, receiving his B.A. in 1903. He earned an M.F. from the Yale School of Forestry in 1905 and served as a U.S. FOREST SERVICE forest ranger until 1910, when he became district forester for the Northern District, headquartered in Missoula, Montana.

Silcox earned a particularly high reputation as a manager of fire fighting, and in 1917, he also proved himself a master labor organizer when he negotiated with the International Workers of the World to end a general strike against local lumber companies and recruit loggers as fire fighters. After serving briefly in World War I, as captain in the 20th (Forestry) Engineers, Silcox's reputation as a negotiator prompted his move to the Department of Labor. He did not return to the Forest Service until 1933, when he was persuaded to assume the leadership of the service following the death of Robert Y. STUART.

An enthusiastic believer in FRANKLIN DELANO ROOSEVELT's New Deal, Silcox oversaw the work of some 3 million young men in the CIVILIAN CONSERVATION CORPS, fighting fires, planting trees and building roads and recreational facilities. Silcox also led the Forest Service in the creation of tree "shelterbelts" to combat soil erosion in the Dust Bowl of the Great Plains.

Realizing that the Depression-racked lumber companies were not adequately reforesting the land they worked, Silcox pushed for better forest management and more public ownership of forests. Under his leadership, cooperative programs between the public and private sectors were expanded, and the national forests were significantly enlarged.

Silkwood, Karen (February 19, 1946– November 13, 1974)

Karen Silkwood was killed when her automobile skidded off a road near Crescent, Oklahoma, crashed through a guardrail and hurtled down an embankment. She had been driving to meet *New York Times* reporter David Burnham, to whom she was to deliver a manila folder containing a report of alleged health and safety violations at the Kerr-McGee Cimarron River nuclear fuel-rod manufacturing facility, where she worked as a technician.

Authorities, including the local police and, subsequently, the U.S. Department of Justice, ruled Silkwood's death an accident. However, no trace of the manila folder was ever found, and an investigation by a private detective concluded that she had probably been forced off the road by another car, perhaps deliberately rammed from behind. Congressional hearings and a lawsuit successfully brought against Kerr-McGee by Silkwood's family later revealed the likelihood that she had been under surveillance for some time and that her phone had been tapped. It

was well known that she herself expressed fears that "someone was out to get her."

Why?

Karen Silkwood made an unlikely target for corporate terrorism. Born in Longview, Texas, Silkwood had wanted to be a scientist. She excelled in high school, especially in chemistry, and, after graduating, attended Lamar College in Beaumont, Texas, for a year until she eloped with Bill Meadows, an oil industry employee. After years of financial struggle, Silkwood left Meadows in 1972 when she discovered that he was having an affair with one of her friends. Giving him custody of her three children, she moved to Oklahoma City, where she found employment at the Kerr-McGee Cimarron River plant in the town of Crescent. Silkwood joined the Oil, Chemical and Atomic Workers Union and was active in a 10-week 1972 strike protesting low wages and seeking increased safety provisions and improved employee training.

The union made serious allegations against Kerr-McGee. The Cimarron River facility manufactured nuclear reactor fuel rods, using highly toxic plutonium. Workers, the union alleged, were poorly trained and inadequately advised of safety and health concerns. The company, according to the union, monitored radiation levels poorly and failed to minimize contamination; high levels of uranium dust, for example, were found in the plant lunchroom. Under pressure to step up production, the plant, according to union allegations, also deliberately disguised faults in fuel rods that should have been rejected as defective.

Faced with production and scheduling problems, management at the Cimarron River plant attempted to break the union. Clearly, Kerr-McGee could ill afford to tolerate whistleblowers like Karen Silkwood, who, emerging as a local labor leader, traveled to Washington, D.C., in September 1974 with two other union officials to confer with the Atomic Energy Commission and national union leaders on conditions at the Cimarron River facility.

Following this meeting, according to her friends, Silkwood became obsessed with her mission to uncover and document safety violations. On November 4 and 5, 1974, she was contaminated by radioactivity (she had been contaminated earlier as well, in July), and her apartment also showed high levels of contamination. She and her roommate were sent to federal laboratory facilities at Los Alamos, New Mexico, for testing and treatment. Their levels of exposure were deemed not serious.

Just a few days after returning from Los Alamos, she was ready to deliver to *New York Times* reporter

Burnham the results of seven weeks of documenting safety violations at the plant.

Following her death, allegations flew thick and fast. Kerr-McGee accused Silkwood of having deliberately contaminated herself to support her allegations of unsafe conditions at the plant. Company spokesmen claimed that she stole plutonium. Union officials, Silkwood's family and others accused Kerr-McGee of, at the very least, harassment and, at the worst, murder—though no indictments or formal charges were ever made against anyone.

Silkwood's death and the resulting controversy came at a critical time for the nuclear industry, which was under fire by increasingly influential anti-nuclear activists. The Atomic Energy Commission confirmed three violations at the Cimarron River plant, which was ultimately shut down. In May 1979, a jury awarded the Silkwood estate over $10 million in punitive damages against Kerr-McGee and cleared her name of accusations that she had stolen plutonium. The corporation was also found negligent on several counts. An appeals court overturned the decision, which, however, was reinstated by the U.S. Supreme Court.

Throughout all of this, Karen Silkwood emerged posthumously as a symbol and rallying point for the anti-nuclear movement, which steadily gained ground. Many regard Silkwood as a grass-roots hero and martyr to the closely allied causes of individual rights, worker safety, public safety and the defense of the environment.

Further reading: Howard Kohn, *Who Killed Karen Silkwood?* (New York: Summit, 1981); Richard Rashke, *The Killing of Karen Silkwood* (Boston: Houghton Mifflin, 1981).

Simon, Julian L. (February 12, 1932–   )

Julian L. Simon is an author and an expert on marketing and demography, who has written two important studies of the relationship between economics and population growth: *The Effects of Income on Fertility* (1974) and *The Economics of Population Growth* (1977).

Born in Newark, New Jersey, Simon was educated at Harvard University (B.A., 1953) and the University of Chicago (M.B.A., 1959 and Ph.D., 1961). He has taught at several universities, including the University of Illinois and Hebrew University in Jerusalem.

Singer, Peter (Albert David) (July 6, 1946–   )

While he was teaching at Oxford University during the early 1970s, Peter Singer met a group of vegetarians who avoided meat not because of any personal distaste for it, but because they believed, as Singer subsequently related, that "there was no way in which [mistreatment of animals by humans] could be justified ethically." Singer was soon persuaded by their arguments, joined in their beliefs and set about writing his passionate documentary treatise on animal rights, *Animal Liberation,* which appeared in 1975 and was revised in 1990.

Animal Liberation was the first modern book to argue that anyone who professes opposition to human suffering must also oppose inflicting suffering on animals. Singer did not make this point with abstract philosophical theory, but by documenting in detail the pain suffered by animals in scientific, military and commercial research as well as in the processes through which meat is commercially produced. Singer's book is widely credited with bringing the animal rights movement into being.

Essential to Singer's vision is the concept of "speciesism," which the philosopher defines as "a prejudice or attitude of bias toward the interests of members of one's own species and against those of members of other species." Only rarely, Singer argues, is speciesism "either necessary or moral." According to him, most medical experimentation on animals, for example, is utterly unnecessary; nor is meat the only viable source of protein in the human diet. If speciesism is, then, almost always unnecessary, the imperative against it is urgently compelling, because "there is every reason to believe, and no good reason to deny, that animals feel pain. . . . Whatever reasons we have for not inflicting pain on innocent and helpless humans extend equally well to animals."

Peter Singer was born in Melbourne, Australia, the son of a businessman and a physician. He was educated at the University of Melbourne (B.A., with honors, 1967; M.A., 1969) and at University College, Oxford (B. Phil., 1971). He was a lecturer in philosophy at University College, Oxford, from 1971 to 1973; visiting assistant professor of philosophy at New York University from 1973 to 1974; senior lecturer in philosophy at La Trobe University (Bundoora, Victoria, Australia) from 1974 to 1976; and has been professor of philosophy at Monash University (Clayton, Victoria) since 1977. He also directs the university's Centre for Human Bioethics. Singer is active in the Animal Liberation movement, as president of Animal Liberation (Victoria) and vice-president of the Australian and New Zealand Federation of Animal Societies.

In addition to *Animal Liberation* (1975; 1990), Singer has published *Democracy and Disobedience* (1973), *Practical Ethics* (1979), *Marx* (1980) and *The Expanding Circle* (1981). He has edited a number of other volumes, including *Test-Tube Babies* (1982, with William Walters) and *Animal Rights and Human Obligations* (with Tom REGAN, 1975).

Further reading: Singer, *Animal Liberation,* 2nd ed. (New York: New York Review Books, 1990).

Smith, Robert (December 11, 1873–August 28, 1900)

Influenced by his study with the French botanist and plant geographer Charles Flahault, Scottish naturalist Robert Smith initiated the creation of a Botanical Survey of Scotland, the first detailed mapping of vegetation communities in the British Isles. Although Smith died at 26, after completing only two sections of the survey, his brother William Gardner SMITH carried on his work, and their ambitious project proved a keystone in the development of the British ecology movement.

A Forfarshire native, Smith studied botany at the University College of Dundee and worked as an assistant at the institution's zoological museum. During the 1890s, Smith furthered his education with field research and laboratory work at the Botanical Institute of the University of Montpellier, where Flahault had begun a thorough cartographical study of the vegetation and forests of France. When he returned to Dundee, Smith became a college lecturer in botany and adapted Flahault's surveying methods to record the plant carpet of the Scottish countryside. In 1898, his *Plant Associations of the Tay Basin* was published, and in 1900, the first sections of the Botanical Survey—covering the Edinburgh district and the northern Perthshire district, and including meticulously colored vegetation maps—appeared in the *Scottish Geographical Magazine.* Only months later, after returning from a field expedition, the young botanist died suddenly of appendicitis. Thanks to Smith's groundwork, however, his brother William and other plant scientists continued the Scottish vegetation survey and extended it to several districts in England. Gathering together to coordinate their efforts, the botanical workers formed the British Vegetation Committee in 1904, and nine years later, the group invited zoological researchers to join with them as the British Ecological Society.

Smith, William Gardner (March 20, 1866–December 8, 1928)

While continuing work on the pioneering *Botanical Survey of Scotland* his brother Robert had begun, Dundee-born botanist and plant geographer William Gardner Smith became a founding member of the British Vegetation Committee and the British Ecological Society.

Smith studied botany and zoology at the University College of Dundee, graduating with a bachelor of science in 1890. After a year as assistant science master at Dundee's Morgan Academy, Smith taught botany at Edinburgh University, then lectured in agriculture for the county of Forfar. In 1893, he traveled to the University of Munich for further study in botany; there he translated a volume on plant diseases and earned his Ph.D. in 1894. After his return from Germany, Smith taught plant physiology at the University of Edinburgh for three years, then joined the university at Leeds as an assistant lecturer in botany. In 1908, Smith began lecturing in biology at the Edinburgh and East of Scotland College of Agriculture, where he then taught for 18 years and undertook research on the cultivation and nutritive value of hill pasture. In 1926 he was named advisory officer in agricultural botany.

Smith's younger brother, the botanist and plant ecologist Robert SMITH, died suddenly in 1900, after publishing only the first two sections of his projected cartographical study of Scotland's plant communities. This comprehensive and detailed overview, the first of its kind to be undertaken in Great Britain, was inspired by the "plant sociology" studies of early 19th-century continental botanists and by Smith's first-hand observation of Charles Flahault's primary forest and vegetation surveys of France. After Robert's death, William Smith took up his brother's work, completing the unfinished manuscripts and colored vegetation maps for the *Botanical Survey; III and IV,* which covered the Scottish districts of Forfar and Fife (*Scottish Geographical Magazine,* 1904-5). Smith also began a survey of Yorkshire vegetation, forming a special committee of the Yorkshire Naturalists Union to help collect and codify local data. In 1903, with former Leeds students C. E. Moss and W. Munn Rankin, he issued the first vegetation maps of England, describing the plant carpets of the Leeds, Halifax, Harrowgate and Skipton districts. For this work, Smith was awarded the Back Bequest of the Royal Geographical Society. Also in 1903, Smith published the paper "Botanical Survey for Local Naturalist Societies," promoting the creation of similar mapping projects by other regional groups.

In December 1904, at the suggestion of the Cambridge botanist A. G. TANSLEY, a small group of interested plant workers met at Smith's house in Leeds to discuss the coordination of various surveys even now in progress throughout the country. With Smith as secretary, the plant scientists formed the Central Committee for the Study and Survey of British Vegetation, a name soon simplified to the British Vegetation Committee. Over the next years, the group met periodically in cities throughout the British Isles for informal conferences and field trips, published an introductory pamphlet to share their methodology with a wider audience of nature-study enthusiasts and organized a series of International Phytogeographical Excursions to exchange field visits and information with botanists and plant ecologists in Europe and North America.

Responding to increased interest in the broader study of natural communities, the group elected to change its name to the British Ecological society in April 1913, and for his contributions to the original group's activities, William Gardner Smith was named an honorary life member. He served as president of the society in 1918 and in 1919, when he also headed the Yorkshire Naturalists Union.

Snyder, Gary (May 8, 1930–)

Among the most enduring and highly respected creative writers to come of age in the so-called Beat Generation, Gary Snyder has produced poetry and prose that are steeped in the natural world and speak of the values of simple living, hard physical work and respect for the environment. Snyder's writing is also strongly reflective of his lifelong interest in Asian culture, religion and mythology. Novelist Jack Kerouac used his friend Snyder as the model for the fictional hero of *The Dharma Bums* (1958), a mountain-climbing Beat poet with a learned passion for things Asian. But if Snyder was closely associated with the Beats, particularly in their rejection of the status quo and Establishment values, his form of literary protest was far less emotionally harrowing than that of poet Allen Ginsberg, prose writer Neal Cassady or Kerouac himself. Whereas their response to modern technocracy tended toward the frenetic, destructive and self-destructive, Snyder looked more constructively to nature, self-reliance and the quiet values of the East for alternatives to mainstream American culture.

Gary Snyder was born in San Francisco but raised on a marginal farm near Seattle, Washington, during the hardest years of the Depression. At 12, Snyder moved with his family to Portland, Oregon, where he attended high school and worked at a variety of odd jobs. He read widely and was especially captivated by the works of Ernest Thompson SETON, a writer on American Indian life, the wilderness and woodcraft. Young Snyder sewed his own moccasins and made his own bows and arrows. A love of the frontier came naturally to Snyder, whose father's family included homesteaders and whose mother numbered pioneers among her ancestors. Departure from the social mainstream was also a tradition Snyder was familiar with. His grandfather had been a political radical and a labor organizer for the International Workers of the World (IWW).

Snyder was educated at Reed College (B.A., 1951) and also attended Indiana University (1952–53) and the University of California, Berkeley (1953–56). During the summers of 1952, 1953, 1954 and 1955, he worked as a fire lookout on Crater and Sourdough mountains in Washington State, as a choker setter (a junior logger who loops a hauling cable around logs for transportation) at Camp A of the Warm Springs Lumber Company and as a trail crew worker at Yosemite National Park. In 1956, he moved to Japan, where he lived for the next 12 years, with occasional visits to the United States. During this period, he became a Buddhist.

Snyder's first collection of poetry, *Riprap*, was published in 1959. As Snyder later explained, " 'Riprap' is really a class of poems I wrote under the influence of the geology of the Sierra Nevada and the daily trail-crew work of picking up and placing granite stones in tight cobble patterns on hard slabs. 'What are you doing?' I asked Roy Marchbanks—'Riprapping' he said. His selection of natural rocks was perfect—the result looked like dressed stone fitting to hair-edge cracks." It is just such a fitting together of natural elements that constitutes Snyder's best and most characteristic poetry, which, drawn from the environment itself, has a natural grace and a simplicity of form verging on minimalism.

Snyder's second book, a long poem titled *Myths & Texts* (1960), was an indictment of virtually the whole of Western civilization. It, too, is firmly founded in nature, and its orientation is richly ecological. Begun in the summer of 1952 at Crater Mountain, the poem consists of three sections—"Logging," which concerns the destruction of forests and evokes the attitudes responsible for the loss of the wilderness; "Hunting," which celebrates the mystical identification between primitive hunters and their prey, exploring the relationship of humankind to the animal world; and "Burning," which uses the concept of wild ecology to build a myth of human renewal and rebirth.

These two early works, which became the basis of Snyder's growing reputation in literary circles, were followed by *Riprap and Cold Mountain Poems* (1965), *Six Sections from Mountains and Rivers without End* (1965, a work in progress), *A Range of Poems* (1966), *The Back Country* (1967), *Earth House Hold* (1969), *Regarding Wave* (1969), *Turtle Island* (which was awarded the Pulitzer Prize; 1974), *The Old Ways: Six Essays* (1977), *He Who Hunted in His Father's Village: The Dimensions of a Haida Myth* (1979) and *The Real Work: Interviews and Talks, 1964–1979* (1980).

Gary Snyder now lives in California's Sierra Nevada, where he writes and studies and is also active in environmental causes. In 1971, he delivered a paper titled "The Wilderness" at the Center for the Study of Democratic Institutions in Santa Barbara, and in 1972, he participated in the United Nations conference on the Human Environment in Stockholm, Sweden. In 1983, he delivered the E. F. Schumacher (*Small Is Beautiful*) lectures in England. He lectures widely on environmental issues.

Further reading: Bert Almon, *Gary Snyder* (Boise: Boise State University Press, 1979); Bob Steuding, *Gary Snyder* (Boston: Twayne, 1976).

Society of American Foresters (Founded: 1900)
5400 Grosvenor Lane, Bethesda, Maryland 20814; (301) 897-8720

Founded in 1900 with seven members and Gifford PINCHOT as president, the Society of American Foresters works to promote forestry as a profession by issuing publications, codifying terminology and setting educational standards. The society reaches its membership of 21,000 foresters and scientists through a variety of quarterly publications, including *Forest Science, Northern Journal of Applied Forestry, Southern Journal of Applied Forestry,* and *Western Journal of Applied Forestry* and through a monthly entitled *Journal of Forestry*.

In 1919, the group began to standardize forestry terminology and 25 years later issued its first edition of *Forestry Terminology* (1924). *Forestry Handbook,* a 1,200-page volume that first appeared in 1955, includes standards for forestry practices. The organization also accredits educational programs for foresters and maintains a code of ethics governing the professional conduct of members.

Further reading: Ralph S. Hosmer, "The Society of American Foresters: An Historical Summary," *Journal of Forestry* 38 (November 1940): 837–854.

Soil and Water Conservation Society
(Founded: 1945)
7515 N.E. Ankeny Road, Ankeny, Iowa 50021; (515) 289-2331

The Soil and Water Conservation Society's 13,000 members include researchers, planners, educators, technicians, conservation officials, farmers, ranchers, students and other specialists in land and water management. With headquarters in Ankeny, Iowa, an office in Washington, D.C., and 120 local chapters, the organization advocates the conservation and responsible stewardship of soil and water resources in the U.S. and abroad. Society task forces conduct and synthesize scientific research on erosion and sediment control, evaluate existing and forthcoming conservation legislation and formulate policy recommendations for the protection of privately owned wetlands and other fragile ecosystems. SWCS also publishes books and educational materials promoting practices of contour farming, maintenance of native ground covers and other techniques for sustainable agriculture.

In 1990, the society released an in-depth study of the implementation and potential long-range impact of the 1985 farm bill, which introduced conservation requirements for farmers receiving price supports, crop insurance and other federal program benefits. The report concluded that although these conservation measures could significantly improve and protect soil and water conditions on the nation's croplands and virtually eliminate serious soil erosion by 1995, public awareness and U.S. Department of AGRICULTURE monitoring and enforcement of the bill's provisions were not yet adequate for widespread compliance.

The Soil and Water Conservation Society holds conferences and workshops, bestows awards and scholarships and (in conjunction with the American Society of Agronomy) offers professional certification in erosion and sediment control.

SWCS publishes the bimonthly *Journal of Soil and Water Conservation* and *Conservogram,* a member newsletter. As part of its educational program, the group has also produced an award-winning series of cartoon booklets introducing elementary school children to basic concepts of resource conservation.

Soil Conservation Service, U.S. (Established: 1935)
P. O. Box 2890, Washington, D.C. 20013; (202) 205-0027

The United States Soil Conservation Service was a development of the Great Depression and the Dust Bowl disaster of the 1930s. In 1930, Congress passed an Agriculture Appropriation Bill that included funds for a study of the causes of soil erosion and its possible solutions. With an appropriation of $160,000, the U.S. Department of AGRICULTURE established the Bureau of Chemistry and Soils, headed by Hugh Bennett, a long-time member of the department's Bureau of Soils. Bennett set up erosion experiment stations at 10 different locations and set out to gather the necessary information on soil and water loss.

In the meantime, funds were made available to the U.S. Department of the INTERIOR for public work projects in rural areas. Secretary of the Interior Harold ICKES created the Soil Erosion Service in 1933 and

Wildlife wetland, Cerro Gordo Soil Conservation District, Iowa. *USDA Soil Conservation Service, courtesy of Soil and Water Conservation Society*

hired Bennett to head the program. With an initial budget of $5 million, Bennett conducted a research project aimed at gathering information on the condition of soils across the United States and then set up 40 demonstration projects. Throughout this period, the service was a temporary government agency, one whose funding was to be halted with the arrival of economic recovery. Bennett, however, realized that the problems of soil erosion would not be cured by an end to the Depression, and he continued to push for the permanent status of his agency.

The impetus for conferring such status came from the great dust storm of 1934. Called upon to testify before Congress on March 6, 1935, Bennett related how 300 million tons of soil from the Great Plains had disappeared in the wind during the 1934 dust storm. Even as he testified, a huge dust cloud was gathering over the nation's capital—the second occurrence of this phenomenon in less than a year. Congressional support for making Bennett's program a permanent office was unanimous. The Agicultural

Act of 1935 provided for a permanent Soil Conservation Service within the Department of Agriculture, and the service was given responsibility for developing a long-range program of soil and water conservation.

Over the next year, Bennett set up 147 demonstration programs of approximately 25,000 acres each. In addition, he established 48 soil conservation nurseries and 23 research stations. Through the rest of the decade, the service received manpower assistance from the CIVILIAN CONSERVATION CORPS. In 1937, Bennett received the president's approval for a model state law to set up conservation districts, which 22 states quickly adopted.

With the need for soil conservation projects firmly established, the Soil Conservation Service abandoned its demonstration projects and turned to a new progam of providing technical assistance to farmers and other landowners through their soil conservation districts. Over the years, the districts have proved to be an effective medium for carrying out national policy on soil erosion and water conservation. Today under the direction of Judith Johnson, the service is responsible not only for technical assistance programs on soil and water use but also for preventing floods, controlling pollution and maintaining the natural beauty of America's farmlands. Other programs of the service deal with erosion problems caused by suburban development.

Another major responsibility was added with the passage of the 1985 Farm Bill. The law requires farmers who wish to continue to receive government farm subsidies to implement soil conservation plans developed for them by the service. The new law has propelled the service from a strictly advisory role to an enforcement role as well. Between 1985 and 1991, the service developed more than 1.3 million conservation plans for individual farmers—although many of these farmers have not implemented the plans. A survey by the Soil and Water Conservation Society found that 41% of the nation's farms did not comply with the plans developed for them.

Further reading: D. Harper Simms, *The Soil Conservation Service* (New York: Praeger, 1970).

Sparrowe, Rollin D. (January 21, 1941–   )

President of the WILDLIFE MANAGEMENT INSTITUTE, Rollin D. Sparrowe graduated from Humboldt College in 1964 with a B.S. in game management. He went on to earn a master's degree in wildlife management from South Dakota State University in 1966 and a Ph.D. in wildlife ecology from Michigan State University in 1969.

During his college and graduate school years, Sparrowe worked as an aide with the California Fish and Game Department and, from 1964 to 1966, was a research assistant with the South Dakota Cooperative Wildlife Research Unit. After a brief stint as a ranger-naturalist with the NATIONAL PARK SERVICE at Yellowstone National Park during 1966, he was a research assistant at Michigan State University. From 1969 to 1976, Sparrowe worked for the Missouri Cooperative Wildlife Research Unit of the U.S. FISH AND WILDLIFE SERVICE, becoming supervisor of the unit in 1976, and chief of the Division of Cooperative Research Units in 1979. From 1983 to 1984, he was chief of the Division of Wildlife Research, then moved to the Office of Migratory Bird Management, as chief from 1984 to 1989. Before becoming president of the Wildlife Management Institute in 1991, Sparrowe was deputy assistant director of Refuges and Wildlife for the U.S. Fish and Wildlife Service.

Sparrowe has written numerous articles and papers on a variety of wildlife topics, most recently focusing on harvest management of migratory birds.

Rollin D. Sparrowe, president of Wildlife Management Institute. *Wildlife Management Institute*

Spencer, Herbert (April 27, 1820–December 8, 1903)

Herbert Spencer was the father of evolutionary philosophy. His first contribution to this field was the 1851 *Social Statics; or the Conditions Essential to Human Happiness Specified*. This work was followed by many others, including *A New Theory of Population* (1852), the 10-volume *System of Synthetic Philosophy* (1862–93), *The Classification of the Sciences* (1864), *The Man versus the State* (1884) and *The Factors of Organic Evolution* (1887). Throughout his vast and varied works, Spencer held to a single principle—the "persistence of force"—as the agent of change, form and organization in the universe. He maintained that human society is itself an evolving organism and that all "organisms," whether individual or collective, progress from homogeneity to heterogeneity. A profound influence on many 19th-century ecological and social

President J. Gustave Speth, World Resources Institute. *World Resources Institute*

thinkers, Spencer is credited with coining the phrase "survival of the fittest."

Spencer was born in Derby, England, and died at Brighton.

Further reading: Spencer, *Autobiography* (New York: D. Appleton, 1904).

Speth, James Gustave (March 3, 1942–)

President of the WORLD RESOURCES INSTITUTE since he and others founded the organization in 1982, James Gustave Speth also served as chairman of the COUNCIL ON ENVIRONMENTAL QUALITY from 1979 to 1981 and as a professor of law at Georgetown University from 1981 to 1982. A native of Orangeburg, South Carolina, he was a cofounder of the NATURAL RESOURCES DEFENSE COUNCIL and served as that organization's senior attorney from 1970 to 1977.

In his 1991 World Resources Institute annual report, Speth observed that six transitions are necessary for sustaining human society: a global transition to stable populations; a move away from wasteful and polluting technologies, particularly those of energy production and consumption; a shift in world economies to reflect the full cost of production and use; a sharing of environmental and economic benefits among nations; increased understanding of the requirements for sustainability; and more effective partnerships between environmental organizations and government. The report continued: "The WRI staff and board are convinced that the only real hope of sustaining the earth and its people lies in addressing the underlying problems of rapid population expansion, poverty and inequity, short-sighted economic signals, outdated technologies and institutions and inadequate information and training."

A graduate of Yale University (B.A., 1964), Speth attended Balliol College, Oxford University, on a Rhodes Scholarship, earning an M. Litt. in economics in 1966. He graduated in 1969 from Yale Law School and served as law clerk to Supreme Court Justice Hugo L. Black from 1969 to 1970.

Stafford, Robert T. (August 8, 1913–)

As Republican senator from Vermont from 1971—when he was appointed to fill a vacancy—to 1989, Robert T. Stafford played a key role in much of the important environmental legislation of the 1970s and 1980s. He was especially effective in defending the gains on the environmental front won during the 1970s from the resolute efforts to weaken environmental regulations by the REAGAN administration in the 1980s.

Stafford served as chairman of the committee on Environment and Public Works. He was instrumental in the passage of the first legislation authorizing the Superfund to identify and clean up the nation's most urgent toxic waste sites in 1981. He also spearheaded efforts to reauthorize the bill in subsequent sessions of Congress. Stafford played a major role in the passage of other environmental legislation, most notably the strengthening of the Clean Water Act and the reauthorization of the Clean Air Act—the latter involving months, then years, of patient maneuvering and negotiation.

A native of Rutland, Vermont, Stafford was educated at Middlebury College, earning a B.S. in 1935. He attended the University of Michigan (1935–36) and Boston University, from which he received a law degree in 1938. He served in the U.S. Navy during World War II (1942–46) and the Korean War (1951–53) and was Rutland County state's attorney from 1947 to 1951. Stafford was deputy attorney general for Vermont from 1953 to 1955 and attorney general from 1955 to 1957. Lieutenant governor from 1957 to 1959, he was elected governor in 1959. Stafford served in the U.S. House of Representatives from 1961 to 1971 before he was appointed to fill a Senate vacancy.

Stafford was named distinguished scholar by the University of Vermont in 1989 and, the same year, was made distinguished professor of public affairs at Castleton State College.

Startzell, David N. (June 16, 1949–   )

A native of Washington, D.C., David N. Startzell was educated at Miami University of Ohio in 1971, earning a B.A. in sociology. He took a master's degree in planning from the University of Tennessee in 1976. During the period of his graduate studies, he worked as a planning consultant at the university's Technical Assistance Center, was an assistant to the state chapter of the American Institute of Planners' legislative affairs committee and a planning consultant to the office of the mayor of Knoxville.

In 1977, Startzell worked as an assistant in the planning department of the city of Oxnard, California, and in 1978 joined the APPALACHIAN TRAIL CONFERENCE as director of trail management services. He became director of resource protection in December 1979 and was appointed associate director of the conference in 1981, with a wide range of responsibilities, including congressional liaison, public affairs management, fund-raising and building management. In 1986, Startzell became executive director (and chief executive officer) of the Appalachian Trail Conference.

Startzell is involved with other trail and conservation group coalitions and served as chairman of the task force that produced *Trails for All Americans,* a report on national trails planning that was the centerpiece of the National Trails Agenda Project of the NATIONAL PARK SERVICE and American Trails, with additional support from the American Hiking Society.

Sternglass, Ernest Joachim (September 24, 1923–   )

Ernest Sternglass is best known in environmental circles for his studies of the biological effects of radiation from atomic bomb testing and, most recently, from fallout resulting from the Chernobyl nuclear reactor accident.

Emeritus Professor of Radiological Physics at the University of Pittsburgh, Ernest Joachim Sternglass has conducted extensive research in secondary electron emission, the physics of electron tubes, electron and elementary particle physics, electronic imaging devices for astronomy and medicine, radiation physics and the biological effects of radiation. Born in Berlin, Germany, he was a physicist with the U.S. Naval Ordnance Laboratory from 1946 to 1952, and then returned to Cornell University—where he had taken his undergraduate and graduate degrees—as a research associate from 1951 to 1952. From 1952 to

1967, he worked for the Westinghouse Corporation as a physicist, and again returned to the academic world when he became professor of radiation physics at the University of Pittsburgh from 1967 to 1980.

Sternglass and statistician Jay Gould, an Environmental Protection Agency advisor during the Carter administration, sent shock waves through the environmental community during the late 1980s when they reported that 35,000 to 40,000 more Americans died in the summer of 1986 than anticipated by standard mortality statistics. In addition, Sternglass reported the research of California ornithologists, who cited a decrease in bird populations during the same time. Sternglass and Gould attributed these findings to the fallout circulating around the globe after the April 1986 Chernobyl nuclear accident in the Ukraine.

Sternglass is the author of *Secret Fallout* (1982), in which he argues that infant and fetal mortality rates corresponded closely to the radiation levels of nuclear weapons testing, and that such radiation can also cause mental retardation in those infants who survive the exposure. In earlier articles, Sternglass stated that 400,000 children had died in the United States due to the exposure to fallout from nuclear bomb tests in the 1950s and 1960s.

Stevens, Christine Gesell (March 10, 1918–   )

St. Louis-born Christine Gesell Stevens was a founder of the ANIMAL WELFARE INSTITUTE in 1951 and has served as its president since then. Stevens has been engaged in campaigns to advance the humane treatment of laboratory animals and to limit suffering of animals on traplines and in slaughterhouses. At the institute, she has edited *Animals and Their Legal Rights, Animal Expressions: A Photographic Footnote to Charles Darwin's "Expression of the Emotions in Man and Animals," The Endangered Species Handbook, Physical and Mental Suffering of Experimental Animals* and other Animal Welfare Institute publications.

In 1954, Stevens was a founder of the Society for Animal Protective Legislation. As secretary of the organization, she was active in securing passage of federal laws protecting animals. Stevens is the president of SAVE THE WHALES, an organization founded in 1971 to save whales from extinction, to inform the public about the lives of whales and to oppose commercial whaling. She has been a delegate to seven annual International Whaling Commission meetings and four biennial meetings of the Convention on International Trade in Endangered Species of Wild Fauna and Flora. In addition, she is a member of the board of the Society for Animal Protective Legislation and an honorary director of the New York State Humane Association.

Stewart, Alice Mary (October 4, 1906–   )
The British epidemiologist Alice Mary Stewart has conducted exhaustive research on the effects of X-rays on fetuses, concluding that the children of mothers who had been X-rayed during pregnancy were predisposed to developing leukemia, and that the likelihood of contracting the disease increased in proportion to the amount of radiation exposure.

In addition to studying the effects of radiation on fetuses, Stewart also researched the effects of low-level radiation on adults after she discovered, in 1975, a high incidence of cancer among workers at the Hanford nuclear weapons plant. Together with two colleagues, she published her research in *Health Physics* and immediately went to war with the American government and the weapons industry. After Stewart's findings were presented to the Atomic Energy Commission early in 1976, the commission canceled the government grant that had funded the project in question. Stewart continued her work in the area, testifying before Congress in 1988, when she blasted the U.S. Department of ENERGY, successor to the Atomic Energy Commission, for locking up files on worker health. She also pointed out a conflict of interest within the department, which not only operated nuclear power and weapons plants, but was also responsible for researching the effects of radiation, and therefore had an interest in deeming potentially dangerous levels of radiation safe. Partly in response to pressure Stewart had brought to bear, the Department of Energy announced in March 1990 that it would open its records on worker health and that it would transfer responsibility for research on worker health to the Department of Health and Human Services.

Born in the Yorkshire city of Sheffield, England, Stewart received her M.D. degree from Cambridge University and served on the staff of four British hospitals. She joined the faculty of Oxford University in 1941 and was almost immediately engaged by the British government to study the health problems of workers at munitions plants. The government had found that workers who filled shells with TNT during World War I had developed liver damage, anemia and other blood disorders. To study the problem, Stewart hired Oxford University students to work in a munitions plant. After one month, she examined them, concluding that exposure to TNT impaired the body's ability to produce blood cells. The plants under study changed their manufacturing processes and equipment to reduce exposure levels.

In 1956, Stewart tackled the problem that would catapult her to international fame. She found that children who died of cancer between 1953 and 1955 had been exposed to twice as many prenatal X-rays as those without cancer. Scientists and doctors around the world attacked her findings. It was widely accepted that a radiation dose of 500 rems or more caused disease, but low-level radiation, such as that used in medical X-rays, was deemed safe. Over the next 20 years, other scientists examined Stewart's findings and conducted studies of their own. By the mid-1970s, her conclusions were widely accepted.

In 1986, Stewart was awarded the Right Livelihood Award by the Swedish parliament; the award honors individuals who have developed and implemented practical solutions to world problems. She is currently the chief researcher for the Three Mile Island Public Health Fund.

Stockman, David (November 10, 1946–   )
David Stockman—Ronald REAGAN's point man in his war on government bureaucracy—considered the EN-VIRONMENTAL PROTECTION AGENCY a primary target when he was named director of the OFFICE OF MANAGEMENT AND BUDGET in 1981.

Stockman's attack came on two fronts. As budget director, Stockman slashed the EPA's budget, from $1.4 billion in 1981 to $1.2 billion in 1982, to $916 million in 1983. And as a member of the President's Task Force on Regulatory Relief, Stockman prepared a list of regulations that were deemed to be unnecessarily hampering industry. By a 1981 executive order, the OMB director had the power to reject regulations whose economic liabilities were deemed to outweigh their environmental benefits. Stockman's rejection and revision of environmental regulations, along with the budget cuts, effectively crippled the EPA. It no longer had the money or personnel to adequately investigate violations of existing environmental laws in such areas as air and water quality, pesticide use and hazardous waste disposal, amounting to what was a de facto repeal of those laws without a single vote in Congress.

Stockman was born in Fort Hood, Texas, raised in Michigan, and graduated from Michigan State in 1968. After graduate studies at Harvard, Stockman became involved in politics, eventually serving as a U.S. representative from Michigan from 1977 to 1981. When Reagan modified his budget-cutting and deregulating profile in preparation for the 1984 election, Stockman singlemindedly refused to go along. He resigned in 1985 and went into private business.

Straus, Robert Ware (July 22, 1909–August 25, 1991)
A founder and president of the Accokeek Foundation, a preservation organization working in Prince George's County, Maryland, Robert Ware Straus was instrumental in the successful battle to preserve the Potomac woodlands across from Mount Vernon.

Born in Hinsdale, Illinois, a suburb of Chicago, Straus graduated from Harvard University in 1931 and worked in the Office of Price Administration, the U.S. Department of the INTERIOR and the U.S. Maritime Commission before serving in the U.S. Navy during World War II. After the war, he established Galaxy Inc., a corporation that promoted American technology abroad, and served as its president until his retirement in 1985.

Stuart, Robert Young (February 13, 1883–October 23, 1933)

Robert Stuart Young earned his M.F. in forestry from Yale University in 1906 and immediately joined the U.S. FOREST SERVICE, going to work in the Rocky Mountains. In 1910, he became assistant district forester and in 1912 accompanied his chief, William B. GREELEY, to Washington, D.C., as assistant chief of silviculture. Stuart served two years with the 10th and 20th (Forestry) Engineer regiments during World War I, then returned to the Forest Service.

In 1920, Stuart resigned his Forest Service position to become deputy commissioner of forestry in Pennsylvania under Gifford PINCHOT. When Pinchot was elected Pennsylvania's governor in 1922, Stuart was made commissioner of forestry, then, in 1923, secretary of forests and waters. He rejoined the U.S. Forest Service in 1927 and succeeded Greeley as its chief in 1928.

During his tenure as chief of the Forest Service, Stuart enlarged federal forest holdings, but backed off from promoting federal regulation of cutting on private lands, preferring to urge the states to intervene. Under Stuart, the nationwide forest survey mandated by the McSweeney-McNary Act got under way, and the service issued its *National Plan for American Forestry* in 1933. Stuart was working feverishly to establish the first CIVILIAN CONSERVATION CORPS camps for forestry work when he succumbed to a heart attack.

Student Conservation Association (Founded: 1957)

Box 550, Charlestown, New Hampshire 03603; (603) 826-4301

The Student Conservation Association engages high school and college students in volunteer activities in the nation's parks and public lands. Working with natural resource conservation agencies, the association identifies volunteer opportunities and places 900 resource assistants in those agencies each year. Designed for individuals 18 years old and older, the resource assistant positions are 12-week, expense-paid internships at such agencies as the NATIONAL PARK SERVICE, the U.S. FOREST SERVICE, the U.S. FISH

Student Conservation Association revegetation work in Yellowstone National Park. *Photo by Janet Warren, Student Conservation Association, Inc.*

AND WILDLIFE SERVICE, the Bureau of LAND MANAGEMENT and various state wildlife departments and private organizations. The association's high school programs, for students 16 to 18 years old, engage participants in four to five weeks of summer work. Organized in crews of six to 10, the students work on trail, campsite or revegetation projects and live in tent camps. The association and participating agencies provide food, lodging and equipment to the student workers.

In addition to its volunteer placement programs, the Student Conservation Association conducts a Wilderness Work Skills Program for professional resource managers at 10 to 15 locations throughout the country.

Since 1957, the Student Conservation Association has placed an average of 1,300 volunteers each year in participating agencies. In addition, the association publishes *JOB-SCAN*, a listing of paid positions available in resource management, and a semiannual *Newsletter*.

T

Talbot, Lee Merriam (August 2, 1930–   )
Lee Merriam Talbot is a research fellow at the Environment and Policy Institute of the East-West Center in Honolulu and visiting fellow at the WORLD RESOURCES INSTITUTE. A native of New Bedford, Massachusetts, Talbot holds a B.A. in wildlife conservation and an M.A. and Ph.D. in ecology from the University of California, Berkeley. In 1954, working for the INTERNATIONAL UNION FOR CONSERVATION OF NATURE AND NATURAL RESOURCES (IUCN), he began conducting conservation surveys in Europe, Africa and Asia. In 1959, he and his wife, Mary, initiated pioneering ecosystem research projects in the Serengeti-Mara Plains of East Africa. He was responsible for the IUCN's Southeast Asia conservation program from 1964 to 1965. In 1966, he was named resident ecologist and field representative for international affairs at the Smithsonian Institution. When President Nixon created the President's COUNCIL ON ENVIRONMENTAL QUALITY in 1970, Talbot was named senior scientist. He remained on the council through the administrations of three presidents and was responsible for the group's international activities. In 1978, he joined the staff of World Wildlife Fund International, headquartered in Switzerland, as director of conservation and was elected director general of the IUCN.

Talbot has conducted environmental research in more than 100 countries and has consulted with governments and organizations around the world, focusing especially on international conservation, wildlife ecology and management, tropical land use and savannah ecology, conservation of renewable natural resources, methodology of ecological research and survey, environmental impact analysis, endangered species and environmental impact of economic development.

In "Feeding the Earth: An Agroecological Solution," a 1988 article published in *Technology Review,* Talbot and coauthor Michael J. Dover criticized policies that encourage poor farmers in Third World countries to adopt the agricultural methods of Western developed nations. The authors characterize those farming methods as capital-intensive and claim that, although the caloric intake of wealthy urban residents in Third World countries has increased substantially, the intake of the growers of food in those countries has increased only slightly. In addition, they argue that Western methods do not work in the tropics and that they may, in fact, destroy the croplands. They advocate the development and implementation of new, more affordable agricultural methods that are ecologically sound for tropical farmlands.

Talbot has received awards from the WILDLIFE SOCIETY and the ANIMAL WELFARE INSTITUTE.

Tansley, Arthur George (August 15, 1871– November 25, 1955)
The London-born editor and author of *The British Islands and their Vegetation* and father of the notion of ecosystems, Arthur George Tansley was a pioneer in plant ecology and instructor at various British universities.

After graduating from Trinity College, Cambridge, in 1894, Tansley worked as an assistant to Professor Francis Oliver and as a demonstrator in botany at University College until 1906. During this time, he visited Ceylon, the Malay Peninsula and Egypt, where he studied native flora. Returning to England, he founded *The New Phytologist,* a journal he edited for the next 30 years. In 1907, he was named university lecturer in botany at Cambridge University. In 1927, he moved to Oxford University and Magdalen College, where he served as the Sherardian Professor of Botany until his retirement in 1939.

Tansley's most important work focused on the flora of the British Isles. Between 1903 and 1907, he coordinated a project to map vegetation and established a prototypical mapping technique. He and the other scientists working on this project produced *Types of British Vegetation* in 1911. Next, he and his team of scientists founded the British Ecological Society in 1913 and created the *Journal of Ecology*, which Tansley edited from 1916 to 1918.

Tansley revised *Types of British Vegetation* and published it as *The British Islands and their Vegetation* in 1939. This substantially new work explored the ways in which vegetation is affected by soil composition, climate, animal populations and human uses. Ten years later, he published a shorter, popular version of the 1939 book, calling it *Britain's Green Mantle*. His other publications include several guides, among them *Practical Plant Ecology* (1923).

Tansley served as chairman of the NATURE CONSERVANCY from 1949 to 1953 and as president of the Council for the Promotion of Field Studies (currently named the Field Studies Council) from 1947 to 1953. For his work in ecology, he was honored with several awards, including a fellowship from the Royal Society of London, the Gold Medal of the Linnaean Society and a knighthood.

Tansley was critical of Frederic CLEMENTS's theories of successional climaxes in plant life, and the notion of a monoclimax. Tansley argued that any number of conditions might affect vegetation: soils, animal use and fires, among others. To these causes of climaxes, Tansley added the "anthropogenic" climax, one in which humans create an artificial biological system that is stable and balanced. He cited as an example an agricultural system. He conceded that human populations had changed the course of natural ecological successions, but he contended that the changes made by humankind were no different from the changes made by other, more "natural" factors, such as soil composition and animals.

In 1935, Tansley launched a further attack on Clements's organismic theories in an essay arguing that ecology, as a mature science, must necessarily divide up the "units of nature" into its separate parts. Nature was to be viewed not as the single living organism Clements proposed, but as a composite of separate entities. In addition, Tansley opposed the use of the term *community* to describe any particular grouping of plants and animals. He objected to the anthropomorphic connotations of the term and feared that those who used it viewed human communities and plant "communities" as parallel. For Tansley, *community* connoted images of psychic bonds and social orders, which did not exist in the plant world. By purging the term from ecological descriptions, Tansley hoped to ban all trace of romanticism and moralizing from the science of ecology. In place of *community*, Tansley used the term *ecosystem*. By studying the natural world as an ecosystem instead of as an organic community, he sought to describe the exchanges of energy and chemical substances among the various components of the system. The study of these components was thus reduced to a study of energy in the form of nutrients, and the resulting ecological model could be measured and quantified.

Taylor, Walter Penn (October 31, 1888–March 29, 1972)

Born in Elkhorn, Wisconsin, Taylor became a biologist, ecologist and educator. He went to work for the California Museum of Vertebrate Zoology in 1911 while he was still a student at the University of California, Berkeley. Two years after receiving his Ph.D., he joined the staff of the Biological Survey (later the U.S. FISH AND WILDLIFE SERVICE) as an assistant biologist. Over the next 35 years with this federal agency, he produced more than 300 technical publications and taught a generation of wildlife managers at the University of Arizona (1932–35), Texas A & M (1936–47) and Oklahoma Agricultural and Mechanical College (1947–51).

After retiring from the U.S. Fish and Wildlife Service, Taylor continued his teaching career at Claremont Graduate School (California) and Southern Illinois University, coauthored *The Birds of the State of Washington* (1953) and edited *Deer of North America* (1956).

Organizations that benefited from Taylor's service include the ECOLOGICAL SOCIETY OF AMERICA (president, 1934), the American Society of Mammalogists (president, 1941–42), the Outdoor Writer's Association and the WILDLIFE SOCIETY (president, 1943). He was honored with the Aldo LEOPOLD Award from the Wildlife Society in 1943 and received the U.S. Department of the INTERIOR's Gold Medal in 1951 for distinguished service.

Tennessee Valley Authority

Created by federal legislation on May 18, 1933, the Tennessee Valley Authority, part of Franklin Delano ROOSEVELT's New Deal, is rooted in the earlier conservation programs of President Theodore ROOSEVELT, during whose administration the Inland Waterways Commission proposed a program for improved resource use in the Tennessee River basin. One of the TVA's first activities was reforestation to improve soil conservation. More than 7,500 men hired by the CIVILIAN CONSERVATION CORPS (CCC) worked in reforestation in the region, and their efforts were continued by private landowners after the CCC was disbanded. By 1960, private owners were reforesting some 90,000 acres annually.

When the TVA was created, nearly 10% of the forests in the Tennessee Valley basin burned each year. Again, the TVA and CCC cooperated in fighting fires, building fire towers and educating foresters and the public about the need for fire prevention.

At the time of its creation, the TVA did not count power production among its high priorities. Today, however, the agency is the largest utility in the United States, and 97% of its budget is allocated to power. In recent years, the TVA has weathered a storm of criticism directed against its dams, which forced the relocation of many families and the flooding of thousands of acres of farmland; against its coal-fired generators; and against its nuclear power program. The TVA has canceled most of the 19 nuclear power projects it had originally planned. Protests have also halted construction of the Tellico Dam, which threatened the snail darter, an endangered species of fish.

Further reading: Willis M. Baker, "Reminiscing about the TVA," *American Forests* 75 (May 1969): 30–31, 56–60; Richard Kilbourne, "A Quarter-Century of Forestry Progress in the Tennessee Valley," *Southern Lumberman* 195 (December 15, 1957): 100–105.

Thoreau, Henry David (July 12, 1817–May 6, 1862)

Author, Transcendentalist philosopher and self-taught naturalist, Henry David Thoreau was in many ways responsible for infusing the emerging field of ecology with a romantic vision of the world. Educated at Harvard, he worked in his father's pencil factory and as a teacher and surveyor. His true vocation was that of a writer, but his works, now considered classics of American literature, reached only a small circle of readers during his lifetime.

Walden, or Life in the Woods (1854), his masterpiece, describes a two-year experiment in self-sufficiency conducted from 1845 to 1847, when Thoreau withdrew from community life to Walden Pond near Concord, Massachusetts. In its pages are accounts of his daily life, his experiments in agricultural subsistence, his visitors and the plants and wildlife in the area.

While *Walden* is of great spiritual and intellectual significance to modern ecologists, more valuable on a practical level is Thoreau's *Journal*, first published in 14 volumes in 1906. Compiled during the 1850s, the 2- million-word work develops Thoreau's ecological philosophy. Thoreau was attracted to the new model of ecology emerging in the mid-19th century, a model that emphasized change and turbulence. He

Henry David Thoreau

wrote that every organism, whether plant, animal or human, is "contending for the possession of the planet." Keeping such contentions in check were natural foes and climatic changes. Nature, for Thoreau, was exuberant and rich with apparent excess. As an example, he noted that vegetation, left unchecked, would cover the world. Yet he believed that nothing in nature was "wasted." To him, every animal and plant had its niche, its necessary role to play in the grand natural scheme: "Every decayed leaf and twig and fibre is only the better fitted to serve in some other department, and all at last are gathered in her compost-heap."

The woods held a particular fascination for Thoreau. He described the dense forest cover of the 17th century in New England, where white and pitch pines, hemlocks, chestnuts, maples, birches and oaks created a green canopy over most of the terrain. He noted estimates that, within a given 10-square-mile forest area could be found five black bears, two pumas, two gray wolves, 200 turkeys, 400 white-tailed deer and 20,000 gray squirrels. By Thoreau's epoch, this forest region had been reduced by 60%. The changes wrought by human society were not yet irreversible in the mid-19th century, but recovery of the pristine state would require accommodations that ran counter to an age that heedlessly embraced industrial progress.

In 1860, Thoreau presented a lecture entitled "The Succession of Forest Trees" at the Middlesex Agricultural Society's annual cattle show in Concord. Widely reprinted, the essay developed the theme of the ecology of the seed. Noting how the woodland sustained itself—through seeds buried by squirrels and other animals and by the blowing of seeds to new planting spots—Thoreau called on society to emulate nature in woodland management. He advocated the planting of seeds according to the plan manifest in nature, a process that would result in a perpetual woodland crop for farmers.

Thoreau also advocated the preservation of woodland areas. He proposed that each town take responsibility for the preservation of a "primitive forest" within its boundaries. Measuring 500 or 1,000 acres, each area would be a preserve for both plants and animals and would provide a place for the study of nature and for recreation. "As some give to Harvard College or another institution, why might not another give a forest or huckleberry field to Concord?" he wrote in his later journals.

Throughout his studies and writings, Thoreau's purpose was to reconstruct "the actual condition of the place where we dwell" as it appeared in the centuries before the arrival of Europeans in the New World, and his advice to humankind was to accommodate to the natural order. This romantic, arcadian infusion was to remain in ecological studies for decades to come.

Further reading: Sherman Paul, *The Shores of America: Thoreau's Inward Exploration* (Champaign-Urbana: University of Illinois Press, 1958); F. N. Sanborn, *The Life of Henry David Thoreau* (Boston: Houghton Mifflin, 1917).

Tindall, Barry Sanford (June 29, 1939–   )

A native of Edinburg, New Jersey, Barry Sanford Tindall entered the conservation field in 1963 as a research aide in watershed management, a program of the U.S. FOREST SERVICE. Four years later, he joined the staff of the National Recreation and Park Association and worked as a conservation program specialist and director of public affairs before being named director of public policy. He holds an A.A.S. in forestry from Paul Smith's College of Arts and Science, a B.S. in recreation and park administration from North Carolina State University and an M.A. in urban and regional planning from George Washington University.

Tindall has applied his expertise in park management and conservation issues to projects of various conservation organizations. In 1970, he served as project director and editor of *State Park Statistics* and two years later as project director of *Island of Hope: Parks and Recreation in Environmental Crisis*. From 1974 to 1975, he assisted the NATURE CONSERVANCY in its analysis of policies affecting natural areas, both public and private. That work resulted in *The Preservation of Natural Diversity: A Survey and Recommendations*. He has served as an instructor in the politics of conservation at the U.S. Department of AGRICULTURE's Graduate School.

Tindall has served on the board of directors of the Audubon Naturalist Society of the Central Atlantic States and has been honored with awards from the NATIONAL PARK SERVICE, the Heritage Conservation and Recreation Service and North Carolina State University's School of Forest Resources.

Titus, Elizabeth Cushman (April 3, 1933–   )

A native of Long Island, New York, Elizabeth C. Titus was educated at the genteel Green Vale School in Glen Head, Long Island (1939–48), and at Miss Porter's School, Farmington, Connecticut (1948–51), before going on to earn a B.A. at Vassar College (1951–55). Her senior thesis was entitled "A Proposal for a Student Conservation Corps," which embodied her response to articles she had read concerning the plight of the nation's parks and difficulties suffered by the chronically understaffed NATIONAL PARK SERVICE. While experiencing the western outdoors personally by working on two "dude ranches" during the summers of 1955, 1957 and 1958, Titus put her bachelor's thesis to practical work by organizing the Student Conservation Program in cooperation with the NATIONAL PARKS AND CONSERVATION ASSOCIATION. The program gave students an opportunity to earn academic credit while serving as interns at Grand Teton National Park and Olympic National Park, building and maintaining trails, repairing park structures, organizing office files and learning about the wilderness.

From 1957 to 1960, Titus served as the director of the program under the auspices of the National Parks and Conservation Association, then, from 1961 to 1962, as director under the auspices of the NATIONAL PARK SERVICE. She worked as consultant to the program between 1962 and 1965, then established it as an independent organization—the STUDENT CONSERVATION ASSOCIATION—in 1965, serving as executive director and president until 1969, then as president and today as founding president.

Elizabeth C. Titus is also active in the Garden Club of America, the Vermont Nature Conservancy and the Vermont Natural Resources Council. She is a

Russell E. Train, chairman of the board, World Wildlife Fund. *Courtesy of World Wildlife Fund*

member of the board of trustees of Merck Forest and a member of the president's advisory council of the University of Vermont.

Train, Russell Enrol (June 4, 1920–   )

A native of Jamestown, Rhode Island, Russell Enrol Train graduated from Princeton University in 1941. He served in the United States Army during World War II and then enrolled in Columbia University, receiving an LL.B. degree in 1947. After working on the staffs of several congressional committees, he was named assistant to the secretary of the treasury in 1956. The following year he was appointed judge in the U.S. Tax Court, a position he held until 1965. Because of his life-long interest in African wildlife, Train founded the African Wildlife Leadership Foundation in 1961 and became its first president and chairman of the board. He also took an active role in the leadership of the CONSERVATION FOUNDATION as trustee in 1964 and president from 1965 to 1969.

Train was appointed under secretary of the U.S. Department of the INTERIOR in 1969. The following year, he was named chairman of the President's COUNCIL ON ENVIRONMENTAL QUALITY. Between 1973 and 1977, he was administrator of the ENVIRONMENTAL PROTECTION AGENCY. He was president and chief executive officer of the WORLD WILDLIFE FUND from 1978 to 1985, when he became chairman of the board of the organization, which had merged with the Conservation Foundation.

Train has figured importantly in other environmental groups, including the BOONE AND CROCKETT CLUB, the British Fauna Preservation Society, the American Conservation Association, the AMERICAN FORESTRY ASSOCIATION, the INTERNATIONAL UNION FOR THE CONSERVATION OF NATURE AND NATURAL RESOURCES and the Year 2000 Committee.

Train has received numerous awards for his conservation work, including the Albert Schweitzer Medal of the ANIMAL WELFARE INSTITUTE (1972), the Aldo LEOPOLD Award of the WILDLIFE SOCIETY (1975), the Conservation of the Year award of the NATIONAL WILDLIFE FEDERATION (1975), the Environmental Leadership Medal of the UNITED NATIONS ENVIRONMENT PROGRAMME (1982) and the ENVIRONMENTAL LAW INSTITUTE award (1986).

In May 1990, Train addressed the North American Conference on Religion and Ecology in Washington, D.C., calling for churches to take an active role in transmitting environmental values to society.

Trees for Tomorrow Inc. (Founded: 1944)

611 Sheridan Street, P. O. Box 609, Eagle River, Wisconsin 54521; (715) 479-6456

Trees for Tomorrow Inc., founded by a consortium of nine pulp and paper mill companies in Wisconsin, has planted or distributed more than 24 million trees since 1944. The group, which includes some 200 individual members and a staff of 16, also designs forest management plans for owners of woodland areas, oversees harvesting in forests and sponsors a scholarship program for students of forestry. The organization's Resources Education Center conducts more than 100 workshops and camp programs for the public, and by 1980, the organization estimated that 130,000 people had attended one of its education programs. The group's publications include *Northbound,* a quarterly journal, and a newsletter on natural resources.

Trees for Tomorrow's activities are restricted to the state of Wisconsin and the Upper Peninsula of Michigan.

Further reading: Folke Becker, "Trees for Tomorrow," *Wisconsin Magazine of History* 36 (Autumn 1952): 43–47.

Trust for Public Land (Founded: 1972)

116 New Montgomery Street, 4th Floor, San Francisco, California 94105; (415) 495-5660

With a staff of 170, the Trust for Public Land is dedicated to acquiring and preserving land in urban as well as rural areas for public use. The trust acquires recreational, historic and scenic lands for conveyance to local, state and federal agencies as well as non-profit organizations for protection as open spaces and for other public uses. It also provides assistance, training and technical advice on land acquisition to community and urban groups, and it assists ranchers and farmers to preserve agricultural lands.

Martin J. Rosen is president of the trust, which publishes an annual report and a magazine, *Land and People*, three times a year.

Turner, John F. (March 3, 1942–   )

A former Wyoming state senator, John F. Turner is director of the U.S. FISH AND WILDLIFE SERVICE of the Department of the INTERIOR.

Born in Jackson Hole, Wyoming, Turner received his bachelor of science in biology from Notre Dame University in 1964. After postgraduate study in zoology at the University of Innsbruck and the University of Utah, he earned his master's degree in wildlife ecology at the University of Michigan (1970). Turner was elected to the Wyoming State Assembly in 1970, and in the next two years, he was honored with the Outstanding Freshman Legislator award (1971) and the Wyoming Press Award (1972). He remained House representative for Teton County until 1974, when he won his seat in the Wyoming Senate. During his 15 years as state senator, the legislator served terms as Senate caucus chairman, majority floor leader, Senate vice-president and president of the Senate. The author of more than two dozen research studies on wildlife, particularly the grizzly bear and the bald eagle, Turner has advised on numerous wildlife-related committees, including the National Wetlands Policy Forum, the National Park System Advisory Board, the Take Pride in America Campaign and the Hovenweep Task Force for the National Park Service. He was named 1984 Citizen of the Year, Teton County, and in 1985, he received the Friend of Mental Health Award and a Special Achievement Conservation Award from the National Wildlife Federation.

Turner was made director of the Fish and Wildlife Service in August 1989, and he currently serves as chairman of the Standing Committee of the United Nations Convention for Wetlands of International Importance, vice-chairman of the secretary of the interior's National Parks Advisory Board and a board director of the Wyoming Waterfowl Trust. In addition to his work in the public sector, Turner is a rancher and outfitter with his family's Triangle X dude ranch in Moose, Wyoming, and is a member of the advisory council of the College of Agriculture at the University of Wyoming.

Further reading: Turner, *The Magnificent Bald Eagle: Our National Bird* (New York: Random House, 1971).

U

Udall, Morris King (June 15, 1922–   )
A congressman from Arizona (he was born in rural St. Johns), Udall served as chairman of the House Interior and Insular Affairs Committee. From this position he steered through Congress a series of environmental and wilderness protection acts between 1977 and May 30, 1991, when ill health forced him to resign from Congress. His most significant victory was a federal law protecting 100 million acres of wilderness in Alaska.

Udall made two unsuccessful bids for speaker of the House and, in 1976, campaigned for the Democratic Party's presidential nomination, losing to Jimmy Carter. He is the author of *Arizona Law of Evidence* (1960), *Education of a Congressman* (1972) and *Too Funny to Be President* (1988). He is the brother of Stewart Lee UDALL.

Udall, Stewart Lee (January 31, 1920–   )
First elected to Congress in 1954, Stewart Lee Udall served on the House Interior and Insular Affairs Committee where he became known as one of the members of the "conservation bloc."

In 1962, President John F. Kennedy appointed Udall secretary of the interior. In this role, he worked for improved protection of water quality and public lands and expanded parks and recreation areas. During his leadership of the U.S. Department of the INTERIOR, more than 3.8 million acres of land were added to the NATIONAL PARK SERVICE's holdings. Among his other achievements as secretary of the interior are the creation of the Bureau of OUTDOOR RECREATION in 1962 and the Land and Water Conservation Fund in 1964, and the passage of the 1964 Wilderness Act, the 1966 Endangered Species Preservation Act, the 1968 Wild and Scenic Rivers Act and the 1969 National Trails System Act. In 1965, he helped Mrs. Lyndon Johnson convene the White House Conference on Natural Beauty, which resulted in the passage of the Highway Beautification Act.

Udall is the author of two books, *The Quiet Crisis and The Next Generation* (1963), a work that outlines his belief in preserving beauty not only in wilderness areas but in urban regions as well, and *1976: Agenda for Tomorrow* (1968), an exposition of man's ethical responsibility to his environment.

Udall has been honored with awards from the WILDLIFE SOCIETY and the NATIONAL AUDUBON SOCIETY. After leaving public service, he founded Overview, an environmental consulting firm. Like his brother, Congressman MORRIS KING UDALL, Stewart Udall was born in the rural Arizona town of St. Johns.

Further reading: Barbara Le Unes, "The Conservation Philosophy of Stewart L. Udall, 1961–1968," Ph.D. dissertation, Texas A & M University (1977).

Union of Concerned Scientists (Founded: 1969)
26 Church Street, Cambridge, Massachusetts 02238; (617) 547-5552

With more than 100,000 scientists, engineers and other professionals as members, the Union of Concerned Scientists advocates the adoption of national policies on global warming, energy, nuclear power safety and nuclear arms control. Calling for an accounting of fossil fuel costs that includes global warming, air pollution, oil spills, acid rain and health problems, the union engages teams of scientists to work on the energy problem and promotes the use of renewable sources of energy. Other union studies have focused on the use of pesticides, the problems inherent in transporting liquefied natural gas, waste disposal options for nuclear power and the strategic arms race.

The union's research on nuclear power safety has indicated that the power source is not a viable solu-

Howard Ris, executive director of the Union of Concerned Scientists. *Photo by Koby-Antupit Studio, courtesy of the Union of Concerned Scientists*

Since 1969, the Union of Concerned Scientists has compiled studies on global warming and nuclear power and organized a "Billion Pound Diet" campaign, in which communities in all 50 states were engaged in programs to reduce carbon dioxide emissions. The union has published and distributed more than 3 million copies of brochures, including "How YOU Can Fight Global Warming," designed to educate the general public on energy-related issues. In 1990, the union published the *Appeal by American Scientists to Prevent Global Warming*, signed by 52 Nobel Laureates and more than 700 members of the National Academy of Sciences. Presented to President George Bush, the document asserts that global warming is the most serious environmental threat facing the world today.

The Union of Concerned Scientists publishes an eight-page quarterly, *Nucleus*, with articles on global warming, transportation problems, nuclear reactors and arms control. Other publications include *Cool Energy: The Renewable Solution to Global Warming*, *The Energy Switch: Alternatives to Nuclear Power*, *Safety Second: The NRC and America's Nuclear Power Plants*, *Steering a New Course: Transportation, Energy, and the Environment* and a video entitled *Greenhouse Crisis: The American Reponse*. Howard Ris is executive director of UCS.

United Nations Environment Programme
(Established: 1972)
Executive Director Dr. Mostafa K. Tolba, P.O. Box 30552; Nairobi, Kenya; (254) 2-333930
New York Regional Office for North America, UNEP Liaison Office, UNDC Two Building, Room 0803, Two United Nations Plaza, New York, NY 10017; (212) 963-8138

UNEP was established on December 15, 1972, by act of the United Nations General Assembly in response to a report of the secretary-general on the U.N. Conference on the Human Environment. It began operations from a temporary headquarters in Stockholm, Sweden, then moved to its permanent headquarters in Nairobi, Kenya.

UNEP aims to promote international cooperation in the field of the environment and to recommend appropriate policies, provide general policy guidance, coordinate environmental programs with the United Nations system, keep under review the world environmental situation, promote the exchange of environmental information among nations, maintain under review the international impact of the environmental activities of the various nations and review the effect of development plans of developing nations.

tion to the country's energy needs. Scientists engaged in the research claim that nuclear power is too expensive and too dangerous. In 1987, the group called on the Nuclear Regulatory Commission to close eight nuclear reactors similar in design to the faulty reactor at the Three Mile Island plant. The reactors, manufactured by the Babcock & Wilcox Corporation, were called "the most dangerous of all pressurized-water designs" by the union's nuclear experts, who cited at least 30 accidents at the eight plants. In a study undertaken after the NRC's suspension of new power plant construction and the closing of some exisitng sites, union scientists considered three new designs for reactors and recommended design changes that improved safety and noted others that increased the likelihood of accidents or that were vulnerable to sabotage. Headed by Gregory C. Minor, the union's study group said that no matter how many safety features were incorporated into the design of reactors, risk of malfunctions and accidents would always be present.

UNEP maintains a special program called Earthwatch, which is designed to provide early warning of significant environmental risks and opportunities. UNEP ensures that all governments have access to this information. Earthwatch monitors the state of the environment through the Global Environment Monitoring System (GEMS), the International Environmental Information System (INFOTERRA) and the International Register of Potentially Toxic Chemicals (IRPTC).

UNEP does not restrict its activities to providing official aid to government agencies, but also works to raise public awareness of environmental issues and to encourage community and nongovernmental action to address global, regional and local problems. To these ends, the organization offers an array of programs that provide information, education, training and technical assistance. It organizes a World Environment Day each June 5th.

UNEP administers the Fund of the United Nations Environment Programme and is governed by a council of 58 member nations, which convenes every two years. Permanent paid staff of the program numbers approximately 500.

V

Vajk, Joseph Peter (August 3, 1942–   )
A consultant, lecturer and writer with Space Energetics Inc. in Walnut Creek, California, Joseph Peter Vajk was born in Budapest, Hungary. He holds an A.B. degree from Cornell University and a master's degree and Ph.D. from Princeton University. From 1968 to 1976, he was the senior physicist in the Theoretical Physics Division of the Lawrence Livermore Laboratory in Livermore, California. In 1976, he moved to Science Applications Inc., Pleasanton, California, where he was senior scientist.

Vajk's *Doomsday Has Been Cancelled* was published in 1978 by Peace Press. In it, Vajk argues for a "more humane and positive future," asserting that the colonization of space and the use and development of energy resources and raw materials from space will bring about a new period of hope for humanity.

Vajk's recent research has focused on the strategic and technical analyses of defense, both space-based and ground-based.

W

Walcott, Frederic Collin (February 19, 1869–
April 27, 1949)
A founder of the American Game Protective and
Propagation Association, Frederic Collin Walcott
served that organization from 1911 to 1935 as a mem-
ber of the board of directors. A native of New York
Mills, New York, he was elected U.S. senator from
Connecticut in 1929 and over the next six years played
a key role, as chairman of the Special Committee for
Wildlife, in drafting and securing passage of the
Walcott-Kleberg Duck Stamp Act, the Forest Wildlife
Refuge Act, the Pittman-Robertson Federal Aid in
Wildlife Restoration Act, the Whaling Treaty, the
Cooperative Wildlife Research Unit Program and the
Migratory Bird Treaty with Mexico. In addition, he
worked on legislation that established the Patuxent
Wildlife Research Center of the Bureau of BIOLOGICAL
SURVEY and that combined the Bureau of Biological
Survey and the Bureau of Sport Fisheries into the
U.S. FISH AND WILDLIFE SERVICE. In 1935, he and
other senators persuaded President Franklin D. ROO-
SEVELT to convene the first international American
Wildlife Conference. Walcott was president of the
American Wildlife Institute and the North American
Wildlife Foundation. He also chaired the Connecticut
Board of Fisheries and Game.

Walker, John Ernest (October 14, 1942–   )
John Walker is president of DUCKS UNLIMITED INC.,
an organization of environmentally minded sportsmen dedicated to preserving North America's waterfowl.

After earning a bachelor's degree in business administration, Walker worked for the American National Insurance Company as an investment analyst.
He is now an independent investment manager in
Galveston, Texas. For the past 20 years, Walker has
been active in DU, serving as the first DU Texas state

chairman in 1971. He has also served as a national
trustee for the organization, regional vice-president
and senior flyway vice-president.

As a concerned sportsman, Walker is the typical
Ducks Unlimited activist. He is also associated with
the Migratory Game Bird Association, which was
responsible for the passage of the Texas Duck Stamp
Act of 1990.

Wallace, Catherine (January 17, 1952–   )
A warrior in the battle against "environmental van-
dalism," Catherine Wallace of New Zealand has called
for the creation of a world park on Antarctica in order
to preserve the continent by regulating tourism and
industry. As of 1991, 12 nations have endorsed her
plan for the park.

The daughter of a marine biologist and agricultural
scientist, Wallace first entered the environmental field
when the government of New Zealand granted to a
private mining company the right to explore the
forest lands of her family's sheep ranch. She protested the action and succeeded in getting the proposed mining program halted.

In 1991, Wallace was one of seven environmentalists awarded a Goldman Environmental Prize of
$60,000.

Wallace, Henry Agard (October 7, 1888–
November 18, 1965)
Born in Adair County, Iowa, of a prominent farm
family—his father, Henry C. Wallace, was secretary
of agriculture under Warren G. Harding and Calvin
Coolidge—Henry Agard Wallace became associate
editor of *Wallace's Farmer* after graduating from Iowa
State College in 1910. During his early years, Wallace
produced a study of farm prices, which was developed into the first hog-ratio charts, and he experimented in agricultural genetics, developing a hybrid

Henry A. Wallace

corn that his family marketed. In 1924, he was named editor of the magazine, which in 1929 merged with another publication, becoming *Wallace's Farmer and Iowa Homestead*.

In 1933, President Franklin D. ROOSEVELT named Wallace secretary of agriculture. Working through New Deal programs, Wallace developed soil conservation and controlled production programs. After serving Roosevelt through two terms as secretary of agriculture, Wallace was named the president's running mate when Roosevelt ran for his third term in 1940. He was replaced by Harry S Truman on the fourth-term ticket in 1944, but was named secretary of commerce in 1945. Wallace resigned from that post less than a year later because of differences with Truman, who had succeeded Roosevelt upon the latter's death.

After leaving office, Wallace edited the *New Republic* and then decided to run for the presidency on the Progressive ticket. He received more than 1 million popular votes, but no electoral ballots. After his defeat, he returned to his home in South Salem, New York, where he continued to conduct experiments in agricultural genetics until his death.

Further reading: Russell Lord, *The Wallaces of Iowa* (Boston: Houghton Mifflin, 1947). Frederick H. Schapsmeir, *Henry A. Wallace of Iowa: The Agrarian Years, 1910–1940* (Ames: Iowa State University Press, 1968) and *Prophet in Politics: Henry A. Wallace and the War Years* (Ames: Iowa State University Press, 1971).

Ward, Lester Frank (June 18, 1841–April 18, 1913)

Sociologist and author Lester Frank Ward was born in Joliet, Illinois, and was raised there and in Iowa. After serving in the Union Army during the Civil War, he worked for the Treasury Department and studied at Columbian College (now George Washington University), graduating in 1869 and receiving a law degree in 1871. Rather than practice law, Ward turned to the study of geology, paleontology and botany, disciplines in which he was largely self-taught. In 1881, he was named geologist with the U.S. GEOLOGICAL SURVEY and was appointed paleontologist in 1892. During his tenure at the U.S. Geological Survey, Ward wrote *Dynamic Sociology*, a work that explored evolutionary sociology and for which he became known as the "father of American sociology."

Ward believed that civilization demanded the rational management of nature. In *The Psychic Factors of Civilization* (1893), he called for science to reorder nature and thereby "redeem" it from its primitive state. He claimed that "nature has no economy," citing the meandering of rivers, the prolific laying of eggs by herrings and the anachronistic redwoods. Ward saw man as the potential instrument through which a higher order might be introduced into the otherwise chaotic natural world.

Warming, Johannes Eugenius Bulow (November 3, 1841–April 2, 1924)

Born in Mandø, Denmark, Johannes Eugenius Bulow Warming is credited with the establishment of plant ecology as a discipline within the study of botany. Although it was Ernst HAECKEL who coined the term "ecology" in 1866, Warming was the person most responsible for firmly establishing a basis for the study of the interrelationships of plant species.

Warming studied at the universities of Copenhagen, Munich and Bonn. He received his doctoral degree from the University of Copenhagen in 1871 and, two years later, took a position as a botany instructor. From 1873 to 1882, he served as professor of botany at the Royal Institute of Technology in Stockholm, Sweden. Then, from 1885 until his retirement in 1911, he was professor of botany at the University of Copenhagen and director of the Botanical Gardens.

While still a student at the University of Copenhagen, Warming assisted the Danish zoologist P. W. Lund in an excavation of fossils in Brazil. During this expedition, Warming studied tropical vegetation and, over the next several years, compiled his research, which was published in 1892 as *Lagoa Santa: A Contribution to Biological Phytogeography.* Other expeditions in which Warming participated were to Greenland (1884), Norway (1885) and the West Indies and Venezuela (1890–92).

Warming's most significant work was developed in *Plantesamfund,* published in 1895 and revised and translated into English in 1909 as *The Oecology of Plants: An Introduction to the Study of Plant Communities.* The work begins with a thorough description of the factors that determined which habitat groups were present within a region: light, heat, humidity, soil, terrain and animals. Each of these factors, Warming believed, had a determining effect on the composition of the plant community, by which he meant the group of several species sharing the same environmental conditions. A large portion of the book discusses the communal life of organisms, for, according to Warming, the interrelationships among plants and animals can take on several different forms. Of the more than a dozen interrelationships Warming identified, the most common was "commensalism," a state in which different species complement each other, one using nutrients provided by the other. Another interrelationship was "symbiotic"—for example, the combination of algae and fungus to form lichen, or the nondestructive parasitic dependence of some species of plants on host species. The importance of these natural linkages would be explored for years to come in the new field of ecology.

Warming was the first botanist to adopt Charles DARWIN's proposition that nearly every species is sustained to some degree by other species, and that the different species battle each other for primacy.

In his *Oecology,* Warming also developed a system for classifying plant communities, primarily in relation to the water content of soil. He named those plants that required a large amount of water "hydrophytes," while plants that thrived in arid conditions, he called "xerophytes." Those in regions with moderate amounts of annual rainfall, he labeled "mesophytes." Others he classified according to the amount of salt or acid present in the soil. The process of plant succession was yet another part of Warming's *Oecology.* He wrote that each such succession in nature progressed toward a "climax" or final community, which was diverse, stable and self-perpetuating. Any number of factors could alter the existing plant and animal community. People might set fire to a forest or introduce new animals to graze in the region. Beavers might change the amount of water within a region by damming a stream. Years of drought might forever alter the water content of the soil. This concept of sucessional development became an integral part of the new study of ecology and was to be debated, examined and elaborated upon for decades to come.

Waste Watch (Founded: 1979)

P. O. Box 298, Livingston, Kentucky 40445

Waste Watch, a volunteer arm of the Technical Information Project, engaged private citizens and government agency employees in community action projects on waste management. With 2,000 members and 12 regional groups, the organization worked to increase public knowledge about waste issues and to engage citizens in advocacy programs. Waste Watch offered a consulting program and conducted seminars and workshops on waste disposal and other environmental issues. A. J. Fritsch was director of the organization, which became inactive in 1992.

Water Pollution Control Federation (Founded: 1928)

601 Wythe Street, Alexandria, Virginia 22314-1994; (703) 684-2400, Fax (703) 684-2492

An international educational and technical organization, the Water Pollution Control Federation represents over 60 member societies of water system professionals, including municipal and industrial engineers, facility superintendents and operators, chemists, researchers, educators and equipment manufacturers. Established in 1928 as the Federation of Sewage Works Associations, the group's initial purpose was to create the *Sewage Works Journal,* and today the WPCF continues to produce a number of professional periodicals—*Water, Environment, and Technology, The Research Journal of the WPCF, Operations Forum, The Bench Sheet, Safety and Health Bulletin, Washington Bulletin, Literature Review* and *The Job Bank*—as well as the book series *Manuals of Practice,* several audiovisual training courses, public information materials and a Water Environment Curriculum for middle-school students.

The federation seeks to preserve and improve water quality and resources throughout the world and to increase public awareness of water pollution control. The group's volunteer committees formulate recommendations on individual water quality issues and report on technical advances in the design, operation and management of water processing facilities. Representatives of the WPCF meet with government officials to discuss environmental policies and comment on regulations affecting public and industrial wastewater treatment. The organization sponsors the WPCF Research Foundation, maintains an extensive library of water-related volumes, bestows awards and holds annual and specialty conferences for water system professionals.

Watkins, James David (March 7, 1927–   )

In 1989, Admiral James D. Watkins (ret.), a native of Alhambra, California, succeeded John S. Herrington as secretary of the U.S. Department of ENERGY in the cabinet of President George Bush. Among his top priorities were the operation and modernization of the department's defense production program and associated problems of cleaning up production sites. Before taking office, he declared his intention of revitalizing nuclear power as a viable source of energy in the United States. Environmentalists have been concerned that Watkins's efforts on behalf of nuclear energy production would overshadow nuclear waste clean-up. But, in 1991, Watkins issued the National Energy Strategy, the Bush administration's proposed energy plan, which addresses energy efficiency, the use of natural gas, oil and electricity, the generation of nuclear power, renewable energy sources, alternative fuels and industrial innovations in addition to the generation of nuclear power. With the end of the Bush presidency, Watkins was replaced as secretary of energy by Hazel R. O'Leary.

In the Navy, Watkins had served under Admiral Hyman Rickover, the father of the Navy's nuclear propulsion program. Watkins studied at the Navy's reactor school in West Milton, New York, and graduated from the reactor training program at Oak Ridge National Laboratory. He served as commander of the Pacific Fleet from 1981 to 1982 and as chief of Naval Operations from 1982 to 1986. In 1987, President Ronald Reagan appointed him to a 13-member commission on AIDS, and later that year, he became the commission's chairman.

Watt, James Gaius (January 31, 1938–   )

In 1969, James Gaius Watt, a native of Lusk, Wyoming, went to work for the U.S. Department of the INTERIOR as a deputy assistant secretary for water and power development, and in 1972, he was named director of the department's Bureau of OUTDOOR RECREATION, a post he held until 1975. With Ronald REAGAN's election to the presidency, Watt became secretary of the interior in 1981.

As secretary, Watt came under fire from environmentalists for his stance on the exploitation of natural resources. Almost immediately after taking office, he announced plans to ease the regulation of oil and gas drilling leases on federal lands and offshore waters, to open federal lands to grazing, timber cutting and oil exploration and to stop new acquisition of land for the National Park Service. He also planned to ease the regulation of strip mining and concessions in national parks and to suspend additions to the list of endangered species. Following these announcements, by October 1981, several environmental organizations filed lawsuits against him, and the SIERRA CLUB began circulating a petition calling for his removal. In response, Watt backed down on some of his plans, only to announce in July 1982 a five-year program to open 1 billion acres of coastline to offshore drillers. By 1983, Watt's policies had created such a furor that President Reagan removed him from office.

After leaving government service, Watt became a business consultant in Washington, D.C., and Jackson Hole, Wyoming, and served as chairman of the boards of Environmental Diagnostics (1984–87) and Disease Detection International (1986 to the present).

Watts, Lyle Ford (November 18, 1890–June 15, 1962)

A native of Clear Lake, Iowa, Lyle F. Watts studied forestry at Iowa State College, earning his B.S. in 1913, and joined the U.S. FOREST SERVICE. Watts served as supervisor of three national forests in Idaho between 1918 and 1926 and was promoted to assistant chief for forest management in the Intermountain Region, serving until 1928. He left the Forest Service for 15 months to organize and head the department of forestry at Utah State Agricultural College in Logan, then returned to the service as senior silviculturalist.

After serving as director of the forest experiment station in Missoula, Montana, from 1931 to 1936, Watts was appointed North Central regional forester, overseeing a major expansion of national forest holdings in that region. He became regional forester for the Pacific Northwest in 1939, and in 1943 became chief of the Forest Service.

Watts was a believer in strong federal regulation of forest lands, as well as cooperation among states, private owners, and the federal government. Although he was unsuccessful in introducing federal regulation of private use on a large scale, he did reduce cattle grazing on national forest lands by 20% and managed to achieve a reasonable balance between the greatly increased postwar demands for lumber and the need to preserve the national forests.

Watts was instrumental in advancing international forestry when he helped start the forestry program under the United Nations Food and Agriculture Organization. For his services to the United Nations effort, the French government decorated him with the Croix du Chevalier de la Mérite Agricole, and the U.S. Department of AGRICULTURE presented its Distinguished Service Award.

Watts retired from the Forest Service in 1953 to chair Oregon's Water Resources Committee, which achieved environmentally sound reform of the state's water law by 1955. Active in the IZAAK WALTON LEAGUE, Watts served as conservation adviser to Oregon Senator Richard L. Neuberger and his wife, Maureen, after she succeeded him in 1960. Watts served on the executive board of Conservationists for Stevenson-Kefauver during the 1956 Democratic presidential campaign. He was also an adviser to the 1960 Kennedy-Johnson campaign.

Waxman, Henry Arnold (September 12, 1939–   )
A native of Los Angeles, Henry A. Waxman was elected to represent California's Twenty-fourth Congressional District (Hollywood and part of the San Fernando Valley) in 1974 and has served since. A liberal Democrat, Waxman has been a strong environmental legislator. He is credited with maintaining a strong pro-environment voice during the difficult REAGAN years and with playing a key role in forging the strengthened Clean Air Act of 1990. For nearly a decade, Waxman sparred with Michigan Congressman John D. DINGELL, who, while inclined toward much in the environmentalist agenda, held out for relaxation of auto emission standards and anti-smog and anti-acid rain measures. On the eve of the passage of the Clean Air Act, Waxman and Dingell arrived at a workable compromise that helped launch the bill.

Waxman is a member of the House Committee on Energy and Commerce and chairman of the Health and the Environment Subcommittee. He is a strong advocate of legislation to fund education, testing and treatment programs to combat AIDS.

Educated at the University of California, Los Angeles, Waxman received a B.A. in political science in 1961 and his J.D. in 1964. He was admitted to the California bar in 1965 and served on the California State Assembly from 1969 to 1974. He is a member of the SIERRA CLUB.

Wayburn, Edgar (September 17, 1906–   )
Born in Macon, Georgia, Wayburn moved to California, where he practiced medicine and became a longtime supporter of the SIERRA CLUB, first joining the organization in 1939. He played a key role in establishing Redwood National Park and the Golden Gate National Recreation Area and in designing the Alaskan National Interest Lands Conservation Act of 1980.

A member of the board of directors of the Sierra Club since 1957, vice-president for three terms and president for two, Wayburn also chaired the club's Eighth Biennial Wilderness Conference and the Conservation Committee. Other organizations he served include the FEDERATION OF WESTERN OUTDOOR CLUBS and Trustees of Conservation. He received the American Motors Conservation Award in 1964, the John Muir Award from the Sierra Club in 1972 and the NATIONAL PARKS AND CONSERVATION ASSOCIATION'S Marjory Stoneman Douglas Award in 1987. His articles on conservation have appeared in the *Sierra Club Bulletin, Sierra* and *California Medicine*.

Weyerhaeuser, George (July 8, 1926–   )
A native of Seattle, George Weyerhaeuser worked his way up the corporate ladder from logger to president of his family's company, the lumber and paper giant Weyerhaeuser Corporation. Although the company has come under fire for importing woods from endangered tropical forests, it has maintained generally high standards of stewardship of the land it manages. As the world's largest owner of private timberland, Weyerhaeuser has developed a program to increase yields of natural second growth in its forests.

George Weyerhaeuser holds a B.S. in industrial engineering from Yale University and has been president of the family business since 1966.

Wheeler, Douglas Paul (January 10, 1942–   )
Douglas Paul Wheeler was born in Brooklyn and educated at Hamilton College, Clinton, New York, earning an A.B. in government (with honors) in 1963. He took his law degree at Duke University in 1966 and was admitted to the North Carolina bar the same year. He practiced in Charlotte from 1966 to 1969, when he moved to Washington, D.C., to become legislative attorney to the assistant legislative counsel of the U.S. Department of the INTERIOR. In 1972, Wheeler was appointed deputy assistant secretary in the department, serving until 1977, when he became executive vice-president of the National Trust for Historic Preservation. From 1980 to 1985, Wheeler was president of the American Farmland Trust, and then became executive director of the SIERRA CLUB from 1985 to 1986. He returned to Washington as vice president of the Land Heritage and Wildlife Conservation Foundation, becoming executive vice president in 1989.

In addition to his position with the Land Heritage and Wildlife Conservation Foundation, Wheeler has been director of the Wildlife Enhancement Council since 1988 and a member of the advisory committee on hazardous substances for the research and training division of the U.S. Department of Health and Human Services since 1987. He has been director of the Resources Development Foundation since 1984 and a member of various national commissions and boards concerned with recreation and the environment.

Wheeler received a commendation from the Department of the Interior in 1976 and that department's Achievement Award in 1980. Gulf Oil Corporation presented him with its 1985 Conservation Award. He is a lifetime member of the SIERRA CLUB.

Wheeler, William Morton (March 19, 1865–April 19, 1937)

"There are, in fact, no truly solitary organisms." Through his intensive study of ants and other insect species, turn-of-the-century entomologist and author William Morton Wheeler advanced a philosophy of the ultimate interrelatedness of all living beings, a concept that remains one of the underlying principles of ecology. Wheeler's contribution to the theory of emergent evolution—which asserts that radical, unprecedented leaps may occur in the origins and development of biological forms—emphasized the unpredictable creative potential of the social structures found in nature. Association, within and among species, may fundamentally modify the behavior and character of individual organisms, so when biological communities interact at aggregate levels, Wheeler proposed, progressively more complex patterns of organization and ecological cooperation may spontaneously emerge.

Born in Milwaukee, Wheeler attended that city's German-American Normal College, and after graduating in 1884, he catalogued zoological specimens at taxidermist Henry Augustus Ward's Natural Science Establishment in Rochester, New York. There he met and befriended Carl Akeley, who went on to fame as a modernizer of the craft. In June 1885, Wheeler returned to Wisconsin, and over the next few years, while teaching German and physiology at Milwaukee High School, he was introduced to the latest principles and techniques of developmental morphology by leading researchers at the nearby Lake Laboratory. Wheeler undertook an embryological study of the cockroach *Blatta germanica*, and this was published in 1889.

From 1887 to 1890, Wheeler worked as custodian of the Milwaukee Public Museum, then traveled to Worcester, Massachusetts, to pursue a research fellowship at Clark University, where he published 10 entomological papers and earned his Ph.D. in 1892. His doctoral thesis, "A Contribution to Insect Embryology," (1893) is considered a classic in its field. Before commencing his duties as an instructor in embryology at the University of Chicago in 1894, Wheeler spent an acadamic year abroad, visiting the Zoological Institute of the University of Wurzburg, the Naples Zoological Station and the Institut Zoologique at Liège in Belgium. In Chicago, he continued his independent research in entomology, and in 1899, he became a professor of zoology at the University of Texas. During the next four years, he created several of the first field studies of the region's insects and further concentrated his longtime interest in ant species.

Wheeler moved again in 1903, when he was chosen for the curatorship of invertebrate zoology at the American Museum of Natural History in New York. Developing the museum's research collection of insects and designing the exhibition displays for the Hall of the Biology of Invertebrates, he continued to write, and produced over 75 papers, mainly on ants. Wheeler synthesized many of these studies in his first major volume, *Ants: Their Structure, Development and Behavior* (1910).

In 1908 the peripatetic scientist finally settled permanently as a professor of entomology at the Bussey Institution, Harvard University's graduate school of applied biology in Forest Hills, Massachusetts. He held this position for nearly 30 years, and was dean of faculty from 1915 to 1929. The Bussey Institution transferred to Harvard's newly opened Biological Laboratories in Cambridge in 1931, and after his retirement from teaching three years later, Wheeler continued his research at the Laboratories. He died of heart failure in 1937.

Over the course of his career Wheeler authored more than 450 publications. A member of the American Academy of Arts and Sciences and the American Philosophical Society, he was awarded four honorary doctoral degrees, the Eliot Medal of the National Academy of Sciences, and the French Legion of Honor. A man of philosophy and letters as well as science, Wheeler found great significance in the patterns of the social insects, and he promoted an organismic view of ecological interdependence. He believed that biological communities—from the ant colony to the human family to the nation state—become so thoroughly integrated in quality and coordinated in function that the societies themselves may be seen as new, comprehensive organisms from which higher, unforeseen development may evolve. Perhaps because of his respect for the interrelation of all species, Wheeler never applied his knowledge of insects to their agricultural control, and in 1920 he wrote: "As the earth becomes more densely covered with its human populations, it becomes increasingly necessary to retain portions of it in a wild state, i.e., free from the organizing mania of man . . . and return to a Nature that really understands the business of organization."

Further reading: Wheeler, *Social Life among the Insects* (New York: Harcourt, Brace, 1923); *The Social Insects, their Origin and Evolution* (London: K. Paul, Trench Trubner, 1928); *Demons of the Dust* (New York: Norton, 1930); *Foibles of Insects and Men* (New York: Knopf, 1928).

White, Gilbert (July 18, 1720–June 26, 1793)

With the rediscovery, in the 1820s, of *The Natural History and Antiquities of Selborne*, originally published in 1789, Gilbert White became, posthumously, a symbolic leader of the arcadian school of ecology. The arcadian school and the imperial school were the two most important ecological traditions of the 18th century. The arcadian view, which White epitomized, advocated the need for mankind to adopt a simple life in order to achieve peaceful coexistence with nature. The imperial school, best represented by Carolus LINNAEUS, was more in line with popular European philosophies extolling man's faculty of reason and stressing man's dominion over nature. White and Linnaeus represent the conflicting views of man's relationship to nature that would contend for dominance through the next two centuries.

White attended Oriel College in Oxford and received his M.A. degree in 1746. Over the next few years, he served as a curate in various country churches. In 1751, he returned to his native Selborne, where he was curate of St. Mary's.

From his home in Selborne, he carried on a lively correspondence with Thomas Pennant, a zoologist, Daines Barrington, a barrister and judge, and others. These men urged White to collect and publish his letters on the wildlife, seasons and antiquities of his hometown. The resulting book became a cornerstone of naturalist thought and was the prototype of the natural history essay, a hybrid literary-scientific genre especially popular in the 19th century. *Natural History* portrays the unity in diversity that White found in his corner of the universe. His purpose was to discover how many different creatures lived in his parish and how they were related.

For 30 years after its publication, White's book was largely ignored, but by 1830, it had been rediscovered by naturalists, and a "cult of Gilbert White and Selborne" developed. Prominent poets and scientists, including James Russell Lowell and Charles DARWIN, made pilgrimages to Selborne, which had become a symbol of the arcadian ideal of life in harmony with nature.

Further reading: Cecil S. Emden, *Gilbert White in His Village* (London: Oxford University Press, 1956); Walter Johnson (ed.), *Journals of Gilbert White* (Cambridge, Mass.: MIT Press, 1977).

White, Gilbert Fowler (November 26, 1911–   )

Professor and director emeritus of the Institute of Behavioral Science, Chicago-born Gilbert Fowler White began his career as a geographer with the Mississippi Valley Committee of the Public Work Administration (PWA) from 1934 to 1935. He next worked for the Natural Resources Planning Board from 1935 to 1940 and the Bureau of the Budget from 1940 to 1942. During World War II, he was a volunteer in France and India with the American Friends Service Committee, and upon returning to the United States, he was named president of Haverford College (1946–55). He was next a professor of geography at the University of Chicago, then accepted a professorship at the University of Colorado, where he also became director of the Natural Hazards Information Center (1978–84) and was named director emeritus of the Institute of Behavioral Science.

Between 1950 and 1951, White served as vice-chairman of the President's Water Resources Policy Commission, and between 1965 and 1966, he was chairman of the Bureau of the Budget's Task Force on Federal Flood Policy. White has also chaired the board of RESOURCES FOR THE FUTURE, the Commission on Natural Resources, and the NATURAL RESOURCES COUNCIL OF AMERICA. He was executive editor of *Environment*, and, since 1986, he has been a member of the advisory group on greenhouse gases of the World Meteorological Organization. Since 1987, he has chaired the technical review committee of the Nevada Nuclear Waste Project, and in 1989, he was named chairman of the national review committee on the Status of U.S. Floodplain Management.

Among White's many published works are *Human Adjustment to Floods* (1942), *Science and the Future of Arid Lands* (1960), *Social and Economic Aspects of Natural Resources* (1962), *Choice of Adjustment to Floods* (1964) and *Strategies of American Water Management* (1969).

White has been honored with awards from the American Geographical Society, the American Water Resources Association, the National Council for Geographic Education, the International Geographical Union and other national and international organizations.

Whitehead, Alfred North (February 15, 1861– December 30, 1947)

The British mathematician and philosopher Alfred North Whitehead (born in Ramsgate, Isle of Thanet, Kent) is familiar to ecologists for his theories of organicism. In *Science and the Modern World* (1925), he noted that scientists over three centuries have emphasized the mechanism of nature. In place of this, he proposed an organic approach, concentrating on process, creativity, indefiniteness and relativity. He claimed that the parts of nature are closely interdependent and that by extracting one organism for analysis, thereby removing it from its context, scientists altered the very nature of that organism. In *Science and the Modern World,* Whitehead used a Brazilian rainforest as a microcosm illustrative of nature's interconnectedness. "A forest is the triumph of the organisation of mutually dependent species," he wrote. Although he did not use the term *ecology* himself, his alternative holistic approach prefigured the ecological movement, which sees nature as an interdependent whole.

Whitehead became friends with Bertrand Russell at Trinity College in Cambridge. After reviewing Russell's first draft of *Principles of Mathematics,* he joined the great philosopher in the project, which resulted in the monumental three-volume *Principia Mathematica* (1910–13). Whitehead immigrated to the United States and became a professor of philosophy at Harvard University in 1923.

In addition to *Science and the Modern World,* which remains the most cogent exposition of his philosophy, and his works on mathematics, Whitehead also wrote *An Enquiry Concerning the Principles of Natural Philosophy* (1919), *The Concept of Nature* (1920) and *The Principle of Relativity* (1922).

Further reading: Paul Grimley Kuntz, *Alfred North Whitehead* (Boston: Twayne, 1984); Nathaniel M. Lawrence, *Alfred North Whitehead: A Primer of His Philosophy* (New York: Twayne, 1974); Victor Lowe, *Alfred North Whitehead: The Man and His Work, 1861–1910* (Baltimore: Johns Hopkins University Press, 1985); Paul Arthur Schilpp (ed.), *The Philosophy of Alfred North Whitehead,* Evanston and Chicago: Northwestern University Press, 1941).

Whitesell, Dale Edward (October 12, 1925–   )

After serving in the U.S. Army Air Corps during World War II, Dale Edward Whitesell attended Ohio State University and graduated with a B.S. in agriculture and an M.S. in wildlife management. In 1951, this native of Miamisburg, Ohio, went to work for the Ohio Division of Wildlife as a wildlife district game-management supervisor and in 1963 was named chief of the division. From 1965 to 1987, he served as executive vice-president of DUCKS UNLIMITED INC. and, during his tenure, upgraded the organization's fund-raising programs and recruited a staff of wildlife professionals. Under his leadership the annual income of Ducks Unlimited rose from its 1965 level of $876,000 to more than $34 million in 1982. Whitesell

devoted nearly 80% of that income to habitat development. As a result, more than 3 million acres of wetlands in Canada have been preserved for wild waterfowl. Other organizations Whitesell has served include the Safari Club International Conservation Foundation in Tucson, Arizona, the Ohio Wildlife Management Association and the International Association of Fish, Game, and Conservation Commissioners.

Wild, Peter (April 25, 1940–   )

The American poet Peter Wild uses surrealistic images of the American Southwest to present myths and legends of Native Americans and to contrast the smallness of human beings in relation to the vastness of their environment. A professor of English at the University of Arizona in Tucson, Wild has also written nonfiction prose works on conservation, including *Pioneer Conservationists of Western America* (1979) and *Pioneer Conservationists of Eastern America* (1980). He is a contributing editor to the environmental newspaper *High Country News.*

Wilderness Society (Founded: 1935)
900 17th Street NW, Washington, D.C. 20006-2596; (202) 833-2300

Founded by eight conservationists (including Robert MARSHALL, Benton MACKAYE, Harvey BROOME and Aldo LEOPOLD) concerned over highway development in the Appalachian Mountains, the Wilderness Society today has a membership of 375,000, a staff of more than 130, 16 field offices and an annual budget of $17 million. Early battles were waged against the construction of an aqueduct tunnel through the Rocky Mountains, the building of CIVILIAN CONSERVATION CORPS (CCC) trails through the Adirondacks and the construction of a skyline parkway in the Green Mountains of Vermont. Later, the society mobilized its members against the building of Echo Park Dam and in support of the Wilderness Act. More recent efforts have been directed toward devising an agreement between the state of Florida and the federal government for improved management of Everglades National Park and the expansion of the Big Cypress National Preserve; supporting the Arizona Wilderness Act of 1990, which transferred 2.3 million acres of wilderness to federal holdings; continuing to press for protection of the Arctic National Wildlife Refuge and the forests of the Pacific Northwest; and generating support for protection of woodlands in northern New England.

The organization publishes a quarterly journal, *Wilderness,* and a magazine, *The Living Wilderness.* Today, it concentrates its efforts on lobbying, research, public education and developing grass-roots support for conservation issues.

Wildlife Conservation International (Founded: 1897)

c/o New York Zoological Society, Bronx, New York 10460; (212) 220-5155

Wildlife Conservation International works to preserve wildlife habitats and ecosystems. With a staff of 25, the organization conducts field investigations, offers training opportunities to field biologists and prepares recommendations for the management of wildlife and protected areas for national parks. Formerly called the Animal Research and Conservation Center, the organization publishes a bimonthly magazine entitled *Wildlife Conservation*. John G. Robinson serves as director of the organization, which has 40,000 members.

Wildlife Management Institute (Founded: 1911)

1101 14th Street NW, Suite 725, Washington, D.C. 20005; (202) 371-1808

The Wildlife Management Institute promotes improved management and use of natural resources by supporting research activities and the establishment of wilderness areas, and by publishing the biweekly *Outdoor News Bulletin*. Originally named American Game Protective and Propagation Association, and founded by sportsmen and conservationists, the group first devoted its attention to importing exotic game birds. Today, the Wildlife Management Institute monitors timber operations and their effect on wildlife habitats and sponsors an annual North American Wildlife and Natural Resources Conference.

Wildlife Society (Founded: 1936)

5410 Grosvenor Lane, Bethesda, Maryland 20814; (301) 897-9770

Serving as the professional organization for wildlife managers, the Wildlife Society was originally called the Society of Wildlife Specialists. Today the group's 8,500 members include wildlife biologists, scientists, enforcers of conservation laws and natural resource managers. The group publishes the *Journal of Wildlife Management*, *Wildlife Society Bulletin* and *Wildlife Monographs*, as well as *Wildlifer*, a bimonthly newsletter. In addition, it certifies wildlife biologists, publishes an annual *Directory and Certification Registry* and serves as an information clearinghouse for scientific information needed by wildlife managers.

Further reading: Daniel L. Leedy, "The Wildlife Society," *Journal of Forestry* 54 (December 1956): 821–823.

Lonnie L. Williamson, vice president of Wildlife Management Institute. *Wildlife Management Institute*

Williamson, Lonnie Leroy (November 12, 1939–   )

Vice-president of the WILDLIFE MANAGEMENT INSTITUTE and free-lance writer of articles on conservation and wildlife, Lonnie Leroy Williamson, a native of Jackson County, Georgia, holds a degree in journalism from the University of Georgia, a master's degree in wildlife management from the University of Georgia's School of Forest Resources and has done postgraduate work in natural resource economics at the University of Maryland's Department of Agricultural Economics. From 1966 to 1970, he worked as a research associate with the Southeastern Cooperative Wildlife Disease Study, College of Veterinary Medicine, University of Georgia. In 1970, Williamson became editor of *Outdoor News Bulletin*, published by the Wildlife Management Institute, was named secretary of the institute in 1975 and vice-president in 1987.

Williamson has won awards for writing and editing from the Mason-Dixon Outdoor Writers Association, the NATURAL RESOURCES COUNCIL OF AMERICAN and the Outdoor Writers Association of America. In addition, the U.S. FOREST SERVICE conferred on him its Distinguished Service Award in 1988.

In addition to his work for the Wildlife Management Institute, Williamson serves as editor-at-large for *Outdoor Life*. He has frequently testified before Congress as an expert witness.

Wirth, Conrad Louis (December 1, 1899–)

Conrad Louis Wirth, director of the NATIONAL PARK SERVICE from 1951 to 1964, first became involved in scenic preservation as a member of the National Capital Park and Planning Commission in 1928. Three years later, he was appointed assistant director in charge of land planning for the National Park Service. In 1933, Wirth worked with the CIVILIAN CONSERVATION CORPS (CCC) as the supervisor of state and county park activities, and two years later, his position was expanded to include all park activities throughout the U.S. Department of the INTERIOR.

As director of the National Park Service, Wirth initiated Mission 66, a program designed to protect, improve and extend the service's holdings. After his retirement from the park service, he directed the Hudson River Valley Commission from 1965 to 1966, served as a commissioner of the Palisades Interstate Park Commission from 1964 to 1972, chaired the New York State Historic Trust from 1966 to 1970 and served as a consultant on conservation to LAURANCE S. ROCKEFELLER and the Rockefeller Brothers Fund. In 1980, he founded the American Academy of Parks and Recreation Administration.

Wirth, Timothy Endicott (September 22, 1939–)

In 1992, Democrat Timothy Wirth retired as senior senator from Colorado (elected in 1986), having served as a powerful advocate of environmental legislation. He was, however, uncompromising and, some critics say, even intolerant of differing points of view on certain environmental issues. For example, he refused to yield on strict standards for reducing auto emissions and researching alternative fuels in revising the Clean Air Act during the 101st Congress. Wirth not only broke with pro-environment members of his own party over this issue, but with some environmental lobbyists as well, who feared that his uncompromising stance would sink the entire bill. Most embarrassingly, ultraconservative and environmentally hostile South Carolina Senator Jesse Helms supported Wirth's amendment, presumably hoping it would bring about the defeat of the new clean air measures. In the end, the new Clean Air Act of 1990 was signed into law, but without Wirth's amendment.

A member of the Energy and Natural Resources Committee, Wirth presided over committee hearings to draft legislation to alleviate the "greenhouse effect," global warming caused by upper-atmosphere pollutants. As chairman of the Energy Regulation and Conservation Subcommittee, Wirth worked to create environmentally sound energy policy.

While Wirth was uncompromising on various environmental issues, he did nod to his Colorado constituents in his support for western water projects and for measures aimed at benefiting the oil-shale and energy industries of his region.

Wirth was born in Santa Fe, New Mexico. Educated at Harvard University (A.B., 1961 and M.Ed., 1964) and Stanford University (Ph.D., 1973), Wirth was a White House fellow, working as special assistant to the secretary of health, education and welfare in 1967. He was assistant to the chairman of the National Urban Coalition in 1968 and deputy assistant secretary for education, Department of Health, Education, and Welfare, in 1969. Wirth returned to the private sector from 1970 to 1973 and was elected to the U.S. House of Representatives in 1974, serving from 1975 to 1987, when he took office as senator.

Woodwell, George Masters (October 23, 1928–)

George Masters Woodwell, who was born in Cambridge, Massachusetts, took his Ph.D. in botany at Duke University and served as a member of the faculty of the University of Maine from 1957 to 1961. He worked as an assistant ecologist and senior ecologist at the Brookhaven National Laboratory from 1962 to 1975 and founded the Ecosystems Center at the Marine Biological Laboratory in Woods Hole, Massachusetts, of which he was director from 1975 to 1985. In 1985, Woodwell founded the prestigious Woods Hole Research Center. He has been a lecturer at the School of Forestry at Yale University since 1969.

Woodwell was active in the founding of several environmental organizations, including the ENVIRONMENTAL DEFENSE FUND, the NATIONAL RESOURCES DEFENSE COUNCIL and the WORLD RESOURCES INSTITUTE. In 1981, he became the chairman of the WORLD WILDLIFE FUND. From 1976 to 1978, he served as vice-president, then president, of the ECOLOGICAL SOCIETY OF AMERICA, and from 1982 to 1983, he was chairman of the Conference on Long Term Biological Consequences of Nuclear War.

Woodwell has studied terrestrial and marine ecosystems for many years, concentrating on their structure, function and development. He has also conducted research on the way pesticides, nutrients, radioactive isotopes and organic compounds are cycled through the environment and the environmental problems caused by carbon dioxide. Woodwell's books include *Ecological Effects of Nuclear War* (1965), *Diversity and Stability in Ecological Systems* (1969), *Carbon and the Biosphere* (1973), *The Role of Terrestrial Vegetation in the Global Carbon Cycle: Measurement by Remote Sensing* (1984) and *The Earth in Transition: Patterns and Processes of Biotic Impoverishment* (1990).

World Resources Institute (Founded: 1982)

1709 New York Avenue NW, Suite 700, Washington, D.C. 20006; (202) 638-6300

With a staff of 35 research professionals, World Resources Institute analyzes global resources and environmental conditions to provide information on likely trends and to develop strategies for handling the problems it identifies. The organization publishes books, reports and papers; sponsors seminars and conferences; and provides the media with information on environmental issues. Of primary concern to the institute are the deterioration of natural resources and the effects of that deterioration on economic development. The institute focuses on such research areas as climate, energy and pollution; forests and biodiversity; economics; and technology. James Gustave SPETH is president of the organization, which annually devotes $7.5 million to research activities.

World Wildlife Fund (Founded: 1961; merged 1985 with the CONSERVATION FOUNDATION)

1250 24th Street NW, Washington, D.C. 20037; (202) 293-4800

The World Wildlife Fund studies environmental trends, arbitrates disputes over the resolution of environmental problems, protects wildlife habitats and supports activities aimed at biodiversity, sustainable development and the control of air pollution and toxic substances. The organization was created in 1985 when the World Wildlife Fund and the Conservation Foundation merged. KATHRYN S. FULLER is the current president.

The organization has a staff of 150 professionals and an annual budget of $50 million. It publishes the *WWF Letter, Resolve* and *Successful Communities*; it sponsors conferences and workshops and produces films on wildlife studies.

Worldwatch Institute (Founded: 1975)

1776 Massachusetts Avenue NW, Washington, D.C. 20036; (202) 452-1999

Worldwatch Institute serves as a clearinghouse for information on global trends in human and natural resources. Culling data on current projects from more than 200 periodicals and 100 newsletters from around the world, Worldwatch Institute annually publishes *State of the World,* an assessment of the world's resources and a report on projects and initiatives established to manage them. The publication is translated into 25 languages and each year sells more than 200,000 copies. Among the topics covered are energy, food policy, population, development, technology, environment, human resources and economics.

In addition to the annual *State of the World,* Worldwatch Institute has published more than 15 books and 100 position papers on environmental issues. The organization's bimonthly magazine, *World Watch,* publishes feature stories on energy, population research, food production, social trends, the environment and sustainable development. Orville Freeman is chairman of the board, and Lester R. Brown is president of the organization.

Worldwide Fund for Nature (Founded: 1961)

World Conservation Centre, Avenue du Mont-Blanc, CH-1196 Gland, Switzerland; (22) 649111

With 1.5 million members in 23 national groups (including WORLD WILDLIFE FUND, in the U.S.) and an annual budget of 25 million Swiss francs, WWF is a large organization dedicated to promoting the conservation of the natural environment and ecological processes essential to life on earth.

WWF emphasizes heightening public awareness of environmental issues through programs of education, and it supports and encourages public action based on scientific priorities. To this end, WWF maintains a library of 10,000 books, 500 periodicals and 35,000 photographs of wildlife and natural areas. Through its education department, headed by Peter Martin, WWF sends out specially written literature to schools on request and also works with commercial publishers to produce teaching materials for sale to schools and school systems.

WWF publishes *The New Road,* a quarterly; *WWF Conservation Yearbook,* a biennial; *WWF News,* a bimonthly; *WWF Reports,* a bimonthly; the quarterly *Special Reports;* and the annual *Year Review.* Its director general is Charles de Haes.

Worster, Donald E(ugene) (November 14, 1941–)

Donald E. Worster is a historian of environmentalism and ecology. Born in Needles, California, he was educated at the University of Kansas (B.A., 1963; M.A., 1964) and at Yale University (M. Phil., 1970; Ph.D., 1971). Worster taught in the speech and drama department at the University of Maine, Orono, from 1964 to 1966; at Brandeis University, as assistant professor of American Studies from 1971 to 1974; at the University of Hawaii at Manoa, as associate professor from 1975 to 1980, and as professor from 1980 to 1983; and as professor of American Studies at Brandeis since 1984.

Worster's writings on the history of ecology include *American Environmentalism: The Formative Period, 1860–1915*, which Worster edited in 1973, and *Nature's Economy: The Roots of Ecology*, which appeared in 1977 and was revised and updated in 1984. He has also written a history of the Dust Bowl—*Dust Bowl: The Southern Plains in the 1930s* (1979)—and a history of water use in the American West, *The Rivers of Empire: Water and Society in the American West* (1985). For *The Dust Bowl*, Worster received the Bancroft Prize.

Worster's interest in the history of environmentalism is not merely academic. He told the editors of *Contemporary Authors* that he is "interested in finding ways for myself, family, and others to live on this fragile planet with the least impact, the fullest humanity, and the greatest amount of personal freedom compatible with ecological integrity."

Further reading: Worster, *Dust Bowl: The Southern Plains in the 1930s* (New York: Oxford University Press, 1979); *Nature's Economy: The Roots of Ecology*, 2nd ed., (New York: Cambridge University Press, 1984).

Wright, R. Michael (July 12, 1943–   )

Named western regional counsel for the NATURE CONSERVANCY in 1972, R. Michael Wright initiated the organization's International Program in 1974. As director of the program, Wright, a native of Eugene, Oregon, worked to gain protected status for new regions, including the Archbold addition to Dominica's Morne Trois Pitons National Park, Corcovado National Park, Costa Rica National Wildlife Refuge and Long Point National Wildlife Refuge in Canada. In 1979, he left the Nature Conservancy to become vice-president and general counsel of the WORLD WILDLIFE FUND. During President Jimmy CARTER's administration, he was named assistant director of the Task Force on Global Resources and Environment. Wright is a member of the Costa Rica Conservation Foundation and the Asa Wright Nature Centre in Trinidad. In 1974, he was awarded a Rockefeller Foundation fellowship in environmental affairs, and in 1979, he was a member of the U.S. Delegation to the Governing Council of the UNITED NATIONS ENVIRONMENT PROGRAMME.

Wuori, Matti Ossian (July 15, 1945–   )

A native of Helsinki, Finland, Matti Wuori earned a reputation in his country as an effective civil rights

Matti Wuori, chairman of Greenpeace International. © *Greenpeace/Goldblatt*

lawyer and environmental affairs consultant. When David MCTAGGERT resigned as chairman of GREENPEACE INTERNATIONAL on September 2, 1991, Wuori was named as his successor.

Matti Wuori has practiced law as a licensed advocate and junior lawyer with a firm in Kerava, Finland. Since 1970, he has been senior partner in his own Helsinki firm, and in 1979 received a master of laws degree from Helsinki University. From 1970 to 1983, he served as ombudsman and arbitrator for the Helsinki Journalists Association and is a member of various state commissions and committees. Wuori is a member of the Finnish Bar Association, the International Bar Association and since 1988 has been vice-president of the Helsinki chapter of the International Commission of Jurists. Since 1986, he has served as president of the Human Rights Commission of the International Union of Advocates.

In 1988, Wuori was appointed counselor to the International Board of Directors of Greenpeace International. Under the leadership of David McTaggart, the organization earned a reputation for radical confrontation marked by its guerrilla-style approach to settling environmental issues by means of "direct actions." Often, it seemed, Greenpeace protested capitalism as much as it attempted to confront offenders against the environment. While this stance gave the organization a nearly mythic reputation for daring, determined and effective militancy—an environmental organization of uncompromising conscience and courage—it also alienated some governments, influential leaders, other environmental groups and various potential allies. Wuori, a moderate, has the difficult mission of bringing Greenpeace International nearer to the mainstream of environmentalism without drastically diluting its fervor.

Y

Yard, Robert Sterling (February 1, 1861–May 17, 1945)

As publicity chief for the NATIONAL PARK SERVICE (1914–19), Yard helped establish and expand the service. His illustrated books—*The National Parks Portfolio* (1916), *The Top of the Continent* (1917), *The Book of the National Parks* (1919) and *Our Federal Lands* (1928)—were instrumental in spreading public appreciation of and support for the parks. In 1919, he left the service to found the NATIONAL PARKS AND CONSERVATION ASSOCIATION, where he edited the *National Parks Bulletin* until 1936. He defended the park system against encroachment by commercial interests, but—more controversially—also criticized recreational overuse and campaigned for greater selectivity in the acquisition of park land. Yard was a founder of the WILDERNESS SOCIETY.

Further reading: Stephen Fox, *John Muir and His Legacy: The American Conservation Movement* (Madison: University of Wisconsin Press, 1985).

Youth Conservation Corps, U.S. (Established: 1979)

During the 1970s and early 1980s, federal conservation and environmental programs received vital assistance from the Youth Conservation Corps and its associated program, the Young Adult Conservation Corps. Created by Congress as a jobs program, the corps employed young Americans in state and national parks, forests, wildlife refuges and rangelands. Participants planted trees, constructed and repaired trails and improved wildlife habitats—work valued at more than $341 million.

In 1980, 90,000 young people were employed by the corps. While an analysis of their work revealed that for every dollar invested in the program, the corps returned work valued at $1.20, the necessity of the agency was called into question during hearings on the federal budget in 1981. Although several environmental and wildlife organizations, including the DEFENDERS OF WILDLIFE, ENVIRONMENTAL ACTION COALITION, FRIENDS OF THE EARTH, the LEAGUE OF CONSERVATION VOTERS, the SIERRA CLUB and the WILDERNESS SOCIETY, supported continuation of the programs, both the Youth Conservation Corps and the Young Adult Conservation Corps were eliminated.

Z

Zahniser, Howard Clinton (February 25, 1906–May 5, 1964)

After working briefly as a teacher and newspaper reporter, Zahniser, a native of Franklin, Pennsylvania, joined the U.S. BIOLOGICAL SURVEY in 1930 as a researcher, writer and editor. In 1942, he joined the Bureau of Plant Industry, Soils, and Agricultural Engineering (U.S. Department of AGRICULTURE) as director of publications and research reporting. His work with both agencies inspired his wholehearted commitment to conservation causes, and in 1945, he left the bureau to become executive secretary (later executive director) of the WILDERNESS SOCIETY as well as editor of the society's journal, *The Living Wilderness*, which became the forum that developed much of the public's awareness of national environmental issues. It was through the journal and other publications, as well as lectures and congressional testimony, that Zahniser helped lay the foundation for the Wilderness Act of 1964.

Zero Population Growth (Founded: 1968)
1400 16th Street NW, Suite 320, Washington, D.C. 20036; (202) 332-2200

Zero Population Growth works to garner popular support for achieving the goal of a sustainable balance of population, resources and the environment. The organization monitors legislation and judicial decisions that affect population issues, studies population trends around the world and disseminates population statistics to the media and the public. In addition, the organization sponsors training workshops for teachers and produces and distributes teaching kits.

Zero Population Growth advocates the universal availability of family planning services; the development of new contraceptives that are safe and effective; and full legal, educational and social equality for women. The organization works to achieve improved survival rates for infants and children.

Among the group's publications are *Media Targets, Teacher's PET Term Paper, The ZPG Activist* and *The ZPG Reporter*. Zero Population Growth has approximately 30,000 members and an annual budget of $1.3 million. Susan Weber is currently executive director.

Susan Weber, executive director of Zero Population Growth. *Zero Population Growth*

Zon, Raphael (December 1, 1874–October 27, 1956)

One of America's foremost forest scientists, Raphael Zon was born in Simbirsk, Russia. As a medical student and a student of the natural sciences at the University of Kazan, Zon espoused a political radicalism that prompted his arrest by the czar's police and conviction for subversive activity. The young man escaped from captivity, fled briefly to Germany and Belgium, then settled in London, where he worked in the British Museum.

Zon immigrated to the United States during the late 1890s and studied forestry at Cornell University under Professor Bernhard FERNOW and Filibert Roth. Fernow recommended Zon as a student assistant in the Special Investigations Section of the U.S. Bureau of Forestry (predecessor of the U.S. FOREST SERVICE), where he was profoundly influenced by bureau chief Gifford PINCHOT. Zon achieved quick promotion in the bureau, becoming assistant forest expert and, subsequently, forest assistant.

From 1907 to 1914, Zon served as head of the bureau's Office of Silvics, and from 1914 to 1923, he was head of the Office of Forest Investigations. Zon was instrumental in gaining acceptance of the idea of staffing each national forest with trained researchers, and he established a system of forest experiment stations, starting with the one at Coconino National Forest in Fort Valley, Arizona, in 1908. Zon also played a key role in the creation of the Forest Products Laboratory in Madison, Wisconsin, and was one of the writers of the Capper Report of 1920, which recommended the creation of a comprehensive national forest policy.

Zon was editor of the *Proceedings of the Society of American Foresters*, and succeeded his mentor Bernhard Fernow as editor of the prestigious *Journal of Forestry* in 1928. From 1928 to 1944, Zon directed the Lake States Forest Experiment Station in St. Paul, Minnesota. During these years he did prodigious research on forest protection, economics and management, which not only stimulated much activity on the state level, but led to the creation of a so-called shelterbelt of trees along the 99th meridian from the Canadian border down to Texas.

Zon retired from the U.S. Forest Service in 1944, devoting himself during the late 1940s and 1950s to work with the United Nations Relief and Rehabilitation Administration, the FOOD AND AGRICULTURAL ORGANIZATION and the journal *Unasylva*.

INDEX

National Energy Strategy, 238
National Environmental Policy Act, 53, 64, 171
National Environmental Satellite, Data, and Information Service, 164, 165
National Forest Commission, 182
National Forest Management Act of 1976, 181
National Forest System, 58, 89, 182
National Forestry Commission, 208
National Freshwater Fishing Hall of Fame, 138–39
National Geographic Society, 54, 55, 95, 98, 135, 164, 171,
National Geophysical Data Center, 164
National Heritage Trust Task Force, 185
National Hunting and Fishing Day, 139
National Industrial Pollution Control Council, 136
National Institute for Occupational Safety and Health, 22, 86
National Institute for Urban Wildlife, 185
National Institute of Arts and Letters, 21
National Institute of Bank Management, 145
National Institutes of Health, 30, 186, 199
National Lumber Manufacturers Association, 8
National Mapping Program, 96. *See also* Geological Survey, U.S.
National Marine Fisheries Service, 165
National Museum of the United States, 111
National Museums of Southern Rhodesia, 63
National Natural Heritage Inventory, 169
National Ocean Survey, 165
National Oceanic and Atmospheric Administration, 25, 164, 165, 185, 186
National Oceanographic Data Center, 164
National Park Foundation, 165
National Parks and Conservation Association, 17, 27, 34, 35, 37, 52, 72, 112, 166, 177, 185, 239, 248
National Parks and Wildlife Refuges in Hawaii, 47
National Parks Association, 30, 33, 34, 135. *See also* National Parks and Conservation Association
National Parks Mining Act, 46
National Park Service, 1, 6–7, 27, 36, 57, 65, 66, 70, 71, 89, 106, 107, 109, 116, 148, 149, 151, 154, 157, 158, 160, 165–166, 175, 177, 178, 183, 192, 196, 197, 199, 200, 222, 224, 228, 230, 231, 238, 244, 248
    Division of Education and Forestry, 106
    Field Division of Education, 106
    Land and Water Conservation Fund, 57
    National Capital Park and Planning Commission, 244
    Wild and Scenic Rivers planning program, 57
National Park Service Act of 1916, 6, 175
National Park System, 191, 197, 230
National Parks, The, 93
National Plan for Outdoor Recreation, 178
National Power Survey, 1974, 86
National Press Club, 168
National Reclamation Association, 170
National Recovery Administration, 114, 148
National Recreation and Park Association, 228
National Recycling Advisory Council, 126
National Register of Historic Places, 116
National Research Council, 100, 157, 193–194, 212
    Committee on Preservation of Natural Conditions, 52
    Committee on Wastewater Management for Coastal and Urban Areas, 78
National Resources Council of America, 167–168
National Rifle Association, 200
National Science Board, 95
National Science Foundation, 30, 35, 91, 174
National Skeet Shooting Association, 200
National Society for Park Resources, 66
National Trails Agenda Project, 222
National Trails System Act, 1969, 231
National Trust for Historic Preservation, 239
National Tuberculosis Association, 71
National Urban Coalition, 196, 244
National Voter, 132
National War Garden Commission, 179
National Weather Service, 165
National Wetlands Policy Forum, 230
National Wetlands Technical Council, 81
National Wild and Scenic Rivers System, 9, 10

National Wilderness Act of 1964, 213
National Wilderness Preservation System, 10, 192, 213
National Wildflower Research Center, 122
National Wildlife Federation, 2, 11, 36, 37, 47, 58, 61, 65, 98, 105, 106, 166–167, 179, 181, 229
    Resources Defense Division, 179
National Wildlife Foundation, 30, 47
National Wildlife Refuge System, 18, 204
National Wildlife Week, 62, 167
National Youth Administration, 123, 180
Native Americans, xii–xiii, 42
Natural Areas Association, 85
Natural Bridges National Monument, 201
Natural Environment Research Council, 110
Natural Hazards Information Center, 241
Natural Heritage Protection Campaign, 198
Natural Land Institute, 85
Natural Resources Council of America, 17, 27, 36, 47, 151, 180, 183, 194, 196, 205, 212, 241, 243
Natural Resources Defense Council, 3, 15, 22, 24, 36, 47, 98, 163, 171, 193, 221, 224
Natural Resources Institute, 136
Natural Resources Planning Board, 241
"Nature" series, 139
Nature Conservancy, 65, 71, 79, 85, 91, 98, 168–169, 174, 177, 193, 206, 212, 226, 228, 246
NatureQuest, 167
NatureScope, 167
Navajo Trail Association, 106
Naval Ordnance Laboratory, U.S., 222
Nearing, Louis, 169
Nearing, Minnie, 169
Nearing, Scott, 169–170
Nebraska Aircraft Corporation, 135
Neitzche, Friederich, 137
Nelson, Gaylord Anton, 170, 191
Neuberger, Senator Richard L., 239
Nevada Nuclear Waste Project, 115
New Alchemy Institute, 170
New England Environmental Network, 65
New England River Basins Commission, 51, 103
New Land Foundation, 107
New Melones Dam (California), 92
New River Gorge, 199
New Tide, 47
New York College of Physicians and Surgeons, 100
New York Department of Environmental Conservation, 123
New York Environmental Advisory Board, 126
New York Forest Commission, 86
New York Lawyers Alliance for Nuclear Arms Control, 4
New York Lyceum of Natural History, 100
New York State College of Forestry, Syracuse, 3
New York State Forest Preserve, 104
New York State Humane Association, 46
New York State Historic Trust, 244
New York State Museum, Albany, 3
New York Zoological Park. *See* Bronx Zoo
New York Zoological Society, 12, 156, 161, 178
Newell, Frederick Haynes, 170–171
Newhall, Nancy, 2
Newlands, Francis G., 170
Next Whole Earth Catalog, The, 26
Niagara Falls, New York, 96
Niagara Falls State Reservation, 176
Nicholas I, Czar, 112
Nicholl, Jack, 40
Nixon, Richard, 21, 36, 37, 38, 41, 52, 53, 82, 83, 151, 171–172, 196, 202, 206, 225
North American Conference on Religion and Ecology, 229
North American Radon Association, 172
North American Waterfowl Management Plan, 71
North American Waterfowl Management Plan Implemention Board, 51
North American Wetlands Council, 51
North American Wildlife Foundation, 51, 120, 172, 183, 235
North Carolina State University School of Forest Resources, 228
North Cascades National Park, 29
Northeast Association of Fisheries and Wildlife Agencies, 51
Northeast Corridor Regional Modeling Program, 48
Northern Forest Lands Study, 47

Northern Overland Expedition, 130
Northington, David, 122
Northwest Association for Environmental Studies, 39
Northwestern Labs, Battelle Memorial Institute, Columbus, Ohio, 50
Nuclear Regulatory Commission, 22, 80, 172–173, 232
    Special Inquiry Group, 90
Nuttall, Thomas, 173
NWF Wildlife Camps, 167

Oak Ridge National Laboratory, 52, 174, 238
Oberholtzer, Ernest Carol, 174
Ocean Dumping Act, 123
Ocean Research and Education Society, 21
Oceanographic Institute and Museum, 53
Occupational Safety and Health Agency (OSHA), 52, 162, 174
    Environmental Conference, 151
Odum, Eugene Pleasants, 174–175
"Oeconomy of Nature, The," 137
Office of Management and Budget, 171, 175, 192, 206, 223
Office of Technology Assessment, U.S., 27
    Advisory Panel on Superfund Implementation, 48
    Panel on Industrial Waste Reduction, 48
Ohio Division of Wildlife, 242
Ohio Hazardous Substance Institut, 22
Ohio River Water Sanitation Commission, 136
Ohio Wildlife Management Association, 242
Oil, Chemical, and Atomic Workers Union, 214
Oldham, Sally, 207
O'Leary, Hazel R., 80, 238
Olmstead, John, 175
Olmstead, Frederick Erskine, 175
Olmstead, Frederick Law Jr., 174, 175–176, 205
Olson, Sigurd Ferdinand, 176–177
Olympic National Park, 33, 75, 200, 212, 228
Olympic National Park Expansion Act, 209
Onthank, Karl William, 177
Open Space Institute, 177
Operation Firestop, 13
Ordre National des Architects, 55
Ordway, Samuel H. Jr., 51
Oregon County Parks Asociation, 177
Oregon Dune National Seashore, 177
Oregon Water Resources Board, 177
"Organic Living," 200
Organization of American States, 18
O'Riordan, Timothy, 177
Osborn, Fairfield, 51, 177–178
Outdoor Recreation and Heritage Conservation and Recreation Service, U.S. Bureau of, 60, 178, 180, 185, 231, 238
Outdoor Recreation Resources Review Act of 1958, 212–213
Outdoor Recreation Resources Review Commission, 180, 200
Outdoor Writers Association of America, 27, 138, 226, 204
Outlook Tower, 96
Overseas Development Council, 30, 31
Overview, 231
Owens Valley, 5
Owings, Margaret Wentworth, 178
Oxford University Bureau of Animal Population, 78
Oxford University Department of Zoological Field Studies, 79

Pacific Coast Borax Company, 148
Pacific Creek Redwoods State Park, 178
Pacific Fur Company, 173
Pacific Gas and Electric Company, 207
Pack, Arthur Newton, 179
Pack, Charles Lathrop, 10, 179
Packwood, Robert, 15
Paley, Willam, 179
Palisades Interstate Park Commission, 244
Pan American Airways, 136
Parenteau, Patrick Aloysius, 179
Park, Orland, 7
Park, Thomas, 7
Park Commission, U.S. Senate, 175
Passano Foundation, 71
Pasteur, Louis, 63
Patterson, Clair Cameron, 180
Patuxent Wildlife Research Center, 235

Pelican Island Refuge, 126
Penfold, Joseph Weller, 180
Pennant, Thomas, 241
Pennsylvania Association for the Advancement of Science, 200
Pennsylvania Department of Environmental Resources, 78
Pennsylvania Department of Forests and Waters, 45
Pennsylvania Forestry Association, 202
Pennsylvania Game Commission, 99
People for Parks Charitable Fund, 40
People's Bicentennial Commission, 198
Perlas, Nicanor, 198
Perring, Franklyn Hugh, 180
Perry, Robert J., 131
Persian Gulf, 110, 113, 141
Persian Gulf War, 211
Peruvian Conservation Foundation, 156
Pesticide Action Network, 189
Pesticides, U.S. Office of, 83
Pesticides, Wildlife, and Fish, U.S. Office of, 83
Peterson, Ralph Max, 180–181
Peterson, Roger Tory, 167, 181
Peterson, Russell Wilbur, 181
Pew Charitable Trusts, 81
Pharmaceutical Industries, 71
Phelan, J.A., 88
Philippines, 5
Philippines School of Forestry, 5
Photographic Society of America, 2
"Physiographic Ecology of Chicago and Vicinity," 56
Pierce, Atwood, Scribner, Allen, Smith & Lancaster, 95
Pigeon River Watershed, 174
Pillar Dome, 170
Pinchot Institute for Conservation Studies, 93
Pinchot, Gifford, 5, 17, 100, 101, 112, 115, 128, 137, 147, 152, 170, 175, 181–182, 184, 185, 207, 218, 224, 250
Pinchot, James W., 182
Pinchot, Mary Eno, 182
Pineapple Research Institute, 134
Pius IX, xii
Planet Drum Foundation, 19
Planned Parenthood Foundation, 47
Planning Commission for New Directions, 30
Plant Industry, Soils, and Agricultural Engineering, Bureau of, 249
Plant Variety Protection Program, 5
Pledge of Resistence, 17
Ploughshares Fund, 107
Plumas National Forest (California), 180
Point Foundation, 26
Point Lobos (California) Reserve, 47
Pollution Prevention Pays, 136
Pomerance, Rafe, 29, 182
Poole, Daniel Arnold, 182–183
Population Council, 183
Population Crisis Committee, 47, 181
Population-Environment Balance Inc., 58–59
Population Institute, 183
Porter, Eliot, 150
Post, Diana, 183–184
Potter, Albert Franklin, 184
Pound, Roscoe, 184
Powell, John Wesley, 115, 184–185
Powers, Roger W., 124, 185
Prairie Center, 100
Prairie Creek State Park, 206
President's Science Advisory Committee, 122
Prevost, J., 110
Price, Overton Westfeldt, 185
Primarily Primates Inc., 156
Prince William Sound, 108
Pritchard, Paul Clement, 185–186
Industry, The, 1
Professional Association of Diving Instructors, 56
Project Censored, 46
Project Ocean Search, 55
Project on the Nuclear Weapons Complex, 115
Project on the Predicament of Mankind, 90
Project on the Protection of the Global Atmosphere, 115
Project Work, 204
Proposal for a Student Conservation Corps, 228
Proposition 20. *See* California Coastal Zone Conservation Inititative
Proposition 65, 24